22nd IAPRI World Conference on Packaging 2020

Industry 4.0-UDEM

Online
30 June – 31 December 2020

ISBN: 978-1-7138-5251-3

Printed from e-media with permission by:

Curran Associates, Inc.
57 Morehouse Lane
Red Hook, NY 12571

CURRAN ASSOCIATES INC. proceedings.com

Some format issues inherent in the e-media version may also appear in this print version.

Universidad de Monterrey
Av. Ignacio Mornoes Prieto 4500 Pte.,
San Pedro Garza García,
N.L. México. C.P. 66238

Phone: +52 (81) 8215-1000
Fax: +52 (81) 1790-0872

www.udem.edu.mx

Additional copies of this publication are available from:

Curran Associates, Inc.
57 Morehouse Lane
Red Hook, NY 12571 USA
Phone: 845-758-0400
Fax: 845-758-2633
Email: curran@proceedings.com
Web: www.proceedings.com

PACKAGING LATEST INVESTIGATIONS

IAPRI MEXICO 2020

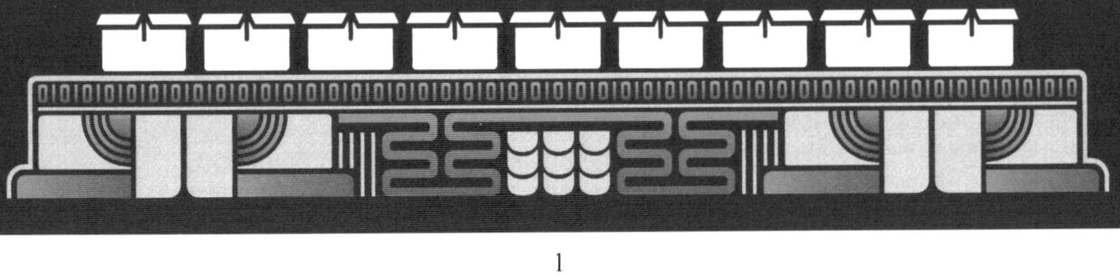

IAPRI MEXICO
Av. I. Morones Prieto 4500 Pte., 66238
San Pedro Garza García, N.L. México
Conmutador +52 (81) 8215-1000
Admisiones +52 (81) 8215-1010
Línea sin costo 01-800-801-UDEM
www.udem. edu.mx

Edited and published in Mexico

IAPRI MEXICO 2020

22ND WORLD PACKAGING ONLINE CONFERENCE

Industry 4.0 - UDEM

UNIVERSIDAD DE MONTERREY

HOMO HOMINIS IN MINISTERIO PERFICITUR

MONTERREY

MÉXICO

CONVENTION AND VISITORS BUREAU

SPONSORS

PARTNERS

Preface

We are delighted to welcome the international packaging community to IAPRI Online Conference 2020, hosted by Universidad de Monterrey.

This year, 2020, we have faced a challenge, the whole world has been affected by the coronavirus pandemic. The latest changes in the world have taught us that every industry needs to adapt, and as we know packaging plays a primordial role, being an essential industry with high demands on food, medicines, and supply chain.

Universidad de Monterrey was very excited to have the privilege to host the 22nd IAPRI World Packaging Conference for the first time here in Mexico, but the health and safety of the community comes first. Therefore, Universidad de Monterrey decided to cancel the physical event and adopt an online format. It has been our pleasure to organize the first IAPRI Online Packaging Conference, where leading researchers and global experts gather to share their research findings in the field of packaging, sustainability, distribution and logistics. The IAPRI Conference promotes the state of the art of packaging research and the exchange of knowledge among its researchers.

The conference theme is industry 4.0. Interconnectivity through the Internet of Things (IoT), automation, machine learning, and real-time data are pillars for manufacturing and supply chain management that allow technology to become a part of physical production and operations. Thanks to the packaging industry integration of IoT technologies, it was possible to adapt to the changes required by the global pandemic. We were ready to start remote activities and businesses with more automated processes continued their labors without greater impact.

For this Conference edition we accepted a total of 85 abstracts. Over 200 promising packaging researchers participated in the call for papers for the conference, representing 24 countries including Australia, Brazil, Chile, China, Colombia, Denmark, Finland, France, Germany, Hungary, Italy, Japan, Mexico, Netherlands, Norway, Portugal, Singapore, Spain, Sweden, Switzerland, Thailand, Turkey, United Kingdom and the United States. Due to the world pandemic most of the authors had limited resources, making it impossible to complete their researches. We are glad to count with 45 participations of the scientifics who could complete their papers.

The Online Conference consisted of 4 webinar conferences, 4 keynote speakers, 8 cycle of conference speakers, 26 oral video presentation and 9 poster video presentations. The digital conference proceedings include 45 papers (28 full papers and 17 abstracts). The investigations have been distributed in 11 topics: Industry 4.0, Sustainability, recycling and renewable materials, Packaging dynamics (vibrations and shocks), Packaging materials, Active and intelligent packaging, Packaging design and innovations, Food packaging, barrier properties and migration, Packaging logistics, Consumer research and marketing, Testing analysis and quality control and Packaging education.

We would like to thank our sponsors, IAPRI's Board of Directors and Vice-rectory of Art, Architecture and Design of Universidad de Monterrey for making the first edition of IAPRI's Online Conference possible.

We thank the International Scientific Committee for their hard work reviewing each of the research papers. We want to give a special thanks to the authors and speakers for their trust and support.

On behalf of the conference organization team, we would like to thank you for your participation on the first IAPRI Online Conference.

Cristina F. Guzmán Siller, Ph.D.
IAPRI Conference Coordinator

ID Diana Sofía Chapa Chapa
IAPRI Conference Logistics

ID Paola Ivonne Cáceres Alvarado
IAPRI Conference Academics

Hello and greetings to my respected colleagues and friends from around the world and welcome to a wonderful educational experience hosted by University of Monterrey.

Whether it is physically, emotionally, or financially, all of us have been impacted by the coronavirus pandemic this year. Despite these unprecedented circumstances, University of Monterrey, my friend Cristina and her exceptional team have salvaged this excellent virtual event. While applauding their great amount of unrecognized effort over the past few years towards organizing what surely would have been an IAPRI World Conference to remember for years, I would like to thank University of Monterrey, Cristina and her team in putting the health and safety of all attendees ahead of personal emotions and investment.

While we all were looking forward to network, communicate and develop ideas as well as to exchange experiences with our national and international peers in physical environment, I am thankful to the hosts of this event for putting on a first ever virtual IAPRI Conference.

With the significant changes in the consumer and customer preferences as well as the disrupted global supply chains due to the COVID-19 pandemic, the packaging industry, needless to say, has been greatly impacted. With food and healthcare being amongst the packaging industry's largest sectors, the over 900 billion dollar global industry is now more than ever at the frontlines. While the demand for packaging for groceries, healthcare products, and e-commerce, are emerging as the lifelines in this dramatically transforming world, demand for industrial, luxury and B2B transportation packaging are experiencing declines.

The perception of packaging has also been dramatically impacted by the global pandemic. The skeptical headlines related to packaging from just earlier this year such as ocean plastics, environmental compromises, and recycling economies, have drastically changed to where packaging is being reflected as the lifeline towards addressing global health and safety concerns.

While rapidly navigating through the current pause, the packaging industry is already planning for the comeback and to shape the next normal that will emerge from this pandemic. This is an opportunity for all packaging value chain players, including the industry, researchers, and academics at this event, to reflect and prepare for a more robust future.

I would also like to take this opportunity to formally thank the hosts, the sponsors, the keynote speakers and all presenters for making this virtual Conference a success.

I hope that all of the attendees will enjoy the incredible virtual program put together for us by the University of Monterrey, Cristina and her team.

On behalf of IAPRI, I wish you, your teams and your loved ones health and safety through this difficult period. It is challenging operating under the current restrictions; however, I am confident we will get through this, together.

We hope to see you all in the near future at another IAPRI event.

Best Wishes,

Jay Singh
President

iapri

June 16, 2020

Dear IAPRI World Conference participant,

As the Secretary General of IAPRI, I would like to send my sincere thank you to you for your participation in this first venture for IAPRI with an online, on demand conference. We would have preferred the networking opportunities of a face to face conference but given the Covid -19 pandemic that has affected us all, that was not possible. I genuinely want to thank the University of Monterrey and Dr. Cristina Guzman for all the extra effort they have had to put forth to make this online event possible.

As a longtime friend, I know Cristina had dreamed for a long time of holding a World Conference in Mexico. She and the University with a great amount of effort over the past 18 months was ready for us all to be in Monterrey. Then when it had to be cancelled, they switched gears and quickly moved forward planning the webinar, the on-demand videos of research presentations and posters, and the production of these conference proceedings.

Again, thank you for participating.

Sincerely,

Edward A. Church
Secretary General

Content

CHAPTER I

Industry 4

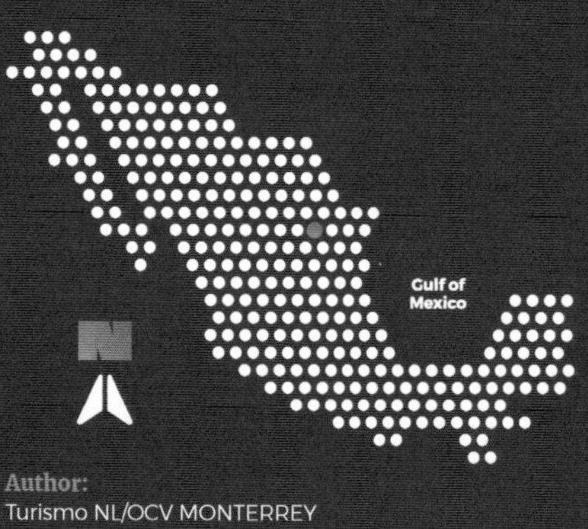

Author:
Turismo NL/OCV MONTERREY

Location:
Monterrey, NUEVO LEÓN

Description:
Monterrey's downtown has so much to offer: a simple stroll through the Macroplaza lets you see how the city has grown and evolved throughout the years. Right next to Monterrey's Cathedral you have another site of worship, this one for art, the Museum of Contemporary Art (MARCO).

Deployable Kirigami Cushion Design for E-Commerce Packaging [9]

Euihark Lee* 1, Xingguang Pan 1, Kazuko Fuchi 2
1 School of Packaging, Michigan State University, East Lansing, MI 48824, USA
2 University of Dayton Research Institute, Dayton, OH 45469, USA

Abstract: In packaging, cushion barriers are needed to provide content protection in a disposable form. However, conventional cushioning materials and designs typically require a large volume, which decreases shipping and storage efficiency and increases environmental impact. Especially in e-commerce, where "shipping and handling" occur at an exceedingly rapid pace in large-scale operations, many packages suffer from being over or under packed through the fulfilment process. To solve this issue, this paper presents deployable kirigami-based cushion designs that can be collapsed or deployed depending on the distribution situation. Kirigami is a variation of origami that involves both cutting and folding of paper. The advantage of this design is that the kirigami cushion can be applied on the outside of a shipping container, instead of inside. Therefore, the shipping container itself can be more compact and the cushioning can be accessed and deployed when it is needed. The deployable kirigami cushion design was evaluated using compression and vertical impact tests, and the testing results are presented.

Keywords: kirigami, deployable structure, cushioning, distribution, e-commerce.

***Correspondence to:** Euihark Lee, School of Packaging, Michigan State University, East Lansing, MI 48824, USA. E-mail: leeeuiha@msu.edu

1. Introduction

In a packaging system, a cushioning structure provides protection, one of the most important packaging functions. Cushioning prevents physical damage of the products during distribution. In general, polymeric foam [1]-[3] and fiber [4],[5] materials have been used widely in package cushioning. Polymeric foam is well developed to optimize the cushioning function [6]; however, it has a negative environmental impact because of recycling issues [7]. On the other hand, fiber materials are used as alternative solutions to polymeric foam but the corrugated cushioning design cannot provide good cushioning function, especially for repeated shocks.

Cushioning is becoming more important to the e-commerce industry. In 2014, the value of U.S. retail e-commerce sales, including digital services, was $298.26 billion (U.S.), and by 2023 is expected to grow to $969.7 billion (U.S.) [8]. The growth of e-commerce creates more challenges for packaging for many reasons. First, the distribution environment of e-commerce is tougher than for brick and mortar distribution since most products are delivered through single-parcel distribution systems. Second, the handling process for packages associated with the e-commerce environment requires more steps than for the brick and mortar distribution system. According to an Amcor report in 2016,[9] the minimum handling point for e-commerce distribution is at least three times more than for brick and mortar distribution, and could be exposed to more potential hazards during the distribution. Lastly, e-commerce may require different types of packaging systems than regular package systems for the same products. For example, Amazon gives incentives to their vendors if the packaging is certified by Amazon to meet the Frustration-Free Packaging (FFP), Ships in its Own Container (SIOC), and Prep-Free Packaging (PFP) Program guidelines [10]. Because of these reasons, the packages in e-commerce tend to be oversized and over protective, which impacts the shipping efficiency.

To help resolve these packaging issues for e-commerce, a deployable kirigami cushion design is proposed in this paper. Kirigami is a variation of origami that involves cutting and folding of paper into the desired shape, whereas origami only involves folding [11]. The main advantage of the kirigami design is that the deployable structure can be constructed from a simple pattern. By implementing the kirigami structure into a cushion design, the cushion can be changed when more cushioning is needed. As a result, the overall shipping volume can be controlled based on the shipping conditions. The conceptual design of the deployable cushion is shown in Figure 1. For example, when the product ships as a pallet, all cushions can be collapsed to maximize shipping efficiency. However, when each package is distributed as a single parcel, the cushion can be deployed at the distribution center to maximize the product protection.

Testing was performed on the deployable kirigami cushion structure to verify the cushioning function. First, the compression test was performed to measure the compression strength of the kirigami cushion. Next, the vertical impact test was performed to verify the benefits of the kirigami cushion design. The major aim of this research was to investigate the effectiveness of two types of the kirigami cushion design to increase shipping efficiency and content protection through a sustainable solution. The findings of this investigation can be applied to packaging distribution broadly, but especially in e-commerce packaging.

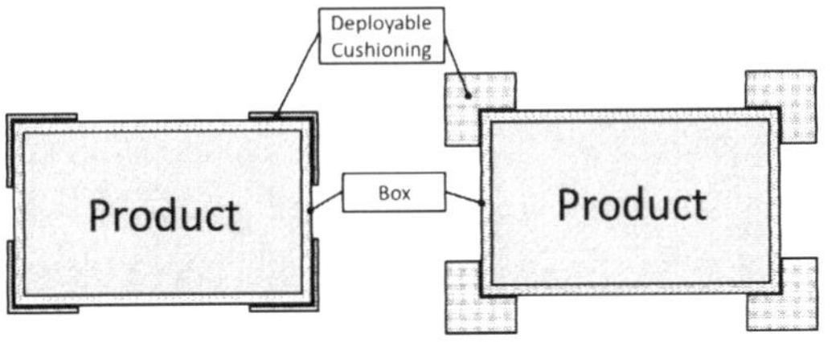

Figure 1 *Conceptual configuration of deployable cushioning.*

2. Kirigami Cushion Design

The proposed deployable kirigami cushion design is shown in Figure 2, with photos of the collapsed and deployed cushion. This kirigami cushion can be attached to the current packaging system in the collapsed form and then be deployed when needed. This kirigami design can be made with paper using a simple pattern that creates a honeycomb structure when it is deployed. The honeycomb structure provides the cushioning function, and that function can be controlled by the number of honeycomb cells in the kirigami design. When the kirigami design has more honeycomb cells in a given cushioning space, it will be stiffer. The number of honeycomb cells is determined by the gluing pattern for the flat sheets.

Figure 2 *A deployable 6-partition kirigami cushion design.*

In this study, two different types of kirigami cushion samples of the same size were prepared with a 4- or 6-partition design. These different kirigami cushions were used to demonstrate how the number of partitions affects the material properties using same size of the cushion. This kirigami cushion is composed of 30 individual 4 × 4 inch paper sheets that are folded in half and glued in specific configurations. For this study, each 4 × 4 inch sheet was folded in half to convert to 4 × 2 inches, and after folding all sheets the glue lines were applied to the inside and outside; the four-partition design has 3 glue lines and the 6-partition design has 5 glue lines. Glue was applied along the glue lines on alternate sides of the sheets, as shown in Figure 3. The red line represents the fold line and green lines indicate the glue application lines. Each folded sheet was attached to another sheet until all 30 folded sheets were glued. For this study, 10 specimens of each partition design were prepared as described.

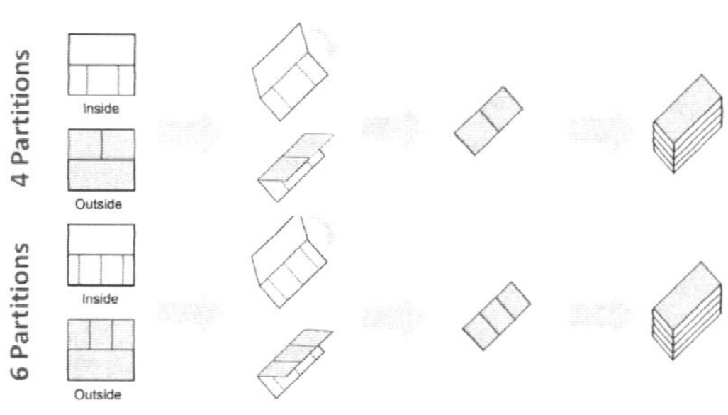

Figure 3 *Fold line and glue line applications for the kirigami cushion design.*

3. Compression Test of the Deployable Kirigami Cushion

To measure the compression strength of the proposed deployable kirigami cushion, compression tests were performed on 4-partition and 6-partition specimens using an Instron 5605 Universal Testing Machine. Five specimens of each partition design were tested.

3.1 Compression Testing Method

Each specimen was placed on top of the compression fixture in a 180-degree deployed shape, as shown in Figure 4. The compression rate was set at 0.5 inches per minute, and compressive extension and compressive load were measured during the test. The compression motion was ended after 0.8 inches of compressive extension, or when the sensitivity of rate of load is 40 percent.

Figure 4 *Compression test set up using Instron 5605.*

3.2 Compression Testing Results

The relationship between compressive extension and load for the 4-partition cushion is shown in Figure 5. When the compressive extension is less than 0.2 inches, the major compression happened in the arc space area between the bottom fixture and the deployed kirigami cushion. Once the cushion started to support the compressive load, then the curve shows a steeper slope between compressive extension and load. The maximum compressive loads are marked with a rectangle on each curve, and the average maximum load was 162.4 ± 11.2 lbs (standard deviation). Because this 4-partition kirigami cushion has a multiple honeycomb structure, the cushion maintains a certain percentage of maximum compressive strength even when the compressive extension passed the maximum compression load.

To demonstrate the different compression strength of the kirigami cushion with 6 partitions, specimens were tested at the same conditions and the results are shown in Figure 6. The relationship between compressive extension and load was similar for the 6-partition and 4-partition cushions. However, the average maximum compressive load for the 6-partition samples was 243 lbs, which is about 80 lbs more than for the 4-partition samples. This result shows that the compression strength can be controlled easily by changing the number of partitions with the same volume and materials for the kirigami cushions.

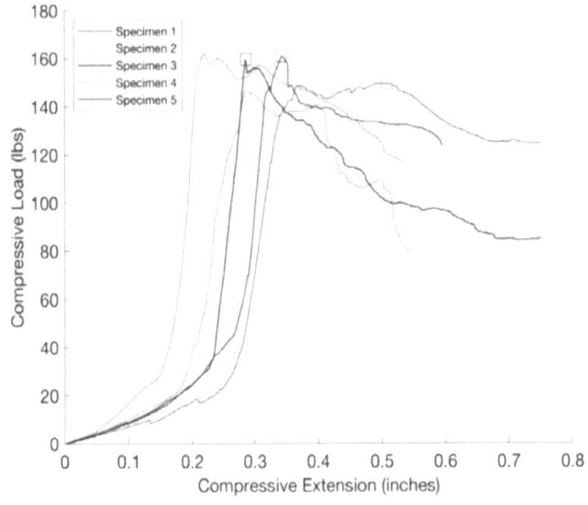

Figure 5 *Compression strength for 4-partition cushion.*

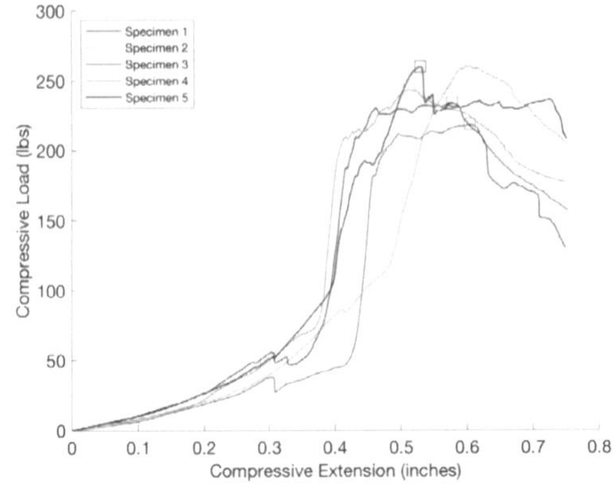

Figure 6 *Compression strength for 6-partition cushion.*

4. Vertical Impact Test of the Deployable Kirigami Cushion

The vertical impact test was performed on 4-partition and 6-partition cushion specimens using the Lansmont Vertical Impact Tester. Five specimens of each partition design were tested.

4.1 Vertical Impact Test Method

The vertical impact test set up is shown in Figure 7. A 12-inch drop height was used for the entire test and the drop weight was 12.8 lbs. Each kirigami cushion was placed on the impact surface in a 180-degree deployed shape. Each specimen was tested with 5 drops, and the transmitted shock (G's) was measured for every drop to evaluate the cushioning function of the kirigami cushion design.

Figure 7 *Vertical impact test set up*

4.2 Vertical Impact Test Results

The vertical impact test results for the 4-partition cushion are shown in Figure 8 and Table 1. The x axis represents the drop number, from 1 to 5, and the y axis shows the impact acceleration (G). The average impact acceleration of the first drop was 19.85 ± 5.88 G (SD).

At drop number 2, specimens 2, 3, and 5 showed less impact acceleration than at the first drop because the integrity of the kirigami cushion structure was largely maintained at the first drop. The acceleration increased dramatically when the integrity of the structure was lost. From the results, the acceleration started to increase at drop number 2 for specimens 1 and 4, at drop number 3 for specimens 2 and 5, and at drop number 4 for specimen 3. The changes in the kirigami cushion structure through the five drops are shown in Figure 9.

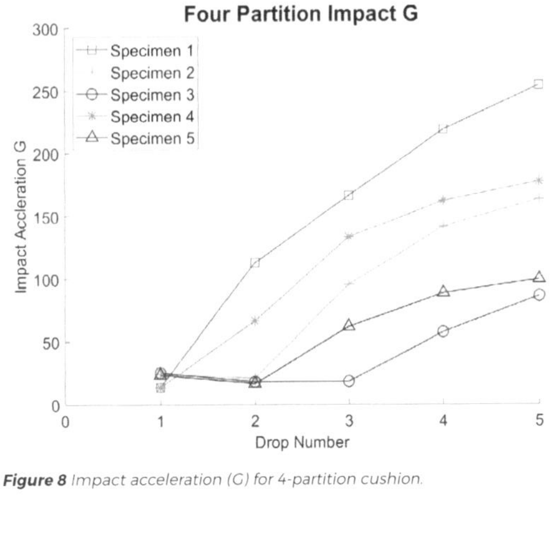

Figure 8 *Impact acceleration (G) for 4-partition cushion.*

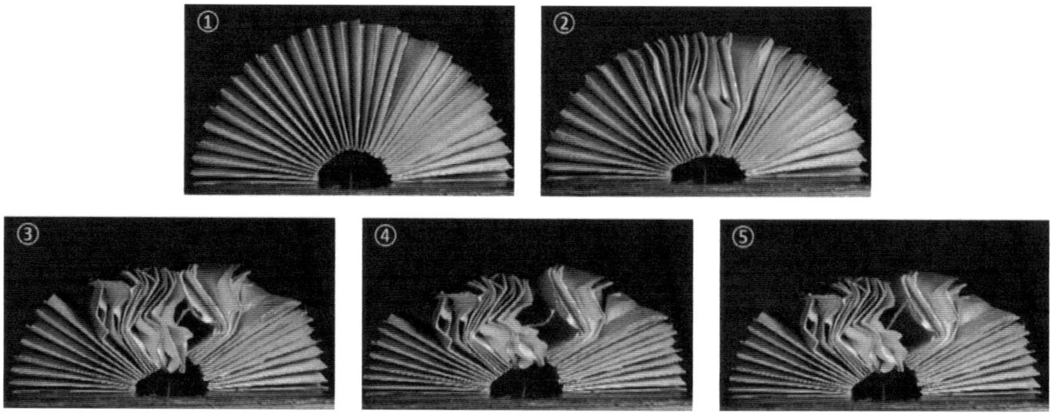

Figure 9 *The changes in kirigami cushion structure through drops 1 to 5.*

To demonstrate the different cushioning function of the kirigami cushion made with the same materials but with 6 partitions, specimens were tested and the vertical impact test results are shown in Figure 10 and Table 2. The 6-partition and 4-partition cushion vertical impact test results were similar; however, because of more glue lines, the structural integrity of the 6-partition kirigami cushion was maintained better than that of the 4-partition kirigami cushion. As a result, all five specimens had less acceleration at drop 2 and started to increase at drop 3. The average impact acceleration of the first drop was 35.33 G with 2.27 standard deviation, and the average of the second drop was 19.71 G with 5.35 standard deviation. The 6-partition cushion results show more clearly that the impact acceleration of the second drop was less than for the first drop. As explained previously, the first drop crushes some of the honeycomb structure and the structure provides more cushioning function. In the case of specimen 1, the impact acceleration was maintained well below the first impact acceleration. This result shows that as long as the kirigami cushion maintains structural integrity, it maintains the cushioning function. This function could be beneficial for distribution environments with repeated impacts.

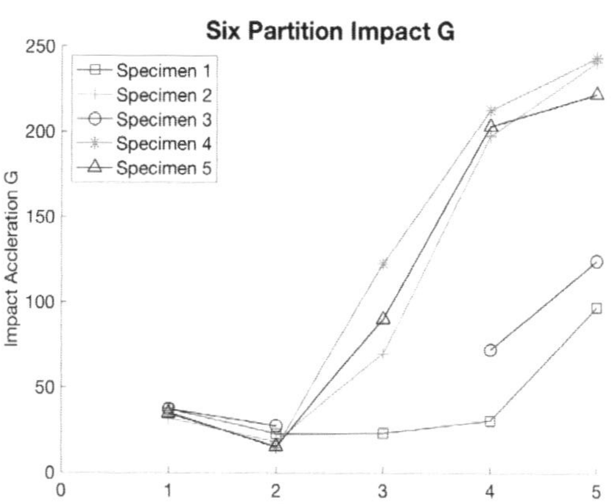

Figure 10 *Impact acceleration (G) for 6-partition cushion.*

5. Conclusions

In this paper, the deployable kirigami cushion is presented with prototype designs. The main advantage of the kirigami cushion is the deployable function, which can enhance shipping efficiency depending on the distribution situation. Moreover, it is easy to control the cushioning properties of the kirigami cushion as shown in the comparisons between the 4-partition and 6-partition kirigami designs. Therefore, depending on the cushioning needs, the designer can simply modify the partitions to ensure the cushioning properties match the products to protect. Additionally, the kirigami cushion can be attached to the current packaging systems used for brick and mortar vendors, and e-commerce vendors do not have to prepare different packaging systems for the same products.

6. References

[1] Miltz J, Ramon O. Energy absorption characteristics of polymeric foams used as cushioning materials. Polymer Engineering and Science 1990; 30: 129–133. DOI:10.1002/pen.760300210.

[2] Singh J, Ignatova L, Olsen E, Singh P. Evaluation of stress-energy methodology to predict transmitted shock through expanded foam cushions. Journal of Testing and Evaluation 2010; 38(6): 724–730.

[3] Navarro-Javierre P, Garcia-Romeu-Martinez MA, Cloquell-Ballester VA, de-la-Cruz-Navarro E. Evaluation of two simplified methods for determining cushion curves of closed cell foams. Packaging Technology and Science 2012; 25(4):217-231. DOI: 10.1002/pts.969.

[4] Marcondes J. Cushioning Properties of Corrugated Fiberboard and the Effects of Moisture Content. Transactions of the ASAE 1992; 35(6): 1949–1953. DOI: 10.13031/2013.28821.

[5] Daum M, Darby D, Batt G, Campbell L. Application of the Stress-Energy Method for Generating Corrugated Board Cushion Curves. Journal of Testing and Evaluation 2013; 41(4): 590-601.

[6] ASTM D1596-14. Standard Test Method for Shock Absorbing Characteristics of Package Cushioning Materials 2014; E.E.U.U. www.astm.org.

[7] Sustainable Packaging Coalition. (2009). Environmental technical briefs of common packaging materials: Polymers. Charlottesville, VA.

[8] eMarketer. (June 24, 2019). Retail e-commerce sales including digital services in the United States from 2014 to 2023 (in billion U.S. dollars) [Graph]. In Statista. Retrieved May 8, 2020, from https://www.statista.com/statistics/183750/us-retail-e-commerce-sales-figures/#statisticContainer

[9] Amcor Flexibles North America. (2016) Packaging for a new era of ecommerce: How ecommerce will transform the role of consumer packaging. http://www.bemis.com/Bemis/media/Library/pdf/restricted/amcor-ebook-ecommerce-na.pdf. Accessed 11 May 2020.

[10] Amazon. (2019). Amazon Frustration-Free Packaging Program Certification Guidelines. https://d39w7f4ix9f5s9.cloudfront.net/35/92/d21b63d5447e90627abebd01ebc6/amazon-frustration-free-pack aging-program-certification-guidelines-v10.2 2019_FINAL.pdf. Accessed 11 May 2020.

[11] Temko, F. 1962. Kirigami: The creative art of paper cutting. New York: Platt & Munk.

Carbon dioxide concentration in carbonated beverages: a comparison between Zahm & Nagel ™ e LAB.CO ™ methods [30]

Paula F. Janetti Bócoli *1, Léa M. Oliveira1, Bruno F. Gasparino 1, Sandra Balan M. Jaime 1, Marcio Amazonas 2
1 Packaging Technology Center, Institute of Food Technology - Cetea/Ital - Avenida Brasil, Campinas/SP - Brazil
2 ACM Beverage Processing Instrumentation, Corp., USA

Abstract: A carbonated beverage must have in its formulation controlled concentrations of carbon dioxide (CO_2), a non-toxic, inert, colorless and tasteless gas that gives efferervescence and contributes to freshness feeling when it is consumed. Carbonation levels, or the concentration of carbon dioxide dissolved in the beverage, are defined depending on the type of product and generally range between 1.2 and 4.6 CO_2 volumes (% v/v, or 1.97 times in g/L); carbonation loss is a critical factor that affects the product acceptability, thus requiring the evaluation of CO_2 barrier during the development of new or lighter packaging. The reference method used to determine carbonation in beverages is the Zahm & Nagel ™ system (Z&N), a mobile punch device coupled to a pressure gauge which, after manual perforation of the closure, allows to check the dissolved gas pressure in the beverage. Using pressure and temperature, CO_2 volume is calculated based on standard tables. Its use is widespread, however, its disadvantages regarding the time required for sample preparation, testing and product disposal, have motivated the development of nondestructive technologies. This study aimed to comparatively evaluate the Z&N (destructive method) and the LAB.CO™, an equipment that allows direct measurements of CO_2 volume in beverage packaging headspace using laser light, non-destructively and quickly. Samples tested included cola beverage, with sugar and sugar- free, in two sizes, 200 mL and 2L, in clear PET bottle presentations, and carbonated water in glass and PET bottles. The bottles were kept at 23 °C for 8 weeks and periodically evaluated. LAB.CO results showed good repeatability. When analyzed CO_2 volumes, comparatively with Z&N method, some small differences in results were observed.

Keywords: carbonated beverage, CO_2 measurement; LAB.CO ™, nondestructive testing, laser absorbance, Zahm & Nagel ™

***Correspondence to:** Paula F. Janetti Bócoli, Packaging Technology Center, Brazil Avenue, Brazil. E-mail: paula@ital.sp.gov.br

1. Introduction

In Brazil, the carbonated drinks market is quite expressive, even with a drop in consumption, mainly in soft drinks, observed in the period from 2014 to 2017. On the other hand, in the same period, bottled water had a considerable increase, leading to a perspective of change in the consumption habit of Brazilians [1-2], representing the second largest segment of non-alcoholic beverages in Brazil [3].

Carbonated drinks are characterized by the presence of carbon dioxide (CO_2), a non-toxic, inert, colorless, tasteless, and water-soluble gas. Its high solubility, especially at low temperatures, allows it to remain in solution and confer an effervescent characteristic to the drink and, consequently, the sensation of freshness that the consumer feels when ingesting the product. In addition to enhancing the flavor, the presence of CO_2 also helps to conserve the drink because, in contact with water, carbon dioxide is transformed into carbonic acid, contributing to the acidity of the product and controlling microbiological growth [4-5].

The levels of dissolved CO_2 (volume of gas absorbed by an equal volume of water, at an atmospheric pressure of 0 psi and at a temperature of 16° C (60 F) vary between 1.2 to 4.6 volumes (% v/v, or 1.97 times in g/L) [6] for different types of drink, taking into account the ideal taste for the consumer. Historically, according to many manufacturers, a 15% carbonation loss limit in 12 weeks of product storage is still acceptable [7], given that only a few products and distribution routes reach the expiration date due to low rotation. Bottles and closures are designed to ensure CO_2 loss is controlled to reach the "sell by" date at acceptable carbonation levels; advanced technologies are being developed to improve such gas barrier, requiring quick studies, 9-week shelf life studies or long-term testing.

The carbonation process can be done directly on the product or by mixing carbonated water with syrup [8]. Some production parameters need to be controlled to ensure good carbonation: temperature of the drink, gas pressure in the saturator, water quality, type of syrup (in the case of soft drinks) and packaging. Another essential procedure is reduce to the minimum achievable the levels of air/oxygen dissolved in the beverage drink and in the packaging headspace, since small concentrations of oxygen can decrease up to 50 times the volume of CO_2 dissolved in the product. Until the 1930s, carbonated drinks were packaged only in glass bottles, usually returnable, with thick walls and high weight. Even then, the first metallic steel packaging was introduced. As time passed, the glass bottles started to lose weight and the cans started to be manufactured also in aluminum. The first PET bottles were introduced to the market in the 1970s and, in Brazil, the first disposable bottle was marketed in 1987 [8].

Currently PET packaging is the main presentation used for this segment, in different volumes, shapes and colors, including returnable and refillable bottles. Glass packaging has remained strongly present in the market, mainly for carbonated alcoholic beverages, such as beers, sparkling wines and mixed drinks, beverages for which the control of the dissolved CO^2 content is extremely important to maintain the organoleptic properties appreciated by the consumer.

There are methods on the market to determine the CO_2 content dissolved in drinks, the most traditional and considered as a reference being the manometric method known as Zahm & Nagel ™ (Z&N). This system consists of a mobile device with a piercing tip coupled to a manometer, in which after perforation of the lid, there is the release of the pressure of dissolved gas in the drink, in order to allow the calculation of CO_2 volume correlating the pressure registered in function of the drink temperature at the time of analysis. Its use is widespread worldwide, however, its disadvantages regarding the destruction of the sample / loss of product and generation of packaging waste, as it is a destructive method, is still a matter of concern. Another factor that may raise doubts about the results obtained by this method is the definition of the correct execution of the analysis. Normative references mention the importance of agitating the packaging for at least one minute, after drilling, to homogenize the temperature and pressure of the gas dissolved in the product, released into the headspace. However, after drilling, many bottlers release the gas pressure, a process known as snifting, meant to eliminate foreign gases present in the headspace, which should not be considered in the determination of the CO_2 dissolved in the product. With this step, the CO_2 volume calculated will be based on a second pressure measurement, obtained after shaking the package several times, until the pressure reading on the pressure gauge stabilizes.

In view of these factors, some companies have been seeking to develop new, non-destructive technologies to reduce such occurrences. With this type of equipment, after checking the gas content, the product packaging can return to the process line and, in the case of shelf-life studies, CO_2 loss can always be monitored in the same bottle, reducing the number of samples and the necessary storage space, while presenting more real results due to reduced variability. In addition, due to it is an automatic device, it reduces the probability of analyst errors since all measurements are performed directly by the device and the results can be transferred directly to spreadsheets. An example of nondestructive equipment is the LAB.CO ™, developed by the Austrian company ACM GmbH. The operating principle is to read the CO_2 concentration in the bottle headspace, without contact with the packaging, with a CO_2-selective laser, after shaking the sample to release the carbon dioxide dissolved in the product and reach pressure equilibrium with the gases dissolved in the liquid. The CO_2 concentration is determined based on the Beer-Lambert law (Figure 1), according to which it there is a direct correlation between the light absorbed by CO_2 molecules and its concentration in the medium. The temperature is determined by a pyrometer that measures the heat radiated by the outer face of the package. With the information obtained, the equipment quickly calculates the dissolved carbon gas content, expressed in volume, as well as the pressure and temperature values, using Henry-Dalton's law of gases, converting partial pressures into volume of dissolved CO_2 using normative tables or the equation below:

$$c^*_{CO_2} = \xi^*_{CO_2} * p^*_{CO_2}$$ where:

- $c^*_{CO_2}$ = CO_2 is the concentration in equilibrium
- $\xi^*_{CO_2}$ = CO_2 is the solubility coefficient (depends on the type of beverage and temperature)
- $p^*_{CO_2}$ = CO_2 is the partial pressure of the headspace in equilibrium

For water:

$$CO_2[g/l] = (P+1)*10*EXP(-11.073+2725/(T+273.15))$$

(to convert in CO_2 Vol. [% v/v] = CO_2[g/l]/1.97)

For soft drinks (with sugar):

$$CO_2[g/l] = (0.0002607*(T+273.16)*(P/1.03321)+[(0.01898-0.000047591*(T+273.16)/(0.03275*(T+273.16)-7.9567)]*[(P/1.03321)+1)*(T+273.16)]*1.976$$

P = Partial pressure
T = Temperature in °C

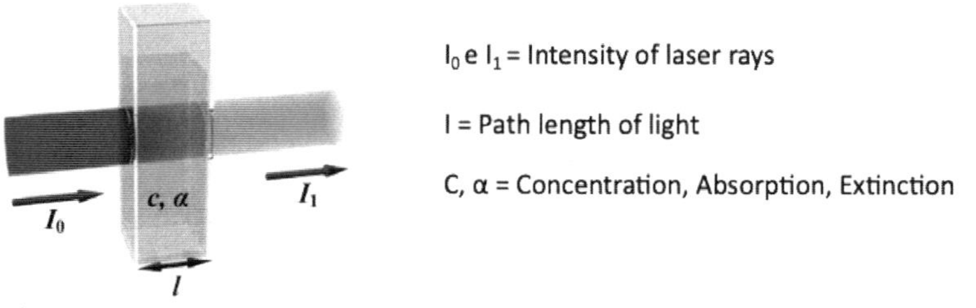

Figure 1 *Beer-Lambert law.*

Non-invasive or non-destructive methods apply for glass and plastic bottles, transparent or colored, of different shapes, volumes, and products.

Considering the characteristics of most carbonated products, such as the amount of dissolved solids, the presence of sugars, dyes, etc., and the packaging used, such as material, color and wall thickness, the equipment was developed with different methodological options, in addition to allowing different packaging positions to ensure that measurements are performed correctly.

In order to assist the market in reducing losses, eliminating differences in methodologies and modernizing production controls, the study sought to correlate the results of the dissolved CO_2 content in carbonated beverages obtained by the reference method (Z&N) with results generated by the LAB.CO.

2. Materials and Methods

At first, LAB.CO repeatability and reproducibility (R&R) were determined using 60 units of cola beverage in clear 2 L PET bottles, being 30 traditional and 30 sugar-free.

The LAB.CO performance evaluation during storage time was made using cola beverage samples, traditional and sugar-free in clear 200 mL PET bottles and carbonated water clear and green PET bottles and in flint and green glass bottles. Thirty units of each samples were kept at 23 °C for 8 weeks and periodically evaluated. At the beginning of the storage period, all units were analyzed by LAB.CO. Weekly, 5 units of cola beverage (traditional and sugar-free) and 3 units of carbonated water in each type of bottle were randomly selected and analyzed by non- destructive equipment. Part of them were also analyzed by Z&N in even weeks.

Prior of the determinations, the bottles were homogenized on an IKA Labortechnik shaker, model HS250 basic, for a period of 3 minutes and were left to stand for 1 minute. The combination of LAB.CO software analysis methods was determined according to the Table 1.

Table 1 *LAB.CO operation conditions.*

Sample	Metho d	Materi al
Traditional Cola PET 2 L and 200 mL	Henry	PET1
Sugar-free Cola PET 2 L and 200 mL	Henry	PET1
Water – clear PET	Henry	PET1
Water – green PET	Henry	PET1
Water – flint glass	Henry	Glas1
Water – green glass	Henry	Glas1

For the Z&N method, a digital manometer brand IQM Instruments and a digital immersion Testo thermometer were used. The evaluation of the bottles was made 5 minutes after the end of the readings at LAB.CO, without releasing the initial pressure (no snifting) and shaking the bottles until the pressure registered on the manometer stabilized. With the pressure and temperature data, the CO_2 volume was calculated using Table X1 (Carbonation Volumes Tables) of the ASTM F 1115 - 95 (2001) - Standard Test Method for Determining the Carbon Dioxide Loss of Beverage Containers [9].

The results obtained were analyzed statistically using the Action software, version 2.9.29.368.534 and version of R: 3.0.2, using the Anderson-Darling and Wilcoxon tests, Bartlett and Anova variance.

3. Results and Discussions

Figure 2 shows the individual results obtained, in triplicate, for cola beverages packaged in 2 L PET bottles, traditional and sugar-free, with the nondestructive method (LAB.CO). For each bottle, there was no statistical difference (95% confidence interval) among the three repetitions.

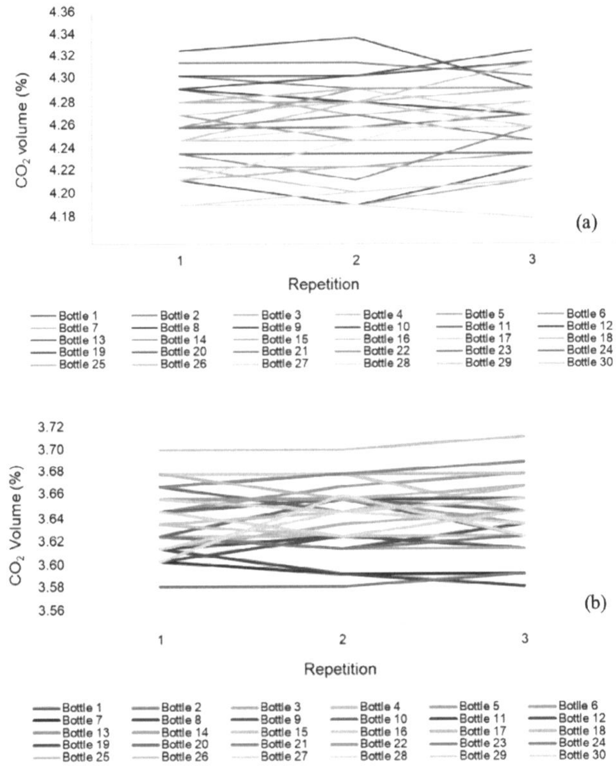

Figure 2 *Individual results obtained in the determination of the CO_2 volume by LAB.CO. in triplicate, of 2 L PET cola beverages: (a) traditional and (b) sugar-free.*

In the comparison between analysts (reproducibility), it can be observed, as illustrated in Figure 3, that the results were similar, with no statistical difference, at the 95% confidence level, with each other, for all 2 L bottles of cola beverage, traditional and sugar-free. Similarly, in the evaluation of the method's repeatability, no statistical difference was observed for the same results, at the 95% confidence level.

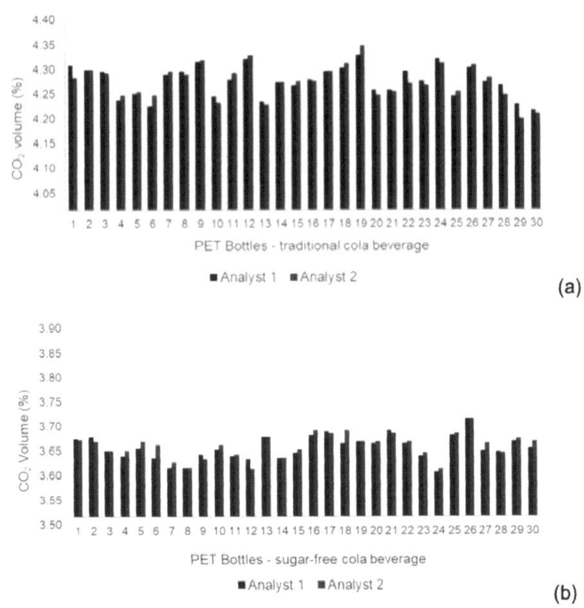

Figure 3 *Average results of CO_2 content obtained in the comparison between analysts (reproducibility) of 2 L PET cola beverages: (a) traditional and (b) sugar-free.*

The weekly evaluations of the same 5 bottles of traditional and sugar-free cola beverages, 200 mL nominal volume, and of the 3 clear and green PET bottles, containing carbonated water, showed decreases in the CO_2 volumes obtained by LAB.CO (Figures 4 and 5).

In each analysis period, in practice, there was no variation between the CO_2 volumes for traditional cola beverages (Figure 4b) and carbonated water samples (Figures 5a and 5b), which indicates good method repeatability for these products, as verified for the 2 L PET colas. For sugar-free cola samples there was variation between the bottles used in each period, which may be due to the heterogeneity of the batch, produced on August 5, 2019.

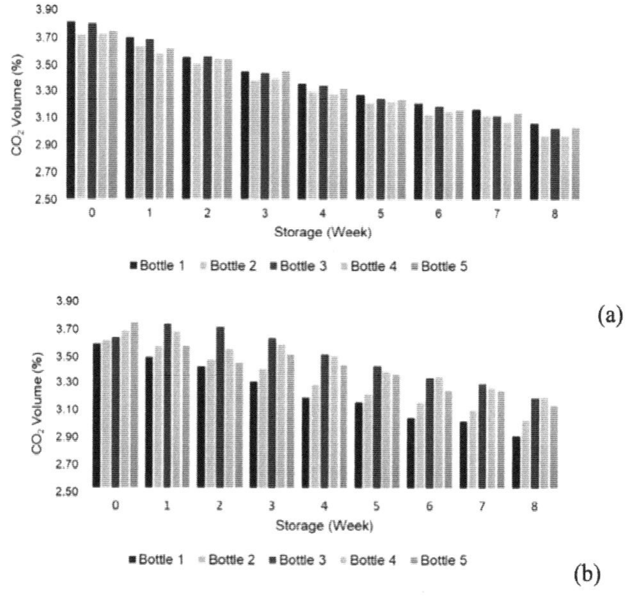

Figure 4 *Weekly CO_2 volume control: (a) 200 mL traditional cola and (b) 200 mL sugar-free cola, in clear PET.*

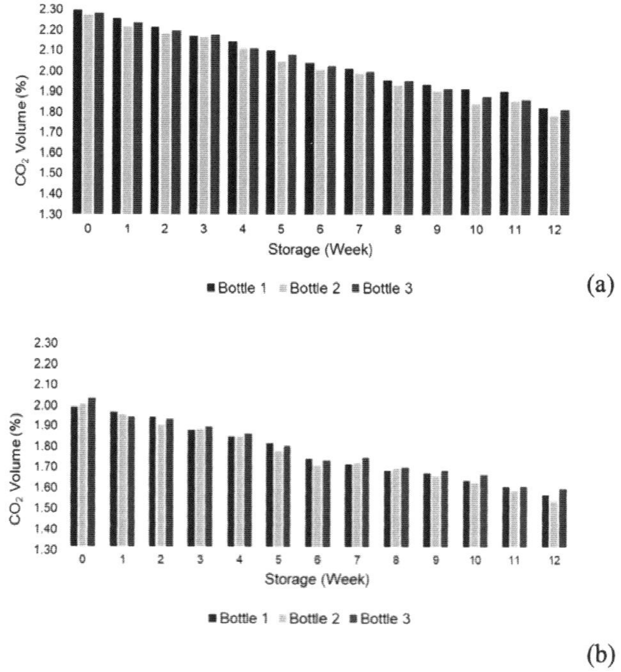

Figure 5 *Weekly CO_2 volume control: (a) 500 mL carbonated water in clear PET and (b) 510 mL carbonated water in green PET.*

In Figure 6, it can be seen, CO_2 volumes determined in the traditional and sugar-free cola beverages. The results showed no statistical differences between the methods in all the analyzed periods, for both samples. The higher Z&N punctual values may be due to the fact that the technique considers all gases present in the packaging as CO_2. In the determination of the gaseous composition (O_2, N_2 and H_2) inside the packages, in the periods of 0 days and 4 and 8 weeks in an Agilent gas chromatograph [1], the presence of nitrogen and oxygen was observed in concentrations similar to the air composition, in all periods, which demonstrated that there is no free space inertization and it proves that the quantification by the Z&N method considers the pressure of other gases besides CO_2.

The results obtained in the evaluation of carbonated water stored in green and clear PET bottles (Figure 7) were similar, with no statistical difference, at the 95% confidence level, regardless the technique used in the determination.

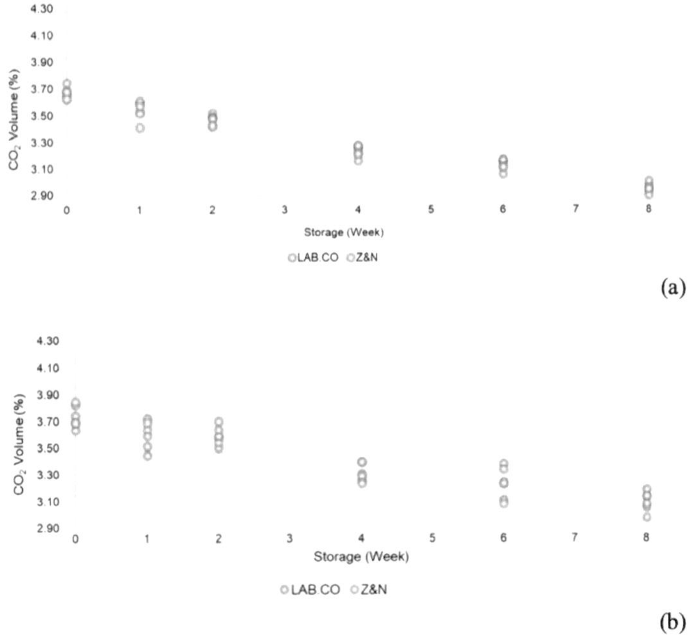

Figure 6 *Volume of CO_2 determined periodically in cola beverages, 200 mL, by the LAB.CO and Z&N methods: (a) traditional and (b) sugar-free.*

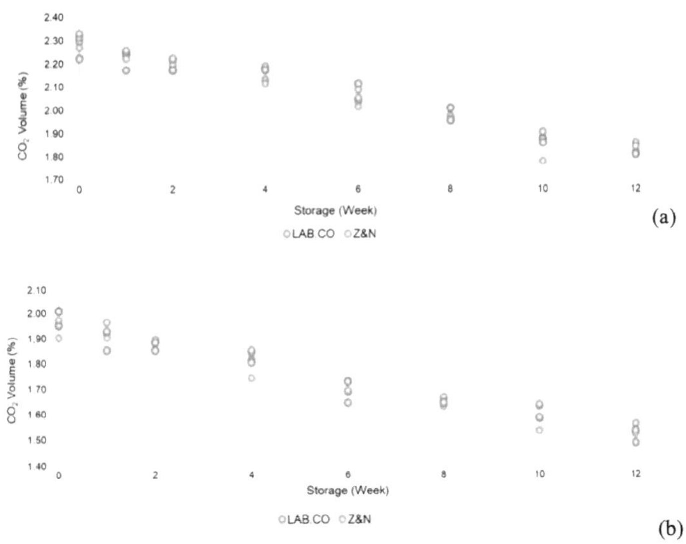

Figure 7 *Volumes of CO_2 determined periodically by the LAB.CO and Z&N methods in carbonated waters packed PET: (a) clear and (b) green bottles.*

1: Model 7890, operating with a thermal conductivity detector at 150 °C, columns (Molecular Sieve) 13X and Porapak N) at 40 °C and injector at 70 °C, using the Chemstation / Agilent program, version B 03.01.

In flint glass bottles (Figure 8a), statistically different results were found when comparing the methods, the results of LAB.CO being higher than Z&N, in most periods. However, for green glass bottles (Figure 8b), there was no statistical difference, at the 95%, comparing the techniques.

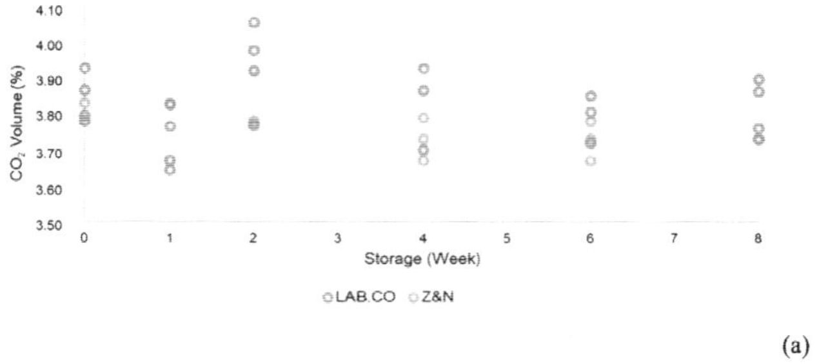

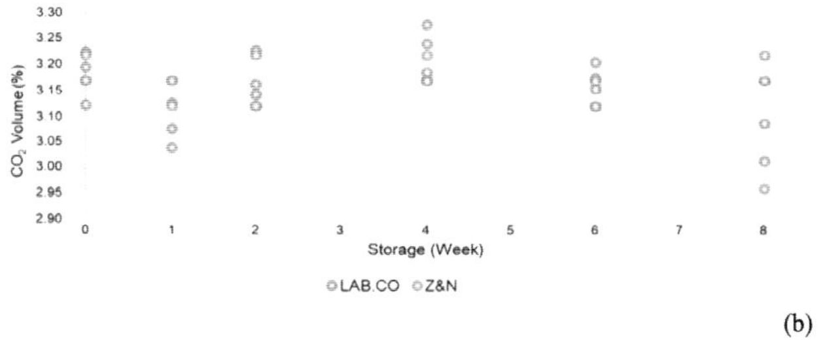

Figure 8 *Volumes of CO_2 determined periodically by the LAB.CO and Z&N methods in carbonated waters packed: (a) flint and (b) green glass bottles.*

4. Conclusion

The results of the CO_2 volumes obtained in cola beverage samples, traditional and sugar-free and in carbonated water, determined by the destructive (Z&N) and nondestructive (LAB.CO) methods, allow us to raise the following considerations:

1. The triplicate readings obtained with the LAB.CO provide information on good method repeatability.

2. The comparison between analysts with the 2 L PET cola bottles, evaluating the nondestructive method, did not show statistical difference, at the 95% confidence level, indicating good reproducibility of the method and absence of the influence of operator in performing the analysis.

3. In most comparisons between destructive and nondestructive methods, there can be no statistically significant difference, at the 95% confidence level, of the results, except for samples of carbonated water in a flint glass bottle.

4. The nondestructive method (LAB.CO) has advantages when compared to the traditional destructive method (Z&N) and with potential to replace it in beverage and packaging testing, since the results obtained were satisfactory.

5. References

[1] MOBLICCI, N. Panorama of the Brazilian alcoholic beverages market. São Paulo: Sintec, 2018. 4 p. Available at h ttps://sintec.com/pt-br/p_innovador/ panorama-do-mercado-brasileiro-de-bebidas-nao- a lcoolicas/. Accessed on: 06 May 2020.

[2] FARIAS, T. Soft drink consumption in Brazil falls and China takes 3rd place. Meio & Mensagem. Feb 28 2019. Available at: h ttps://www.meioemensagem.com.br/home/ultimas-noticias/2019/02/28/consumo-de-refrigerantes-no-brasil-cai-e-china-assume-3-lugar.html. Accessed on: 06 May 2020.

[3] BRASIL beverage trends 2020. Campinas: Ital, 2016. 302 p.Available at: h ttp://www.brasilbeveragetrends.com.br/files/ assets/basic-html/page-1.html. Accessed on: 06 May 2020.

[4] ASHURST, P. R.; HARGITT, R.; PALMER, F. Soft drink and fruit juice problems solved. 2nd. ed. Duxford: Woodhead, 2017. 232 p.

[5] WHITE MARTINS. Carbonation: the life of the drink. Curitiba: White Martins, 1998. 10 p

[6] ROBERTS, I. S. Containers and closures. In: FORMULATION and production of carbonated soft drinks. Glasgow: Blackie and Son, 1990. Chapter 9, p. 140-173.

[7] ASHURST, P. R. Carbonated beverages. Reference Module in Food Science, 2016. 5 p. Available at: h ttps://doi.org/10.1016/ B978-0-08-100596-5.03240-6. Accessed on: 06 May 2020.

[8] OLIVEIRA, L. M. (Ed.). Protection requirements for products in rigid plastic packaging. Campinas, SP: Ital / Cetea, 2004. 327 p

[9] ASTM INTERNATIONAL. ASTM F 1115-16: standard test method for determining the carbon dioxide loss of beverage containers. West Conshohocken: ASTM, 2016. 11 p.

E-commerce packaging: Challenges, opportunities, and trends [89]

Diana Sofía Chapa Chapa *, Cristina F. Guzmán Siller
Universidad de Monterrey, NL, Mexico

Abstract: The packaging for e-commerce has emerged during the last decade due to the purchase of goods immediately through the Internet, considering that it requires less effort and less waste of time for the consumers. Industries face constant challenges and customers demand immediate solutions. E-commerce packaging represents great challenges and opportunities from production to distribution processes. The pros and cons should be taken into account when making the selection of packaging material, avoiding over-packaging or missed packaging of the product. Companies are focusing on sustainable packaging solutions to reduce waste, turning into responsible companies. Currently, some challenges that we can see in e-commerce are: avoiding shipping damage, reducing the return rates of damaged products and reducing shipping costs by having excessive dimensions or material.

The purpose of this research is to provide an overview of past researches about e-commerce packaging. Showing a study of the current challenges that can be turned into opportunities and share information about future trends.

Keywords: e-commerce packaging, packaging trends, materials for e-commerce, sustainable materials, industry 4.0

***Correspondence to:** Diana Sofía Chapa Chapa, Universidad de Monterrey, NL, Mexico. E-mail: diana.chapa@udem.edu

CHAPTER II
Sustainability, recycling & renewable materials

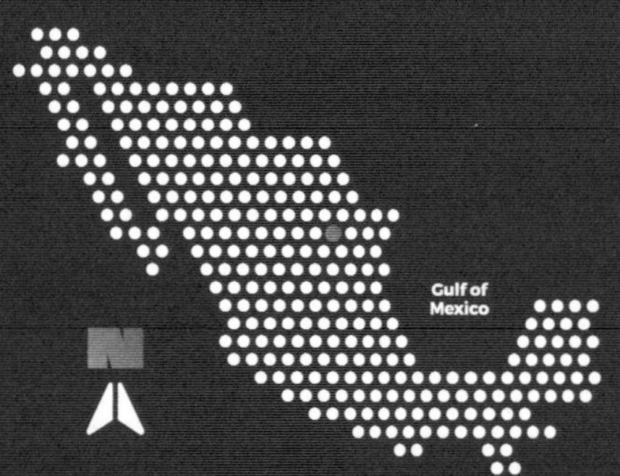

Author:
Oscar Alan Ríos Guajardo

Technique:
Digital photo with wide angle

Location:
San Pedro Garza García, NUEVO LEÓN

Description:
This is the Gate of Creation of Latin America, the place where tomorrow's leaders in Art, Design and Architecture will acquiere all the needed knowledge to make the right decisions tomorrow, following both their minds and their hearts.

Improved Recyclability of Multi-Layer, Dyed, and Contaminated Packaging by Low-Temperature Plasma Processing [6]

Alexander Bardenstein *, Jens Kromann Nielsen, Stanislav Landa, and Kenneth Kisbye
Danish Technological Institute, Gregersensvej 1, 2630 Taastrup, Denmark

Abstract: The most optimal use of packaging materials in the circular economy would ideally be reached using only mono-materials. However, numerous packaging products across industries comprise different materials to achieve required functionalities. In general, only clean "conventional" mono-plastics (PE, PP, and PET) are recycled and the use of recycled materials is restrained. The aim of this study is to improve recyclability of multi-material and contaminated plastic packaging waste by development and laboratory validation of an industrially relevant selective processing technology based on accelerated decomposition of polymers and inks and surface sterilization in chemically active plasmas. Controlling temperature of processed materials was proved to be important for achieving both selectivity and high process speed. The plasma technology can be divided into thermal (high-temperature) and non- thermal (low-temperature) plasma processing. A thermal plasma exhibits high energy density thermal reactions, while lacking chemical selectivity. On the other hand, the non-thermal plasma demonstrates selectivity with relatively slow processing. In order to find optimal processing regimes, the conditions have been explored between the thermal and non-thermal modes by tuning such plasma parameters as gas pressure and feeding gases, geometry of a plasma reactor, and electrical power. The selectivity of oxygen plasma processing regarding etching of different commonly used polymers (PET, PE, PP, and PS) has been proved and characterized by material- specific etching rates. It was shown that under the optimized conditions the processing time of the order of a few minutes is required for thin films (< 100 μm) typically used in food packaging. For instance, the total of LDPE barrier coatings can be etched away from a milk or juice carton in 4 minutes using 0.047 kWh of electrical energy (see Figure 1). Similarly, etching of a sealing LDPE layer from a PET meat tray takes about 3 minutes and requires the energy of about 0.017 kWh.

This study has been supported by a project "Improved recyclability of complex plastic waste by using selective low-temperature plasma technology" (2018-2021) granted by Ministry of Environment and Food of Denmark under the Environmental Technology Development and Demonstration Program (MUDP) and a grant from Danish Technological Institute's performance contract B4 (High-value plastic – Recycling and sustainable substitution), 2019- 2020, entered with the Danish Agency for Institutions and Educational Grants under The Ministry of Higher Education and Science of Denmark.

Keywords: Packaging recyclability, plasma processing, etching of polymers, bleaching, decontamination

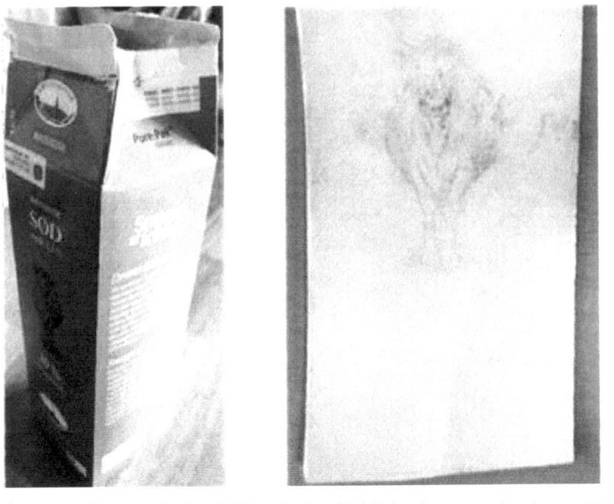

Figure 1 *Milk carton before (left) and after (right) 4-min processing in oxygen plasma of a capacitively coupled 250-W radio-frequency electrical discharge.*

***Correspondence to:** Alexander Bardenstein. E-mail: alb@dti.dk

Recyclable mono materials for packaging of fresh chicken filets- new design for recycling in circular economy [12]

Marit Kvalvåg Pettersen *1, Magnhild Seim Grøvlen 1, Nina Evje 2, Tanja Radusin 1
1 Nofima - Norwegian Institute of Food, Fisheries and Aquaculture Research, 1430 Ås, Norway
2 Nortura, Lørenveien 37, 0585 Oslo, Norway

Abstract: To ensure a uniform test level during design type testing and production line leak testing and therefore a comparable safety level as required by the Dangerous Goods Regulations, it is necessary to include a more precise specification in these regulations. This requires, on the one hand, information about the sensitivity of the bubble test and, on the other hand, the inclusion of a list of suitable, equally effective industrial test methods with their specific boundary conditions. Focus on sustainability and circular economy are leading to a need for development of new food packaging concepts, including recyclable materials which ideally consist of a single material in a monolayer system. This research was focused on possibility of replacing complex multi-layered material (amorphous-polyethylene terephthalate/polyethylene-APET/PE) with simple recyclable mono material (high density polyethylene-HDPE) for packaging of chicken fillets in modified atmosphere packaging MAP (CO_2/N_2-60%/40%). Bacterial growth measured as total viable count (TVC), Lactic acid bacteria (LAB) and Enterobacteriaceae, Brochothrix thermosphacta and Escherichia coli for chicken fillets packed in HDPE mono materials were compared with chicken fillets packed in APET/PE.

TVC increased during the storage period (24 days) with high level of TVC count (7 $\log_{10}$CFU/g) recorded at day 19-20 of storage in both HDPE and APET/PE material. No significant differences were recorded in off-odour between chicken stored in APET/PE compared to HDPE in CO_2/N_2 atmosphere during the storage period (samples were regarded as acceptable at 24th day of storage). The drip loss increased in all samples during storage and no significant differences between samples stored in different materials was recorded.

Significant differences in bacterial growth were recorded between samples with different gas volume to product volume (G/P) ratio (day 17) implying that higher G/P ratio is resulting in lower TVC count. The lowest G/P ratio caused the highest drip loss, while addition of CO_2 emitter reduced the drip loss to some extent.

This research is very encouraging as it provides new insight into the use of monolayer materials as well as importance of design for recycling in circular economy.

Keywords: sustainability, packaging, materials

PTS Special Edition: https://onlinelibrary.wiley.com/page/journal/10991522/homepage/iapri_papers

***Correspondence to:** food packaging, shelf life, active packaging, recyclable, circular economy, design for recycling

Flexible plastic packaging for instant coffee: product characteristics and packaging properties [27]

Raquel Massulo Souza [1], Thainá Bianchi Mazzarella [2], Christiane Quartaroli Moreira [3], Leda Coltro [4], Rosa Maria Vercelino Alves [5]

Packaging Technology Center, Institute of Food Technology - Cetea/Ital - Brazil Avenue, Campinas, São Paulo, Brazil

Abstract: Instant coffee is the second most consumed coffee product in Brazil, which is currently marketed in glass bottle and stand-up pouch flexible packaging. Cost reduction, increased convenience and use packaging structures with less negative environmental impact are highly desirable. Post-consumed flexible packaging usually causes environmental problem due to the difficulty of materials separation and incompatibility in the recycling lines. Therefore, the aim of the study was to evaluate the influence of the instant coffee process (spray and freeze dried, with and without a surface application of coffee oils to enhance the headspace aroma), packaging material barrier in the quality and shelf life of the product. For this, the residual oxygen of the headspace of commercial packages of instant coffee was analyzed and the products themselves in relation to moisture content, water activity, and moisture sorption isotherms at 25°C. The barrier properties of the packages were analyzed too. Results showed differences in the composition of the headspace gas and in the moisture sorption isotherms. Brazilian packages presented air composition in the headspace. One imported glass bottle showed modified atmosphere in the headspace. Spray dryer coffees (agglomerated and powder) showed higher water activity and initial and critical moisture than freeze dryer coffees. Spray dryer presented changes in the characteristic aspects at 12% d.b moisture and freeze dryer at 5 and 7% d.b. WVTR between 0.021 - 0109 g water.m-2.day-1 at 25C/75%RH for instant coffees were estimated to stand-up pouches with 50 g net weigh product through the moisture sorption isotherms adjusted. These results will allow outlining alternatives of flexible plastic packaging materials for instant coffee packages, preserving quality requirements and product shelf life as well as generating less negative environmental impact.

Keywords: instant coffee, shelf life, sustainable packaging, flexible packaging

*Correspondence to: raquel.souza@ital.sp.gov.br [1], thainabianchi@gmail.com [2], christiane@ital.sp.gov.br [3], ledacolt@ital.sp.gov.br [4], rosa@ital.sp.gov.br [5]

Development of peach pit waste-filled polyolefin biocomposite with maleic anhydride coupling agent [40]

Caralyn Wong [1], Joongmin Shin [*1], Stephanie Jung [2], and Ajay Kathuria [1]
1 Industrial Technology and Packaging, California Polytechnic State University, San Luis Obispo, USA
2 Food Science and Nutrition, California Polytechnic State University, San Luis Obispo, USA

Abstract: It is estimated that roughly 103, 515 tons of peach waste is produced annually in the US. The majority of the waste is disposed of in landfills, which contributes to climate change as they release 93 million metric tons of CO2 equivalent. Peach waste principally consists of remaining stone and seed after flesh removal. The agro-waste includes both cellulose and lignin, which can be utilized as a filler in plastic packaging to reduce carbon footprints and material cost. The objectives of this research are (1) to develop peach flour (PF)-filled biocomposites with a polyolefin matrix using maleic anhydride-g-high density polyethylene (MAH-g-HDPE) coupling agent resin and (2) to investigate the composites' physicomechanical, thermal, and water absorbance changes. First, a range of PF concentrations (5-50%) and MAH concentrations (0-20%) was tested to narrow the variability of PF and MAH loading mixture in an HDPE matrix. Response surface methodology (RSM) was utilized to analyze and optimize the tensile strength of the PW composite. The RSM parameters were MAH loading (5-20%) and PF loading (2.5-10%). The properties of optimized PF-HDPE biocomposites were analyzed using several instrumental analyses. Mechanical strength (including tensile strength and elongation) and thermal properties (thermal degradation, melting point, and crystallinity), and water resistance with the addition of PF and MAH were investigated. The thermal analysis suggested that thermal stability increased with PF loading. Tensile strength displayed an optimized maximum of PF and MAH loadings. Additionally, tensile test results demonstrated that PF-composites of comparable tensile strength to a commercially available control can be produced with 2.5% PF.

Keywords: Biocomposite, Peach stone, Maleic anhydride

***Correspondence to:** Joongmin Shin, California Polytechnic State University, San Luis Obispo. E-Mail: jshin20@calpoly.edu

1. Introduction

Food is lost and wasted along the entire supply chain with agricultural production and consumer consumption stages accounting for a majority of food wastage. The fruit industry generates large volumes of waste and byproducts from processing fresh fruit into juices, nectars, jellies, and canned foods. Fruit byproducts such as peels, stems, and seeds account for more than 50% of fresh fruit weight and may have a higher nutritional or functional content than the final product [1, 2]. Landfilling remains the main technology for managing food waste, but this method results in landfill gas and leachate production with the risk of contaminating ground water [3]. Landfill gas is generated from disposing biodegradable materials in landfill and is composed of 55-65% v/v methane and 40-45% v/v carbon dioxide [4]. In 2017, the United States peach industry produced 103,515 tons of by-product (15% total weight) after processing 690,100 tons of peach, which is primarily sent to landfill [5,6]. Biochemical analysis indicated that drupe seeds contain nearly twice as much lignin as wood and possess high mechanical properties, which opens opportunities for drupes in materials research [7]. During the past decade, the number of published scientific articles on biocomposites has increased each year by roughly 17.5%. Applications for biocomposites include household items (chairs, containers), automotive parts (door panels, bumpers), and moderate strength construction materials.

2. Research Goals / Objectives

The objectives of this research were (1) to develop PF-filled biocomposites with an HDPE matrix using MAH as a coupling agent resulting in a biocomposite with maximum tensile strength and (2) to investigate the biocomposites' physico-mechanical, thermal, and water resistance properties of the PF- filled biocomposites.

3. Research Method

Peach stones were donated by Del Monte Foods, Inc. (Modesto, CA). Peach stones were ground into flour via mechanical grain mill and sieved to a particle size of 195μm. A preliminary experiment investigated a range of PF concentrations (5-50%) and MAH concentrations (0-20%) compounded into an HDPE matrix to narrow the levels of PF and MAH loading. Response surface methodology (RSM) was utilized to analyze and optimize the tensile strength of the PF-filled biocomposite. The RSM parameters were MAH loading (5-20%), PF loading (2.5-10%). Samples were labeled as "PE" followed by the PF loading percentage. For example, PE10 is the sample for an HDPE sample with 10% PF loading. The properties of PF-HDPE biocomposites were investigated using several instrumental analyses. Mechanical strength was analyzed using a tensile tester and thermal properties were analyzed using thermogravimetric analysis and differential scanning calorimetry. Water resistance was measured according to ASTM D570.

4. Results and conclusions

The PF-HDPE biocomposites displayed no change in thermal stability compared to its control, except for the composites with 5%PF, which may be attributed to sample variability. The addition of a coupling agent may not increase thermal stability as MAH-g-PLA has previously decreased thermal stability because MAH molecules can destroy polymer crystal structures to promote thermal composition [8]. A previous study that developed a coconut shell powder-PLA composite discovered an increase in thermal stability in the presence of their natural fiber. This increase was attributed to the char formation during fiber pyrolysis, as char may act as a protective barrier from thermal decomposition [9, 10]. The addition of PF immediately decreased biocomposite crystallinity. The addition of fibers may act as an obstacle for crystal formation as it limits polymer chain movement [9]. PF had no influence on T_c and T_m suggesting there was no interaction or negligibly weak interaction between filler and matrix.

The addition of PF decreased tensile strength, extension at break, and young's modulus. A decrease in tensile strength is associated with poor adhesion between filler and polymer, which concentrates stress and accelerates sample break [11]. A decrease in Young's modulus may be due to the weak interactions between polymer and fiber. With the addition of natural fibers and coupling agents, the rigid particles and enhanced interfacial adhesion ultimately decreases polymer plasticity to decrease the extension at break.

As fiber loading increased, water absorption increased. This was expected due to the hydrophilicity of cellulose fibers [12]. These fibers contain a hollow center, which absorbs water through capillary action. Therefore as loading increases, the interfacial area increases to absorb more water.

Overall the addition of PF into a polyolefin matrix is best with a 2.5% fiber loading as it produces a tensile strength comparable to virgin polymer. A 2.5% PF composite could divert approximately 2,500 tons of organic waste from landfill and used for non-structural commodities such as packaging, construction, and automotive parts.

5. Future Research

Future research should explore morphological properties of a PF-HDPE biocomposite to understand the composite's physical and chemical structure. This information would give insight to further analyze composite mechanical, thermal, and water retention properties. Another research opportunity is to investigate other drupe waste to utilize as filler in a polyolefin biocomposite and compare performance properties.

6. References

[1] Ayala-Zavala JF, Vega-Vega V, Rosas-Domínguez C, et al (2011) Agro-industrial potential of exotic fruit byproducts as a source of food additives. Food Res Int 44:1866–1874. doi: 10.1016/J.FOODRES.2011.02.021

[2] Torres-León C, Ramírez-Guzman N, Londoño-Hernandez L, et al (2018) Food Waste and Byproducts: An Opportunity to Minimize Malnutrition and Hunger in Developing Countries. Front Sustain Food Syst 2:1–17. doi: 10.3389/fsufs.2018.00052

[3] Kaur G, Luo L, Chen G, Wong JWC (2019) Integrated food waste and sewage treatment – A better approach than conventional food waste-sludge co-digestion for higher energy recovery via anaerobic digestion. Bioresour Technol 289:121698. doi: 10.1016/J.BIORTECH.2019.121698

[4] Aghdam EF, Scheutz C, Kjeldsen P (2019) Impact of meteorological parameters on extracted landfill gas composition and flow. Waste Manag. doi: 10.1016/j.wasman.2018.01.045

[5] D. J. Hills, D. W. Roberts (1982) Conversion of Tomato, Peach and Honeydew Solid Waste into Methane Gas. Trans ASAE 25:0820–0826. doi: 10.13031/2013.33621

[6] USDA (2018) Noncitrus Fruits and Nuts 2017 Summary. United States Dep Agric - Natl Agric Stat Serv 112p.

[7] Mendu V, Harman-Ware AE, Placido A, et al (2011) Identification and thermochemical analysis of high-lignin feedstocks for biofuel and biochemical production. Biotechnol Biofuels 4:43. doi: 10.1186/1754-6834-4-43

[8] Zhang L, Lv S, Sun C, et al (2017) Effect of MAH-g-PLA on the Properties of Wood Fiber/Polylactic Acid Composites. Polymers (Basel) 9:5–8. doi: 10.3390/polym9110591

[9] Perinović S, Andričić B, Erceg M (2010) Thermal properties of poly(l-lactide)/olive stone flour composites. Thermochim Acta 510:97–102. doi: 10.1016/J.TCA.2010.07.002

[10] Chun KS, Husseinsyah S, Osman H (2012) Mechanical and thermal properties of coconut shell powder filled polylactic acid biocomposites: Effects of the filler content and silane coupling agent. J Polym Res 19:. doi: 10.1007/s10965-012-9859-8

[11] Essabir H, Bensalah MO, Bouhfid R, Qaiss A (2014) Fabrication and characterization of apricot shells particles reinforced high density polyethylene based bio-composites: Mechanical and thermal properties. J Biobased Mater Bioenergy 8:344–351. doi: 10.1166/jbmb.2014.1447

[12] Alamri H, Low IM (2012) Mechanical properties and water absorption behaviour of recycled cellulose fibre reinforced epoxy composites. Polym Test 31:620–628. doi: 10.1016/J.POLYMERTESTING.2012.04.002

Packaging and its impact on the value chain towards circular models [44]

Irma Elizabeth Peñúñuri García *1,
1 Universidad de Monterrey, NL, México
Doctorado, Universitat Politecnica de Valencia, Spain

Abstract: This article presents a study of topics and concepts related to the product value chain (PVC) with a focus on packaging and its relevance in circular economy models. This exploratory research generates a preamble of existing concepts and methodologies for the development of products with a life cycle approach, comparing systemic methodologies in relation to packaging-product development and circular strategies of packaging.

Keywords: Circular Economy, Ecodesign, packaging, Life Cycle Assessment, Responsible Consumption and Production, recycling.

***Correspondence to:** Irma Peñúñuri. E-Mail: irmaepg@gmail.com, irma.penunuri@udem.edu

1. Introduction

Our consumption habits have been modified, consequently the demand and speed of production and response in the value chain face challenges and transformations derived from the use of technology, population growth, pressure towards resources and the environment.

Between 2011 and 2050 the world population is expected to be 9.3 million, a 33% increase (UN DESA, 2011), and the demand for food will increase by 60% (Alexandratos and Bruinsma, 2012) generating greater pressure on natural resources that we have.

A large part of these demanded foods is lost and wasted at some stage of the food supply chain (FSC). In general terms, the flow of food throughout FSC stages generates loses of 54% in the early stages (production, post-harvest and storage) and 46% during the final stages (processing, distribution and consumption). (FAO, 2011).

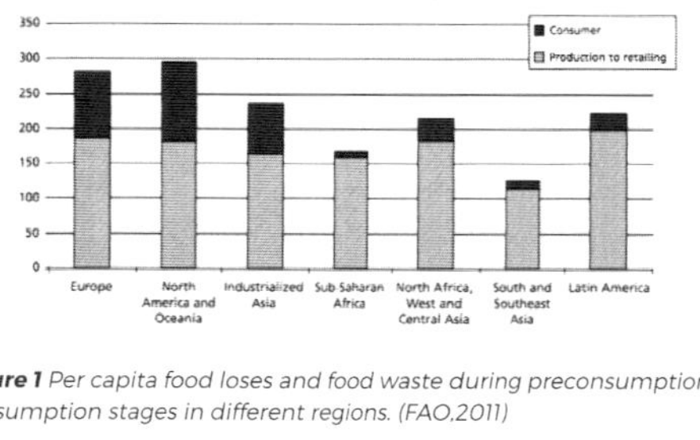

***Figure 1** Per capita food loses and food waste during preconsumption and consumption stages in different regions. (FAO,2011)*

The reasons for these losses and waste are diverse; in developing countries with low purchasing power they are related to financial, administrative and technical limitations that restrict storage capacity and conservation of food that is hindered due climate conditions, infrastructure, packaging and supply chain (SC) management issues; In countries with high purchasing power, consumers behavior is driven by different factors in the food supply chain, such as quality standards that reject food for not having a desired shape or appearance, unplanned purchases where the expiration dates generate a great amount of food waste and discard, as well as discarded items due to damaged packaging and presentation aspects.

The packaging industry is the third largest industrial sector in the world, behind only the food and petrochemical industries. In this sense, 69% of the entire subsector concentrates on the manufacture of packaging aimed at the B2C consumer; divided 50% for food packaging and 19% drinks and softs. (Grijalva, S.2018). Because of this, far from being a secondary element, packaging is one of the main processes involved throughout the FSC. In it is the heart of diverse industries. By designing it integrally, substantial loses and inefficiency can be avoided, and these benefits extend to other stages of the supply chain and life cycle (LC).

In Europe, during 2014 an approximate of 82.5 million metric tons per year of packaging waste was generated; in the United States, it was 69.6 million metric tons. Of these, between 65.5% and 51.5% are recycled respectively. (Geuke, J. et Al., 2018)

The application of sustainability criteria in the development of primary, secondary and tertiary packaging is paramount. The production and its final management must be able to adapt to current needs, eco-efficiency and the adaptation of technology such as digital transformation 4.0 to improve processes in the Product Value Chain (PVC).

This article seeks to generate a comparison of concepts, methodologies, tools and techniques available for the development of a circular design for packaging and product-packaging combinations (PPC). Describing the approach of concepts, definitions and strategies of the circular design towards the practical application in the perspective of Responsible Consumption and Production (RCP).

Objectives

- Analyze the concepts related to packaging from an integral approach to circular economy considering stakeholders.

- Compare packaging development methodologies and sustainability assessment in the PVC and life cycle.

Material and methods

The purpose of this exploratory and descriptive research is to generate the preamble for the comparison of concepts, tools and methodologies related to the circular economy (CE), as well as the impact of packaging on the PVC. This comparative diagnosis of tools for the development of product-packaging, will allow to start towards the development of a proposal for future application and validation.

Results and discussion

1. Impact of packaging

The United Nation Program in the 2030 Agenda for Sustainable Development, established 17 Sustainable Development Goals (SDGs), refers to the concept of CE particularly in the SDG RCP, making references to the new business models and production based on no-linear approach. (UNDP, 2015)

The need for guidelines and compliance with sustainability standards and circular design is recognized by the industry, as well as the international agenda and are significant when evaluating, designing and developing packaging in the PVC.

Traditional pollution management models in linear models have not been sufficient for the management and control of waste, due the speed with which they are generated. That is, it has caused delays and externalities in the management of resources, as well as an imbalance in the inputs and outputs of the product-systems.

Referring of the packaging industry, it represents almost 40% of the plastics we consume in the world. (Gongora, 2014). Considering that the packaging has a very short life, compared with the useful life of other plastic products such as electronic or automotive parts, they make packaging and ideal and crucial element to be recovered. The choice between circular strategies should focus and compare the fulfillment of the function commonly called Functional Unit (FU) in Life Cycle Assessment (LCA)

Fundamental approaches towards the circularity of resources:

1. Reduce cycle speed by **extending the life of products**.

2. Close cycle through the creation of circular flows thorough **recycling** or **reuse**

3. Reduction of material flows through **reduction** and optimization.

The weigh, volume, material composition, are crucial in different stages of the LC, mainly in the distribution and end of life. Alternatives of circularity should be considered; however, the premises of circular guidelines and environmental aspects should be defined in early stages of product-packaging development.

Considering extending life, most product and packaging have not been designed for recycling, reuse or any other circular scenario. The lack of strategies clearly derives a speed and lack of control of resources, where the consumption is greater than the resources that we are able to regenerate, just as the waste is greater than what we are capable of assimilating or managing. This linear model is clearly unsustainable and requires a different perspective in the usual sustainability approach tools.

The packaging approach must be a fundamental element that is increasingly relevant (Luttinkhuis, E. et Al., 2013) when talking about CE. The reason is that though an LCA, there is inherent dependence between the product and the package.

The LC of the product-packaging are more complex according to the concurrence of two parallel LC. In Figure 2. We can observe the phases where cycles overlap forming an iterative entity, where the container helps fulfill part of the function of a product either partially or totally. Since these functions are strongly related to the product, it is inevitable not to take it into account when analyzing the product.

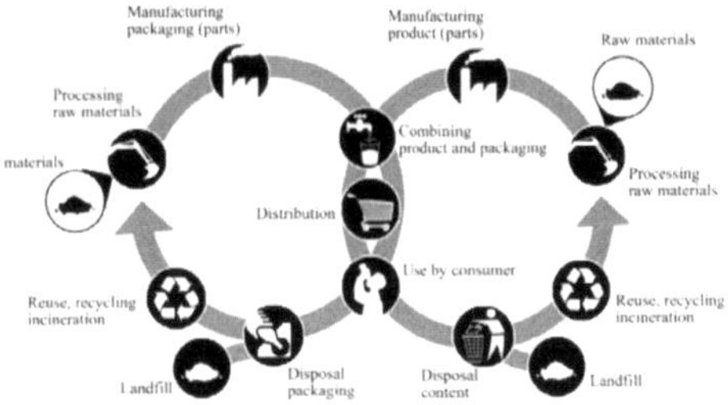

Figure 2 *Global Product/packaging life cycle. Luttinkhuis, E., et all.(2013).*

Packaging is a critical element when conducting LCA studies. It is important to consider it carefully in the LC inventory. The packaging impacts directly during phases of the LC such as storage, transport, distribution, marketing and, in some cases, even the efficient use of the actual product comes to depend on the packaging.

These cases, when the product depends directly on a package to be used effectively, they are called PPC. PPC cases, where a direct correlation and interdependence is evident, are commonplace in the packaging industry. This makes it even more important to considerer the following.

2. Circular models

According to different authors, CE models respond to closed cycle scenarios through the valorization of their materials and optimization of their function. We talk about products that flow in a system, on a smaller scale we talk about the flow and balance of their materials.

There are several strategies and guides to apply principles of circular design. According to Siem Haffmans (Haffmans, 2018), which describes the strategies of 4R's to generate value thorough products of high volume of consumption or Fast Moving Consumer Good FMCG, anticipating the end of linear life and the loss of value in the packaging means:

- Recycling: when the packaging elements are separated and transformed into new materials for the same or different purpose.

- Reuse: when packaging elements are collected, reconditioned and reused for the same purpose, either by simply filling or repackaging elements.

- Renewable: when the packaging elements are designed to use renewable and/or biodegradable materials.

- Redesign: rethinking or renew products and packaging applications in order to improve their environmental performance focusing mainly on the function.

In its application it is recommended to complement the development and design through ecodesign and LCA to support decision-making by comparing possible circular scenarios where it is fundamental to correctly define the package FU to make an adequate evaluation and innovation in the PVC.

2.1.Recycling

The waste management demands an extra energy and resources, from recovery of the product-packaging, the disassembly, separation, collection, classification of the different materials (either manual or automated), to its reprocessing until the transformation into a new material and the manufacture of a new packaging. Therefore, it is necessary to calculate the potential environmental impacts throughout the LC before considering recycling over another circular strategy.

Recycling design considers the following characteristics:

- Separability: Poor separability and disassembly can make recycling, repairing or repacking impossible.

- Compatibility: In cases where it is not possible to separate the elements of the packaging and it has reached its end of life, recycling is considered to be based on different properties and different materials and processes management should be considered.

In some cases, the material considered recycled or post-consumer, does not maintain the quality required for the same application in the packaging. When this happens, it is considered a material with downcycling.

In all the cases discussed previously, we need to ensure the separability and a clear identification system for the material composition, as well as the end of life scenario with correct symbols and ecolabelling if it applies. One example of these symbols is the mobius triangle, that through its variants it can indicate the type of material and/or the percentage of composing materials like recycled or post-consumer.

The importance of standardization with symbology that represents and objectively communicates the characteristics of compostable, biodegradable, recycled, or raw materials, is seen across the entire supply chain and product life cycle. This life cycle involves several stakeholders, including producers, consumers and third-party waste disposal/recovery entities.

The following statements provide further context to the need of clear identification and symbology:

- Many consumers base their purchasing decision according to the perceived sustainability information obtained by symbology for material identification and do not necessarily reflect any sustainability characteristics of the materials used in the packaging or the product itself. Furthermore, consumers also assume shared responsibility in the waste management process, since in many countries they are responsible for the separation and classification of the materials at the end of product-packaging life. This makes the correct interpretation of relevant symbology and ecolabeling information so important.

- A producer needs to be certain of a material's composition to be able to properly recycle for the same purpose, repurposing or, as a worst case scenario, for downcycling.

- In many countries, third party companies or the government itself are responsible for the recollection, classification, processing and transportation of recyclable materials. Once again, the correct interpretation of relevant symbology and ecolabeling information would simplify the waste management effort across entire supply chains, therefore supporting the circular economy approach.

The technology around waste management, identification and separation by automated systems, traceability and other concepts regarding Industry 4.0 have helped pave the road towards circular economy. However, focusing on manual systems will allow a greater part of the supply chain and stakeholders to understand the importance of this element to be able to take advantage of the available resources and materials, as well as their reevaluation for recycling optimization and the use of renewables. There is also an environmental education challenge implementing waste management on developing countries that needs to be considered.

2.2. Reuse

Even with the current efforts for recycling in the packaging industry, only 60% is recycled (Eurostats, 2019). For this reason, before recycling, the intention is to extend the life of any packaging as long as possible through product life optimization strategies, so we can later apply reusability principles; in which case we can talk about two types of scenarios:

- Reuse: Preserving the value of the material though repair, refurbishment or reuse without any change in the function thereof.

- Repurposing: When we sometimes reuse primary or tertiary packaging with a purpose different than the original.

In these cases, we can find strategies in the reuse and repurposing like the service design, and the extending of useful life. In addition, the extending of product life implies the delay of the stage of decline and focus on reliability of the product for the intended purpose or functional unit.

We see many examples of products that now are visualized as a system-product packaging, incorporating the value chain of the product and its stakeholders to offer an intangible product accompanied by the tangible called service design. Some recent examples are refill systems, reuse systems through rental of packaging and retail items.

To ensure these systems success it is necessary to design for reliability and for the prolongation of life itself that it will be important to consider when analyzing its life cycle with LCA and its potential environmental impacts, as well as economic and social issues involved in the value chain.

2.3. Renewable

The use of renewables, refers to the application of the following materials:

- Biobased: They are derived totally or partially from biomass. It refers to the origin of the carbon source of the material, from renewable resources or agroindustrial subproducts for its use and revalorization.

- Renewable: They are those that can regenerate in a human scale time and that do not come from fossil fuels.

In recent years, the use of bioplastics has grown significantly. During 2015 the production capacity of biobased and biodegradable plastic reached about 1%; production for 2020 is estimated at 2.5% as described Figure 3.

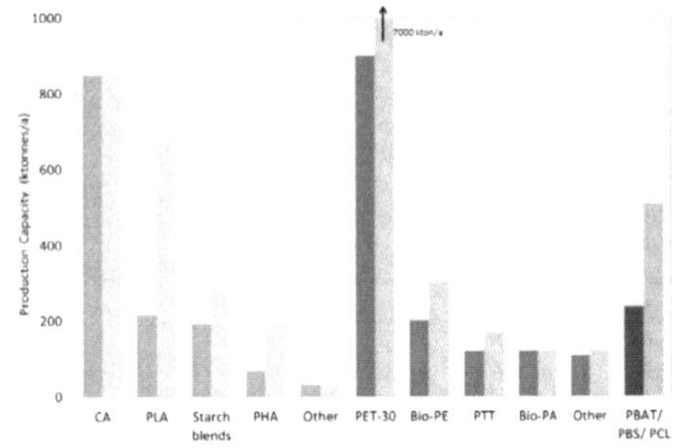

Figure 3 *Biobased Biodegrabale plastics (gren), biobased Non-biodegrabale plastics and Biodegradable fossil plastics: global production capacity 2015/2016 and 2020 prediction). IfBB, 2016; EuBP, 2016) (Over, M. et Al., 2018)*

The term bioplastic and biobased, are not synonymous, a bioplastic refers to either the biobased origin or the biodegradable nature of the plastic (Over, M. et Al., 2018). Some materials are biodegradable in almost any scenario, while others require special conditions, such as thorough composting systems where it is important to differentiate industrial or domestic systems because in both the process are different. In Figure 4, we can observe this classification. (Delft University of Technology, 2018)

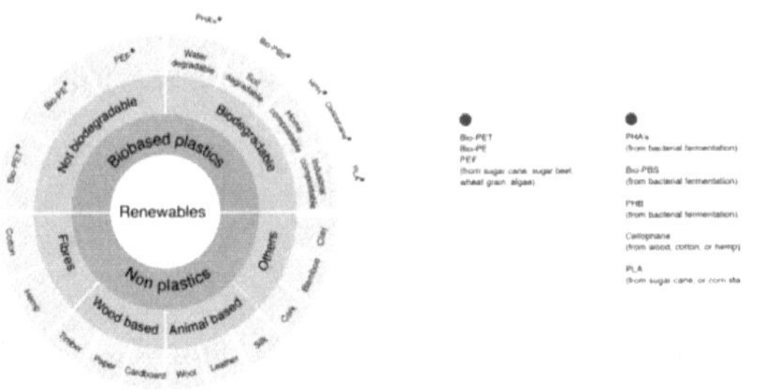

Figure 4 *Diagrama de clasificación de selección de materiales renovables utilizados en el empaques. Fuente: DelftX, 2019.*

The application of renewable materials in packaging has not been clear, there is confusion between technical characteristics, as well as communication with consumers through symbols or ecolabels, this mainly affects the correct and efficient management of the packaging during the end of life and, during purchase, generates greenwashing or disinformation.

In all previous cases using renewable materials it is again crucial to be able to identify which is the optimal material for the application in a product-system packaging, as well as to be clear about its end-of life scenario for the user or consumer, as well for the producer to ensure proper management. With this information we contribute to the development of materials and their responsible applications, obtaining relevant quantitative information in the LCA and the selection of circular strategies.

2.4 Redesign

2.4.1. Techniques, methodologies and existing tools

Numerous sustainability assessment tools exist for product-packaging development. These tools, as shown in Figure 5, are divided into four large groups, differentiated by the type of results and the stage of maturity of the project for accessing information required during the application of each of these.

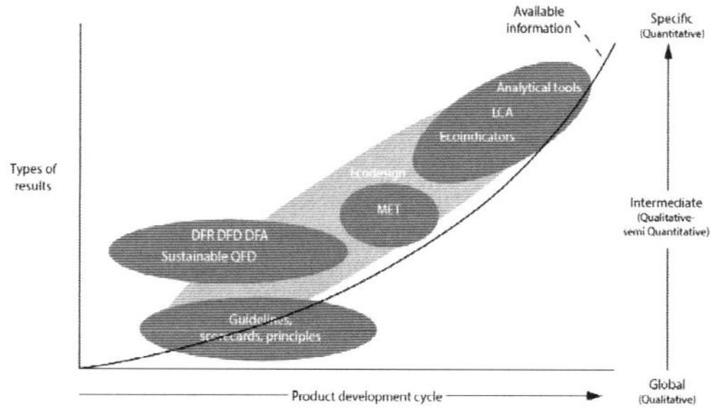

Figure 5 *General vision of tools and applicability. Modified from Luttinkhuis, E., et Al. (2013)*

Some of the tools mentioned in figure 5 describe guidelines or principles applied in the sustainability-focused design of materials, production processes, packaging, distribution, use and end of life. Tools like the family of "Design for X" where "X" is a characteristic to improve or a key development feature used in circular strategies: recyclability, assembly, disassembly, reusability, reliability, remanufacturing or other key development and design characteristics used in circular strategies.

A product or packaging that is difficult or impossible to separate or to disassemble will prove difficult to properly repair or recycle. For this reason, efforts on their fronts favor the use of the 4 R's: Recycling, Reuse, Renewal and Redesign and need clear and cumulative actions throughout the packaging design process. Another group describes guidelines or principles applied in packaging design with a life cycle approach regarding the product packaging system.

When considering intermediate qualitative-quantitative results we find tools like the MET Matrix (Materials, Energy and Toxicity), which is an analysis tool used to classify information on qualitative terms divided in inputs and outputs on the columns of the matrix, while using the respective rows to list the stages of the life cycle, this allows you to structure information for the inventory required for the LCA. An alternative matrix is the Quality Function Deployment, QFD is a structured approach to define requirements or needs and translating them to specific plans for products with a focus on sustainable considerations.

On another more specific side of the tool spectrum, we have ecoindicators and LCA that use inventories and calculations to provide quantitative information of potential environmental impacts, which allows for objective scenario comparisons. However, they require precise data of the scenario with certain confidence, as a result these tools are usually used on the final stages of the product development cycle.

All these considerations when using each of the tools in Figure 5, adding the complexity and lack of life cycle approach of some processes, highlights the importance of selecting and correctly applying these tools, especially in the early stages of packaging design. A better understanding of the environmental aspects to improve on a specific product-packaging development will allow for appropriate tool selection at the time of the development of the product-packaging.
The packaging ecodesign challenge is to articulate and integrate systemically to improve circular model proposal. Adapting circular model requirements and reaching the environmental performance of product-packaging and PVC to the early design and development processes.

Future research

Packaging decision making requires reaching the environmental performance and the translation of CE objectives and standards to early design and development processes and these definitions need to be aligned to the sustainability goals without leaving aside technical feasibility, functional optimization, competitiveness and market needs. However, in practice these applications are not obvious, because of the particularities of the packaging LC or PPC.

As shown in Figure 6, the incorporation of design methodologies and guidelines for application of actions and environmental qualitative-quantitative input that improve desirable characteristics for circular strategies like: recyclability, separability, compatibility, disassembly, as well as the use of materials with post-consumer or renewable content should be considered in the development of packaging.

The characteristics of renewable, recyclable or recycled materials must be clearly identified by the consumer, whose purchasing decision is sometimes swayed due this confusion. This confusion also risks the correct application or success of circular models during the end of life since the consumer is either wholly or partially responsible for classifying and managing waste. These methodologies should also consider an integration of value chain and stakeholders parallel to the maturity of the design project itself.

In Figure 6. Compares strategies and actions where redesign and ecodesign intend to develop a future integration for a proposal of a systematic model of circular approach that considers quantitative and qualitative elements in the PVC towards and application of RCP y CE. (Ellen Mcarthur Foundation, 2014)

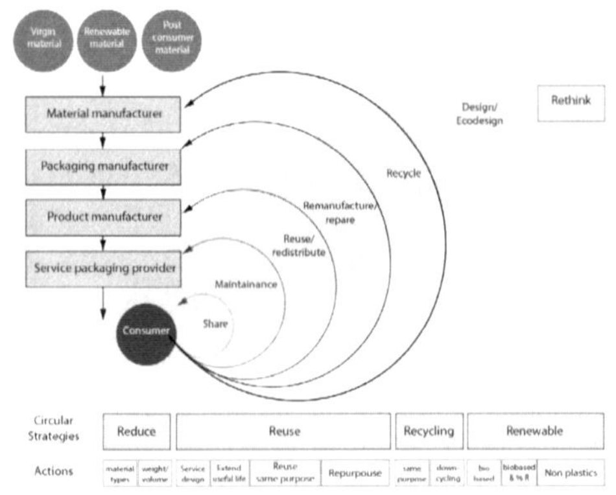

Figure 6 *Circular economy diagram with packaging strategy and action adaptation. Adapted from Ellen Mcarthur Foundation (2014)*

Future research could use a technical and qualitative perspective to develop a mythological proposal incorporating circular design strategies during earlier design phases. When discussing CE, we need to look further than just product-packaging, to the critical role of the consumer behavior, which is often underconsidered in the LCA. The successful implementation of a CE model relies on the consumer during the end of life, since he is either wholly or partially responsible for classifying and managing waste.

References

[1] UN DESA United Nation Department of Economic and Social Affairs (2011) World Urbanization Prospects: The 2011 Revision. NY. UN. http://www.un.org/en/development/desa/population/publications/pdf/urbanization/WUP2011_Report.pdf

[2] Alexandratos, N. y Bruinsma, J. (2012). World Agriculture Towards 2030/2050: The 2012 Revision. ESA Working Paper No. 12-03. FAO. Rome.

[3] FAO (2011). Global food loses and food waste. Rome. Retrieved from http://www.fao.org/3/mb060e/mb060e.pdf

[4] Grijalva, S. F., (2018) La Naturaleza del Embalaje. Spain. Caligrama Editorial.

[5] Geuke, B., Groh, K. & Muncke, J. (2018) Food Packaging in the circular economy: overview of chemical safety aspects for commonly used materials. Journal of Cleaner Production. 193, 491-505. https://doi.org/10.1016/j.jclepro.2018.05.005

[6] UNDP United Nations Development Programme (2015) Sustainable development goals. NY. Retrieved from https://www.undp.org/content/undp/es/home/librarypage/corporate/sustainable-development-goals-booklet.html

[7] Gongora, J. P. (2014). La industria del plástico en México y el mundo. Revista Comercio Exterior Vol. 64, No. 5. México. Retrieved from http://revistas.bancomext.gob.mx/rce/magazines/761/3/la_industria_del_plastico.pdf

[8] Luttinkhuis, E., De Lange, J., Klooster, R., Lutters, E. (2013). Towards integrating sustainability in the development of product/packaging combinations. Conference 23rd. CIRP

[9] Haffmans, S. (2018) A Circular Perspective for Packaging, Delft University of Technology. Retrieved from https://delftxdownloads.tudelft.nl/SPCEx_Sustainable_Packaging_in_a_Circular_Economy/Module_1/SPCEx_Module_1_1-2_A_Circular_Perspective_for_Packaging-transcript.pdf

[10] Eurostat (2019). Packaging waste statistics. Eurostat Statistics Explained. Retrieved from https://ec.europa.eu/eurostat/statistics-explained/index.php/Packaging_waste_statistics#Recycling_and_recovery_targets

[11] Over, M., Molenveld, K., Zee, M., Bos, H. (2018) Bio-based and biodegradable plastics. Netherlands. ISBN 9789463431217

[12] Delft University of Technology (2018) Renewables [Figure] Retrieved from https://prod-edxapp.edx-cdn.org/assets/courseware/v1/e0db875871489ad21a1eea47c13c0f20/assetv1:DelftX+SPCEx+1T2019+type@asset+block/renewables-06.png

[13] Ellen Macarthur Foundation (2014) Towards the circular economy: Accelerating the scale- up across global supply chains, [Figure Pag. 15]. Retrieved from https://www.ellenmacarthurfoundation.org/assets/downloads/publications/Towards-the-circular-economy-volume-3.pdf

A forensic approach to Life Cycle Assessment [47]

Alan Campbell *

Faculty of Engineering Technology, University of Twente, Enschede, the Netherlands

The LCA Centre, Beuningen, the Netherlands

Abstract: Research into methods for collecting product economic inventory data for inclusion in to a comparative product life cycle assessment (LCA) are limited. While the rules, governing such LCA based comparative product studies, are strict in their requirements. As comparative assertions are to be made it would seem appropriate that such studies be approached in a robust manner.

Reference is made to the use of product stakeholders as the source of product economic inventory data for input into LCA and yet research reveals numerous examples of studies in which these stakeholders were evidently absent. Research shows that it is highly likely that, in studies of comparative products, the stakeholders of some or all of the products may be absent, unable or unwilling to cooperate in a comparative product study.

Alternatives to stakeholder cooperation in product data collection are limited, leading to the question as to how a comparative product LCA, in support of a comparative product environmental claim statement, could be addressed from a product economic inventory data collection perspective.

The criminal justice system has been shown to use a variety of analytical instruments to convict individuals based on "beyond reasonable doubt" evidence. To what extent could this forensic approach be used to derive product economic inventory data for input to a comparative LCA study and how would this data differ from the alternative collection methods? To what extent can such a forensic type method be used to establish intended product like-functionality for comparison purposes and to identify the individual products materials composition, associated conversion processes and country-of-origin? All of this information being of value as product economic inventory data for LCA input.

Research shows a significant difference in comparative product ranking when a forensic approach is applied to an existing study that was reliant on assumptions in the absence of stakeholders. Many of these existing studies also show that their authors were potentially lacking in product technologically relevant knowledge, this being a reported critique of LCA. Interpretation of the results of forensic studies would require the study author to have such knowledge in order to interpret the results.

The use of technologically relevant product knowledge and a forensic approach to product economic inventory data collection could help in rendering comparative product environmental claims more robust.

***Correspondence to:** Alan Campbell. E-Mail: alancampbell@thelcacentre.com

Be careful what you ask for; communicating to citizens how to make packaging waste separation decisions in two regions in Sweden and the Netherlands [54]

Thijs van der Linden *1,2, Renee Wever 1, Roland ten Klooster 2

1 Department of Management and Engineering, Linköping University, Linköping, Sweden
2 Faculty of Engineering Technology, University of Twente, Enschede, the Netherlands

Abstract: The global packaging industry is one of the biggest industries worth almost a $1 trillion by 2020. With regards to packaging, society is placing more and more emphasis on sustainability aspects. In 2016, 170 kg of packaging waste was generated per inhabitant in the EU[1]. All that waste needs to be processed and it varies per country how packaging waste is separated and processed. An important aspect when processing is the choice of either source or post-separation of the waste. In the case of source separation many separation rules are drawn up for consumers and often it is not clear for the consumer how to separate the different materials and how the waste processors are dealing with the waste.

Two big leaders in the recycling industry of packaging are Sweden and the Netherlands. Both deal with source separation but still use different separation rules. This exploratory paper looks at the differences of both technical infrastructures of the comparable cities of Linköping (Sweden) and Enschede (the Netherlands) and will take it to a national level. The paper will also look at how the current separation guidelines have been developed and will examine the technical infrastructures for inefficiencies and improvements.

Based on written interviews from different waste separation organizations, an environmental academic expert and public sources, three factors have been identified that determine the current state of the systems. What is communicated in terms of separation rules is a compromise between the technical infrastructure, the legal framework and what the consumer can understand.

The current packaging recycling systems of Sweden and the Netherlands lead to different types of inefficiencies. These inefficiencies are the cause of the legal framework and (perceived) consumer understanding. At last the inefficiencies of the systems are identified and ranked by urgency from an environmental viewpoint.

Keywords: Recycling; sustainability; guidelines; legislation

***Correspondence to:** Thijs van der Linden, Faculty of Engineering Technology, University of Twente, Enschede, the Netherlands. Email: t.b.vanderlinden@student.utwente.nl

1. Introduction

In the packaging world every country deals differently with packaging waste. From source separation to non-separation of waste. In Europe a lot is done on waste separation, but it varies from country to country how they deal with the packaging waste. The most common packaging types of waste based on weight in the EU are 'paper and cardboard (41 %)', 'plastic (19 %)', 'glass (19 %)', 'wood (16 %)' and 'metal (5 %)' [2]. To keep the average recycling (the action or process of converting waste into reusable material) percentage in Europe high, the EU has set targets for the recycling percentage per material type. The statistics show the amount of recycled material divided by the number of packages marketed by producers.

Two countries that are above the EU targets are Sweden and the Netherlands. The EU has set a target for the total recycling of packaging waste at 55% for 2019 [3]. Sweden is on average 78% in 2018 [4] and the Netherlands 79% in 2018 [5], both are therefore far above average. This has to do with the fact that both countries have a good-functioning infrastructure for packaging waste recycling and due to source separation at which a part of the responsibility is placed at the consumer to properly separate the waste per material group. Nevertheless, both countries use different separation rules and process the waste differently. Therefore, it is interesting what the differences are between the systems, how they were designed and what could be improved.

It is often not clear to the consumer how to separate the different materials and how the waste processors are dealing with the waste. Are the separation rules logical and is it true what the consumer thinks that happens in terms of separation and processing of the waste? This paper will start at the differences of both technical infrastructures of the comparable cities of Linköping (Sweden) and Enschede (the Netherlands) and will take it to a national level. The paper will also look at how the current separation guidelines have been developed and will examine the separation guidelines for inefficiencies and improvements. By improvements is meant minimizing the degree of material contamination which leads to higher efficiency in the recycling of materials.

1.1 Problem statement

Currently the technical infrastructure of the separating / processing of packaging waste is not clear from the consumer's point of view in Sweden and the Netherlands. The consumer does not know exactly how to separate the different packaging materials and small mistakes can lead to issues.

Materials that end up in the incorrect material flow leads to a certain degree of material contamination which makes recycling into the purest form of the material more difficult.

This can be solved by applying additional separation methods, but that is not possible in every case.

It is not always easy to recycle materials. It should be logical and economical to do it. The consumer may not know the economic reasons. In addition, what is communicated to consumers does not necessarily correspond to what would be correct from an infrastructure and / or environmental point of view. This is understandable on the one hand because it keeps the system "workable", but on the other hand it could be dangerous because it can lead to a breach of trust of the consumer.

2. Research methodology

The carried-out research is an explorative case study. First both technical infrastructures of Linköping (SE) and Enschede (NL) are investigated from a consumer perspective. How the behavior of the consumer is influenced is investigated by looking at the separation guidelines information and the design of the waste separation location.

The two systems are then compared with each other for similarities and differences. The differences resulted in follow-up questions that were submitted by written interviews to a waste processing company in Linköping, Sweden (Tekniska Verken) and a waste collection organization (Twente Milieu) in Enschede, the Netherlands. With the information from these written interviews, a look has been taken at how the separation guidelines have been developed and which stakeholders influence the development of these guidelines. Subsequently types of inefficiencies in the systems were identified from the various stakeholders. These inefficiencies were then assessed on the basis of an environmental and consumer perspective. At last the types of inefficiencies were ranked by urgency with the help of an environmental academic expert in the Netherlands. The most urgent inefficiencies from the systems can possibly be built on in follow-up research.

2.1. Scope

The focus of this research will be on the consumer packaging waste material separation / recycling infrastructure of the Netherlands and Sweden. Organic and residual waste is not taken into consideration. Because the technical infrastructure is different for each municipality [5], the Dutch city of Enschede and the Swedish city of Linköping are used for field research and examined in this research. Both cities are comparable in size [6] [7]. Because the information from two cities and corresponding waste processors is an example of a municipal recycling system, it is not representative for the entire technical infrastructure of both countries, therefore the available information from both cities has been linked to a national level.

There are many stakeholders who are involved in the technical infrastructure of packaging recycling, this research focuses on part of the chain of the already produced packaging, so from consumer to separation and recycling of packaging. For this study, the brand owner, designer and producer of packaging have been disregarded due to the focus on the consumer perspective on separation guidelines and recycling of packaging waste.

3. Technical infrastructures

The technical infrastructure means the basic physical and organizational structures and facilities to achieve a specific goal, in this case the recycling of packaging waste.

3.1. Technical infrastructure Linköping (Sweden)

To analyse the technical infrastructure of packaging waste recycling of Linköping the involved stakeholders need to be investigated. It can be concluded that there are (within the scope) globally three stakeholders involved. The consumer (source separation), the waste processor (post separation & processing) and the government (legal framework). To determine the current state of the system, the system will be analyzed from the three stakeholder perspectives.

3.1.1. Consumer perspective

To analyse the consumer perspective it is looked at how the consumer is informed how to separate the waste. This is done by visiting two different locations of collection points of waste in Linköping. An example of the waste collection point and rules can be seen in figure 1. In Linköping and Sweden each material group is collected separately.

Figure 1 *Waste collection point and rules Linköping*

The different packaging material groups which are separated are:

· Packaging of uncoloured / coloured glass (colour separated)
· Metal packaging
· Plastic packaging
· Paper-based packaging
· Newspapers
· (Residual waste)

A full overview of the separation guidelines in Linköping as it is communicated to the consumer has been created and can be found in appendix A. It comes down to a few general rules.

· For the glass stream only packaging glass will be recycled, heat-resistant glass such as oven dishes, tea glasses and lamps are therefore not allowed in this stream.

· For the metal stream only packaging metal will be recycled. Everything with propellant gas like spray cans of whipped cream, deodorant and paint cans is excluded. Also packaging with an aluminum coating is excluded from this stream.

· For the plastic stream only packaging plastic will be recycled. Plastic toys and electronics are excluded. Crisps bags are included in this stream.

· For the paper stream only packaging paper which consists for more than half out of the paper will be recycled. All newspapers, office paper, envelopes, post-it's and greasy dirty paper are excluded from this stream.

· For the newspaper stream all paper which is not packaging is collected. Envelopes, post-it's and greasy dirty paper are excluded from this stream.

· In addition, all packaging is expected to be returned clean and empty to prevent odor at the separation point.

3.1.2 Waste processor perspective

In order to gain a better insight into the technical infrastructure of the waste processor, a written interview has been held with a Swedish waste processor near Linköping. This interview shows that each material has its own recycling plant, for example in Hammar (glass), Smedjebacken (metal), Motala (plastic) and Norrköping (paper and newspaper). Addition to this the municipalities, for example Linköping, have no responsibility for collecting and recycling packaging materials. The municipality's responsibility is to collect and recycle food waste and general waste. When collecting food waste and general waste, packaging material is not post sorted. All packaging material in the general waste will not be recycled [8].

For the recycling of packaging material, a different law comes into play, namely the Swedish "Ordinance of producers responsibilities for packaging". According to this law the different packaging materials have to be delivered separately to the recycling plant owned by the producers. Producer responsibility is based on the polluter pays principle [9]. More information about this law will be discussed at the government perspective section.

The producers have an organization called FTI for collecting and recycling packaging materials. FTI stands for "Förpacknings & tidnings insamlingen" which is translated to Packaging & newspaper collection. All companies affiliated with the system pay packaging fees in relation to the amount of packaging material their operations generate [10]. In figure 2 an example can be seen what fees are paid per material group [11].

Packaging fees				
	Item no.	Material	From April 1, 2019 (SEK/kg)	From January 1, 2020 (SEK/kg)
Household packaging	310	Paper (high)	1.92	3.28
	315	Paper (low)	na	2.23
	410	Plastic (high)	3.90	5.22
	415	Plastic (low)	3.15	3.47
	511	Aluminium	2.00	2.21
	512	Steel plate	3.15	3.59

Figure 2 *Packaging fees FTI January 2020*

Residual waste is removed from the packaging stream at the various recycling plants to keep the contamination level low.

3.1.3 Government perspective

The government is responsible for making laws regarding packaging. When recycling packaging material, the aforementioned "Ordinance of producers responsibilities for packaging" is therefore important. This law contains three main points of obligations where companies that produce, import or sell packaged goods are subject to. The business shall [9]:

· Ensure that a collection system exists, through which customers and other end consumers can return used packaging.

· Ensure that customers receive the information they need about the collection of used packaging.

· Ensure that collected packaging is recovered, recycled and put to good use as either new raw material or energy.

All the responsibilities of businesses can be found in chapter 15 of the Swedish environmental code [12].

In addition to the producing company, consumers also have a certain responsibility under the same regulations namely they are required to sort their waste and drop-off used products and packaging [13]. As mentioned before the municipality's responsibility is to collect and recycle food waste and general waste, not packaging waste.

3.2 Technical infrastructure Enschede (the Netherlands)

In the Netherlands, too, the global stakeholders involved in packaging recycling are (within the scope) the consumer (source separation), the processor (post separation & processing) and the government (legal framework). To determine the current state of the system, the system will be analyzed from the three stakeholder perspectives.

3.2.1 Consumer perspective

To establish the consumer perspective, the rules which are communicated to the consumer and the collection points are investigated. The collection points and the separated waste streams differ per municipality. There may be local collection points or personal bins for the different material groups at home. An example of a collection point can be seen in figure 3.

Figure 3 *Waste collection point Enschede (paper left, PMD right)*

In Enschede not every material is separated and sorted. The different packaging material groups which are separated are:

· Packaging of uncoloured / coloured glass (colour separated)

· PMD (Plastic packaging, metal packaging and beverage cartons)

· Paper (Residual waste)

In the Netherlands the stream of PMD; Plastic packaging, metal packaging and beverage cartons (plastic verpakkingen, metalen verpakkingen en drinkpakken) exist but it differs per municipality whether this PMD, PM (plastic packaging and metal packaging), P (plastic packaging) is collected or all materials are collected together and post separated (mixed stream). In the Netherlands, the municipality is therefore free to determine the manner of waste collection, waste processors often determine the agenda due to available equipment and business models [14]. So, it is important to look carefully at how each municipality is separating their packaging waste. There are also online waste separation guidelines which helps consumers in case of doubt.

A full overview of the separation guidelines in Enschede as it is communicated to the consumer has been created and can be found in appendix B. It comes down to a few general rules.

· For the glass stream only packaging glass will be recycled, heat-resistant glass such as oven dishes, tea glasses and lamps are therefore not allowed in this stream.

· For the metal stream within PMD only packaging metal will be recycled. Everything with propellant gas like spray cans of whipped cream, deodorant and paint cans are excluded. Also packaging with an aluminum coating are excluded from this stream.

· For the plastic stream within PMD only packaging plastic will be recycled. Plastic toys & electronics are excluded. Crisps bags, bioplastic / compostable, plastic nets from citrus fruits and black plastic dishes are excluded in this stream. Also, plastic packaging with an aluminum coating are excluded from this stream.

· For the beverage stream within PMD only soda, wine and dairy packaging are allowed. they consist of 75 to 80 percent paper and cardboard and are provided on the inside and outside with a layer of polyethylene (PE) and / or aluminum foil (with long-lasting products). These materials can be recycled.

· For the paper stream newspapers and advertising brochures, print, fax, copy, write and drawing paper, envelopes, egg cartons, paper bags and cardboard boxes, cardboard and paper packaging are allowed. Greasy dirty paper is excluded from this stream. Also, paper packaging with an aluminum coating is excluded from this stream.

3.2.2 Waste processor perspective

In order to gain a better insight into the technical infrastructure of the waste processor, a written interview was held with a Dutch waste processor near Enschede. This interview shows that each material has its own recycling plant, for example in Wijster (residual waste, organic waste and PMD), Heijningen (glass) and Utrecht (paper). Addition to this the municipalities, for example Enschede, have no responsibility for collecting and recycling packaging materials. The municipality's responsibility is to collect and recycle food waste and general waste [15].

The collection and recycling of packaging is funded by the companies that market packaged products in the Netherlands. They do this by paying a levy on their packaging to the Packaging Waste Fund, which reimburses the costs incurred for collection and recycling [16]. This is also mandatory by law, more about this at the government perspective section.

Residual waste is removed from the packaging stream at the various recycling plants to keep the contamination level low. When residual waste is collected and processed, packaging waste is vice versa separated in the residual waste stream in order to increase the recycling percentage [17].

It differs per municipality how this method of waste collection and processing is arranged and is therefore often dependent on what the waste processor can achieve with his waste processing installation. The waste processor often sets the agenda of the municipality in terms of waste separation to get their installations economically running.

3.2.3 Government perspective

The government is responsible for making laws regarding packaging. These laws descend from The Packaging Waste Directive 94/62, where the Netherlands has translated these directives into its own legislation. When recycling packaging material, the Packaging Management Decree (2014) applies [18]. This law says in § 3. Collection, recycling and other waste management, article 5:

· The producer or importer is responsible for the separate collection or the collection and post- separation of packaging placed on the market in the Netherlands and of packaging imported by him from that calendar year.

· The costs of the separate intake or the intake and post-separation of packaging are for the account of the producer or importer.

In the Netherlands, such producer responsibility for packaging also applies. The Packaging Waste Fund plays a major role in producer responsibility, it provides collectively the obligations that the packaging industry has to follow from the Packaging Management Decree law [19].

The responsibility of the municipality in this story is the organization of the collection system for residual waste. The municipalities have no responsibility for collecting and recycling packaging materials. The municipality's responsibility is to collect and recycle food waste and general waste [16].

4. Results

From the analyses of both technical infrastructures of Sweden and the Netherlands, three factors (within the scope) have been identified that determine the current state of the systems. What is communicated in terms of separation rules is a compromise between the technical infrastructure, the legal framework and what the consumer can understand. Now it is known how both systems work, the next step is to analyze both systems for similarities and differences.

4.1. Common characteristics

What both systems have in common is that the consumer takes part in source separation. In addition, each material has its own recycling plant in both Sweden and the Netherlands. In both systems there is a producer's responsibility and an organization for collecting and recycling packaging materials. These organizations work by asking for a packaging fee per material group per kg. In both systems the municipality's responsibility is to collect and recycle food waste and general waste, not packaging waste.

Both systems seem to function well when looking at the average percentages of recycled packaging material compared to the European target. But a number of significant differences are still visible between the systems.

4.2. Differences

The differences between the systems are compared on three points; separation rules, waste processing and recycling rates per material.

4.2.1 Differences in separation rules

Differences in separation rules		
Material	Linköping, Sweden	Enschede, the Netherlan ds
Packaging of uncoloured / coloured glass (colour separated)	Need to be cleaned and caps sorted by material.	Lids and leftovers are no problem.
Metal packaging	Cans are separated separately. The loose lids of glass jars are collected here. Need to be cleaned.	Cans are part of the PMD stream and are not collected separately. No need to be cleaned.
Plastic packaging	Plastic packaging is separated separately. All packaging need to be empty and cleaned. Crisps bags are collected by plastic packaging.	Plastic packaging is part of the PMD, PM or P or mixed stream and is not collected separately. No need to be cleaned. Crisps bags are not collected in the plastic packaging stream or mixed stream.
Beverage cartons	Does not have the PMD stream section they collect it at papers.	Collects this in PMD stream.
Paper	Packaging consists of more than half of paper. All packaging needs to be empty and cleaned. Newspapers and advertising brochures are separated separately. Beverage cartons are collected in the paper stream. Envelopes are not allowed in this stream.	Newspapers and advertising brochures are not separated separately. Beverage cartons are separated in PMD not in paper. Envelopes are allowed in this stream.
Newspapers	-	Does not have this stream.
PMD	Does not have this stream.	-

Figure 4 *Differences in separation rules between Sweden and the Netherlands*

4.2.2 Differences in waste processing

The biggest difference between the two systems is that packaging waste is separated from residual waste in the Netherlands for those municipalities that do not use consumer sorting. This does not happen in Sweden[8]. This packaging material can therefore be partly recovered during the post-separation of residual waste.

In addition, the separation of PMD, PM, P or mixed stream in the Netherlands is done at the processor. In Sweden this is, if all goes well, already collected separately and therefore goes directly to the correct recycle plant. Lastly, envelopes cannot be included in the Swedish paper processing system and crisps bags are included in the plastic packaging stream. In the Netherlands, envelopes are collected and processed with the paper stream and crisps bags are collected at residential waste. The choice to collect crisps bags (aluminum foiled plastics) at the plastic stream in Sweden and sort them out later probably has to do with understanding

the consumer. The consumer sees a bag of crisps as something of plastic, but often does not know that the multi- layer material makes it difficult to recycle.

4.2.3 Differences in recycle rates

The research was first focused on two different cities from Sweden and the Netherlands with associated waste processors. The two cities are part of the bigger picture, because it differs per municipality how waste is collected and recycled, it has been looked at the national level in terms of recycling rates and is compared to the European goal.

Figure 5 shows the resulting recycling rates for different materials from Sweden (2018) and the Netherlands (2018) and the recycle rate target for each material to EU objective (2019). The statistics show the amount of recycled material divided by the amount of packages and magazines marketed by producers [3][4].

Sweden scores slightly higher in terms of glass recycling percentage, the Netherlands, on the other hand, scores higher in the paper sector. The Netherlands does not have a separate material flow for newspapers, which is why they cannot be compared nor has the EU set an objective for this. In the field of plastic packaging recycling, the Netherlands scores slightly higher than Sweden. In the recycling of metal packaging, the Netherlands also scores slightly higher than Sweden. What is striking is that both countries score well above the EU objective.

Recycling statistics packaging waste			
Material	Result 2018 Sweden	Result 2018 the Netherlands	EU 2019 objective
Glass	93%	86%	60%
Paper and cardboard	80%	88%	60%
Newspapers	91%	-	-
Plastic	42%	52%	22.5%
Metal	82%	95%	50%

Figure 5 *Recycling statistics packaging waste Sweden and the Netherlands*

4.3 Inefficiencies in the systems

Despite the fact that the systems of Sweden and the Netherlands score above the European objective, there are still a number of inefficiencies in both systems. What is communicated in terms of separation rules is a compromise between the technical infrastructure, the legal framework and what the consumer can understand. Inefficiencies can occur in the communication between these stakeholders. Examples of these inefficiencies can be:

Material which is separated in a certain stream which is not right. Cause is wrong behavior of the consumer.

· Packaging ends up in wrong packaging material group.

· Packaging ends up in residual waste.

· Residual waste ends up in packaging material stream.

Material could be in a certain material stream but is not due to legislation. Cause is wrong legal framework.

· The law stipulates that certain material does not belong in a certain material stream but through both the eyes of the infrastructure and the eyes of the consumer it is possible.

4.4 Inefficiencies in the Netherlands

The inefficiencies of the technical infrastructure of the Netherlands by consumer behavior is divided into non packaging in the packaging stream, packaging in residual waste and size and shape by policy waste processor.

4.4.1. Inefficiencies by behavior consumer

Non packaging or wrong packaging in packaging stream inefficiencies by wrong consumer behavior

Packaging of uncoloured / coloured glass

· None packaging glass (drinking glasses, vases)
· Mirrors
· Heating resistant glass
· Oven dishes
· Lamps Metal packaging
· None packaging metal
· Not empty packaging
· Metal packaging with KCA logo (small toxic waste)
· Spray cans of whipped cream
· Spray cans deodorant
· Paint cans
· Spray cans of chemical agents Plastic packaging
· None packaging plastic
· Blister packs of medicines
· Toothbrush
· Crisps bags
· Disposable cups
· Plastic disposable tableware
· Plastic packaging with aluminum inside
· Bioplastic, compostable
· Plastic nets from citrus fruits or onions
· Styrofoam meat / fish dishes
· Black plastic dishes Paper
· Paper cups
· Paper coffee bag with aluminum inside
· Packaging with food leftovers
· Beverage cartons
· Laminated board like Pringles can

Packaging in residual waste inefficiencies by wrong consumer behavior

Residual waste: 180kg per person per year but 42 kg is real residual waste[20].
· 57kg GFT
· 24kg plastic
· 21kg paper
· 10kg textile
· 9kg glass
· 8kg metal
· 5kg wood
· 2kg devices

Size / shape does not belong in the stream by policy processor (misunderstanding consumer)

Plastic, if the size is larger than an A4, it is recycled. Smaller pieces are taken out and burned.

· Small plastic foils (for example of vegetables)
Plastic nets from citrus fruits or onions at plastic stream (misunderstanding consumer).

· The nets turn around the blades of the grinding mills, so that the machine must be stopped, and the nets must be cut off from the blades. Other waste also gets stuck in the nets, so you don't get clean sorting flows.

4.5 Inefficiencies in Sweden

The inefficiencies of the technical infrastructure of Sweden is divided by inefficiencies by law and by consumer behavior like non packaging in the packaging stream, packaging in residual waste and size and shape by policy waste processor.

4.5.1 Inefficiencies by law

The law stipulates that certain material does not belong in a certain material stream but through both the eyes of the infrastructure and the eyes of the consumer it is possible
· Envelopes
· Tealights

The problem is the fact that envelopes are not considered as a packaging - paper industry can process it but are not paid because the producers of envelopes do not fall under the "Ordinance of producers responsibilities for packaging". The same problem applies to the metal container that encloses a tealight. This creates a misunderstanding among consumers.

4.5.2 Inefficiencies by behavior consumer

Non packaging or wrong packaging in packaging stream inefficiencies by wrong consumer behavior

Packaging of uncoloured / coloured glass
· None packaging glass (drinking glasses, vases)
· Mirrors
· Heating resistant glass
· Oven dishes
· Glass cups
· Lamps Metal packaging
· None packaging metal
· Spray cans of whipped cream
· Spray cans deodorant
· Paint cans
· Spray cans of chemical agents
· Crisps bags Plastic packaging
· None packaging plastic (toys)
· Blister packs of medicines
· Toothbrush
· Disposable cups
· Plastic disposable tableware
· Bioplastic, compostable Paper
· Envelopes
· Post-it Notes
· News papers
· Office paper
· Paper cups
· Paper coffee bag with aluminum inside
· Packaging with food leftovers
· Beverage cartons Newspapers
· Envelopes
· Post-It notes
· Postcards
· Paper packaging

Packaging in residual waste by wrong consumer behavior "Unfortunately for plastic packaging it is also the case that more than half of all packaging ends up in the normal waste and therefore does not get the chance to be recycled" [8].

The proportion of plastic packaging that nowadays becomes new plastic products is around 15-20 percent of the plastic packaging that is marketed by our affiliated manufacturers. One of the reasons for this is that too many plastic containers end up in the garbage bag at home. About 55 percent of the plastic packaging that Swedish people submit for recycling can be sorted at the Swedish plastics recycling plant in Motala and thus recycled [8].

5. Perspective on inefficiencies

Now that it is known which inefficiencies are present in both systems, it is important to view them on different perspectives. This view on the inefficiencies will be done from a consumer and environmental perspective.

5.1 Consumer perspective

Consumers quickly associate packaging with waste, even though the share of packaging in the waste flows is low. Consumers can also be irritated if they discard packaging. For example, because they are left with too much packaging, separation rules are not clear, there are no understandable / good functioning facilities or because the packaging cannot be properly separated with the waste [21].

From a consumer perspective, it does not directly make much difference whether the materials are separated correctly. The government does not impose a fine when not sorted correctly. On the other hand, waste separation is valuable. Not only for the environment, but often also cost wise. Collected paper, glass, metal and textiles generate revenue: this reduces the costs of collection and processing. With plastic it is a bit more complicated: because of the low oil price, new plastic is sometimes cheaper than recycled plastic. But because the producers of plastic packaging contribute to the recycling, separate collection and sorting of plastic is nevertheless cost-effective [22].

Another factor is that there are not enough sorting machines to separate all the waste afterwards. And it costs a lot to build such machines. Municipalities must therefore invest in this. This could be at the expense of the consumer, the budget for the separation machines could also have been spent in a different way for the good of the consumer [22].

From an environmental perspective it does not matter that a small piece of plastic (smaller than A4) in the Netherlands ends up at the plastic stream and is filtered out again to be incinerated, from a consumer perspective it can be a bigger problem because they feel cheated (fact that separated materials are still removed for incineration).

When a material could be in a certain material stream but is not due to legislation because an inefficiency in the legal framework can also be experienced negatively by the consumer. Through logical thinking the consumer tries to contribute to the separation of different material groups, but apparently it is not allowed by law (whether it is a packaging material or not, confusion with tealight and envelope in Sweden).

5.2 Environmental perspective

From an environmental perspective collecting and recycling waste separately is demonstrably better for the environment than collecting and incinerating everything together. While waste incineration provides energy, on balance it causes extra CO_2 emissions and loss of raw materials [22].

Recycling instead of incineration saves resources, for example, trees for paper, petroleum for plastic, (rare) metals for devices and cans. Besides that, recycling usually costs (much) less energy than extracting raw materials and making new materials. For example, new aluminum requires 20 times more energy than melting used aluminum. The quality of recycled materials is usually just as good. At last recycling results in fewer greenhouse gases than waste incineration [22]. It is also important from an environmental perspective that source separation is done and not only post separation.

Post-separation is not the solution for every type of waste. Paper, organic waste, textile and glass can only be recycled if it is collected separately. For example, paper and textiles that are in the residential waste become wet and dirty and that will affect the quality when processing at the recycling plant. Separate waste that is very contaminated can still be incinerated.

This is slightly different for steel cans; processors can take the steel cans out of residential waste by use of magnets. With aluminum cans, trays and foil (30% of all metal packaging), this does not work as well, since aluminum is not magnetic. Installations are succeeding (Eddy current) better and better, but not every waste incinerator has already invested in this, plus thin pieces of aluminum are not taken out with Eddy currents. This is a waste, because the recycling of aluminum gives environmental benefits (the production cost a lot of energy, but the total amount is small) [22].

For plastic packaging and beverage cartons it does matter whether residential waste is post-separated. If this is not the case, these materials will be incinerated.

When a material could be in a certain material stream but is not due to legislation because an inefficiency in the legal framework can also be experienced negatively by the waste processor and is bad from an environmental perspective. The material could be recycled but does not fall within the packaging segment and is therefore incinerated.

5.2 Inefficiency ranking of impact on the environment

There are a number of inefficiencies in both systems that can be viewed from different perspectives. At the moment it is most important to look at which inefficiency has the most impact on the environment. So which material flow / inefficiency is the most disruptive in the recycling system? To determine which inefficiency is the most disruptive, the recycle rates, weight share on the market and the embodied energy of the materials in MJ/kg will be on the level of packaging + share in waste. If the processing to packaging (box, bottle, can, cup, etc.) is also taken into account the indicative MJ/kg key figures can be used (average) [24]. The most disruptive inefficiency needs to be tackled in order to minimize the degree of material contamination and reduce the carbon footprint of the material stream.

5.2.1 Paper and board packaging

Looking at paper and board packaging it is economically feasible to recycle paper/board[23]. The recycling statistics of packaging waste shows high recycling percentages (SE 80%, NL 88%) and paper and board packaging can always be reused for paper. Looking at the weight share it is about 41% [2] in Europe and embodied energy of virgin paperboard virgin 45 MJ/kg and recycled paper/board 25 MJ/kg[24]. So, recycle rates are high, relatively high weight share and average embodied energy.

5.2.2 Metal packaging

The metal packaging industry is also economically feasible and sustainable [23]. It has high recycle rates (SE 82%, NL 95%) and sorted metal packaging is taken up in a wider metal chain. Recycled steel and aluminum can be used to make packaging again. The weight share on the market is about 5% [2] and the embodied energy is for steel 50 MJ/kg, recycled steel 12 MJ/kg, aluminum 140 MJ/kg and recycled aluminum 12 MJ/kg [24]. The recycle rates are thus high, relatively low weight share and for steel average embodied energy. For virgin aluminum the embodied energy is high and for recycled quite low. Therefore, it is of importance that aluminum is separated and processed properly to save energy, but in practice this proves difficult for consumers to explain.

5.2.3 Glass packaging

In the glass industry are lots of impurities like ceramics, plastic and aluminum caps, labels etc. Also, there are issues with led because of the content of bottle banks (table glass). But the recycle rates are high (SE 93%, NL 86%). The weight share is about 19% [2] and the embodied energy 9 MJ/kg [24]. Despite the fact that the embodied energy is relatively low, it is useful to recycle glass. It saves energy, every 10% of cullet saves about 2.5% of energy.

The recycle rates of glass are high and it has an average weight share on the market. Nevertheless the low embodied energy and high recycle rates glass recycling is hard to get economically feasible due the impurities and the led issue in glass [23]. It is therefore very important that everything is separated correctly and that no heat resistant glass is returned with packaging glass.

5.2.4 Plastic packaging

Plastics is a tricky business, the recycle rates are quite low (SE 42%, NL 52%) and plastics have a high embodied energy level. For PE/PP is 80MJ/kg needed, for PET 100MJ/kg and for PA 120MJ/kg [24]. Reuse of all plastic packaging, including refund bottles is ca. 20%, the largest share is PET bottles [23]. The weight share to the market is 19% [2]. The great thing about plastic is that the molecule can be made in such a way that it will perform a certain function. Multiple layers with different functions give a "super" material but the end of the chain (recycling) has not been carefully considered. Consumers also play a major role in this; they often do not know how to separate or are unmotivated. As a result, a lot of plastic ends up in the residual waste and it does not always get the chance to be recycled. There are now all kinds of problems in this field, but the field is in a strong development process. The system is nevertheless not economically feasible due to the layered structures and amount of types of plastic.

5.3 Conclusion inefficiencies

Looking at the different recycle streams, it can be concluded that plastics are currently the most disruptive of all recycle streams. The system is not economically feasible and the recycle rates are quite low. The embodied energy of plastics is also relatively high which can cause a high CO_2 burden. In addition, the poor separation of plastic packaging by the consumer plays a major role and the question here is whether the separation system should be changed, for example, from source separation to complete post-separation. Note the separation of waste is a process and gradually it is beginning to become clear what will soon be the most efficient way of collection. When looking at the future in the Netherlands within ten years, all source separating systems will be probably gone. Cees de Mol van Otterloo, Director Packaging Waste Fund the Netherlands (2017): "Post-separation, in addition to source separation, has been developed into a fully-fledged collection system for plastic packaging waste, ... We expect other large cities to choose post-separation as a solution for more plastic collection." [25]. Post-separation develops better than source separation, people just do not understand it or are not motivated. It is better to adjust the entire system than to optimize one material flow.

In this paper a part of the chain has been analyzed, but to map out the complete complex problem, more stakeholders need to be investigated. Brand owners, designers and producers sit together in initiatives like Plastic Pact [26], The European PET Bottle Platform [27] and CEFLEX [28] so that their packaging can be better recycled in terms of ink, labels, caps, colours etc. A lot is already going on in this field in the form of European guidelines. An example of these European guidelines is Recyclass, their goal is "to help the plastics value chain find the correct way to approach and evaluate the design for recycling of packaging products, with the goal of improving their recyclability." [29].

A lot is going to change at the beginning of the chain so that it comes out well at the end of the chain, especially for plastics. Because of this there is a tension between what brand owners, designers and producers want and what the waste processors can do. The tension of this change is that waste processors have to adapt their installation to the new development and they may lose valuable material flows (due to a refund system) and they need a return on investment on their equipment.

It therefore remains a complicated field in which the whole value chain is built on economic principles, every part of the chain wants to earn something from it but on the other hand, there is a great need to become more sustainable. Major changes will have to occur, it is important that sacrifices are made in the value chain to get the most efficient recycling system.

6. Conclusion

This research looked at packaging waste separation systems of two cities from Sweden and the Netherlands and was taken to a national level. From the analyses of both technical infrastructures of Sweden and the Netherlands, three factors (within the scope) have been identified that determine the current state of the systems. What is communicated in terms of separation rules is a compromise between the technical infrastructure, the legal framework and what the consumer can understand.

The current packaging waste systems of Sweden and the Netherlands lead to different types of inefficiencies. These inefficiencies are the cause of the legal framework and consumer understanding. Inefficiencies from the legal framework are that the law stipulates that certain material does not belong in a certain material stream but through both the viewpoint of the infrastructure and the viewpoint of the consumer it is possible, like envelopes and tealights covers in Sweden.

There are many inefficiencies from consumer behavior like putting non packaging in the packaging stream and putting packaging in the residual waste steam. There are also a number of examples from the processor that it is difficult to process certain materials and shapes which is misunderstood by the consumer (plastics foils smaller than A4 size, plastic nets).

The inefficiencies were then assessed from a consumer perspective and an environmental perspective. From the consumer perspective, separating packaging can pose a number of problems, the consumer does not understand the separation rules or is not motivated. The consumer also deliberately intends to separate properly, but at the waste processor the material is still removed and burned (for example, plastics smaller than A4 size, which are difficult to process). This could lead to demotivation of the consumer.

In that sense, one has to be careful what one asks for. The insight that some common consumer waste materials could very well be recycled in existing streams, but are excluded because they do not constitute packaging (and stakeholders from the packaging value chain have to foot the bill), or the insight that some material is allowed in a recycle stream, because it does constitute packaging, but it is subsequently separated out and not recycled, might cause unwanted attention in the media. Which could indeed erode support for waste separation by consumers.

From the environmental perspective, the inefficiencies pose a number of problems. The incorrect separation by the consumer ensures that part of the material no longer can be recycled and is therefore incinerated. In addition, waste processors have a lot of power in controlling the separation rules on which their installation is based. They instruct the municipality how to collect, and the municipality instructs the consumer how to separate the waste. This is not always the most efficient way from an environmental point of view, there are often economic reasons behind it.

To determine which inefficiency is the most disruptive, the recycle rates, weight share on the market and the embodied energy of the materials in MJ/kg have been looked at. This showed that the plastic packaging stream is currently the least efficient from an environmental point of view due to the low recycle rates, high embodied energy and the current not economically feasible situation.

It is a complex problem in which the whole value chain is built on economic principles. Every country in Europe has a different system but every system has its own inefficiencies. Designing and recycling a sustainable packaging is a chain activity and in the future sacrifices must be made in this chain to make the system environmentally efficient. Each stakeholder has their own critique on the system, but whether each stakeholder has an overview of what is happening and really understands the situation is the question. From an environmental perspective, consumer behavior in a source separating system is often the biggest problem, while from a consumer perspective sustainability actions could be the problem (takes a lot of effort, sometimes poorly communicated, does not always understand the reasoning and does not immediately get anything in return).

It needs time to get all insights in all relevant aspects in the value chain and the aspects have to be balanced out which can be at the expense of some stakeholders. There is a great need to become more sustainable, at the time of writing (4th of May, 2020) Earth Overshoot Day has already passed in the Netherlands, which indicates that all raw materials on earth have already been used for the rest of the year [30]. The most ideal Earth Overshoot Day would be on December 31st. Major changes will have to occur to solve the complex problem of getting more sustainable, it is important that sacrifices are made in the value chain to get the most efficient recycling system. But keep in mind it is an ongoing process of improvement.

7. Future research

It is now clear that the focus for improving the systems must be on the plastic material flow and consumer behavior. Influencing disposal behavior is therefore a recommended field of future research. Motivate people to recycle, let them notice the benefits of waste separation, maybe create social pressure by design. The research by (Lockton, Harrison, & Stanton, 2012) [31] may be interesting in this field of research. The research is about how designers see the users whose behavior they are trying to control. It is also interesting how the users see how designers try to influence them, and then allow or disallow them based on the designer's intention (Tromp, Hekkert & Verbeek, 2011) [32]. All these insights could lead to better control of consumer behavior and consumer understanding with regard to waste separation.

It is also recommended to look at source separation vs post- separation. For example, is going on full post-separation more efficient than source separation in order to minimize the degree of material contamination which leads to higher efficiency in the recycling of materials?

In addition, it must be examined how different stakeholders of the full life cycle influence the value chain and how it can be balanced in the future with a new, more environmentally friendly system that is also economically sound. Brand owners, designers and producers of packaging could also be disruptors of the recycle system by their choices.

Finally, it is very important to look at standardization in the value chain at European level. In this study, two illustrative cities were examined and compared with the national level, the systems are more or less in line with the European directives. Sweden and the Netherlands score relatively high in terms of recycling rates, but throughout Europe there is still room for improvement for recycling systems in other countries. In the future it is preferred to see that all of Europe will have a standard for the design, production, use and recycling of packaging waste and where everyone in the value chain knows what is going on. This is possible by making good and clear agreements with all stakeholders what will require the necessary energy and attention.

As mentioned before a lot is already going on in this field in the form of European guidelines. So, steps are being taken to work towards a better future in the recycling industry.

8. References

[1] European Commission. (2018, May 20). Packaging waste statistics Europa. Retrieved 24 October 2019, from https://ec.europa.eu/eurostat/statistics- explained/index.php/Packaging_waste_statistics

[2] European Commission. (2018, April 24). Packaging waste generated by packaging material, EU, 2017. Retrieved 12 November 2019, from https://ec.europa.eu/eurostat/statistics-explained/pdfscache/10547.pdf

[3] Afvalfonds verpakkingen. (2019, October 15). Recyclingresultaten. Retrieved 12 January 2020, from https://afvalfondsverpakkingen.nl/monitoring/pub lieksrapport

[4] FTI. (n.d.). Återvinningsstatistik - Förpacknings- och tidningsinsamlingen, FTI. Retrieved 12 January 2020, from https://www.ftiab.se/180.html

[5] KIDV. (2018, October 10). Inzameling en recycling. Retrieved 13 November 2019, from https://hoeverpakjeduurzaam.kidv.nl/verpakken- in-de-circulaire-economie/inzameling-en-recycling/

[6] Gemeente Enschede. (2020, April 26). Informatie over Enschede. Retrieved 14 January 2020, from https://allecijfers.nl/gemeente/enschede/

[7] Administrative unit: Östergötlands län. (n.d.). Linköping Population. Retrieved 13 January 2020, from http://population.city/sweden/linkoping/

[8] FTI. (n.d.). Frågor & Svar statistik - Förpacknings- och tidningsinsamlingen, FTI. Retrieved 13 January 2020, from https://www.ftiab.se/2975.html

[9] FTI. (n.d.). Producers responsibilities - Förpacknings- och tidningsinsamlingen, FTI. Retrieved 13 January 2020, from https://www.ftiab.se/1765.html

[10] FTI. (n.d.). For producers - Förpacknings- och tidningsinsamlingen, FTI. Retrieved 13 January 2020, from https://www.ftiab.se/1349.html

[11] FTI. (n.d.). Fees 2020 - Förpacknings- och tidningsinsamlingen, FTI. Retrieved 14 January 2020, from https://www.ftiab.se/2934.html

[12] FTI. (n.d.). Swedish environmental code chapter 15, Waste. Retrieved 14 January 2020, from https://www.ftiab.se/download/18.1d61e9b615d6 104cdb3a7/1501185171336/Chapter%2015.pdf

[13] FTI. (n.d.). Legislations - Förpacknings- och tidningsinsamlingen, FTI. Retrieved 14 January 2020, from https://www.ftiab.se/1653.html

[14] Milieu Centraal. (n.d.). Blik en ander metaal: waar laat je het? Retrieved 14 January 2020, from https://www.milieucentraal.nl/minder-afval/welk- afval-waar/blikken-en-ander-metaal/

[15] Ministerie van Volkshuisvesting, Ruimtelijke Ordening en Milieubeheer. (2019, September 10). Huishoudelijk afval scheiden en recyclen. Retrieved 14 January 2020, from https://www.rijksoverheid.nl/onderwerpen/afval/ huishoudelijk-afval

[16] Afvalfonds Verpakkingen. (n.d.). Recycling van verpakkingen succesvol - Afvalfonds verpakkingen. Retrieved 15 January 2020, from https://afvalfondsverpakkingen.nl/monitoring/ver pakkingsmaterialen

[17] Attero. (n.d.). Onze verwerking - Uw verpakkingsafval wordt grondstof - Onze verwerkingstechnieken - Nascheiden - Attero // Energiek met milieu. Retrieved 15 January 2020, from https://www.attero.nl/nl/onze-verwerking/uw-verpakkingsafval-wordt- grondstof/onze-verwerkingstechnieken/nascheiden/

[18] Overheid. (2016, January 1). wetten.nl - Regeling - Besluit beheer verpakkingen 2014 - BWBR0035711. Retrieved 15 January 2020, from https://wetten.overheid.nl/BWBR0035711/2016- 01-01

[19] Afvalfonds Verpakkingen. (n.d.). Taken van het Afvalfonds Verpakkingen - Afvalfonds verpakkingen. Retrieved 15 January 2020, from https://afvalfondsverpakkingen.nl/organisatie/taken-van-het-afvalfonds

[20] Milieu Centraal. (n.d.). Restafval: wat mag in de vuilnisbak? Retrieved 17 January 2020, from https://www.milieucentraal.nl/minder-afval/welk- afval-waar/restafval/

[21] KIDV. (2020, January 30). Weggooigedrag. Retrieved 2 February 2020, from https://hoeverpakjeduurzaam.kidv.nl/consumente ngedrag/weggooigedrag-2/#1511880619035-7bcd5c7b-d731

[22] Milieu Centraal. (n.d.). Afval scheiden: nut en fabels. Retrieved 2 February 2020, from https://www.milieucentraal.nl/minder-afval/afval- scheiden-nut-en-fabels/

[23] ten Klooster, R. (2018, September 27). Sustainability And the role of packaging [Slides]. Retrieved from https://canvas.utwente.nl/courses/1728/files/2351 94?module_item_id=38536

[24] de Lange, J. (2017, September 28). Roadmap to sustainable packaging design Optimizing the packaging design from viewpoint of sustainability [Slides]. Retrieved from https://canvas.utwente.nl/courses/2679/files/3958 00?module_item_id=52506

[25] Afvalfonds Verpakkingen. (2017, January 10). Afvalfonds Verpakkingen en AEB Amsterdam tekenen intentieovereenkomst voor optimalisatie en verduurzaming recycleketen - Afvalfonds verpakkingen. Retrieved 5 February 2020, from https://afvalfondsverpakkingen.nl/pers/eerste- pers-bericht

[26] European Plastics Pact. (2020, March 25). Plastic Pact. Retrieved 4 May 2020, from https://europeanplasticspact.org/

[27] EPBP. (n.d.). How to keep a sustainable PET recycling industry in Europe - EPBP - European PET Bottle Platform. Retrieved 2 May 2020, from https://www.epbp.org/

[28] Ceflex. (2020, January 17). CEFLEX | A circular economy for flexible packaging. Retrieved 2 May 2020, from https://ceflex.eu/

[29] RecyClass. (n.d.). What is RecyClass? Retrieved 2 May 2020, from https://recyclass.eu/recyclass/

[30] Joosse, B. (2019, July 19). Earth Overshoot Day: Nederland gebruikt bijna 3 aardes aan grondstoffen. Retrieved 4 May 2020, from https://www.duurzaambedrijfsleven.nl/recycling/32065/earth-overshoot-day

[31] Lockton, D., Harrison, D., & Stanton, N. A. (2012). Models of the user: Designer's perspectives on influencing sustainable behaviour. Journal of Design Research 14, 10(1- 2), 7-27.

[32] Tromp, N., Hekkert, P., & Verbeek, P. P. (2011). Design for socially responsible behavior: a classification of influence based on intended user experience. Design issues, 27(3), 3-19.

9. Appendix

Appendix A

Overview of the separation guidelines in Linköping

Material	Rules
Packaging of uncoloured / coloured glass (colour separated!)	**YES** Uncoloured / coloured bottles and cans Cans and bottles should be empty and washed out. Sorting caps and cover by material. **NO** Drinking glasses, porcelain, china polyethylene, filament lamps, fluorescent lamps or mirrors
Metal packaging	**YES** Cans (insert the lid into the bottle) Tubes, for example, caviar (let the Cork sit still to avoid bad smell) Metal lids and caps All packages shall: be empty and if necessary washed out. **NO** Paint and glue residues are dangerous waste and to be left on a recycling center. Empty spray cans
Pastic Packaging	**YES** Plastic bags / bags Plastic tubes Refill package Cling film and film * Vacuum packaging Polystyrene Plastic bottles), for example, ketchup, detergent, shampoo and juice Plastic bunches / boxes, to examples of ice cream and jam Note: Unscrew caps and corks. Put them loose in the vessel. All packages shall: be empty and at needs washed out. **NO**
Paper	**YES** Cereal packages Detergent packaging Corrugated packaging Paper bags Wrapping paper Pasta cartons Household / toilet roll Egg cartons Cardboard boxes Packaging for more than half consists of paper. The packages shall: be empty and at needs washed out. **NO** Newspapers and office paper sorted in the vessel for newspapers.
Newspaper	**YES** Newspapers Weekly newspapers Brochures Catalogs and pocket- books with soft back Telephone directories Advertising papers Writing paper Note: Carrier bags, boxes and cases cartons are sorted as paper packaging;

Appendix B

Overview of the separation guidelines in Linköping

Material	Rules
Packaging of uncoloured / coloured glass (colour separated!)	**YES** Packaging glass (such as preserving jars and wine bottles) Is it glass? And was it packed with drinks, food or cosmetics? Then it belongs in the glass container! Nowadays, lids and leftovers are no longer a problem. So you can safely put the lids on and leave the leftovers in the jars and bottles. This also applies to screw caps and corks. **NO** Flat glass (mirror glass and wire glass) Oven dishes Microwave dishes Pan lids Hot plates Coffee and tea pots Glass vases Heater windows Glass cups Car windows Crystal Porcelain Ceramic
Metal packaging	Since 2015, metal cans have been collected together with beverage cartons and plastic packaging. We call this waste stream "packaging". Collecting cans, beverage cartons and plastic packaging together gives you more convenience and ensures a higher separation percentage. **YES** Cans Dog and cat food cans Cans of soft drinks and beer Soup, meat and vegetable cans Lemonade syrup cans and bottles Empty paint cans (without paint residue) Empty spray cans (without KCA logo = small chemical waste) Lids of jars, screw caps and beer caps
Pastic Packaging	Since 2015, metal cans have been collected together with beverage cartons and plastic packaging. We call this waste stream "packaging". Collecting cans, beverage cartons and plastic packaging together gives you more convenience and ensures a higher separation percentage. There are two types of plastic: one-time use plastic packaging, belonging to the 'packaging' waste stream and 'hard plastic'. Hard plastic can be disposed of at the waste collection point / Environmental park. **YES** Plastic bags and bread bags Pasta and rice bags Candy bags Packaging of meat products and cheese Foils of magazines and advertising brochures Blisters including toothbrushes, cords and screws Butter tubs, sauce trays, spreaded cheese, pâté or coffee milk tubs Vegetable, fruit and salad trays or bags, fries trays Cups of yogurt, custard, whipped cream and ice cream Lids of jars of peanut butter, chocolate spread etc. Squeeze bottles of sauces such as ketchup and mayonnaise Bottles of detergents and cleaning products Bottles of, for example, shampoo, shower gel, bath foam and soap Tubes of, for example, gel, cream, body lotion and toothpaste Bottles of oil and vinegar Bottles of soda, water and dairy Jars of gel, medicines and vitamins Small plastic plant pots

Material	Rules
Plastic packaging	**NO** Paper, cardboard residues Cover materials Chip bags Blister packs of pills or chewing gum Chemical waste packaging (such as make-up packaging, turpentine bottles and kit cartridges) Agricultural film **Hard plastic** Box pallets Roof gutters (PVC) pipes Plastic crates Barrels Garden furniture Buckets Plastic toys Scrap
Paper	**YES** Newspapers and advertising brochures Print, fax, copy, write and drawing paper Envelopes Gift Wrapping Telephone directories Egg cartons Paper bags and cardboard boxes Cardboard and paper packaging **NO** Wallpaper Vinyl Beverage cartons Plasticized paper Foils of magazines and advertising brochures Sanitary paper Contaminated paper (for example pizza boxes, frozen packaging and used coffee filters) Tempex File Stucco
Beverage cartons	Since 2015, beverage cartons have been collected together with plastic packaging material and cans. We call this waste stream packaging. Collecting cans, beverage cartons and plastic packaging together gives you more convenience and ensures a higher separation percentage. **YES** Soda packaging Wine packaging Dairy packaging You can find drink cartons in packaging of dairy products, fruit juices, lemonades, iced tea, sauces and soup. Sometimes they have a kink-and-snap closure, sometimes a separate hard plastic cap. They consist of 75 to 80 percent paper and cardboard and are provided on the inside and outside with a layer of plastic polyethylene (PE) and / or aluminum foil (with long-lasting products). These materials can be recycled..
General packaging	Plastic packaging material, beverage cartons and cans are collected together. We call this waste stream packaging. Collecting cans, drinks cartons and plastic packaging together provides more convenience for you and it results in a higher separation percentage. **YES** **Plastic packaging** Plastic bags and bread, pasta and candy bags Packaging of meat products and cheese Foils of magazines and advertising brochures Blisters including toothbrushes, cords and screws Butter tubs, sauce trays, spreaded cheese, pâté or coffee milk tubs Vegetable, fruit and salad trays or bags, fries trays Beakers of yogurt, custard, whipped cream and ice cream Lids of jars of peanut butter, chocolate spread etc. Squeeze bottles of sauces such as ketchup and mayonnaise Bottles of washing and cleaning products - Bottles and tubes of care products Bottles of oil and vinegar Bottles of soft drinks, water and dairy Jars of gel, medicines and vitamins Small plastic plant pots

Material	Rules
General packaging	**YES** **Metal Packaging** Cans Dog and cat food cans Cans of soft drinks and beer Soup, meat and vegetable cans Lemonade syrup cans Empty paint cans (no cans with hardened paint, you can dispose of this at the Small Chemical Waste) Empty spray cans without logo. Small chemical waste Lids of jars, screw caps and beer caps **Beverage cartons** Soda packs Wine packs Dairy packaging **NO** Packaging with contents Chemical waste packaging - for example make-up packaging, turpentine bottles, kit cartridges and filled paint cans Styrofoam - for example, fast food packaging, meat trays and packaging filling material Paper, cardboard or foil residues - for example, cover materials, chip packages and blister packs (pills or chewing gum) Other plastic products and utensils - for example, garden chairs, toys and agricultural film

Circular "on-the-go" packaging [63]

Kristina Wickholm *, Annika Lindström
RISE, Research Institutes of Sweden, Stockholm, Sweden

Abstract: Single-use packaging and goods create major problems, partly because they are collected only to a limited extent and therefore contribute to littering. Furthermore, as these disposables are not collected, they are not recycled either. These disposables end up high on the top 10 list of the most common litter on land and in the ocean. Much of the litter found in measurements performed annually in urban environments, parks and beaches, is from packaging from "on-the-go" products. We want to create behavioral changes both by consumers and stakeholders in the value chain, so that disposables are handled in a more circular manner, ie source sorted, reused and material recycled and also that the recycled material is demanded and used to a greater extent. Determined actions are required from many actors in society. In this project, actors along the packaging value chain collaborate to develop new solutions, based on user needs, for collecting and sorting packaging in public places. The goals are to decrease littering and increase reuse and material recycling of on-the-go packaging.

The results show that consumers want to sort packaging on-the-go if sorting possibilities is offered in public places. It is important that the sorting is close by and that it is easy to understand how to sort the packaging. Furthermore, a deposit is shown to be an effective incentive to increase source sorting because it gives an added value to the used packaging. Therefor we want to provide the possibility of sorting on-the-go packaging, within a reasonable distance and with clear information on how to sort them. In addition, offer a deposit as an incentive to recycle and reuse these packaging. This is accomplished through an app that also facilitates the sorting for the consumer.

Keywords: packaging, recycling, littering, deposit, behavior

***Correspondence to:** Kristina Wickholm, RISE, E-mail: kristina.wickholm@ri.se

1. Introduction

In May 2018, EU countries approved several measures on waste legislation as part of the overall strategy for a circular economy. The purpose is to prevent waste and, when it is not possible, to significantly increase the material recycling of municipal solid waste and packaging. In a circular economy the collection of material is crucial. Single-use packaging and goods create major problems in society and in nature, partly because they are collected only to a limited extent and therefore contribute to littering. Furthermore, as these disposables are not collected, they are not recycled either which makes the resource efficiency low. These disposables end up high on the top 10 list of the most common litter on land and in the ocean. Much of the litter found in measurements performed annually by The Keep Sweden Tidy Foundation, in urban environments, parks and beaches in Sweden, is from packaging from "on-the-go" products.1 Most of the packaging from on-the-go consumption from public places ends up in waste incineration and have the potential to be handled more resource effective through increased material recycling and reuse.

2. Research Goals / Objectives

The project goals were to develop new solutions to decrease littering and increase reuse and recycling of packaging from on-the-go consumption. The aim is to create behavioral changes both by consumers and stakeholders in the value chain, so that disposable packaging from on-the-go consumption are handled more circularly, ie source sorted, reused and recycled to a higher degree than today and also that the recycled material is demanded and used to a greater extent.

3. Research Method

The project gathered actors along the packaging value chain in Sweden to collaborate with the aim to develop new solutions, based on user needs, for collecting and sorting packaging from on-the-go consumption in public places. Activities performed during the project were:

1. Analysis of the current situation. An analysis of the current situation in Sweden and in other countries were performed in the beginning of the project. The purpose was to get insight in other activities in the field.

2. Waste analysis in parks in the city of Örnsköldsvik, Sweden. This was done to see what kind of packages that end up in the parks.

3. Consumer surveys

a. To get an understanding about consumer behavior and needs an online survey was conducted with respondents all over Sweden. 892 answered the survey and of them 811 respondents completed the survey. The result from the survey served as input to the idea generation workshops.

b. A survey was conducted in parks and online in Örnsköldsvik. The purpose of the survey was to get insights in how to improve the collection of packaging from on-the-go consumption in the parks.

4. Idea generation workshops: In the workshops the actors along the packaging value chain were gathered to develop new solutions for more circular use of packaging from on-the-go consumption. Results from the consumer surveys and learnings from the analysis of the current situation served as input and the idea generation workshops.

5. As a last step, in- depth interviews with consumers were conducted to verify the new solutions.

4. Results and conclusions

The results show that consumers want to sort packaging on-the-go if sorting is offered in public places. Many of the respondents stated that they experienced a lack of possibility to sort the packaging from on-the-go consumption, so the waste ended up in waste bins.
Results also showed that it is important that the sorting is close by and that it is easy to understand how to sort the packaging. Even though the consumers are willing to sort their packaging, results show that it is important that the collection bins are not too far away.

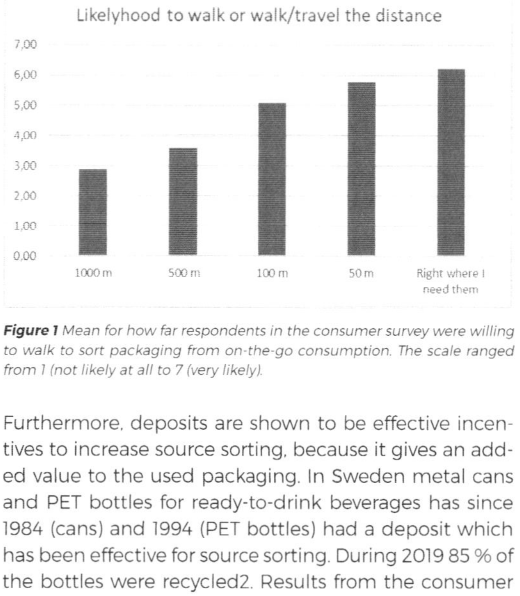

Figure 1 *Mean for how far respondents in the consumer survey were willing to walk to sort packaging from on-the-go consumption. The scale ranged from 1 (not likely at all to 7 (very likely).*

Furthermore, deposits are shown to be effective incentives to increase source sorting, because it gives an added value to the used packaging. In Sweden metal cans and PET bottles for ready-to-drink beverages has since 1984 (cans) and 1994 (PET bottles) had a deposit which has been effective for source sorting. During 2019 85 % of the bottles were recycled2. Results from the consumer survey in the project also showed that packaging with a deposit were recycled to a higher extent. In the parks included in the waste analysis, a complete absence of deposit bottles and -cans was noted. A small test was conducted; bottles and cans with deposit were placed in ten of the parks' bins. Detailed analysis of the collected waste showed that all were removed within 24 hours.

In idea generation workshops new solutions were created, that was built upon the results from the activities in the project. The new solution that we chose to continue with is based on providing the possibility to sort on-the-go packaging, within a reasonable distance and with clear information on how to sort them. In addition, offer deposit as incentives to recycle and reuse these packaging. This should be accomplished through an app that also facilitates the sorting for the consumers by providing information on how to sort the packaging. Furthermore, the app will make it easy for the user to find the closest recycling station and it also offers the possibility to register new recycling stations.

The solution could also be feasible in other countries because the app solution uses the collection system available in the specific country. However, since the collection system differs between countries the solution would need to be tested in the specific country and with their current collection system. The solution also needs to be adjusted to the collection system in that country to reach its full potential.

5. Future Research

Future research should test the effects of the solutions in a real environment. The focus should be to evaluate levels of collected packaging, the quality of the material and how the solution could be adjusted to reach its full potential from both a consumer- and system perspective.

6. Funding

This research was funded by Vinnova, Sweden's innovation agency, and the Swedish Environmental Protection Agency.

7. References

[1] Blidberg, E. (2018). Topp-10-lista över skräp på stränder 2018. Håll Sverige Rents. Retrieved from: https://www.hsr.se/fakta-om-skrap/statistikportal/skrapmatningar-pa-strander/topp-10-lista-over-skrap-pa-strander

[2] Pantamera (2018). About Returpack. Pantamera. Retrieved from: https://pantamera.nu/om-oss/returpack-in-english/about-returpack/

Filamentous Fungi to disappear plastic [88]

Daniela Guadalupe Fernández Leal *
UDEM´s Department of Basic Science and Microbiology Lab. Monterrey, Mexico

Abstract: The consumption of single-use plastic products has created an unmeasured amount of plastic residues worldwide, where only 9% of consumed plastic is recycled (ONU,2018). It was discovered that fungi are capable of metabolizing plastics by its natural growth processes, presenting an opportunity to combat this pollution. Those which are filamentous have been used to produce mycelium, a material capable of substituting foamed materials, mainly for packaging applications. This represents an opportunity not only to substitute plastics but to battle the plastic pollution creating useful products. Several strains of filamentous fungus were tested with polystyrene (PS) as substrate. The samples were analyzed in a 6-week growth-span in, studying it´s plastic samples at a microscopic level. After the growth stage, different tests were made to analyze the plastic degradation in presence of the fungus. Some level of degradation was presented in the samples, but the presence of plastic affected the growth rate. The relevance of this investigation is given the alternative end of life mainly for packaging and single-uses plastic products, given that it presents the 10% of municipal waste worldwide (Barnes, Galgani, Thompson, & Barlaz, 2009). It also presents the possibility to substitute foamed materials used for logistics and packaging. Future investigations regarding the degradation rate should be made to bring this material research for commercial consumption.

Keywords: biomaterial, mycelium, filamentous, fungus, metabolization, microplastics, mushroom, packaging.

***Correspondence to:** Daniela Guadalupe Fernández Leal. E-Mail: daniela.fernandezl@udem.edu

1. Introduction

1.1 Plastics

Plastic comes as a variety of semi-synthetic and synthetic organic compositions, that can be molded and transformed as rigid forms with certain elasticity. (Rocha-Santos & Duarte, 2017) Being also defined by the International Union of Pure and Applied Chemistry as a polymeric material that can contain other substances to enhance its functions or reduce costs. Given its mechanical and chemical properties, plastic substituted the use of other materials, to the extent that in 2015 the production of plastic is over 310 million tons. (PlasticsEurope, 2015)And since it is used mainly as packaging and single-use products, it represents itself globally as 10% of the waste found in municipal waste. (Barnes, Galgani, Thompson, & Barlaz, 2009)

1.2 Plastic waste

Plastic waste is an environmental and economical issue. About 275 million tons of waste were registered worldwide in 2010 (Ritchie & Roser, 2018). Creating a way for this plastic to enter ecosystems that were not meant to live with this pollutant. By introducing itself to marine habitats, it costs between $3,300 to $33,000 dollars per ton globally (Beaumont, et al., 2019).

The fact that we use plastic to dispose of it after a single-use, mainly in landfills or open dumps, creates greenhouse gases (Royer, Ferrón, Wilson, & Karl, 2018) and microplastics. These micro and nano-plastics are ingested first by the organisms living in our environment, especially the ocean, and later (through our food) by us (Rochman, et al., 2016). This intrinsic but sometimes invisible relationship we have created with plastic has changed our ecosystem, creating the plastisphere.

1.3 Plastisphere

The plastisphere is the ecosystem created by living organisms to adapt and live in the presence of man-made plastics. Many species have developed methods to cope and thrive in the presence of plastic. It has been found that some bacteria have created holes in some plastics, metabolizing the polymer to create a living space in them (Zettler, Mincer, & Amaral-Zettler, 2013). Some studies analyze organisms present in the soil which degrade plastic, ranging from bacteria to fungi. Fungi present the most degradation potential due to the enzymes they produce (Barratt, Ennos, Greenhalgh, Robson, & Handley, 2003) Representing an opportunity to harness the power of nature to reduce our plastic footprint.

1.4 Fungi

Fungi create different enzymes that break certain polymeric bonds at a molecular level, presenting the possibility to disappear plastic without creating microplastics, which can be harmful to our health. There are two types of fungi that have been found to metabolize plastic, some yeasts and other filamentous. The Fusarium Culmorum is a yeast and phytopathogen fungi that create cutinase, an enzyme that has shown the ability to mineralize PVC products in 60 hours. Corresponding to the yeasts, Aspergillus Nidulans has shown degradation on LDPE using the same enzyme to degrade said plastic. It must be noted that the degradation can be hard to see without equipment, especially if the exposition to the fungi is short. (Espinoza Arias, 2018) Pleurotus Ostreatus is a basidiomycete fungus, that produces cutinase at a lower rate than the past fungi, but it´s an edible and filamentous fungi. (Conacyt, 2016)Finally, some fungi corresponding to the Pestalotiopsis family have been used to degrade polyurethane (PU), low-density polyethylene (LDPE), and polystyrene (PS).

This family of fungi tends to feed itself by breaking carbon bonds and metabolizing hydrocarbons (Barja, 2016). The Pestalotiopsis Microspora uses enzymes of the family of Serine Hydrolase to degrade PU, and it's an aerobic and anaerobic fungus, so it can live in reduced and sealed spaces (Rodriguez Genes & Rodriguez Sossa, 2015).

1.5 Polystyrene

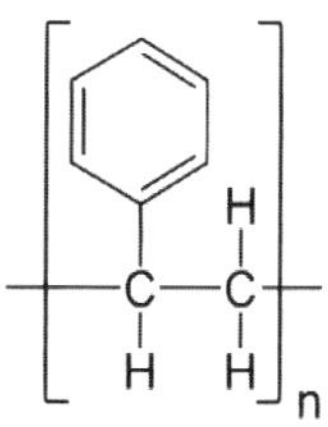

Figure 1 *Chemical structure of PS (Yikrazuul, 2008)*

Polystyrene is one of the plastics that have the most complex polymeric chain since it has an aromatic compound. This compound creates the need for a lot of energy to break the bonds, in comparison to the other plastics such as LDPE or PP. In theory, the cutinase could separate this plastic molecule by breaking the carbon bonds, whilst the serine hydrolase could take the carbon molecules, freeing the hydrogen and aromatic component and generating an aroma and gas as a final product.

Figure 2 *Structure of a fungus. (Mushrooms Are Masters of Design, 2019)*

Mycelium is the vegetative body of the fungi, which produces mushrooms. Mycelium is made from singular multicellular strands called hyphae. Through the tips of the hyphae, the fungus can deliver enzymes to digest its surroundings and absorb the nutrients. These strands branch out to create a vast network called mycelium (Crosby, 2018)

Mycelium is being used as a solution to decrease the use of expanded PS as packaging. While it grows, it acts as a glue to its substrate, which is generally made of wood chips, hemp, or other agro-industrial waste. By doing this it creates a solid material that is malleable and has the potential to produce new materials. Some commercially available products are insulation panels, packaging products, bricks, and some design explorations. Ecovative has been one of the main producers of packaging products that aim to replace products made of expanded PS. This material is compostable and can disappear in just a month (Parra, 2016). It also has acoustic and thermal insulation properties, which makes it a viable substitute for foamed polymers used in construction. (Girometta, et al., 2019) The fungi used to fabricate this material are filamentous, to be able to replicate this material the research focus is on this type of fungi.

2. Research Goals

The objective of this research is to validate if filamentous fungi can degrade PS and create a sustainable material.

To achieve this objective, 4 main goals must be validated, ranging from the degradation of plastic to the properties of the resulting material. The goals are:

1. Understand the natural structure of the fungi, without plastic, to serve as a comparison

2. Grow the fungi in a natural substrate (like the ones used to create commercial mycelium).

3. Evaluate if the PS fragments are affected or not in the presence of the fungi.

4. Evaluate if the traits of the mycelium as a material is kept despite the presence of plastic whilst growing

With these research goals, it can be validated if growing mycelium could be a possible bioremediation alternative for plastic pollution, taking advantage of the already existing mycelium packaging market. Creating a second life to discarded and non-recyclable plastic. It should be noted that this is a first approach to the research objective, and it should continue to be tested both in the matter of the degradation and as a material.

3. Research Method

To reach the objective, there needs to be a confirmation that some kind of degradation is taking place in the PS samples and whether the strain used affects the result or not. Two strains are of interest, the Pleurotus Ostreatus, and the Pestalotiopsis Mircrospora. Both are filamentous fungi that have enzymes that can break some polymeric chains while growing mycelium to create the material structure.

3.1 Pestalotiopsis Microspora

For the P. Microspora, there are to 2 different attempts of growth, given that the sample is delivered in liquid culture. First, 3 ml of the liquid culture were introduced in a premade substrate made of sterilized rye berry. Given that it's a tropical fungus, the sample was placed in an incubator at 37 °C. In the second sample, 9 ml of the liquid culture were added to 800ml of a Sabouraud liquid medium, which was placed in an incubator at 37 °C.

3.2 Pleurotus Ostreatus

This fungus was in germinated sorghum seeds. To evaluate if the fungus could grow with plastic in its substrate, a natural medium was made, composed of agave fibers, coffee, wood, and flour. Different proportions of small pieces of PS, not exceeding 5mm in length, were added. The proportions made by weight began at 0%, 5%, 10%, 20%,30%,40%,50%,60%,70%, and 80% of plastic present in 100 grams of substrate. After the samples are sorted, they are sterilized in an autoclave and inoculated with 10 grams of germinated seeds and left to grow in a space where the temperature was 25°C.

These samples were placed in a space with air conditioning for 6 weeks, and where sprayed with distilled water when needed.

Figure 3 *Substrate samples with different percentages of PS (Author, 2019)*

Figure 4 *Samples of growth per percentage. (Author, 2019)*

The experiment showed different results. After 2 weeks, the fungus grew in all the samples of the substrate. After 4 weeks fruiting bodies were visible. Figure 4 demonstrates that the branching out of the mycelium was reduced as the percentage of plastic present in the substrate grew. All samples had mycelium, but the presence of the plastic did change how it behaved.

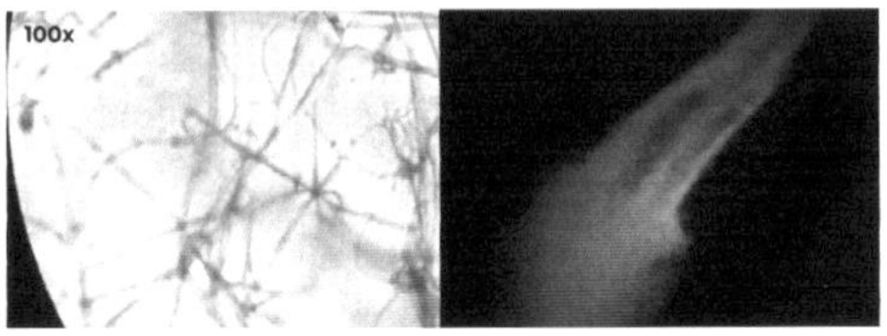

Figure 5 *Control mycelium sample. (Author, 2019)*

In figure 5 we show how the mycelium of this strain grows without the presence of plastic

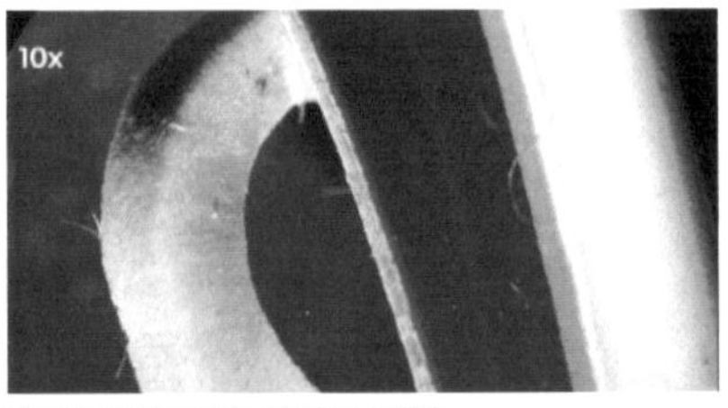

Figure 6 *PS Control sample. (Author, 2019)*

In figure 6 we show how the polystyrene samples are without the presence of the fungus

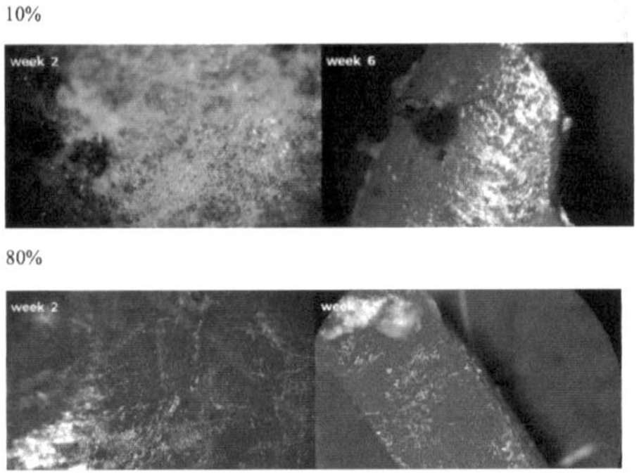

Figure 7 *Development of degradation in samples grown with fungus. (Author, 2019)*

As shown in Figure 7, the presence of the fungus did affect the polystyrene samples. Showing over time the effects from week 2 through week 6. The fungus is growing in the plastic rather than around it, creating pores and melting.

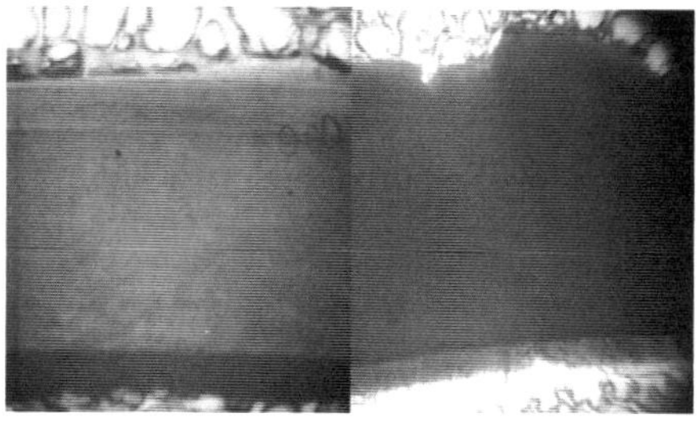

Figure 8 *Comparison between Control and Fungus-Grown PS samples. (Author, 2019)*

A microscopic sample was made, where fragmentation can be seen the occurred between a control plastic sample and one that was with the growing fungus. Hyphae are visible in the outer layers of the sample, validating that the fungus is affecting the plastic and accelerating the degradation process.

3.3 Mycelium properties

Mycelium has thermal insulation capabilities. Some testing was made to evaluate whether our samples of plastic-grown-mycelium had thermal insulation, even in the presence of the plastic pieces.

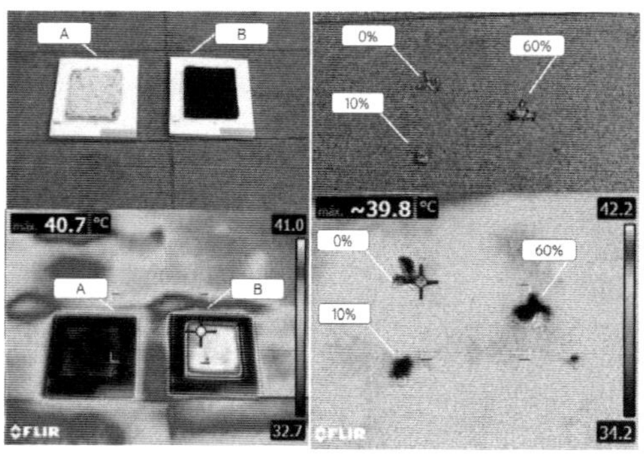

Figure 9 *Insulation tests between commercial mycelium samples and plastic-grown samples. (Author, 2019)*

For 10 minutes of direct sunlight, some commercially available samples of mycelium and small pieces of the plastic-grown-mycelium samples were exposed to validate the thermal insulation traits. With a thermal camera it showed that with the presence of plastic, where there is mycelium, there is insulation. But if the plastic was exposed to the sun, and wasn't protected by the mycelium, it can grow to be a heat focus.

4. Results and conclusions

Analyzing the results of the P. Ostreatus samples, there was some change in the fragments of PS when fungus grew in it. Therefore, it can be concluded that the fungus it's affecting the plastic at a microscopic level. Nonetheless, an elevated percentage of the natural substrate is required, given that the proportion of plastic can affect the behavior of fungus growth. It is recommended to grow the fungus in a 30% - 40% of plastic to the natural substrate if there is a need for long-term results. In the short term, 80% showed the most degradation, but further in time, it did not show any changes after 2 weeks. Also, the fruiting bodies and the branching of the mycelium occurred oddly. The mushroom was weak and could not stand by itself, and the branching was very thin layered, further validating that the percentage is key to obtain results. It was validated that the degradation is taking place, but it is taking longer than estimated and might be an issue to consider as a bioremediation solution. Further research is required to evaluate other conditions that promote mycelium growth in a faster way. And the growth of the mycelium was evaluated to validate its material capabilities, and so far, the thermal capabilities are kept.

5. Future Research

This research presents some feasibility to use filamentous fungi as a bioremediation, but several next steps should be made first. The plastic composition needs to be known before hand, for example in SEM tests, to know the composition before to be able to predict which are the byproducts created by the fungus and the ones created by the degradation of the plastic. Same for the mycelium samples. There must be comprehension of the byproducts created by degradation. For example, if PVC was used. There must be a validation that the chloride molecule is metabolized by the fungus because the damage done from that chemical in the environment could be worse than the stabilized molecule in the plastic. There should also be an analysis to show if the cutinase is the one changing the plastic or if it is a combination of enzymes. This would help to know how to further improve the process. The Pestalotiopsis Microspora should be tried once again as a possible degradation fungus since, in theory, it is the one most capable of metabolizing plastic.

The main reason this research is relevant in packaging is because it offers an alternative end of life to most of the packaging used. Considering even unrecyclable paper and plastic products as substrate, to eradicate the concept of waste in the end of life of a packaging. Including that the byproduct could present itself as an alternative to plastic foamed materials.

6. References

[1] Rocha-Santos, T., & Duarte, A. (2017). Characterization and Analysis of Microplastics (1st ed., Vol. 75). Elsevier.

[2] Barja, C. A. (2016). La eficiencia del hongo Pestalotiopsis spp en la biodegradación de los tipos de plásticos (Poliuretano, polietileno de baja densidad y poliestireno de cristal), a nivel de laboratorio. Retrieved from Repositorio de la Universidad César Vallejo: http://repositorio.ucv.edu.pe/handle/UCV/817

[3] Barnes, D. K., Galgani, F., Thompson, R. C., & Barlaz, M. (2009). Accumulation and fragmentation of plastic debris in global environments. Philosophical Transactions of The Royal Society B Biological Sciences, 1985-1998.

[4] Barratt, S. R., Ennos, A. R., Greenhalgh, M., Robson, G. D., & Handley, P. S. (2003). Fungi are the predominant micro-organisms responsiblefor degradation of soil-buried polyester polyurethaneover a range of soil water holding capacities. Journal of Applied Microbiology, 78-85.

[5] Beaumont, N. J., Aanesen, M., Austen, M. C., Börger, T., Clark, J. R., Cole, M., . . . Wyles, K. J. (2019). Global ecological, social and economic impacts of marine plastic. Marine Pollution Boletin, 189-195.

[6] Conacyt, A. I. (2016, November 17). Investigadores Descubren Hongos Capaces De Degradar Plásticos En Menos De Tres Días. Retrieved from Espacio Joven: http://espacio.fese.mx/investigadores- descubren-hongos-capaces-de-degradar-plasticos-en-menos-de-tres-dias/

[7] Crosby, W. (2018, June 8). What is Mycelium: Nature's World Wide Web Underneath Our Feet. Retrieved from Fungi Ally: https://fungially.com/what-is-mycelium-natures-world-wide-web/

[8] Espinoza Arias, L. M. (2018, May 16). Repositorio USFQ. Retrieved from Evaluación de la degradación de polietileno de baja densidad mediada por diferentes especies de hongos: http://repositorio.usfq.edu.ec/bitstream/23000/7410/1/139174.pdf

[9] Girometta, C., Pico, A. M., Baiguera, R. M., Dondi, D., Babbini, S., Cartabia, M., . . . Savino, E. (2019). Physico-Mechanical and Thermodynamic Properties of Mycelium-Based Biocomposites: A Review. Sustainability.

[10] Mushrooms Are Masters of Design. (2019, March 25). Retrieved from Phenomenal Fungi: https://phenomenalfungi.com/blogs/news/just-how-creative-are-mushrooms

[11] Parra, S. (2016, March 7). El nuevo embalaje ecológico para Ikea estará hecho a base de hongos. Retrieved from Xataka Ciencia: https://www.xatakaciencia.com/medio-ambiente/el-nuevo-embalaje-ecologico- para-ikea-estara-hecho-a-base-de-hongos

[12] PlasticsEurope. (2015). www.plasticseurope.org. Retrieved August 2019, from Plastics – the Facts 2015: https://www.plasticseurope.org/application/files/3715/1689/8308/2015plastics_the_facts_14122015. pdf

[13] Ritchie, H., & Roser, M. (2018, September). Plastic Pollution. Retrieved August 2019, from https://ourworldindata.org/plastic-pollution

[14] Rochman, C. M., Browne, M. A., Underwood, A., Franeker, J. A., Thompson, R. C., & Amaral-Zettler, L. A. (2016). The Ecological Impacts of Marine Debris: Unraveling the Demonstrated Evidence From What Is Perceived. Ecology, 302-312.

[15] Rodriguez Genes, A. L., & Rodriguez Sossa, Y. Y. (2015). BIODEGRADACIÓN DE POLIURETANO MEDIANTE EL USO DEL HONGO Pestalotiopsis microspora. Retrieved from Academia.edu: https://www.academia.edu/14192074/BIODEGRADACI%C3%93N_DE_POLIURETANO_MEDI ANTE_EL_USO_DEL_HONGO_Pestalotiopsis_microspora?auto=download

[16] Royer, S.-J., Ferrón, S., Wilson, S. T., & Karl, D. M. (2018). Production of methane and ethylene from plastic in the environment. PLoS ONE.

[17] Yikrazuul. (2008, May 21). File:Polystyrene.svg. Retrieved from Wikimedia Commons: https://commons.wikimedia.org/wiki/File:Polystyrene.svg

[18] Zettler, E. R., Mincer, T. J., & Amaral-Zettler, L. A. (2013). Life in the "Plastisphere": Microbial Communities on Plastic Marine Debris. Environmental Science & Technology, 7137–7146.

CHAPTER III

Packaging dynamics (vibrations & shocks)

Title:
Pyramid of Chichen Itzá

Author:
Jess Kraft (jkraft5)

Location:
Tinum, YUCATÁN

Description:
Chichen Itzá is considered the heart of the Mayan civilization. Their majestic ruins are an essential visit of any trip through Yucatan. The main building, the Pyramid or Castle of Kukulkán shows the Mayan knowledge of mathematics, astronomy, geometry and acoustics.
It is in this building that during the spring equinox you can see the feathered snake god descend from Heaven to Earth.

International Safe Transit Association's Distribution Environment Data Collection Program [18]

Brian O'Banion *
ISTA Vice President of Research & Education

Abstract: This presentation will be a re-introduction of the ISTA Distribution Environment Data Collection Program, which was presented at the IAPRI 2019 program. This iteration will include summary results from India and an update on our efforts in the European Union, along with an outreach effort to researchers that may be interested in helping us with data collection in China, Japan and Mexico.

ISTA's mission to empower the people and organizations affecting packaging to minimize product damage throughout distribution and optimize resource usage through effective package design continues to be greatly influenced by packaged-product performance testing. As part of our strategic plan to deliver on this mission, ISTA has developed a "Distribution Environment Data Collection Program" with the primary goal of expanding our distribution environment data resources.

ISTA will use the "Distribution Environment Data Collection Program" to expand our distribution environment data resources. This data will then be leveraged to improve current testing protocols, add new testing protocols, and create a world-class data repository that can be leveraged by ISTA, and its members, to better model distribution locally, nationally, and internationally.

Through both directly-funded research and industry collaboration, we will obtain atmospheric, vibration, storage and handling data that meets our established data collection standards for five prioritized global distribution routes. Summary results from our data collection efforts in India will be presented, along with an update on our current efforts in the European Union.

This data will then be developed and implemented into ISTA test procedures as deemed appropriate by the ISTA Testing Council and Technical Division Board.

This approach will yield data that can then be segmented to model global distribution routes. It is also intended to serve as a starting point and not an end goal. We would like to identify and encourage researchers that may be interested in partnering with us as we collect data in other countries, such as China, Japan and Mexico. We are also interested in working with members of the community who own data for routes outside of these identified target areas and have interest in sharing and building the ISTA data repository. This will ultimately serve to improve testing and package design globally.

***Correspondence to:** Brian O'Banion, ISTA Vice President of Research & Education USA. E-mail: bobanion@ista.org

Introduction

The International Safe Transit Association (ISTA) is a trade association that provides the tools needed to ensure packaged-products survive the risky and hazardous global distribution market.

ISTA's vision is to be the leading inspiration and resource for improving our world through transport packaging globally. Packaging enables commerce economies at a micro and macro level, it prevents food waste, it enables healthcare, it prevents disease, it allows us to get food and medicine to populations in critical need, and on and on. But, society and even business doesn't always view packaging in that light. Packaging is often times characterized as a villain, "garbage", an added cost. So packaging needs inspirational voices and it needs champions. Part of our vision is to inspire and project the value of packaging and how it improves our world.

ISTA's mission is to empower the people and organizations affecting packaging to minimize product damage throughout distribution and optimize resource usage through effective package design. ISTA helps members control costs, damage, and resources during the distribution of packaged-products by

- Creating and publishing packaged-product test procedures.
- Certifying packaging laboratories, packaged-products and professionals.
- Providing education, training, and support.

To provide a sense of scale, ISTA's membership consists of over 1,000 companies from over 40 countries. We certify over 500 testing laboratories globally and are an ANSI-accredited standards developer with 22 active standards. These standards can be found in our publication, "Testing Standards and Procedures" for packaged product distribution.

These test procedures include non-simulation screening tests, general simulation testing that is more predictive and enhanced simulation testing using current data, customized to a user.

Objective

ISTA's mission continues to be greatly influenced by packaged-product performance testing. As part of our strategic plan to deliver on this mission, ISTA has developed a new "Distribution Environment Data Collection Program" with the primary goal of expanding our distribution environment data resources. ISTA will use the Distribution Environment Data Collection Program to expand our distribution environment data resources. This data will then be leveraged to improve current testing protocols, add new testing protocols, and create a world-class data repository that can be leveraged by ISTA, and its members, to better model distribution locally, nationally, and internationally.

Approach

Through both directly-funded research and industry collaboration, we've set a goal to obtain atmospheric, vibration, storage, and handling data that meets our established Data Collection Standards for five prioritized global distribution routes. This data will then be developed and implemented into ISTA test procedures as deemed appropriate by the ISTA Testing Council and Technical Division Board.

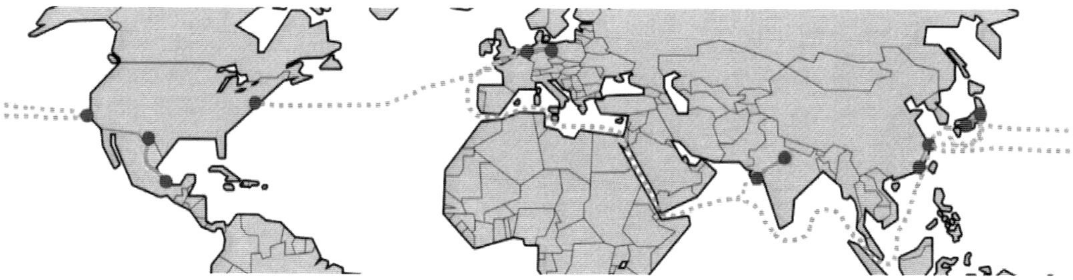

Based on research using trade data from the World Bank and others, ISTA's Technical Division Board decided upon the following approach:

· Gather data for the ocean route of Asia to the EU (Shanghai to Rotterdam). This data can then be adjusted to scale for various ocean transport distances.

· Gather data for two of the top global ports ranging across locations of interest, such as Shanghai and Rotterdam. This data collection effort will determine if there are substantive handling differences at the various ports or if all major ports can reasonably be modeled the same.

· Collect data for the top five inter-regional land routes of interest for which data is currently deemed to be non-representative:

1. China (within and between Shanghai and Guangzhou)
2. India (within and between Jawaharlal Nehru port (Mumbai) and New Delhi)
3. European Union (East/West and North/South routes)
4. Mexico (within and between Veracruz and Mexico City)
5. Japan (within and between Tokyo and Osaka)

· As a first phase, we will focus on data collection for a land route.

This approach will yield data that can then be segmented to model global distribution routes and drive further development of ISTA test protocols and allow development of user-specific test plans through Packsight.

This effort is also intended to serve as a starting point and not an end goal. We are also interested in working with members of the community who own data for routes outside of these identified target areas and have interest in sharing and building the ISTA data repository. This will ultimately serve to improve testing and package design globally.

Methods

As previously mentioned, the data will be collected through both directly-funded research and industry collaboration. We encourage members of IAPRI to participate in this phase, as we will actively solicit bids to perform the field data collection and analysis. Researchers interested in submitting proposals for Distribution Environment Data Collection Project RFPs should contact ISTA directly to note their interest. All RFPs will be sent directly to any researcher with noted interest at the time of publishing.

Directly-Funded Research: The general process is ISTA will develop and issue a RFP describing the scope of work and deliverables, soliciting interested researchers to bid on the project. After receipt of the proposals, ISTA will evaluate them and select a research partner. Part of this evaluation is helping us connect with the right kinds of companies that will allow us access to measure their distribution system. The research partner will work with these companies to collect the field data. Once the data has been collected, the researcher will process the data, providing both raw data and summaries, e.g. PSDs for vibration data, as well as the other deliverables.

Industry Collaboration: ISTA encourages researchers and companies to share their distribution hazard data with ISTA to expand ISTA's dataset. This additional data will improve the quality of ISTA's test procedures to reduce product damage and improve sustainability. Interested parties with data for these targeted ocean, port or land routes can share their data with ISTA, assuming the data meets ISTA's data collection requirements as defined in the ISTA Data Collection Standards.

We are also interested in working with members of the community who own data for routes outside of these identified target areas and have interest in sharing and building the ISTA data repository. This will ultimately serve to improve testing and package design globally. The data we are seeking includes:

- Shock, Vibration, Atmospheric (temperature & Rh)
- Modes
- Route
- Type of Vehicles (Air, Rail, Truck, etc...)
- Suspension and other details
- Time of Year
- Instrumentation & Calibration Details
- Mounting Information

Online data submission is possible through the Data Collection Program webpage or using these links:

Vibration Data
Shock/Drop Data
Atmospheric Data

Data Collection Standards: ISTA has created Data Collection Standards and Data Analysis Guidelines as a way of setting expectations regarding how we wish our data to be collected and analyzed.

The Data Collection Standards were developed by subject-matter-experts and approved by the ISTA Technical Board in 2018. The intent is that these standards will allow ISTA to combine suitable data from different researchers to model custom routes. The Data Collection Standards are available on the ISTA website store and provide the following guidance:

Atmospheric:
- Recording Equipment Requirements
- Calibrated Accuracy
- Range
- Sample Recording Rate
- Date & Time Stamp
- Instrument Placement
- Individual Package
- Unit Load
- Inside a Vehicle (dedicated shipment)

Shock/Drop:
- Documentation of Project & Variables
- Instruments used/setup
- Mounting information
- Vehicle Routes, Speed, Modes
- Photos/Video
- Instrument Mounting
- Instrument Recording Setup
- Threshold Triggering Level

Vibration:
- Documentation of Project & Variables
- Instruments used/setup
- Mounting information
- Vehicle Routes, Speed, Modes
- Photos/Video
- Instrument Mounting
- Instrument Recording Setup

Data Analysis Guidelines: The Data Analysis Guidelines were published in 2020 and are available on the ISTA website store. They have also been developed by subject-matter-experts and will approved by the ISTA Technical Board. As with the data collection standards, the documents provide guidance to the industry and create transparency of analysis methodologies for vibration, thermal and shock/impact data. The original intent was to develop data analysis standards, but as the effort progressed, the team realized that data analysis was a mix of art and science and felt that a guidance document was more appropriate than a standard.

Research Progress

India

The first data collection project awarded was for India and was completed in 2020. The project goal was to collect hazard data for distribution from Jawaharlal Nehru port (Mumbai) to New Delhi. The project scope was as follows:

- Shock, Vibration and Atmospheric - multiple replicates
- Instrumented Trips - 40
- Routes - collected data on several routes
- Modes - Truck, train, air, small parcel delivery
- Number of Companies - 5 CPGs, 1 Retailer, 2 Logistics

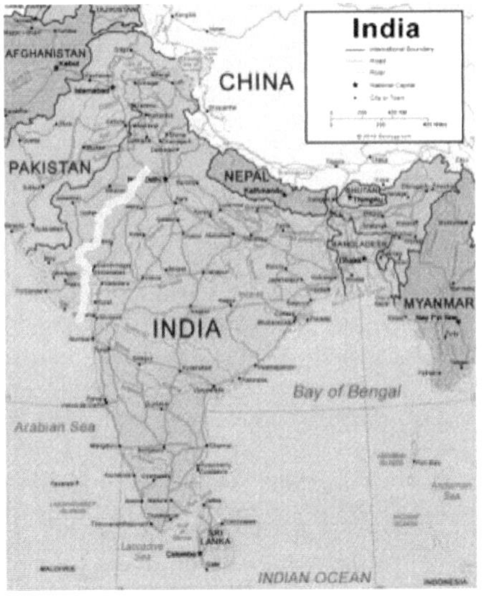

The project was conducted in two portions. The original intent was to collect environmental, shock and vibration data for the Consumer Packaged Goods (CPGs) distribution. However, the researchers recognized that that shock data could not be collected in this distribution channel because the instrumented package (also known as a decoy) was subject to theft and that the loaders could not assure decoy orientation while hand-stacking the load. Therefore, we collected shock data from the small parcel distribution channel as a way of benchmarking the relative shock severity of India as compared with ISTA 3A.

This effort is also intended to serve as a starting point and not an end goal. We are also interested in working with members of the community who own data for routes outside of these identified target areas and have interest in sharing and building the ISTA data repository. This will ultimately serve to improve testing and package design globally.

This paper will present the high-level results of the research but will not include the detailed information at this time. The reason for this restriction is that the data is under review by the ISTA Standards Council for consideration of the development of an India-specific test profile.

Results

Environmental: The average temperature observed during all trips was 94 °F with a range of 66-116 °F, and the relative humidity was observed to be at an average of 50% with a range of 18-85%. The deployment of air-ride suspension trucks as well as palletization and mechanical handling of CPGs is fairly uncommon in Indian distribution environments.

Vibration: Vibration data was collected for all truck, rail, bicycle (rickshaw), and car shipments in the CPG portion of the study. Between the transportation modes, the vertical vibration levels measured during truck shipments were the most intense. The vibration profile measured during car transport was very similar to what was measured during truck transport. Rail shipments had significantly lower intensity levels compared to truck and car shipments, especially at low frequencies. The bicycle shipment measured relatively intense vibration around 5Hz, but the overall vibration level was comparatively low.

Figure 1 shows the average PSD for all truck shipments in the vertical direction. The measured vibration profile was compared to the ISTA 4AB Steel Spring Truck profile and the India Truck profile recommended in the 2007 India Project report by Singh et al.

The average PSD for all truck shipments measured in this study shows that the vibration levels are much more intense in India than they are in North America. The shape of the average truck profile contains much more energy at low frequencies than the standard profile. At low frequencies, the measured levels are very similar to the India Truck profile suggested by Singh et al. based on the summarized data collected in the 2007 project. High acceleration levels at low frequencies produce large displacements that can cause loads to shift. For this reason, the intensity at low frequencies have significant implications for load stability.

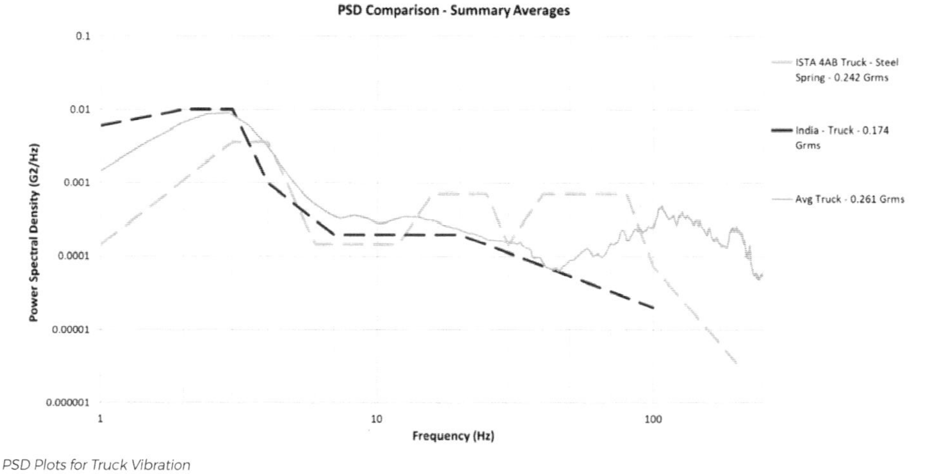

Figure 1 *PSD Plots for Truck Vibration*

Shock: The purpose of the small parcel portion of the study was to measure the dynamic conditions related to the small parcel (express courier) shipping environment in India. 38 one-way air shipments and four one-way surface shipments between four of the major cities in India (Mumbai, New Delhi, Kolkata and Chennai), using two different courier companies over approximately 43,000 miles, were undertaken.

Adopting ISTA's Data Analysis Guidelines for Shock/Impact & Drop, effective free fall drop heights (EFF-DH) for the 1,158 recorded field events were calculated and analyzed towards proposing a lab based drop test protocol for small packaged products shipped via the Indian parcel delivery systems.

The impact orientations and EFFDH were used to develop a proposed drop test protocol for the 90th percentile, 95th percentile and 99th percentile. This proposed drop test protocol is currently under evaluation by the ISTA Standards Council for the possible development of an India-specific test profile.

It may be noted that the drop test protocol proposed for the Indian small parcel distribution environment is substantially different from both ISTA Procedure 3A and the distribution of CPGs through the Indian retail supply channels. ISTA 3A recommends 16 drops for small packaged- products (Test Blocks 3 and 9) with drop heights of 18 (14 drops) - 36 (two drops) inches in flat (three drops), edge (eight drops) and corner (five drops) orientations. Aside from potentially the impact orientations, the drop test protocol proposed by this study varies substantially from ISTA 3A with more and higher drops.

Recall that the study was not able to collect shock data in the CPG portion of the study. However, in an attempt to benchmark the India distribution environment hazard severity, the researcher noted that his previous work with the distribution of CPGs through the Indian retail supply channels found that approximately 85% of all potential drops were estimated to be between 20-48 inches and that approximately 94% of all handling through the distribution was up to 7 times. This information indicates that the India CPG distribution shock severity and frequency exceed the current ISTA test profiles.

European Union

The second data collection project has been started and will collect distribution environment hazard data for CPG distribution in the European Union. The project scope is described as follows:

Shock, Vibration and Atmospheric - multiple replicates
Routes - (2) North/South, (2) East/West routes
Modes - Truck, train, air
Number of Companies - To be determined

The project progress to date is as follows:
Bids were received and a research partner was selected.
The work is just beginning and outreach to potential commercial partners has begun.
The project will extend into 2021, due to the impact of COVID-19 response.

Advocate Council: One additional item of note is that ISTA also sponsors a research consortium consisting of companies involved in packaging, Consumer Packaged Goods, freight, testing laboratories and lab equipment manufacturers. The consortium was established in 2015 and has $1.85m pledged to conduct research and data collection that improves testing and design methodologies to keep pace with the rapidly evolving global supply chain and enhance the knowledge of existing channels. This group also sponsors distribution environment data collection, so please notify ISTA if your research organization would like to be included in the RFP process. All RFPs will be sent directly to any researcher with noted interest at the time of publishing.

Conclusion

ISTA is sponsoring significant data collection efforts and is excited for this opportunity to collaborate with the IAPRI community to continue pushing package performance testing and design forward. You can contact ISTA VP of Research and Education, Brian O'Banion (bobanion@ista.org), directly with any questions or to note interest in participation.

References

[1] International Safe Transit Association (ISTA) at ista.org

[2] ISTA Data Collection Program webpage at https://ista.org/distribution_environment_data.php

[3] ISTA Data Collection Standards. Available from the ISTA website at https://mms.ista.org/members/store_product.php?orgcode=ISTA&pid=22407493.

[4] ISTA Data Analysis Guidelines: Thermal Data available from the ISTA website at https://mms.ista.org/members/store_product.php?orgcode=ISTA&pid=23914219

[5] ISTA Data Analysis Guidelines: Shock Impact Drop Data available from the ISTA website at https://mms.ista.org/members/store_product.php?orgcode=ISTA&pid=24015645

[6] ISTA Data Analysis Guidelines: Vehicle Vibration Data available from the ISTA website at https://mms.ista.org/members/store_product.php?orgcode=ISTA&pid=24016867

[7] ISTA website store: https://mms.ista.org/members/store.php?orgcode=ISTA

[8] Singh, J, Narayanan, P.V. "Distribution Environment Data Collection Project, India, A Transport Environment Data Collection Study" commissioned study for ISTA 2020.

[9] Singh, J, Narayanan, P.V. "Distribution Environment Data Collection Project, India, A Transport Environment Data Collection Study: Small Parcel Shipments" commissioned study for ISTA 2020.

[10] Singh, S. P., Sandhu, A., Singh, J, Joneson, E. "Measurement and Analysis of Truck and Rail Shipping Environment in India," Journal of Packaging Technology and Science, Vol. 20, Issue 6, pp. 381 - 392, November/December 2007

[11] Singh, J., and Narayanan, P. V. "Retail Supply Channels for CPGs In India: An Evaluation of Handling, Storage & Transportation in the Distribution Environment," International Transport Packaging Forum, May 13-16, 2019, Denver, Colorado

Estimation Method of Velocity on Truck Bed [19]

Daichi Nakai *1,2, Katsuhiko Saito 2
1 Sankyu Inc., Kitakyushu, Japan
2 Transport Packaging Laboratory, Kobe University, Kobe, Japan

Abstract: Random vibration tests for packaging are conducted to confirm the safety of packaging during truck shipping. Although the traditional vibration test condition is based on the power spectral density of acceleration, differences exist between traditional vibration tests and real vibrations. While traditional vibration tests stationary and do not include shocks, real vibrations on the truck bed are non-stationary and include shocks.

Many studies that focus on compensating for these differences have been conducted. These studies have considered the power spectral density, root mean square, probability density and kurtosis of the acceleration.

On the other hand, in earthquake engineering, both the maximum acceleration and maximum velocity are correlated with building damage. In impact testing of packaging, the maximum acceleration and velocity change are important factors. Therefore, velocity is assumed to be an important factor in the vibration testing of packaging.

The velocity during the vibration test requires a known vibration velocity on the truck bed as a test condition. To our knowledge, no existing studies have estimated the vibration velocity on a truck bed during shipping.

To estimate velocity, the acceleration is integrated. In this study, we firstly calculated the velocity during the vibration test from acceleration using time series integration. Consequently, we observed that the velocity cannot be accurately estimated by time series integration because of low frequency noises. Therefore, we propose an integration method that employs Fourier transform and low-cut filter to eliminate low frequency noises. The velocity during the vibration test was also estimated by imaging processing using a high-speed camera. The velocity waveforms estimated from acceleration by proposed method were compared with those obtained from displacement by imaging processing, which confirmed the accuracy of velocity estimated using the proposed method.

Keywords: Vibration Test, Vibration Velocity, Low Frequency Noise

***Correspondence to:** Daichi Nakai, Sankyu Inc., Kitakyushu 8050069, Japan. E-mail: d.nakai@sankyu.co.jp

1. Introduction

Product safety from mechanical hazards during distribution is an important factor in packaging. Random vibration tests are conducted for packages to ensure safety during truck shipping. Vibration tests that are more severe than real vibrations will ensure the safety of the product, however these result in high cost because additional cushion materials required. Vibration tests that are milder than real vibrations will occur the product's damage during truck shipping. Hence, it is important to optimize the vibration level.

The traditional random vibration test condition is generally determined from the power spectral density of acceleration (PSD). However, the shocks caused by speed bumps, road roughness and potholes cannot be reproduced by this method. Hence, the test and actual vibrations differ [1].

To solve this problem, many studies have focused on not only PSD but also the probability density of acceleration and acceleration kurtosis [2-6]. The probability density of acceleration during traditional vibration tests is a Gaussian distribution, and the kurtosis value of acceleration is three [7]. The probability density of acceleration measured on the truck bed is non-Gaussian and the kurtosis value of acceleration is greater than 3. Therefore, random vibration tests, where the probability density of acceleration is the same as that measured on the truck bed, are more accurate with respect to the truck bed vibration than traditional random vibration tests.

Velocity is assumed to be an important factor in shock testing for packaging. In earthquake engineering, both maximum acceleration and maximum velocity are correlated with building damage [8]. In impact testing of packages, both maximum acceleration and velocity change are important factors [9]. Therefore, the vibration test, in which probability density of both acceleration and velocity are the same as those measured on the truck bed, can be assumed to be closer to the vibration of the truck bed.

To consider the velocity in a vibration test, it is necessary to know the vibration velocity during truck shipping. To the best of our knowledge, although several studies have been conducted to measure the vibration during distribution, there are no reports about vibration velocity [10-14]. When measuring vibration, accelerometers are mainly used, and the velocity should be calculated from acceleration.

The integral of acceleration over time is the velocity. However, it is possible to accurately estimate velocity from the acceleration measured using an accelerometer through time series integration because of low-frequency noise. In this study, we propose an integration method that uses a Fourier transform and a low-cut filter to eliminate low frequency noises. This method is used in earthquake engineering [15, 16]. We compare the velocity calculated from a camera and the velocity calculated from an accelerometer and evaluate how accuracy of velocity is affected by the cutoff frequency of the low-cut filter.

2. Calculation

2.1 Traditional Method (Trapezoidal rule)

Typically, velocity v can be estimated from acceleration a as shown in equation (1):

$$v_{t+\Delta t} = v_t + (a_t + a_{t+\Delta t})\frac{\Delta t}{2}, \qquad (1)$$

where Δt is the sampling period. However, we cannot accurately estimate the velocity from the acceleration measured with an accelerometer using equation (1) because of low-frequency noise.

2.2 Proposed Method

The Fourier transform of acceleration $A'(f)$ is expressed as:

$$A(f) = \int_{-\infty}^{\infty} a(t)e^{-2i\pi ft}dt \qquad (2)$$

The velocity is expressed as:

$$V(f) = \frac{A(f)}{2i\pi f} \qquad (3)$$

To eliminate low-frequency noise, $V(f)$ is corrected using a low-cut filter $L(f)$. The corrected Fourier transform of velocity $V'(f)$ is expressed as:

$$V'(f) = L(f)V(f) \qquad (4)$$

In this study, a third-order Butterworth filter was used as $L(s)$. The third-order Butterworth filter $L(s)$ is expressed as:

$$L(s) = \frac{\left(\frac{s}{\omega_c}\right)^3}{\left(\frac{s}{\omega_c}\right)^3 + 2\left(\frac{s}{\omega_c}\right)^2 + 2\frac{s}{\omega_c} + 1} \qquad (5)$$

where ω_c is the cutoff angular frequency [16].
We substitute $s = 2i\pi f$ and $\omega_c = 2\pi f_c$ into equation (5) and hence $L(f)$ is expressed by equation (6):

$$L(f) = \frac{1}{1 - 2i\left(\frac{f_c}{f}\right) - 2\left(\frac{f_c}{f}\right)^2 + i\left(\frac{f_c}{f}\right)^3} \qquad (6)$$

where f_c is the cutoff frequency.

The velocity v(t) can be estimated by an inverse Fourier transform:

$$v(t) = \frac{1}{2\pi}\int_{-\infty}^{\infty} V'(f)e^{2i\pi ft}df \qquad (7)$$

3. Test Method

Fig. 1 shows a schematic diagram of the vibration test. An accelerometer DER-1000(Shinyei Technology) was fixed to the vibration table i210(IMV). The sampling period of the accelerometer was 0.25 s. Vibration direction was vertical and vibration duration was 120 s.

Fig. 2(a) shows the target PSD of acceleration during vibration tests. PSD of Test 1 was referred from the JIS Z0232: 2004 annex 1. The PSDs of Test 2, 3 and 4 were 1, 2 and 3 Hz, respectively, higher than that of Test 1. f_{L1}-f_{L4} show the lowest dominant frequency ranges in each test (6, 7, 8, and 9 Hz, respectively). The predominant frequency ranges in tests 1-4 for which the PSD value was 1.15 $(m/s^2)^2$/Hz were 6-20, 7-21, 8-22, and 9-23 Hz, respectively. f_{L1}-f_{L4} show the lowest dominant frequency ranges in each test (6, 7, 8, and 9 Hz, respectively).

To estimate the velocity to be compared, we used a video camera (JVC GZ E355 -T). A 1.5 cm × 1.5 cm square red mark was attached to the side of the accelerometer. The mark was extracted by image processing, and the vertical position x of the center of gravity was calculated.

The velocity v was calculated by equation (8):

$$v_t = \frac{(x_{t+\Delta t} - x_{t-\Delta t})}{2\Delta t} \qquad (8)$$

The sampling period of the camera Δt was 6.67 ms. Image processing was performed using OpenCV 3.1 and scikit-image 0.11.

The accuracies of the velocities calculated from acceleration were evaluated by the differences between the relative frequency distribution calculated from the accelerometer and those calculated from the camera. After the calculation of the velocities, the relative frequency distributions were calculated and these frequencies were 0.01 m/s.

The evaluation value E is defined by equation (9):

$$E = \sum_k |P_k - Q_k| \qquad (9)$$

where P_k and Q_k are relative frequency distributions of the velocities calculated from the accelerometer and the camera, respectively. For a smaller value of E, the velocity can be calculated more accurately through accelerometer.

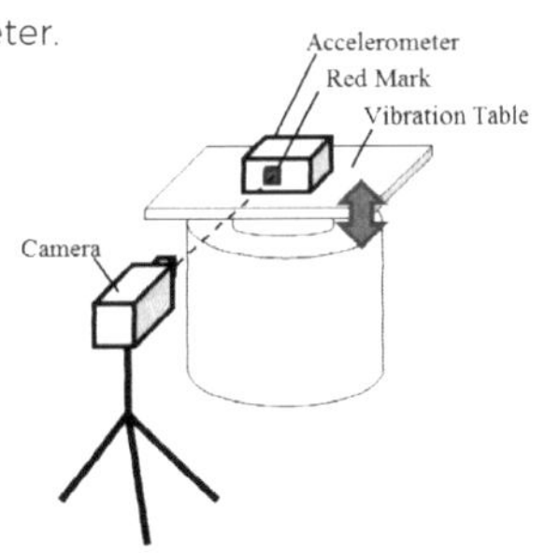

Figure 1 *Schematic diagram of the test*

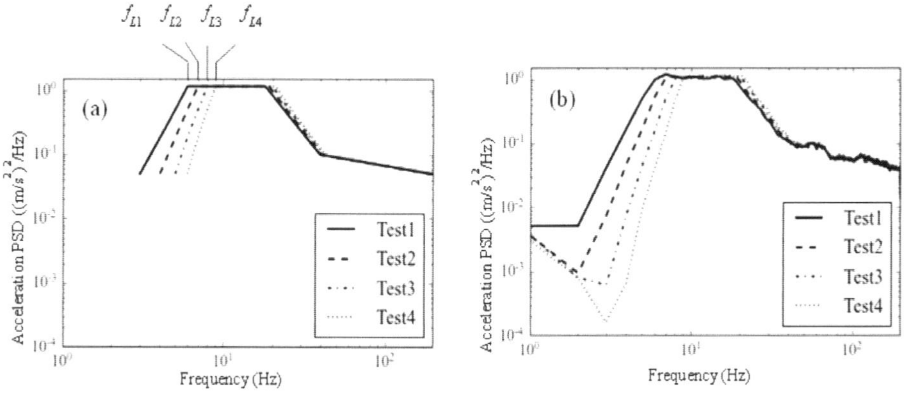

Figure 2 *Acceleration PSD (a) target PSD (b) measured PSD.*

4. Results and Discussion

Fig. 2(b) shows the PSD calculated from the measured acceleration. The measured PSD show a similar trend as the target PSD shown in Fig.2 (a).

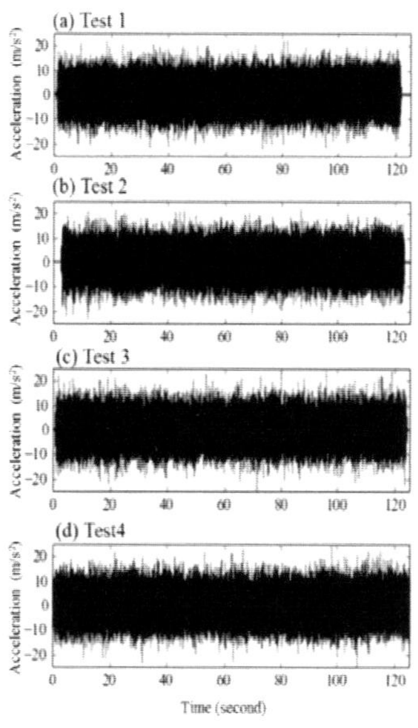

Figure 3 *Times series scceleration*

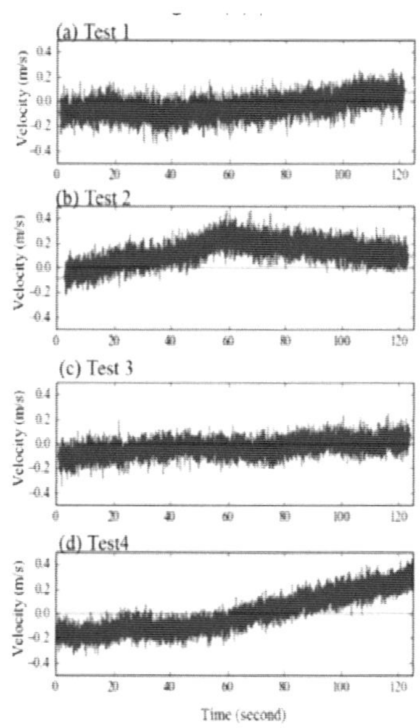

Figure 4 *Time series velocity calculated by trapezoidal rule.*

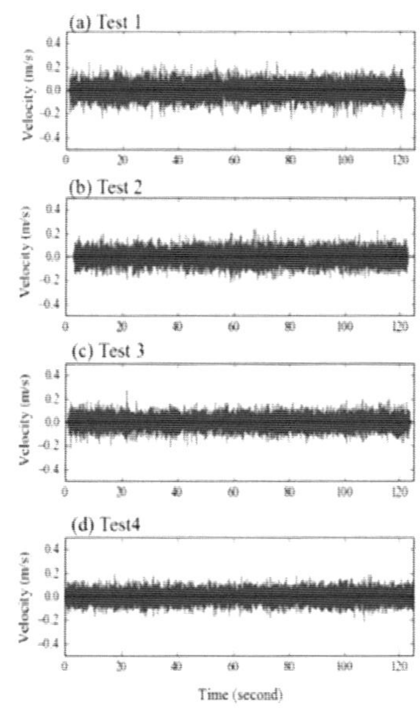

Figure 5 *Time series velocity calculated by proposed method (f_c =1.0 Hz)*

Fig. 3 shows the time series accelerations. Fig. 4 shows the time series velocities calculated using the trapezoidal rule in equation (1). The velocity waveforms calculated by equation (1) meander significantly due to noise in the low- frequency range. In case of Fig. 4 (b), from 20 to 100 s, the upward trend continues for more than 1 min. Considering the properties of the vibration tester, such trends are not expected. Hence, equation (1) cannot be used to accurately estimate the velocities from accelerations.

Fig. 5 shows the time series velocities calculated using equation (3) to (6) (cut-off frequency f_c is 1.0 Hz). There were no visible meandering trends in the velocities.

To understand the suppression of the meandering trends were suppressed, the velocities were calculated from the time series accelerations of Test1 without a low-cut filter (Fig.6). In Fig. 6, there is a meandering trend, which is similar to that in Fig. 4(a). This result shows that a low-cut filter effectively suppresses meandering.

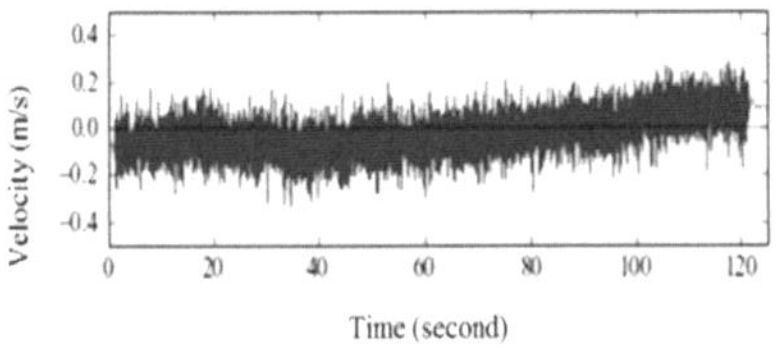

Figure 6 *Velocity time history of Test1 calculated by the proposed method without low-cut filter.*

Fig.7 (a), (b) and (c) show the time series velocities from 0 to 10 s calculated from the acceleration in Test 1 by equation (3) to (6), where the cutoff frequencies are 0.1 Hz, 1.0 Hz, and 6.0 Hz(=f_{L1}), respectively. Fig.7 (d) shows the time series velocities calculated using the camera. The one-sided amplitude of 0.21 m/s is the maximum velocity estimated from the target PSD when the probability density of acceleration is Gaussian [7]. The one-sided amplitude of 0.21 m/s is indicated by a dotted line in Fig. 7.When the cutoff frequency fc is 0.1 Hz (Fig.7 (a)) or 1.0 Hz(Fig.7(b)), the velocity waveform is nearly similar to that of the camera (Fig.7(d)) and the absolute maximum velocity is 0.21 m/s. On the other hand, when cutoff frequency is 6.0 Hz, the velocity waveform is not similar to that of the camera, and the absolute maximum velocity is less than 0.21 m/s.

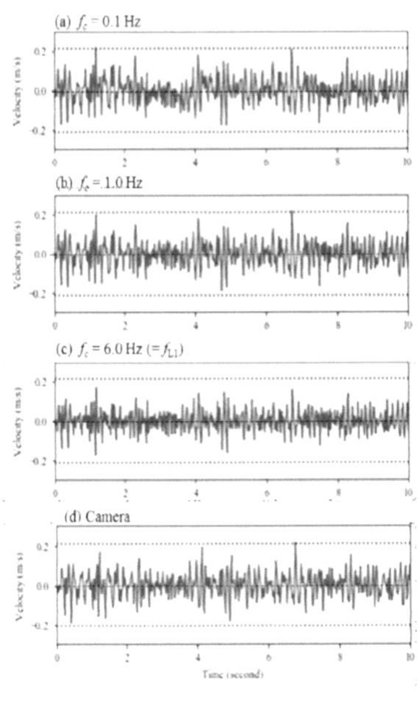

Figure 7 *Velocity time history in Test 1.*

Fig. 8 shows the relative frequency distribution P_k and Q_k of the velocities in Test 1. When the cutoff frequency is 0.1 or 1.0 s, there are no significant differences between P_k and Q_k.

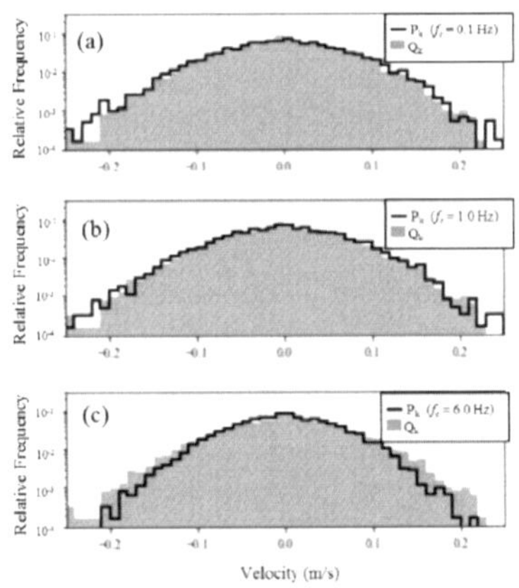

Figure 8 *Relative frequency distribution of velocity of Test1.*

However, when the cutoff frequency is 6.0 Hz, P_k and Q_k differ significantly.

Fig. 9 shows the relationship between the cutoff frequency fc and the evaluation value E. As f_c decreases and approaches 0 Hz, the evaluation value E increases. This indicates that when the cutoff frequency f_c is too low, the velocity cannot be accurately calculated through the accelerometer owing to the effect of low-frequency noises. As f_c increases and approaches f_L, the evaluation value E increases and the difference between the velocities calculated from the camera and accelerometer increases. This is because the necessary vibration is removed when f_c increases.

Thus, the cutoff frequency needs to be set to a large value in the range where the PSD component of the acceleration is sufficiently small.

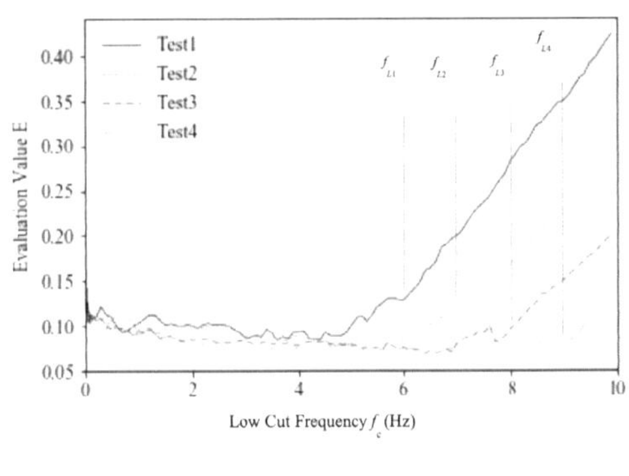

Figure 9 *The effect of low-cut frequency f_c on the evaluation value E.*

5. Conclusions

(1) The velocity cannot be estimated accurately from acceleration by trapezoidal rule integration because of low-frequency noise.

(2) The velocity can be estimated more accurately by the proposed method.

(3) A low-cut frequency must be set below the frequency at which the PSD component is sufficiently reduced and should not be set too low because of low-frequency noise.

Our future objective is to propose the method to generate vibration with arbitrary probability densities of velocity and acceleration.

6. References

[1] J. Lupine, V. Rouillard and M.A. Sek, Review paper on road vehicle vibration simulation for packaging testing purposes, Journal of Packaging Technology and Science 2015; 28(8), pp. 657-671.

[2] A. Hosoyama, K. Saito and T. Nakajima, Non-Gaussian random vibrations using kurtosis, in Eighteenth IAPRI World Packaging Conference, DEStech Publications, Inc.; San Louis Obispo (CA), USA 2012.

[3] V. Rouillard and M.A. Sek, Monitoring and simulating non-stationary vibrations for package optimization, Journal of Packaging Technology and Science 2000; 13(4), pp. 149-156.

[4] K.R. Griffiths, B.J. Hicks, P.S. Keogh and D. Shires, Wavelet analysis to decompose a vibration simulation signal to improve pre-distribution testing of packaging, Mechanical Systems and Signal Processing 2016; 76- 77, pp. 780-795.

[5] H. Zhou and Z.W. Wang, A new approach for road-vehicle vibration, Journal of Packaging Technology and Science 2018; 31(5), pp. 246-260.

[6] Hao Zou and Zhi-Wei Wang, Comparison study on simulation effect of improve methods for packaging random vibration test 2019; Packaging Journal of Technology and Science 32(3), pp.119-131.

[7] JIS Z0232 Packaged freights Method of vibration test 2004.

[8] A. Masuda, K. Nagato and H. Kawase, Study on construction of vulnerability by earthquake response analysis for reinforced concrete buildings, Journal of Structural and Construction Engineering, AIJ 2002; 558, pp. 101-107. (in Japanese).

[9] R.E. Newton, Fragility assessment theory and test procedure, Monterey Research Laboratory Inc., Monterey, California 1968.

[10] Péter Böröcz and S. Paul Singh, Measurement and Analysis of Vibration Levels in Rail Transport in Central Europe, Journal of Packaging Technology and Science; 2017, 30(8), pp. 361-371.

[11] Ran Zhou, Liping Yan, Baiguo Li and Jing Xie, Measurement of Truck Transport Vibration Levels in China as a Function of Road Conditions, Truck Speed and Load Level, Journal of Packaging Technology and Science; 2015, 28(11), pp. 949-957.

[12] S. Paul Singh, K. Saha, J. Singh and A. P. S. Sandhu, Measurement and Analysis of Vibration and Temperature Levels in Global Intermodal Container Shipments on Truck, Rail and Ship, Journal of Packaging Technology and Science; 2012, 25(3), pp 149-160.

[13] Manuel-Alfredo Garcia-Romeu-Martinez, S. Paul Singh and Vicente-Agustin Cloquell-Ballester, Measurement and Analysis of Vibration Levels for Truck Transport in Spain as a Function of Payload, Suspension and Speed, Journal of Packaging Technology and Science; 2008, 21(8), pp. 439-451.

[14] Bundit Jarimopas, S. Paul Singh and Wasan Saengnil, Measurement and Analysis of Truck Transport vibration Levels and Damage to Packaged Tangerines during Transit, Journal of Packaging Technology and Science; 2005, 18(4), pp.179-188.

[15] Hisao Goto, Hiroyuki Kameda, Masata Sugito and Naoto Imanishi, Correction of SMAC-B2 Accelerograph Records by Digital Filter, Japan Society of Civil Engineers; 1978, 277, pp57-69. (in Japanese).

[16] Takeshi Kakishita, Iwao Sasaki and Masashi Kobayashi, An Examination of JMA Formulas for Determining Magnitude using Data Obtained by the JMA-87 Type Electromagnetic Strong Motion Seismograph, Zishin; 1992, 45(3), pp263-277. (in Japanese).

Transmissivity in Broadband Random Vibration Testing [21]

David Shires *1, Changfeng Ge 2, Kyle Dunno2, Ross Battersby 3, Dan Spearman 3
1 Packaging Technology & Science, Wiley, London, UK
2 Department of Packaging Science, Rochester Institute of Technology, Rochester, NY, USA,
3 Smithers, Leatherhead, UK

Abstract:
Introduction: In this paper the authors present new results in support of a previously presented hypothesis that simplified random vibration tests of collated products could be conducted over a narrower bandwidth. The paper explores issues around transmissivity testing and concludes that a new method of transmissivity analysis is needed to produce meaningful fatigue response spectra.
The work supports the potential for simplified vibration test systems, which would be particularly advantageous for multi-axis test systems.

Objective: To explore the potential for simplifying vibration test systems for collated products using narrower bandwidth test methods.
To explore the implications of higher frequency product responses during transmissivity tests.

Methods: Transmissivity data were determined (single vertical axis) for palletised collations of a range of products using different, established, transmissivity test methods. The data were interpreted to show the accumulation of fatigue as a function of frequency and to explore the merits of different methods of testing transmissivity.

Results & Findings: For most products 95% of fatigue is accumulated over a narrow input frequency band supporting the option of simplified test systems.
No established transmissivity test provides a complete evaluation of the fatigue transmissivity response spectrum. This is discussed and a new approach is proposed.

Conclusions: Random vibration tests for most collated products could be conducted over a narrower frequency band, with corresponding simplification of test systems. In particular this indicates the potential for simpler "add-on" pitch and roll systems to extend the test potential of current single axis machines. A more advanced analysis (narrow band input / broad band response) is needed to produce a meaningful fatigue response spectrum for some products.

Keywords: broadband random vibration, fatigue response spectrum, and multi-axis testing

***Correspondence to:** David Shires, Packaging Technology & Science, Wiley, London, UK. E-Mail: pts@shires.me.uk

Kurtosis response spectrum analysis of Gaussian random vibration derived from vehicle vibration [22]

Akira Hosoyama*1, Kazuki Tsuda1, Shogo Horiguchi1
1 Osaka Research Institute of Industrial Science and Technology, Osaka, Japan

Abstract: The objective of this study was to verify the equivalence of the Gaussian random vibrations derived from vehicle vibrations and a vibration controller. To this end, a kurtosis response spectrum analysis was performed to estimate the effect of the natural frequency of a packaged product on the response kurtosis. The results indicate that the response kurtosis of the Gaussian random vibrations derived from a vibration controller is close to three, regardless of the natural frequency, whereas the response kurtosis pertaining to vehicle vibrations may be larger than three, depending on the natural frequency. These findings imply that even when the Gaussian random vibrations derived from the two considered sources have the same power spectral density and Gaussian distribution, the probability density function of a single degree of freedom system response may be different. Therefore, a vibration controller may not be able to accurately reproduce the Gaussian random vibrations derived from the vehicle vibrations in certain cases. Moreover, to overcome the limitations of the current random vibration tests, it may be necessary to additionally perform a time waveform replication test or an actual transportation test. The presented findings can provide an insight into the limitations of the current random vibration tests to formulate recommendations to improve the evaluation accuracy.

Keywords: Kurtosis response spectrum, Non-Gaussian distribution, Random vibration test

***Correspondence to:** Akira Hosoyama, Osaka Research Institute of Industrial Science and Technology. E-mail: hosoyama@tri-osaka.jp

1. Introduction

Packaging vibration tests are conducted to evaluate the durability of packaged products against vibrations by simulating the vibration environment during actual transportation. To this end, currently, the test standards recommend the use of a random vibration test which is performed considering a single power spectral density. Recently, the ISO 4180 [1] and ASTM D 4169 [2] standards were revised to specify a method involving the conduction of sequential tests under multiple power spectral densities. In the revised test method, the actual transport vibrations (non-Gaussian random vibrations) are divided into Gaussian random vibrations with multiple acceleration root mean square (RMS) values. It is assumed that the non-Gaussian random vibrations can be reproduced using the current vibration controller; however, the controller can definitively only generate Gaussian random vibrations. Moreover, although the revised test standard specifies a method involving sequential tests, it is assumed that the vibrations having the same power spectral density (PSD) and probability density function (PDF) are equivalent. In other words, it is assumed that the actual-transport-derived vibrations are equivalent to those generated using the vibration controller. Nevertheless, the equivalence of the vibrations with the same PSD and PDF has not been conclusively established yet.

2. Research Goal

The purpose of this study was to verify the equivalence of vibrations with the same PSD and PDF, derived during actual transport and by using a vibration controller. In particular, a kurtosis response spectrum analysis [3] was performed to determine the response kurtosis for a single degree of freedom (SDOF) system in the natural frequency range of interest. Moreover, the difference between the two types of derived vibrations was clarified.

3. Research Method

The vertical acceleration occurring on the vehicle bed of a small van (Daihatsu HIJET) traveling on a local road in Japan was measured. The acceleration RMS was calculated in intervals of one second and decomposed into several Gaussian random vibrations. A specific decomposed Gaussian random vibration was used as the actual-transport-derived Gaussian random vibration. The vibrations corresponding to the vibration controller were generated to have the same PSD as that of the transport-derived Gaussian random vibration, similar to the process followed in current testing approaches. The kurtosis response spectrum analysis was performed for both the types of vibrations, and the difference between the two vibrations was examined. The analysis was performed in a natural frequency range of 5–100 Hz at a damping ratio of 0.15, assuming the presence of plastic foam cushioning.

4. Results and conclusions

Figure 1 shows the vibrations derived from an actual vehicle and a vibration controller, and Figure 2 shows the corresponding PSD and PDF. It can be observed that both the types of vibrations exhibit nearly the same PSDs and PDFs. Figure 3 shows the kurtosis response spectrum for the vibration inputs. The response kurtosis of the vibration-controller-derived vibration is always approximately three, regardless of the frequency. However, the response kurtosis of the actual-transport-derived vibration varies with the natural frequency. For example, the maximum and minimum response kurtosis of the actual-transport-derived vibration occur at a frequency of 14 Hz and approximately 70 Hz, respectively. We further compared the PSDs and PDFs of the SDOF response to the two types of vibrations at a frequency of 14 Hz and damping ratio of 0.15. Figure 4 shows the SDOF responses to the two types of vibrations shown in Fig. 1, and Fig. 5 shows the corresponding PSDs and PDFs. It can be noted that the SDOF responses to the two types of vibrations exhibit the same PSD but different PDF. The PDF of the SDOF response to the vibration-controller-derived vibration remains Gaussian, whereas that of the SDOF response to the actual-transport-derived vibration changes from Gaussian to non-Gaussian. In general, it is considered that when the actual-transport-derived vibration follows a Gaussian distribution, the SDOF response also follows a Gaussian distribution. However, as shown in Fig. 5, when the actual-transport-derived vibration follows a Gaussian distribution, the SDOF response does not necessarily follow the Gaussian distribution. In other words, even for the vibrations with the same PSD and PDF, the PDF of the SDOF response may be different. Therefore, to accurately reflect the vibrations, it is necessary to consider not only the PSD and PDF, but also the PDF of the SDOF response.

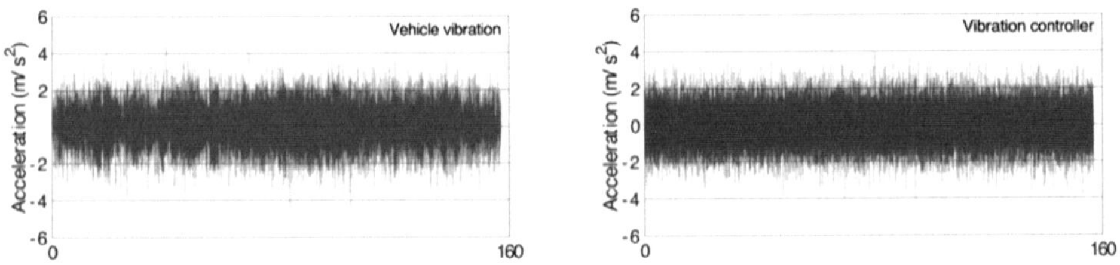

Figure 1 *Gaussian vibrations derived using an actual vehicle (left) and vibration controller (right)*

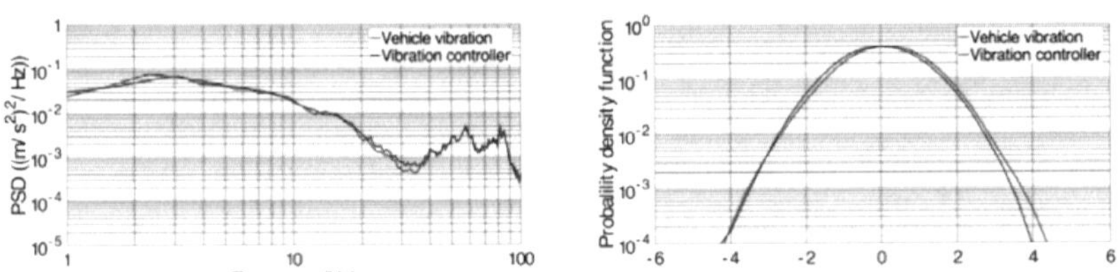

Figure 2 *Comparison between power spectral densities (PSDs, left) and probability density functions (PDFs, right) of Gaussian vibrations derived using an actual vehicle and vibration controller*

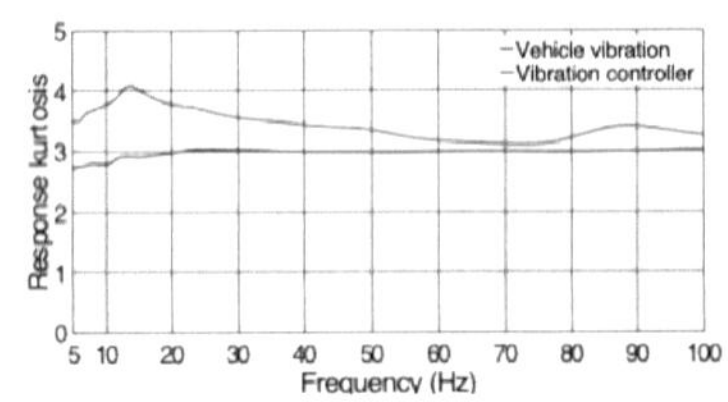

Figure 3 *Kurtosis response spectrum of Gaussian vibrations derived using an actual vehicle and vibration controller*

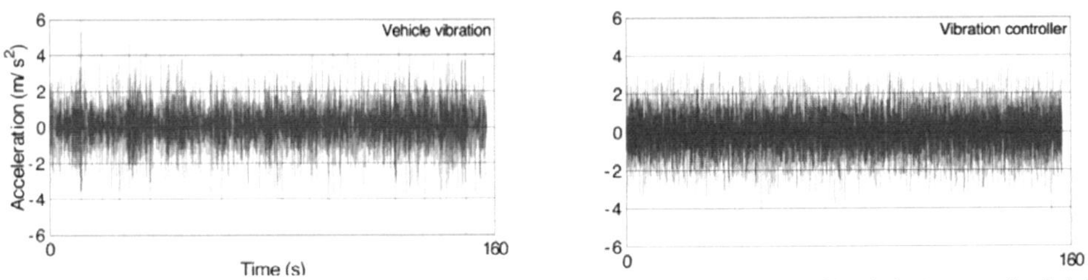

Figure 4 *Single-degree-of-freedom (SDOF) response to Gaussian vibrations derived using an actual vehicle (left) and vibration controller (right); natural frequency = 14 Hz, damping ratio = 0.15*

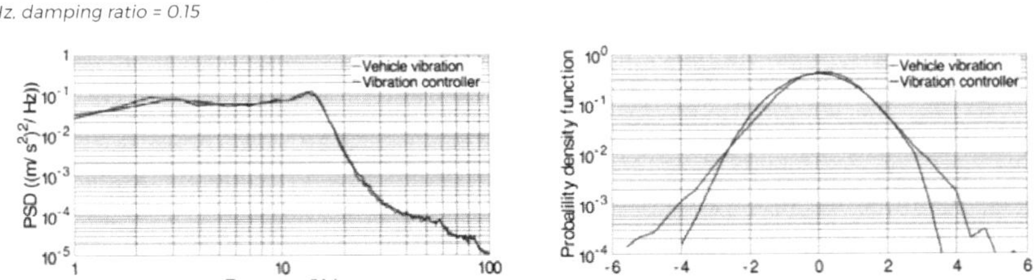

Figure 5 *Comparison between PSDs (left) and PDFs (right) of SDOF response to Gaussian vibrations derived using an actual vehicle and vibration controller*

5 Future Research

The current vibration controller cannot generate random vibrations, considering the non-Gaussian nature of the response. In future work, it is desirable to develop a method to generate random vibrations considering the non-Gaussian nature of the response.

References

[1] ISO 4180:2019, Packaging - Complete, filled transport packages - General rules for the compilation of performance test schedules.

[2] ASTM D4169-16, Standard Practice for Performance Testing of Shipping Containers and Systems.

[3] Hosoyama, A, Tsuda, K, Horiguchi, S. Development and validation of kurtosis response spectrum analysis for antivibration packaging design taking into consideration kurtosis. Packag. Technol. Sci. 2020;33:51-64.

Acknowledgements

This work was supported by JSPS KAKENHI grant number JP18K13964.

Prediction of the service life of expanded polystyrene foam based on Bayesian inference [59]

Hae Chang Gea *1, Hui Ma 1,2, Dawei Xue 1
1 Packaging Engineering Program, Rutgers University, USA
2 College of Mechanical and Electrical Engineering Harbin Engineering University, Harbin, China

Abstract: Expanded Polystyrene (EPS) foam material will change its material properties throughout its service life and consequently affect its functions on product protection. In this study, the prediction of EPS service life was modeled using Bayesian inference. A nonlinear two-degree-of-freedom drop model is established first. Then, a Bayesian inference method is applied to the nonlinear two-degree-of- freedom drop model with uncertainty. The posterior probability of various conditions under the influence of the observation points is calculated. The posterior probability is used to replace the priors in the model to update the prediction distribution sequentially. The simulation results along with the experimental data are presented.

Keywords: Bayesian inference; Bayesian method; drop test; life expectancy; expanded polystyrene foam

***Correspondence to:** Hae Chang Gea, Packaging Engineering Program, Rutgers University, Piscataway, NJ, USA. E-mail: gea@soe.rutgers.edu

1. Introduction

The demands of transportation packaging are increasing with the rapid development of global trade. Various issues such as long transportation distances, large transportation volumes, bumpy roads, and harsh environmental conditions have been often encountered during packaging transportation. At the same time, the product packages need to be stacked, loaded and unloaded multiple times during transportation, which may greatly increase the probability of damage to the shipment as well as the transportation cost. Therefore, it is extremely important to learn how to improve the packaging integrity during transportation.

In order to ensure the integrity of product packages during transportation, it is necessary to understand packaging dynamics. Packaging dynamics provides a theoretical basis for the design of cushioning and vibration-damping packaging. In packaging dynamics, the vulnerability of an item, also called fragility, is used to characterize the ability of the packaged product to resist multiple dynamic loads in the transport. In 1945, R.D. Mindlin[1] consdiered shock and vibration are two main dynamic loading sources experienced during product transportation, and they are also the main cause for package failure and damage.

Expanded polystyrene (EPS) is one of the commonly used cushioning materials in packaging [2]. Compared with other materials, it has the advantages of light weight, easy processing and molding, good thermal insulation properties, and good cushioning properties. It is widely used in home appliances and packaging of industrial products. Athanasopoulos [3] measured dynamic properties of EPS geofoam at cyclic strain amplitude and found that the stress-strain curve of EPS geofoam is linear when the strain is less than 0.1%; when the strain is greater than 1%, the stress-strain curve becomes highly nonlinear. Ozturk [4] studied the deformation-acceleration and deformation-impact force relations of foams with different thicknesses with repeated loading and unloading stress. Chen Ling [5] studied the response of EPS foam under specific loading conditions with finite element method. The results show that the yield shear stress of EPS foam is significantly lower than the yield shear stress under the compression-shear composite load. Keller [6] evaluated the dynamic fatigue of EPS foam during transportation. The principle of hysteresis measurement and evaluation was applied to EPS materials, and its long-term compressive mechanical properties are revealed: when the dynamic load level increases to a critical level above 100 KPa, the mechanical behavior of the compression rate of EPS changes from linear to exponential. Krundaeva [7] obtained the stress-strain curves of EPS foam at different temperatures and densities through static, dynamic compression and crushing experiments. The finite element simulation of the dynamic compression process is performed. The simulation model can simulate the dynamic load of a bicycle helmet. Qin [8] proposed the stress distribution model of EPS foam box, and a structural improvement method for the maximum deformation area, which makes the maximum deformation is reduced and the stress distribution is more reasonable.

Packaging integrity is affected by multiple uncertain factors such as transportation distance and road conditions. Among many uncertainty models, Bayesian inference is widely used to predict the distribution of uncertain parameters [9-12]. Jaydeep M. Karandikar [13, 14] used Bayesian inference to estimate model constants for milling and turning. Yi [15] introduced the likelihood confidence interval and the likelihood confidence region to quantify the identifiability of the parameters with the Metropolis - Hastings algorithm. Liang [16] developed a model for identification of damage parameters based on Bayesian inference theory. Bisaggio [17] applied Bayesian reliability model to evaluate the failure probability considering the uncertainty parameters.

In this study, we will apply Bayesian inference model to predict the service life of transportation packaging. We will first introduce a nonlinear two-degree-of-freedom drop model and then apply Bayesian inference model to update the posterior distribution of predicted serviced life using new testing data. Finally, conclusion remarks are presented.

2. Nonlinear Drop Model

Most packaging drop simulations are performed using a single degree of freedom model for its simplicity. However, in practice, we usually put the product in a primary packaging and then put the primary packaging in a secondary packaging in order to protect the product better. If the entire system is simply reduced to a single-degree-of- freedom system, the calculation results may be inaccurate and cause errors. To overcome this deficiency, a two-degree-of-freedom vibration system is implemented in this study. In our model, the product is regarded as the main mass source mm_2 , the primary packaging is modeled as a nonlinear spring kk_2 with its corresponding deformation xx_2. The secondary packaging is modeled as a small mass source mm_1 and another nonlinear spring kk_1 with its corresponding deformation xx_1. It is important to note that both spring constants kk_1 and kk_2 in the drop model cannot be simply regarded as constants [3].

Assuming that the product drops freely to a rigid ground, the vibration differential equations of the drop system can be established as:

$$mm_1 x\ddot{x}_1 + kk_1 xx_1 - kk_2(xx_2 - xx_1) = 0$$
$$mm_2 x\ddot{x}_2 + kk_2(xx_2 - xx_1) = 0$$

The material we selected in this study is Expanded polystyrene (EPS). The EPS foam has a uniformly closed cavity structure, and its stress-strain curve is measured by an Instron tester first. We can then obtain a nonlinear stiffness-compressive deformation curve as shown in Figure 2. In conjunction with the two-degree-of-freedom drop model we derived earlier, an acceleration-drop height relation can be obtained in Figure 3.

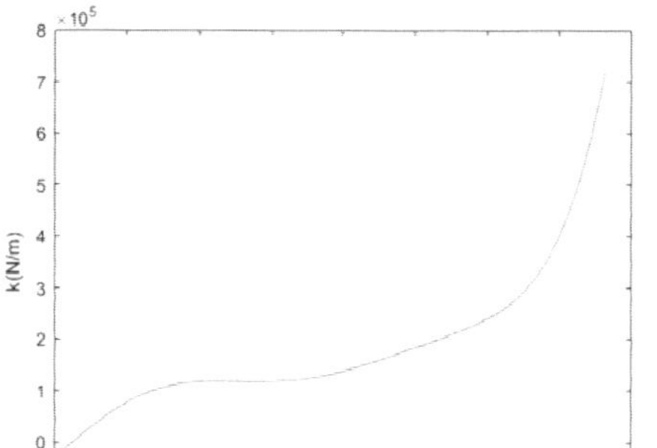

Figure 2 *Stiffness - Deformation curve*

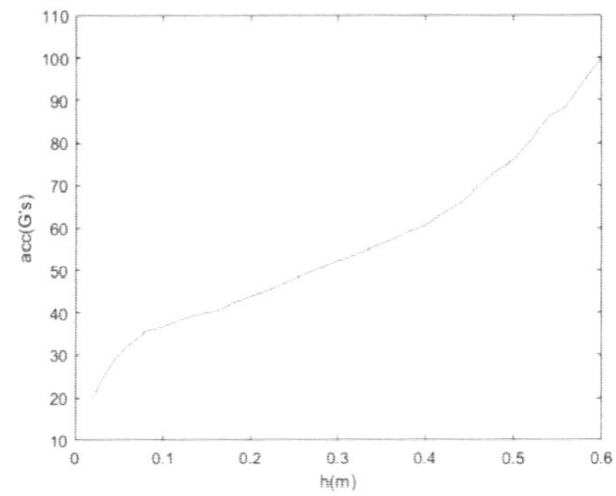

Figure 3 *Acceleration - Drop height curve*

3. Bayesian Inference Model

Bayesian Inference Model is used to evaluate the outcomes of an event that is inferred from the existing evidence and the prior guesses. As the available evidence continues to increase, the speculative results are updated and the confidence of the outcomes continues to improve.

In a Bayesian inference model, the speculative results called the posterior distribution, $pp(ww|YY,aa)$, after taking into account the existing evidence under the given parameters, $pp(YY|aa)$, and the prior guesses, $pp(ww|aa)$ can be expressed mathematically including a likelihood function, $pp(YY|ww,aa)$, as the following:

$$pp(\mathbf{ww}|\mathbf{YY}, \boldsymbol{\alpha\alpha}) = \frac{pp(\mathbf{ww}|\boldsymbol{\alpha\alpha}) * pp(\mathbf{YY}|\mathbf{ww}, \boldsymbol{\alpha\alpha})}{pp(\mathbf{YY}|\boldsymbol{\alpha\alpha})}$$

where ww denotes the event of interests, YY denotes the available evidence and aa represents the given parameters.

To incorporate the uncertainty into the analytical model of a two-degree-of- freedom drop system described in the previous section, the Bayesian Inference method is applied. First, ten acceleration-height curves under different drop times and marked with #1 - #10, are generated under different drop heights between 0.02 m and 0.763 m as shown in Figure 4. To avoid any bias on the Bayesian inference model, the initial prior of all cases is set as 0.1.

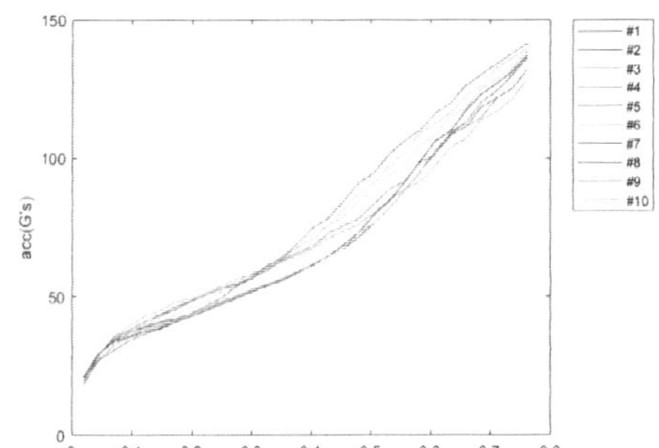

Figure 4 *Height-Acceleration Curve under different drop times*

$$llllkklllllhoooooo = ll - (aaaaaa - aaaaaa_{tttttttt})^2 \; 2\sigma\sigma^2$$

When a new measured acceleration (evidence) is obtained, its likelihood respect to each cases can be calculated as follows:

where $aaaaaa_{tttttttt}$ is the new measured acceleration and $aaaaaa$ is the acceleration at the testing height according to the acceleration- height curves in Figure 4. A control parameter, $\sigma\sigma$, which represents the degree of uncertainty, is introduced into the likelihood function.

In this example, three new test data, #a, #b and #c, are added to the model and they are marked using purple circles in Fig. 5. Two different control parameters, $\sigma\sigma$=1 and 3, are used to represent different degree of uncertainties.

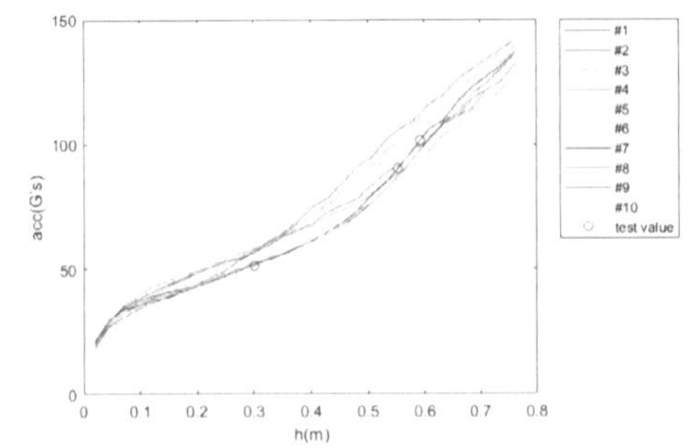

Figure 5. *Height-Acceleration Curve with three new test data*

As new test data is incorporated into the model in sequence, the likelihood probability function can be calculated and their values are listed in Table 1. The bolded numbers represent the cases with higher likelihood probabilities. One can easily observe that as more new test data are included into the model, the higher likelihood cases are converged. However, due to the selection of the degree of uncertainty, the probabilities of those cases are different. For example, the case of the highest likelihood of different degree of uncertainties is the same, Test #7, but the likelihood probability is 0.616 for $\sigma\sigma$=1 and 0.243 for $\sigma\sigma$=3.

Table 1 *Likelihood probability*

Test	a = [0.553,90.5]		b = [0.301,51.3]		c = [0.593,101.6]	
	Likelihood (normalized) $\sigma = 1$	Likelihood (normalized) $\sigma = 3$	Likelihood (normalized) $\sigma = 1$	Likelihood (normalized) $\sigma = 3$	Likelihood (normalized) $\sigma = 1$	Likelihood (normalized) $\sigma = 3$
#1	0.0263	**0.1238**	**0.2252**	**0.2024**	0.0000	0.0575
#2	**0.2487**	**0.1590**	0.0000	0.0394	**0.1920**	**0.2135**
#3	0.0000	0.0002	0.0000	0.0255	0.0000	0.0066
#4	0.0181	**0.1188**	**0.1959**	**0.1993**	0.0000	0.0512
#5	0.0725	**0.1386**	0.0000	0.0197	0.0000	0.0327
#6	0.0000	0.0109	0.0000	0.0145	0.0014	**0.1237**
#7	**0.3574**	**0.1655**	**0.3491**	**0.2125**	**0.6160**	**0.2430**
#8	**0.2499**	**0.1590**	0.0000	0.0390	**0.1906**	**0.2133**
#9	0.0000	0.0000	0.0000	0.0448	0.0000	0.0001
#10	0.0272	**0.1243**	**0.2297**	**0.2028**	0.0000	0.0584

Once the likelihood probability function is calculated for each new test data, the posterior probability of each test cases can be updated using Bayesian inference model. Tables 2 - 4 list the updated posterior probabilities after introduced new test data, #a, #b and #c, sequentially under two different degree of uncertainties, $\sigma\sigma$=1 and $\sigma\sigma$=3.

Table 2 *Posterior probability after adding test point #a*

Test	Prior	Likelihood (normalized) $\sigma = 1$	Posterior (normalized) $\sigma = 1$	Likelihood (normalized) $\sigma = 3$	Posterior (normalized) $\sigma = 3$
#1	0.1	0.0263	0.0263	0.1238	0.1238
#2	0.1	0.2487	0.2487	0.1590	0.1590
#3	0.1	0.0000	0.0000	0.0002	0.0002
#4	0.1	0.0181	0.0181	0.1188	0.1188
#5	0.1	0.0725	0.0725	0.1386	0.1386
#6	0.1	0.0000	0.0000	0.0109	0.0109
#7	0.1	0.3574	0.3574	0.1655	0.1655
#8	0.1	0.2499	0.2499	0.1590	0.1590
#9	0.1	0.0000	0.0000	0.0000	0.0000
#10	0.1	0.0272	0.0272	0.1243	0.1243

Table 3 *Posterior probability after adding test point #b*

Test	Prior $\sigma = 1$	Prior $\sigma = 3$	Likelihood (normalized) $\sigma = 1$	Posterior (normalized) $\sigma = 1$	Likelihood (normalized) $\sigma = 3$	Posterior (normalized) $\sigma = 3$
#1	0.0263	0.1238	0.2252	0.0422	0.2024	0.2014
#2	0.2487	0.1590	0.0000	0.0000	0.0394	0.0503
#3	0.0000	0.0002	0.0000	0.0000	0.0255	0.0000
#4	0.0181	0.1188	0.1959	0.0252	0.1993	0.1902
#5	0.0725	0.1386	0.0000	0.0000	0.0197	0.0220
#6	0.0000	0.0109	0.0000	0.0000	0.0145	0.0013
#7	0.3574	0.1655	0.3491	0.8882	0.2125	0.2825
#8	0.2499	0.1590	0.0000	0.0000	0.0390	0.0498
#9	0.0000	0.0000	0.0000	0.0000	0.0448	0.0000
#10	0.0272	0.1243	0.2297	0.0445	0.2028	0.2026

Table 4 *Posterior probability after adding test point #c*

Test	Prior $\sigma = 1$	Prior $\sigma = 3$	Likelihood (normalized) $\sigma = 1$	Posterior (normalized) $\sigma = 1$	Likelihood (normalized) $\sigma = 3$	Posterior (normalized) $\sigma = 3$
#1	0.0422	0.2014	0.0000	0.0000	0.0575	**0.1111**
#2	0.0000	0.0503	0.1920	0.0000	0.2135	0.0803
#3	0.0000	0.0000	0.0000	0.0000	0.0066	0.0016
#4	0.0252	0.1902	0.0000	0.0000	0.0512	0.0975
#5	0.0000	0.0220	0.0000	0.0000	0.0327	0.0062
#6	0.0000	0.0013	0.0014	0.0000	0.1237	0.0171
#7	0.8882	0.2825	0.6160	**1.0000**	0.2430	**0.4935**
#8	0.0000	0.0498	0.1906	0.0000	0.2133	0.0795
#9	0.0000	0.0000	0.0000	0.0000	0.0001	0.0001
#10	0.0445	0.2026	0.0000	0.0000	0.0584	**0.1132**

Based on the Bayesian inference model, the service life can be predicted to follow the test #7 in both cases although the probability results are different because of two different degree of uncertainties associated with σ =1 and σ=3 as shown in the bolded numbers as 1.0000 and 0.4935 in Table 4, respectively. The proposed model can be easily to apply to other uncertainties, such as measurement error of mass, and measurement error of acceleration, to predict service life.

4. Conclusion

In this paper, the service life of EPS is predicted using Bayesian inference. A nonlinear two-degree-of-freedom drop model is established and a solution method is given. In Bayesian inference, each curve is assigned an initial probability. The distribution is updated with each new data point, and the flat distribution introduced in the prior is changed. A likelihood function is defined to describe the probability distribution of the curve that may occur with the current experimental data. The prior distribution and experimental data are combined to update the probability distribution that each curve may appear. Therefore, based on the current observations and initial guesses, the posterior distribution can be used to predict the service life of EPS.

Acknowledgement

Financial support from Harbin Engineering University Joint Training Foundation and the China Scholarship Council 201806680066 is gratefully acknowledged.

References

[1] Mindlin R D. Dynamics of package cushioning [J]. Bell System Technical Journal, 1945, 24(3): 353-461.

[2] T. Greeley. A review of expanded polystyrene (EPS) properties, performance and new applications [J]. In R. Graves & R. Zarr (Eds.), STP1320-EB Insulation Materials: Testing and Applications,1997, 3, (pp. 224-239).

[3] Athanasopoulos, G.A., Pelekis, P.C. and Xenaki, V.C.. Dynamic properties of EPS geofoam: An experimental investigation [J], Geosynthetics International,1999, Vol. 6, No. 3, pp. 171-194.

[4] Umud Esat Ozturka, Gunay Anlas. Finite element analysis of expanded polystyrene foam under multiple compressive loading and unloading[J], Materials and Design, 2011,32,pp.773-780

[5] Chen Ling, Jan Ivens, Philip Cardiff and Michael D. Gilchrist. Deformation of EPS foam under combined compression-shear loading: experimental and computational analysis[J], DYMAT 2018 - 12th International Conference on the Mechanical and Physical Behaviour of Materials under Dynamic Loading, Volume 183, 2018

[6] Keller, Jan-Hendrik and Volker Altstädt. Influence of mid-stress on the dynamic fatigue of a light weight EPS bead foam[J].e-Polymers, 19.1 (2019): 349-354.

[7] Anastasiia Krundaevaab, GuidoDe Bruynecd, Francesco Gagliardia, WimVan Paepegema. Dynamic compressive strength and crushing properties of expanded polystyrene foam for different strain rates and different temperatures [J], Polymer Testing, Volume 55, October 2016, Pages 61-68

[8] Qin Zhiyuan, Huang Haisong, Zhang Hui. Finite element analysis and optimal design of EPS foam packing case[J], Packaging Engineering,2016,12,37(23),pp:100-104

[9] G D'Agostini. Bayesian inference in processing experimental data: principles and basic applications [J]. Published 11 August 2003 • Reports on Progress in Physics, Volume 66, Number 9

[10] Carl N. Morris. Parametric empirical Bayes inference: theory and applications [J]. Pages 47-55, 12 Mar 2012

[11] Pruzek, Robert M. An introduction to Bayesian inference and its applications [J]. What if there were no significance tests (1997): 287-318

[12] A. P. Dempster. A Generalization of Bayesian Inference. Journal of the Royal Statistical Society: Series B (Methodological) [J].Volume30, Issue2 July 1968

[13] Jaydeep M. Karandikar , Ali E. Abbas, Tony L. Schmitz. Tool life prediction using Bayesian updating. Part 1: Milling tool life model using a discrete grid method[J], Precision Engineering 38 (2014) 9-17

[14] Jaydeep M. Karandikar , Ali E. Abbas, Tony L. Schmitz. Tool life prediction using Bayesian updating. Part 2: Turning tool life using a Markov Chain Monte Carlo approach[J], Precision Engineering 38 (2014) 18-27

[15] Dong HyukYi, Deuk Woo Kim, Cheol Soo Park. Parameter identifiability in Bayesian inference for building energy models [J]. Energy&Buildings198(2019)318-328

[16] Liang Gang, Shi Danyan, Shen Kui shuang. Uncertain damage detection and experimental study of multiple cracks in beams[J], Mechanical Science and Technology for Aerospace Engineering

[17] Helio da Cunha Bisaggio, Theodoro Antoun Netto. Predictive analyses of the integrity of corroded pipelines based on concepts of structural reliability and Bayesian inference[J], Marine Structures, Volume 41, April 2015, Pages 180-199

Correlation between horizontal acceleration testing and tilt testing for load stability [72]

Carlos Mora*, Enrique de la Cruz, Manuel A. García Romeu

Safe Load Testing Technologies, Valencia, Spain

Abstract: In Defining the load stability as the behaviour of a load against an acceleration suffered during transportation, there are two technics to evaluate it: the horizontal acceleration test and the tilt test.

The horizontal acceleration test produces a trapezoidal acceleration transient equivalent to the transient recorded on transport vehicles during emergency braking situations, meanwhile the tilt test inclines the sample.

In an emergency braking, the unit load suffers a dynamic force depending on the level of acceleration, the coefficient of friction between the unit load and the floor of the truck and a coefficient called "Dynamic Amplification Factor". This coefficient varies from 1 to 2 in function of the horizontal natural frequency of the unit load and the duration and shape of the acceleration curve.

During tilt test, the unit load is subjected to a tilt that produces a constant acceleration, that can be calculated to be equivalent to the constant acceleration produced on an emergency braking but lacks of the dynamic force which is up to 2 times the steady force produced on the tilt test. The angle to reach this equivalent force for a single non- deformable block, goes from 16.69° for accelerations of 0.3 g up to 42.37° for 0.7 g. The equivalence obtained could be valid if during the tilting the primary, secondary or full unit load do not tip over and keep their shape and contact between layers and surfaces.

The target of this paper is to define the requirements and boundary limits for a tilt test suitable for evaluate the stability of a unit load subjected to an emergency braking of a vehicle and the considerations that must be took into account in the unit load to be analysed and to compare the results with the deformation obtained in a horizontal stability test.

Keywords: load stability test, horizontal acceleration, tilt test, transport simulation.

***Correspondence to:** Carlos Mora Martín. E-mail: carlos.mora@safeloadtesting.com.

CHAPTER IV
Packaging materials

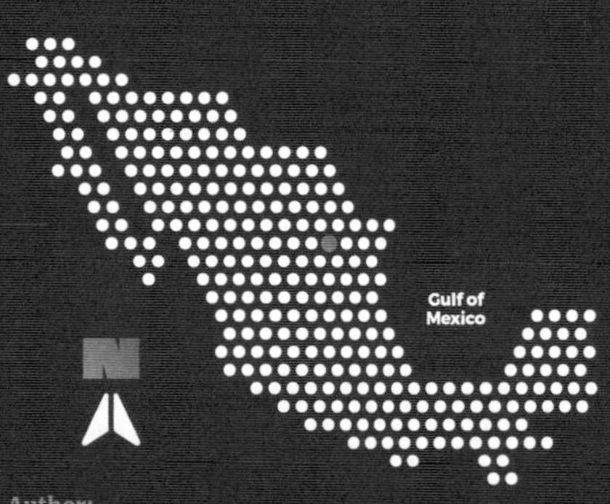

Author:
Turismo NL/OCV MONTERREY

Location:
Santa Catarina, NUEVO LEÓN

Description:
La Huasteca is an ecological park located in Santa Catarina. It has something for everyone: the opportunity to climb its mountains for the fearless ones, the chance to bike through it for the sporty ones, and the chance to just be amazed by its natural peaks and the way light and shadows interact with it.

Estimating Method of Compression Strength for Regular Slotted Container of Any Size [3]

Takashi Takayama *1,2, Katsuhiko Saito 1,
1 Maritime Sciences, Kobe University, Kobe, Japan
2 Kewpie Co., Ltd., Institute of Technology Solutions, R&D Division, Tokyo, Japan

Abstract: The Kellicutt's and McKee's formulas are widely used for estimating the compression strength of regular slotted containers. However, they simplified these formulas by limiting the box sizes to those of typical boxes, which enabled us to easily and conveniently carry out the calculations. For this reason, we cannot estimate the compression strength for boxes with a width or height of 20 cm or less because of the large error involved. The use of small, flat, or narrow boxes whose sizes exceed the range of typical box sizes, such as those used for mail-order sales, has recently been increasing; the need has therefore arisen to estimate the compression strength of these boxes. In this study, in addition to the McKee's formula before simplification, we combined a new formula for collapsing failure and constructed a general formula that can estimate the compression strength for a regular slotted container of any size. The estimated values are compared with the measured values to verify the validity of the new formula. The validation results denote that the new formula exhibits an average error of 6.5% even when considering small, flat, or narrow boxes whose sizes exceed the typical box sizes (the McKee formula exhibits an average error of 6.1%); this accuracy can be considered to be sufficient for practical application. Calculating the compression strength by the McKee's formula before simplification requires knowledge of the bending stiffness (Machine Direction and Cross Direction) and of the edgewise compression strength; these physical values must be obtained for each corrugated board. In this research, we confirmed that the compression strength can be estimated with only the edgewise compression strength instead of the bending stiffness.

Keywords: Regular Slotted Container, General Compression Strength Formula, McKee Formula

***Correspondence to:** Takashi Takayama, Kewpie Co., Ltd., Institute of Technology Solutions, R&D Division, 2-5-7 Sengawa-Cho, Chofu-Shi, Tokyo, Japan. E-mail: takashi_takayama@kewpie.co.jp

1. Introduction

Kellicutt's[1] and McKee's[2] formulas are currently widely used as compression strength formulas for a regular slotted container (RSC). Based on McKee's formula, Wolf's formula [3] has been proposed, which introduced an empirical correction term and improved the accuracy while considering the depth and length-width ratio of the box. When the box is compressed, failure modes can be divided into a case where it collapses as shown in Fig. 1(a) and a case where it buckles as shown in Fig. 1(b). The formulas that represent each of the failure mode cases are to be constructed. Urbanik et al. calculated the compression strength individually according to failure modes, and evaluated the effects of the constraints set up by McKee on the accuracy [4].

In this study, when the box starts to collapse, the upper and lower score lines are crushed into a bellow shape as shown in Fig. 1(a), and these score lines support the load, therefore we assume that the compression strength of the panel is proportional to the panel's width. In the case of buckling, we adopt the McKee's formula before simplification. McKee made the buckling coefficient a constant value to simplify the formula and eliminated the height dimension from the formula.

This makes it impossible to estimate the compression strength of a panel with a width or height values of 20 cm or less. Since the objective of this study is to estimate the compression strength of a panel of any size, we consider it appropriate to apply the McKee's formula before simplification which considers the height dimension. McKee's formula is originally constructed using the concept of the National Advisory Committee for Aeronautics (NACA) formula [5], which is a combination of collapsing and buckling factors. We think it is the best method for a material such as a corrugated board that bulges (buckles) and fails while its internal structure collapses.

To emphasize practicality, we construct the formula that can be applied to any C flute corrugated board that is used mainly for boxes requiring compression strength.

Finally, to verify the validity, we compare the measured and estimated compression strength of a small, flat, or narrow box which could not be estimated by existing formulas. The results show that our constructed formula can estimate with practical accuracy.

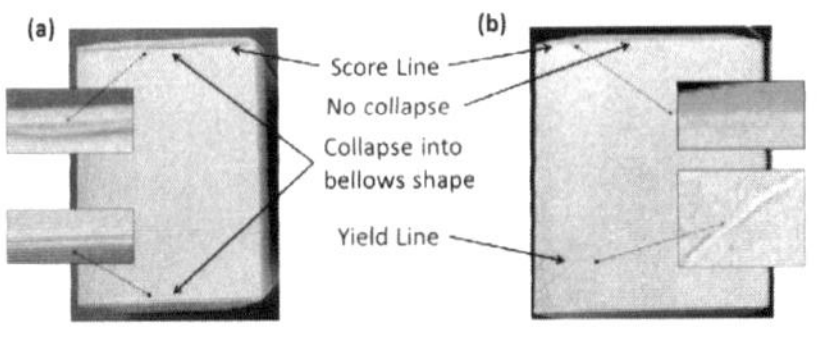

Figure 1 *Box failure modes: (a) collapsing failure and (b) buckling failure*

2. Compression strength formula

2.1. The calculation of collapsing failure panel concept

As shown in Fig. 1(a), the collapsing failure displays that the upper and lower score lines are being crushed like bellows. When the box starts to collapse, the score lines support the load, therefore, we can infer that the compression strength (Ppanel) is proportional to the width (W) of the score lines; furthermore, the constant of proportionality is proportional to the Edgewise compression test (ECT) value. Here, the compression strength formula for the panel due to collapse is:

$$P_{panel} = d\,(ECT) \times W \quad (1)$$

where **d** is a dimensionless coefficient.

2.2. The calculation of buckling failure panel concept

The McKee's formula is constructed based on the formula proposed by NACA as a method of calculating the compression strength of flat plates used for aircraft and is expressed using the following formula (2).

$$P = c(P_m)^b (P_{cr})^{1-b} \quad (2)$$

where **P** is the compression strength per unit width, $\mathbf{P_m}$ is the compression strength of the material, $\mathbf{P_{cr}}$ is the critical stress of plate, and c and b are dimensionless coefficients.

NACA has experimentally found that the compression strength of a panel can be expressed as the weighted harmonic mean of the term Pm for collapsing and the term Pcr for buckling. McKee used the ECT value as Pm and the critical buckling strength formula for the orthotropic panel as Pcr, and transformed formula (2) into the following formula (3):

$$P = c(ECT)^b \left(12k_{cr}\sqrt{D_{MD}D_{CD}} \div W^2\right)^{1-b} \quad (3)$$

where **kcr** is the buckling coefficient, **ECT** is Edgewise compression test value, $\mathbf{D_{MD}}$ is the bending stiffness in the machine direction, $\mathbf{D_{CD}}$ is the bending stiffness in the cross-machine direction, **W** is the panel width, **h** is the panel height, and **n** is the number of half-waves.

$$K_{cr} = \frac{\pi^2}{12}\left(\frac{\sqrt{\frac{D_{MD}}{D_{CD}}} \times h^2}{W^2 n^2} + \frac{W^2 n^2}{\sqrt{\frac{D_{MD}}{D_{CD}}} \times h^2} + 1\right)$$

$$n = j \quad \left(\sqrt{j(j-1)} \le \sqrt[4]{D_{MD}/D_{CD}}\,\frac{h}{W} \le \sqrt{j(j+1)}\right)$$

Since, formula (2) is a compression strength formula per unit width, the compression strength of the panel can be obtained by multiplying with the panel width, W. Therefore, formula (3) is modified as follows:

$$P_{panel} = c(ECT)^b\left(12k_{cr}\sqrt{D_{MD}D_{CD}} \div W^2\right)^{1-b} \times W$$
$$= c(ECT)^b\left(12k_{cr}\sqrt{D_{MD}D_{CD}}\right)^{1-b} \times W^{2b-1} \quad (4)$$

Here, the formula (4) is for calculating the compression strength of a panel in the case of buckling failure.

2.4 Boundary conditions to determine a collapsing or buckling failure

According to Urbanik et al., the boundary conditions that determine whether the panel causes a collapsing or buckling failure can be evaluated using the magnitude of the relationship between the ECT value and the critical buckling strength as follows [4]:

Conditions resulting in collapsing failure:
the critical buckling strength ≥ ECT

Conditions resulting in buckling failure:
ECT value > the critical buckling strength

As the comparison between the ECT value and the critical buckling strength is shown above, failure occurs in the condition with the smaller value. Therefore, in this study, the comparison between collapsing failure and buckling failure values is done, and the smaller value is adopted as the compression strength of the panel.

3. Experiment

3.1. Experimental method

The coefficients d, c, and b of the formulas (1) and (4) will be determined using the measurements in this section. The basis weight of the corrugated boards used is set to three levels: heavy, medium, and light, of C flute, and the changes in compression strength values with the varying panel dimensions are measured. Table 1 shows the physical properties and the measurement conditions for the corrugated boards used.

To determine the compression strength per panel, measurements were carried out on a box with the same width and length values (Fig. 2). Furthermore, to measure the compression strength accurately, a compression test was performed by fixing the inner flaps at the top and the bottom. The measurements are repeated five times under the same condition to obtain an average value, and the compression strength per panel is determined by dividing the measured average strength of the box by 4.

Table 1 The physical properties of materials and test conditions.

Material Supplier: Rengo Co., Ltd.	ECT(kN/m) TAPPI-T811	D_{CD}(kN·m) TAPPI-T836	D_{MD}(kN·m) TAPPI-T836
LC160/MC120/LC160 CF	4.22	4.48×10^{-3}	1.00×10^{-2}
LB210/MC180/LB210 CF	6.88	6.29×10^{-3}	1.41×10^{-2}
LB280/MA200/LB280 CF	9.73	8.32×10^{-3}	2.03×10^{-2}

Compression test condition	
Temperature	23℃
Humidity	50% RH
Compression rate	10 mm/min
Platen type	fixed

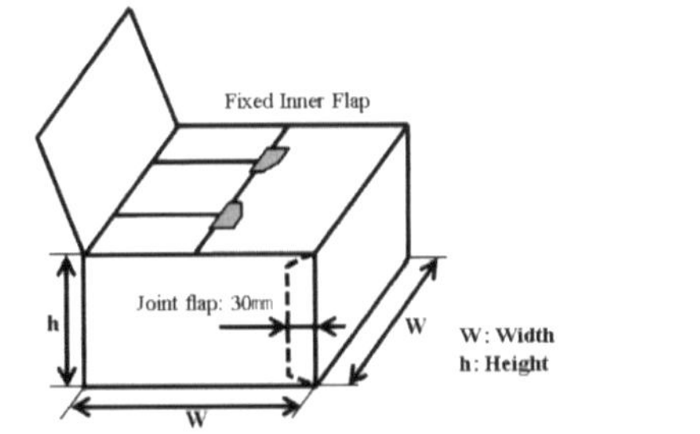

Fig. 2 Schematic of box structure used to measure the compression strength of panels.

3.2 Results

Table 2 shows the results of measured compression strength per panel.

Table 2 Compression strength & failure mode of panels

LC160/MC120/LC160 CF

(m) h \ W	0.075	0.10	0.20	0.3	0.45	0.60
0.075	0.241	0.295	0.514	0.706	0.859	
0.10		0.297	0.503	0.667	0.732	
0.125	0.236	0.275	0.462	0.567	0.655	
0.15		0.281	0.428	0.558		
0.20	0.230	0.285	0.411	0.520		
0.30	0.235	0.317		0.479	0.622	
0.40			0.475	0.512		
0.50	0.233	0.294				0.604

LB210/MC180/LB210 CF — Compression strength (kN)

h \ W	0.075	0.10	0.15	0.20	0.25	0.3	0.45	0.60
0.075	0.569	0.718	0.976	1.161	1.440	1.630		
0.10		0.739	0.967	1.207		1.305	1.521	
0.125	0.569	0.700	0.853	0.951		1.181	1.225	
0.15		0.700		0.847		1.121	1.211	
0.20	0.569	0.728	0.898	1.017		1.046		
0.30	0.567	0.719	0.943			1.133	1.272	
0.40				1.015		1.173		
0.50	0.584	0.736						1.238

LB280/MA200/LB280 CF — Compression strength (kN)

h \ W	0.075	0.10	0.15	0.20	0.25	0.3	0.45	0.60
0.075	0.409	0.503	0.723	0.887	1.018	1.148		
0.10		0.476	0.628	0.831		1.165	1.534	
0.125	0.403	0.514	0.592	0.768		1.104	1.035	
0.15		0.507	0.544	0.654		0.906	0.867	
0.20	0.408	0.515	0.642	0.680		0.860		
0.30	0.414	0.512	0.642			0.850	0.908	
0.40				0.746		0.798		
0.50	0.396	0.497						0.973

(shaded) collapsing failure (unshaded) buckling failure

4. Construction of compression strength estimation formulas

4.1. Estimation formula for collapsing failure panel

All 0.075 m height panels in Table 2 are of collapsing failure mode. From the relationship between the panel width and the compression strength, d (ECT) of formula (1) and the horizontal axis intercepts are obtained from Fig. 3 using the least square method.

From Fig. 3, d (ECT) and the horizontal axis-intercept of each corrugated board is shown below,

LC160/MC120/LC160 CF: d (ECT) = 2.08 kN/m, Horizontal axis-intercept = −0.043 m

LB210/MC180/LB210 CF: d (ECT) = 3.31 kN/m, Horizontal axis-intercept = −0.057 m

LB280/MA200/LB280 CF: d (ECT) = 4.70 kN/m, Horizontal axis-intercept = −0.051 m

According to Fig. 3, the compression strength of the panel is supposed to be approximated using a straight line passing through the origin because the compression strength of the panel is originally proportional to the panel width. But the result shows that the compression strength is proportional to the panel width plus 0.05 m.

Furthermore, the correlation between the ECT value and d (ECT) is determined using the least square method to obtain the coefficient d from Fig. 4.

From Fig. 4, the coefficient d is determined to be 0.483. Therefore, the compression strength formula of the panel that causes collapsing failure is given using the following formula (5).

$$P_{panel} = 0.483(ECT) \times (W + 0.05) \quad (5)$$

Where the unit of **ECT**: (kN/m) and W:(m)

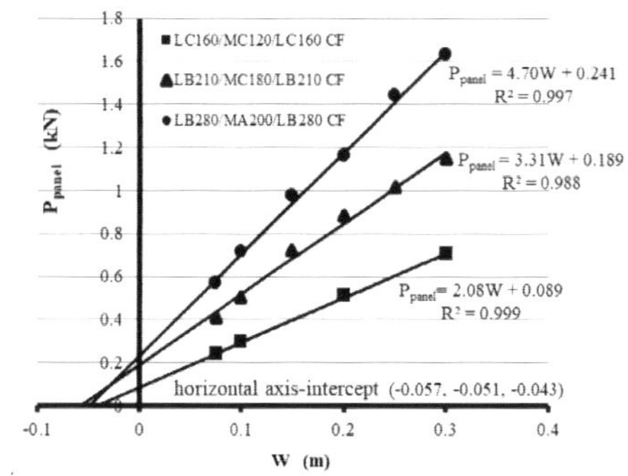

Fig. 3 Relationship between panel width (W) and compression strength (P_{panel}) in the 0.075-m-high panels.

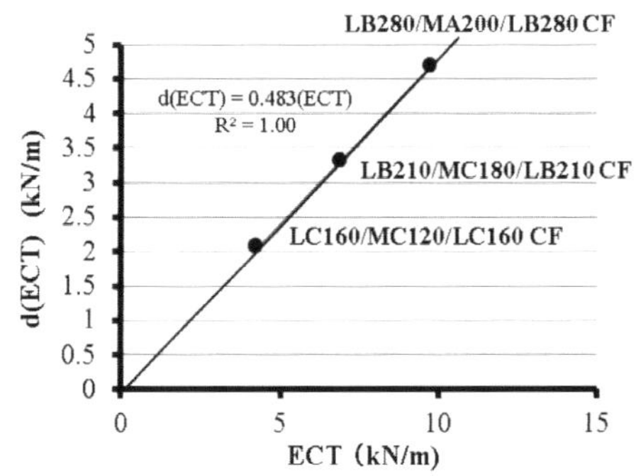

Fig. 4 Relation between ECT and d(ECT).

4.2 Estimation formula for buckling failure panel

Based on the compression strength of the buckling panel in Table 2, the coefficient b and c are determined in such a way that the sum of the % errors of the measured value and the calculated value (|estimated value - measured value | ÷ measured value × 100) is minimized. As a result, c = 0.500 and b = 0.656, and the compression strength formula of the panel causing buckling failure is expressed using the following formula (6):

$$P_{panel} = 0.500(ECT)^{0.656} \times \left(\pi^2 \left(\frac{\sqrt{\frac{D_{MD}}{D_{CD}}} \times h^2}{W^2 n^2} + \frac{W^2 n^2}{\sqrt{\frac{D_{MD}}{D_{CD}}} \times h^2} + 1 \right) \sqrt{D_{MD} D_{CD}} \right)^{0.344} \times W^{0.312} \qquad (6)$$

4.3 Correlation between the estimated and the measured values

By considering the lower value of compression strength estimated using formula (5) or formula (6) to be the compression strength of a particular panel, we obtain the estimated compression strength of the panels used in this experiment and compare with the measured values (Fig. 5).

The average error of the estimated value by McKee's equation is 6.1% [2], whereas the average error in this study is 6.5%. Although it is inferior to the average error of the McKee equation, it can be considered as a practical error range despite applying to a wider range of panel dimensions than that of an existing formula.

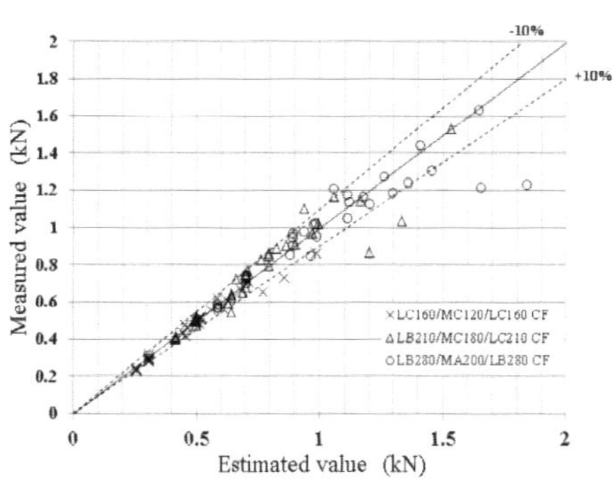

Fig. 5 Comparison of estimated compression strength of panel and measured by boxes.

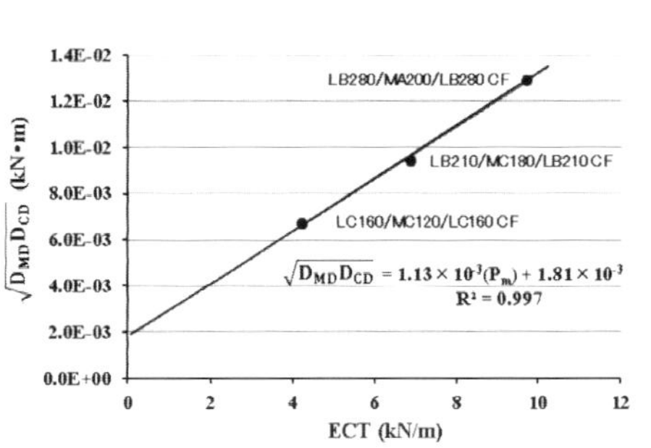

Fig.6 Relation between ECT and the geometric mean of bending stiffness.

4.4 Simplification of compression strength formula

While using formula (6), the ECT value and the bending stiffness in both directions is usually required, and it becomes complicated to measure each time. Therefore, we examine whether the bending stiffness can be estimated from the ECT value. As shown in Fig. 6, the geometric mean of bending stiffness has high correlation with the ECT value, and it can be expressed with the following formula (7):

$$\sqrt{D_{MD} D_{CD}} = 1.13 \times 10^{-3}(ECT) + 1.81 \times 10^{-3} \quad \cdot \cdot \cdot (7)$$

As for $\sqrt{D_{MD}/D_{CD}}$, the average value of 1.52 is applied from Table 1

5. Comparison of the accuracy between estimated strength in this study and the strength in existing formulas

We verify if it is valid that the proposed formula in this study can estimate the compression strength accurately using boxes of different shapes (flat boxes, slender boxes, and boxes with an extremely large ratio of width to length) that cannot be calculated with the existing formulas. Table 3 shows the box dimensions and the measured values, the estimated values using formulas (5) and (6) and the values by McKee's and Wolf's formulas.

Fig.7 shows the correlation between the estimated and measured values according to the results in Table 3. From Fig. 7, the estimated values by McKee's and Wolf's formulas differ significantly from the measured values, while the estimated values using the constructed formulas (5) and (6) show that the accuracy is within ±10%.

Therefore, the constructed formula can be considered to have a practical prediction accuracy.

Table 3 Box dimensions and compression strength of measured and estimated

	Box dimensions				This study	McKee's F.	Wolf's F.
	L (m)	W (m)	H (m)	Measured (kN)	Estimated (kN)	Estimated (kN)	Estimated (kN)
①	0.5	0.1	0.15	3.81	3.63	2.66	-1.07
②	0.3	0.1	0.05	3.31	3.31	2.18	1.87
③	0.3	0.1	0.1	3.35	3.11	2.18	1.81
④	0.3	0.1	0.25	2.17	2.57	2.18	1.75
⑤	0.2	0.15	0.3	2.55	2.68	2.04	2.25
⑥	0.3	0.15	0.3	2.56	2.89	2.31	2.44
⑦	0.4	0.15	0.3	2.62	3.01	2.55	2.32
⑧	0.4	0.25	0.05	4.69	4.97	2.77	2.95
⑨	0.4	0.25	0.1	4.52	4.55	2.77	3.28
⑩	0.4	0.25	0.15	3.24	3.72	2.77	3.19
⑪	0.35	0.25	0.3	3.21	3.20	2.66	3.14
⑫	0.5	0.2	0.05	5.46	5.30	2.87	2.96
⑬	0.5	0.2	0.1	4.54	4.91	2.87	2.87
⑭	0.5	0.2	0.15	3.20	4.02	2.87	2.83
⑮	0.25	0.2	0.1	3.51	3.34	2.31	2.67
⑯	0.25	0.2	0.15	2.52	2.94	2.31	2.63
⑰	0.25	0.2	0.25	2.45	2.94	2.31	2.57

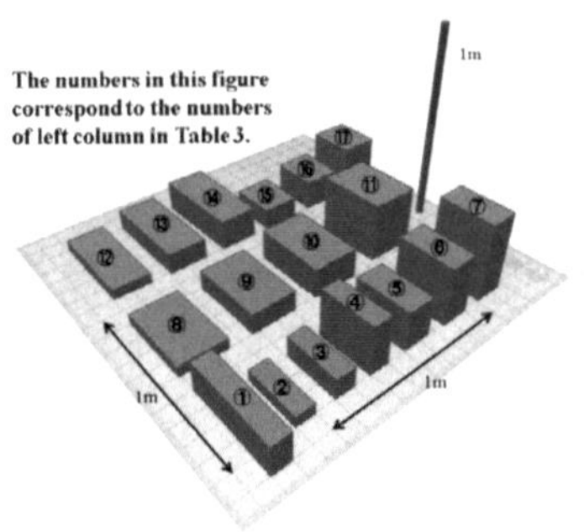

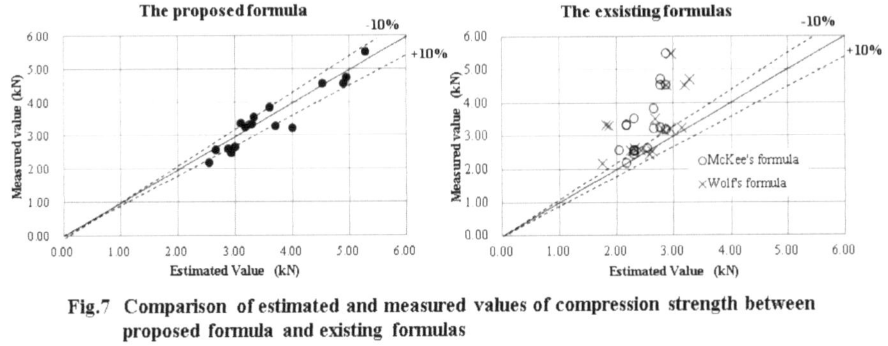

Fig.7 Comparison of estimated and measured values of compression strength between proposed formula and existing formulas

6. Conclusion

In this study, we construct the compression strength estimation formula for RSCs of any size. The formula is constructed according to the two failure modes: collapsing failure and buckling failure, and the least value obtained from both formulas is taken as the compression strength of the panel. Concerning the estimation accuracy, the average error in McKee's formula is 6.1%, whereas in this study it is 6.5%, but there can be a sufficient accuracy for practical use including the panel size area that cannot be estimated using the existing formulas.

We also confirm that the bending stiffness can be predicted using ECT values without measuring the bending stiffness of the corrugated board used. With the estimation method constructed in this study, and with the recent increase in the rate of mail-order sales and home delivery business, an appropriate RSC compression strength can be predicted without measuring the compression strengths of the actual boxes. We believe that it can contribute to increased efficiency.

7. References

[1] Kellicut KQ., Landt EF. Basic design data for the use of fiberboard in shipping containers. Fiber Containers. 1951; 36(12), pp.62-80

[2] McKee RC., Gander JW., Wachuta JR. Compression strength formula for corrugated boxes. Paperboard Packaging. 1963; 48(8), pp. 149-159

[3] Wolf M. How box length, width affects compression strength. Package Engineering. 1971; 16(10), pp.68-70

[4] Urbanik T J. and Frank B., Box compression analysis of world-wide data spanning 46 years, Wood and Fiber Science. 2006; 38(3), pp. 399-416

[5] Norris CB. An analysis of the compressive strength of honeycomb cores for sandwich construction. NACA Technical Note 1251. 1947

Thermoformed containers based on starch and starch/biochar composites [4]

Carlos A. Diaz *1, Tyler Evans 1, Rahul Ketan Shah 1, Thomas A. Trabold 2
1 Packaging Science, 2 Golisano Institute for Sustainability,
Rochester Institute of Technology, Rochester NY, USA

Abstract: Biodegradable containers support zero-waste initiatives when alternative end-of-life scenarios are available (e.g., composting, biodigestion). Thermoplastic starch (TPS) has emerged as a readily biodegradable and inexpensive biomaterial that can replace traditional plastics in applications such as food serviceware and packaging. This study has two aims. First, demonstrate the thermoformability of starch/polycaprolactone (PCL) as a thermoplastic material with varying starch loadings. Second, incorporate biochar as a sustainable filler that can potentially lower the cost and improve biodegradability. Biochar is a stable form of carbon produced by thermochemical conversion of organic biomass, such as food waste, and its incorporation into consumer products could promote a circular economy. Thermoformed cups were successfully made with starch contents from 40 to 60 wt.%. Increasing the amount of starch increased the viscosity of the material, which in turn affected the compression molding (sheet manufacturing) and thermoforming conditions. PCL content reduced the extent of biodegradation in soil burial experiments, and increased the strength and elongation at break of the material. A blend of 50:50 starch:PCL was selected for incorporating biochar. Thermoformed containers were manufactured with 10, 20 and 30 wt.% biochar. The addition of biochar decreased the elongation at break, but did not significantly affect the modulus of elasticity or tensile strength. Preliminary experiments suggest that adding 10 wt.% biochar increased the biodegradation of the material. The results demonstrate the feasibility of using starch and biochar for the manufacturing of thermoformed containers.

Keywords: starch, biochar, polycaprolactone, bioplastics, biodegradation

***Correspondence to:** Carlos A. Diaz, Department of Packaging Science, Rochester Institute of Technology, 29 Lomb Memorial Drive, Rochester NY 14823, USA. E-mail: cdamet@rit.edu

1. Introduction

Zero-waste initiatives call for waste to be either recyclable or compostable. Some municipalities in the US have programs to voluntarily separate organic waste, which is collected and composted. In this scenario, packaging and single-use items that are readily degradable present an opportunity to support and enhance closed loop systems for organic waste.

Thermoplastic starch (TPS) has emerged as a readily biodegradable and inexpensive biomaterial that can replace traditional plastics in applications such as food service and packaging [1]. Our previous study [2] investigated the mechanical performance of blends of TPS and polycaprolactone (PCL). A brittle-ductile transition was observed with the addition of PCL, and the degree of anaerobic biodegradation correlated with the amount of TPS. However, the preparation of TPS using water and glycerol showed inconsistencies from batch to batch and it is susceptible to aging [2]-[4]. Therefore, development of TPS-based products would benefit from a manufacturing process that avoids use of water or glycerol.

Here, a direct mixing of starch and PCL is proposed which bypasses some of the drawbacks outlined with TPS and could facilitate scale-up production. Additionally, the manufacturing of composites using biochar is presented as a means to improve biodegradability and valorize a byproduct from conversion of organic waste, thus promoting a circular economy [5]. Biochar is produced by pyrolysis of organic matter at high temperature under zero-oxygen conditions [6]. This technique creates a carbon-rich material with physical properties such as density, surface area and porosity that can be controlled by selecting critical process parameters, including heating rate, maximum temperature (typically in the range of 400 to 800oC) and residence time [7]. In the process of gasification, some oxygen is introduced to the system (well below the stoichiometric requirement for full combustion), and this may improve biochar quality in some cases, but at the cost of lower yield [8].

2. Methods

2.1 Materials

Corn starch was obtained from MP Biomedicals LLC. Polycaprolactone (PCL) Capa 6800, was supplied by Perstorp. Biochar was derived from spent coffee grounds obtained from the RIT cafeteria. The material was first dried using an in-house batch dehydrator (Ecovim-250) and then processed in a commercial-scale "Biogenic Refinery" manufactured by Biomass Controls (Putnam, CT, USA) and owned by RIT[9]. To produce biochar, dried coffee grounds were fed through a hopper and auger assembly at an average flow rate of approximately 5 kg/h. The temperature setpoint of 800 °C was maintained within ±25 °C over the course of the approximately 3-hour experiment. After thermochemical conversion, a dual auger system transported the final biochar product to the collection box, where samples were quenched with water spray to cool the material and prevent further reaction with ambient air.

2.2 Sample preparation

Thermoplastic starch was made using an internal shear mixer (CWB Brabender Intelli-torque Plasticorder torque rheometer with a 60cc 3-piece mixing head). TPS starch was blended at 30, 40, 50, and 60 wt. % with PCL in the mixer at 100 °C for 8 minutes and 50 rpm. The equilibrium torque was recorded as an indirect measurement of the viscosity of the melt as shown in Table 1. The samples were compression molded with a heated press (Carver 4391). Thermoforming was performed on a Sencorp Cera TEK 810/1-CE sheet fed laboratory thermoformer using a male mold. Optimum forming conditions were achieved through trial and error by adjusting the heating temperature and dwell time and monitoring the wrapping and webbing in the blisters (see Table 1).

***Table 1** Processing conditions for sample preparation*

	Mixing	Compression molding			Thermoforming	
Material Composition PCL:Starch	Equilibrium Torque (Nm)	Temperature (°C)	Pressure (tons)	Time (minutes)	Forming Temperature (°C)	Time (minutes)
60:40	12	200	3	7	110	1.5
50:50	13	200	3.5	8	113	1
40:60	17	180	6.5	15	116	1
30:70	21	210	7	15	138	1

Biochar composites were manufactured using the 50:50 PCL:starch blend as the base material, with 10, 20 and 30 wt.% biochar mixed at 85 °C. Thermoforming was performed at 138 °C, a temperature significantly higher than that of the material without biochar. However, going from 10 to 30 wt.% biochar did not affect the thermoforming temperature.

2.3 Mechanical property characterization

Tensile testing of the blend was carried out using an Instron Universal Testing Machine model 5567 at a crosshead speed of 12.5 mm/min. At least five specimens of each sample were tested according to standard ASTM D638. Samples were conditioned at room temperature for at least 24 hours prior to mechanical testing.

2.4 Soil burial test/ Aerobic degradation

Cellulose, PCL60/Starch40 and PCL40/Starch60 samples were cut into 2.54 cm square pieces to obtain a uniform sample size for degradation. 18 samples of each specimen were prepared and weighed to record their initial weight. The samples were buried in the soil at a depth of about 2.5 cm. The test was carried out at room temperature. Water was sprinkled on the soil surface every three days to ensure that the soil remained humid. The samples were measured for the weight loss every 7 days from the day they were initially buried. 3 samples of each specimen were measured by washing them gently with distilled water and drying the samples at 60°C in a vacuum oven, until a constant weight was obtained. Weight loss percentage was calculated based on Equation 1,

$$Weight\ loss\ (\%) = \frac{W_i - W_d}{W_i} \times 100 \qquad (1)$$

where wd is the dry weight of the film after being washed with distilled water and wi is the initial dry weight of the specimen [10].

3. Results

Table 1 shows the processing conditions for the three stages of sample preparation: mixing, compression molding and thermoforming. As the starch content in the blend increases, the equilibrium torque increases. This indicates that the viscosity of the blend increases due to increase in the starch content. A higher torque requirement for blending with higher starch content also indicates that a higher pressure is required for the conversion process. This can be evidenced in the increase in pressure requirement for the compression molding stage, accompanied with an increase in temperature. Similarly, increase in the starch content increased the forming temperature in the thermoformer (see **Table 1**).

Thermoformed blisters were successfully manufactured with starch contents up to 60 wt.%. Above 60 wt.% starch the material was unsuitable for thermoforming due to decreased pliability and the blend being too fragile (see **Figure 1**).

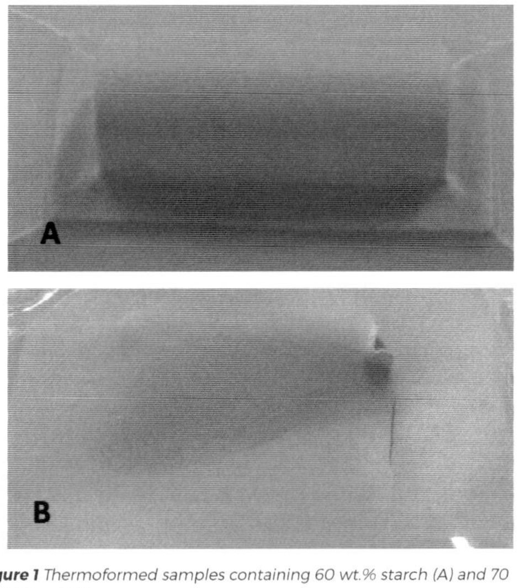

***Figure 1** Thermoformed samples containing 60 wt.% starch (A) and 70 wt.% starch (B)*

Figure 2 shows the effect of PCL:starch proportions on the mechanical properties. Pure PCL has the highest average tensile strength at 55 MPa. The plot displays a U-shape where the strength decreases and then increases at higher starch concentrations (i.e., 70 wt.%). This behavior could indicate an incompatibility of the PCL and starch since the strength of some blends is lower than that of pure PLC and sample with 70 wt.% starch [11]. Similarly, PCL has the highest percentage of elongation at break, which was expected due to its rubbery nature [12]. As the starch content increases, the elongation decreases. Increasing the starch content from 60 to 70 wt.% causes a sharp drop in the elongation from 740% to 26%.

The modulus of elasticity is highest at 70 wt.% starch. The stiffness drops significantly from 70 to 60 wt.% starch. Further decrease in the amount of starch showed a nearly linear increase in modulus of elasticity from 60 to 40 wt.% from 43 to 224 MPa, just above the modulus of elasticity of neat PCL (156 MPa).

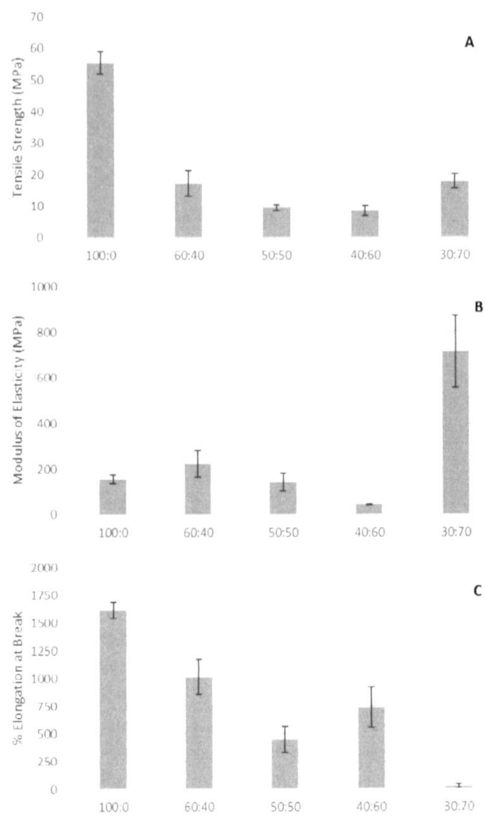

Figure 2 *Effect of blend ratio of PCL:Starch on (A) tensile strength, (B) modulus of elasticity and (C) percentage of elongation at break*

All the mechanical properties drastically changed going from 60 to 70 wt.% starch, suggesting a major change in the structure of the blend where PCL is not the majority component and the properties of starch dictate the properties of the blend. This lack of elongation and high stiffness supports the inability to thermoform the 70 wt.% starch blend.

Figure 3 shows the effect of adding biochar to the TPS containing 50:50 PCL:starch. Adding biochar increased the modulus of elasticity and slightly reduced the tensile strength. Similar results have been observed when reinforcing bioplastics with natural fibers [13]. Varying the biochar content from 10 to 30 wt.% did not have a significant effect on the tensile stress and modulus of elasticity of the material (Figures 3A and B). Conversely, the elongation at break was drastically reduced with the inclusion of biochar. Increasing the amount of biochar from 10 to 30 wt.% further reduced the elongation at break making the composites significantly more brittle.

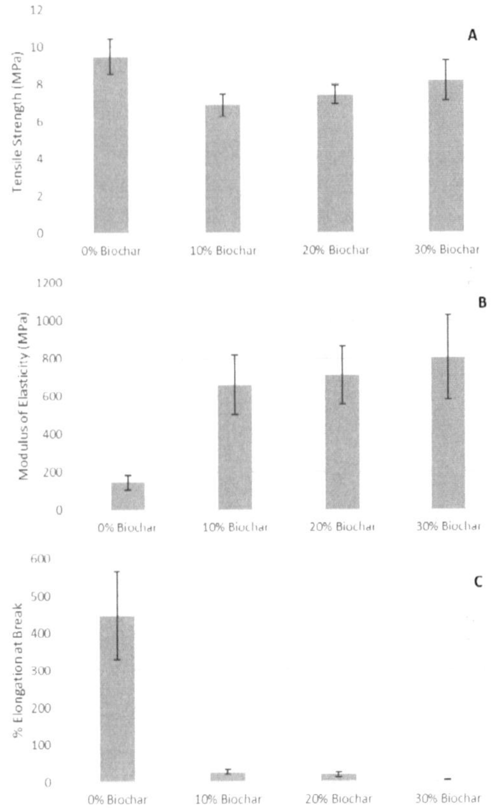

Figure 3 *Effect of biochar content in 50:50 PCL:starch blend on (A) tensile strength, (B) modulus of elasticity and (C) percentage of elongation at break*

To demonstrate the thermoforming ability of the composite with biochar, a male mold of a coffee lid was manufactured to demonstrate a potential application for this biodegradable composite material. All the composites with biochar allowed the sheet to be thermoformedinto coffee lids with loadings up to 30 wt.%. Figure 4 shows a coffee lid containing 10 wt.% biochar. Increasing the biochar load did not affect the thermoforming ability, however the surface was rougher with less resolution of the details of the mold. The results demonstrate the potential to use biochar as a filler material in thermoform containers and packaging. Additionally, this is an example of a product for the coffee shops made from their own waste (i.e., spent coffee grounds). Biochar thus may offer an opportunity for a close-loop economy while displacing plastic or creating fully biodegradable solutions.

Figure 4 *Thermoformed coffee lid made with 10 wt.% biochar from spent coffee grounds*

Ongoing research is looking at structure-property relationships to better understand the changes observed here. Additionally, the rheology of the material should be further studied to expand the findings of this research to other conversion processes such as injection molding and blown film extrusion.

Finally, Figure 5 shows the biodegradation of two samples containing 40 and 60 wt.% starch. Higher starch content resulted in a higher level of degradation. These results agree with previous studies [2]. Preliminary experiments suggest that the addition of biochar enhances the biodegradation, but further experimentation is ongoing.

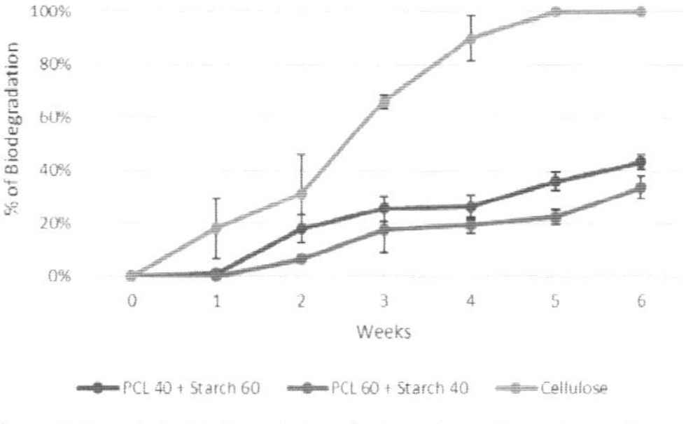

Figure 5 *Cumulative biodegradation of selected samples and a positive (cellulose) control*

4. Conclusion

This study demonstrates the thermoforming of fully biodegradable thermoplastic starch without the use of water or glycerol but instead a rubbery biopolymer (i.e., PCL). The ratio of PCL and starch affected the processing conditions as well as the mechanical properties. Thermoformed blisters were successfully made with starch contents from 30 to 60 wt.%. Increasing the starch content beyond that point drastically changed the properties and rendered the material unsuited for thermoforming. Biochar composites were made using the 50:50 PCL:starch material. Prototype thermoformed coffee lids were made with contents up to 30 wt.% biochar. Manufacturing of composites using biochar demonstrates the possibility to manufacture fully biodegradable items and the valorization of a byproduct from the pyrolysis of organic waste, thus promoting a circular economy model for future sustainable packaging products.

5 References

[1] D. R. Lu, C. M. Xiao, and S. J. Xu, "Starch-based completely biodegradable polymer materials," Express Polym. Lett., vol. 3, no. 6, pp. 366–375, 2009.

[2] R. Nunziato, S. Hedge, E. Dell, T. Trabold, C. Lewis, and C. Diaz, "Mechanical Properties and Anaerobic Biodegradation of Thermoplastic Starch/Polycaprolactone Blends," in 21th IAPRI World Conference on Packaging, 2018, pp. 722–729.

[3] L. Averous, L. Moro, P. Dole, and C. Fringant, "Properties of thermoplastic blends: starch–polycaprolactone," Polymer (Guildf)., vol. 41, no. 11, pp. 4157–4167, May 2000.

[4] O. Lopez, M. A. Garcia, M. A. Villar, A. Gentili, M. S. Rodriguez, and L. Albertengo, "Thermo-compression of biodegradable thermoplastic corn starch films containing chitin and chitosan," LWT - Food Sci. Technol., vol. 57, no. 1, pp. 106–115, Jun. 2014.

[5] A. Zabaniotou, D. Rovas, A. Libutti, and M. Monteleone, "Boosting circular economy and closing the loop in agriculture: Case study of a small-scale pyrolysis-biochar based system integrated in an olive farm in symbiosis with an olive mill," Environ. Dev., vol. 14, pp. 22–36, Apr. 2015.

[6] W. Chen, J. Meng, X. Han, Y. Lan, and W. Zhang, "Past, present, and future of biochar," Biochar, vol. 1, no. 1, pp. 75–87, Mar. 2019.

[7] K. Weber and P. Quicker, "Properties of biochar," Fuel, vol. 217. Elsevier Ltd, pp. 240–261, 01-Apr-2018.

[8] S. Guran, "Sustainable waste-to-energy technologies: Gasification and pyrolysis," in Sustainable Food Waste-to-Energy Systems, Elsevier, 2018, pp. 141–158.

[9] D. Rodriguez Alberto, K. Repa, S. Hegde, C. W. Miller, and T. A. Trabold, "Novel Production of Magnetite Particles via Thermochemical Processing of Digestate from Manure and Food Waste," IEEE Magn. Lett., 2019.

[10] W. Phetwarotai, P. Potiyaraj, and D. Aht-Ong, "Biodegradation of Polylactide and Gelatinized Starch Blend Films Under Controlled Soil Burial Conditions," J. Polym. Environ., vol. 21, no. 1, pp. 95–107, Aug. 2013.

[11] F. Weng, P. Zhang, D. Guo, E. Koranteng, Z. Wu, and Q. Wu, "Preparation and Properties of Compatible Starch PCL Composites: Effects of the NCO Functionality in Compatibilizer," Starch - Stärke, vol. 72, no. 3–4, p. 1900239, Mar. 2020.

[12] J. Z. Liang, D. R. Duan, C. Y. Tang, C. P. Tsui, and D. Z. Chen, "Tensile properties of PLLA/PCL composites filled with nanometer calcium carbonate," Polym. Test., vol. 32, no. 3, pp. 617–621, May 2013.

[13] W. Chaiwong, N. Samoh, T. Eksomtramage, and K. Kaewtatip, "Surface-treated oil palm empty fruit bunch fiber improved tensile strength and water resistance of wheat gluten-based bioplastic," Compos. Part B Eng., vol. 176, p. 107331, Nov. 2019.

Study and characterization of palletizing films used in the field of freight transport [15]

Elora Leguebe *1,2,3, Marie Le Baillif2,3, Victor Huart 1, Jean-Baptiste Nolot 3, Nicolas Krajka 1, Jérôme Pellot 1, Damien Erre 2,3
1 METROPACK, REIMS, FRANCE
2 ITheMM/ Université de Reims Champagne-Ardenne, REIMS CEDEX 2, FRANCE
3 ESIREIMS-ESIEC École nationale Supérieure d'Ingénieurs de Reims, REIMS, FRANCE

Abstract: Nowadays, product protection during transportation has become essential as import-export is increasing drastically. As a result, wrapping is used to stabilize and protect the goods and must be performed properly. The most commonly used wrapping material is the linear low-density polyethylene (LLDPE), either manually or through a mechanical equipment. This study will focus on the understanding of wrapping materials properties during transportations constraints. Both manual and mechanical films were analyzed. As wrapping films are anisotropic materials, it was important to perform the characterization in both the transverse and longitudinal directions. On a first part, tensile properties were measured to determine the elastic fields of the materials, their tensile strength, their elongation at break and their young Modulus. Then, relaxation tests were carried out at several elongation levels to measure the residual stresses corresponding to pallets wrapping applications. Finally, dynamic tests would be performed to highlight the viscoelastic behaviors of the materials during transportation. It was found that both materials showed anisotropic behaviors with a larger elongation capability for the mechanical film in the longitudinal direction. The viscoelastic properties of both materials were found to be affected by the level of elongation prior relaxation and the transport constraints.

Keywords: stretch film; wrapping film; pallets wrapping; stretch film behavior; tensile test; transport

***Correspondence to:** Elora Leguebe, METROPACK 30-32 Rue du Capitaine Georges Madon ZAC Croix Blandin, 51100 REIMS, FRANCE. E-mail: elora.leguebe@metropack.fr

1. Introduction

The present study focused on the understanding of wrapping material properties during transportation constraints. The most commonly used wrapping material is the linear low-density polyethylene (LLDPE), either manually or through mechanical equipment. Both types of films were investigated. Mechanical properties of the materials were measured in order to understand their behaviors during wrapping applications, and to check their possible anisotropy.

2. Research Goals / Objectives

The main goal of this study was to develop an understanding of the wrapping material in transportation conditions but also of transportation constraints. Such knowledge would allow the setting of optimal wrapping parameter for the protection of goods during transportation.

The investigation was focused on measuring mechanical properties of film properties under common wrapping conditions. The final objective would be to be able to choose optimal wrapping parameter as a function of the load transported and the type of transportation.

3. Research Method

• Specimen preparation:

Test pieces of LLDPE were prepared according to IS 14995 standards. The polymer film was set between two sheets of paper prior cutting in order to avoid catching but the cutting machine blade. Specimens of 150 cm were cut in transverse and longitudinal directions. Then each specimen was taped on a cardboard frame prior testing.

prior testing.

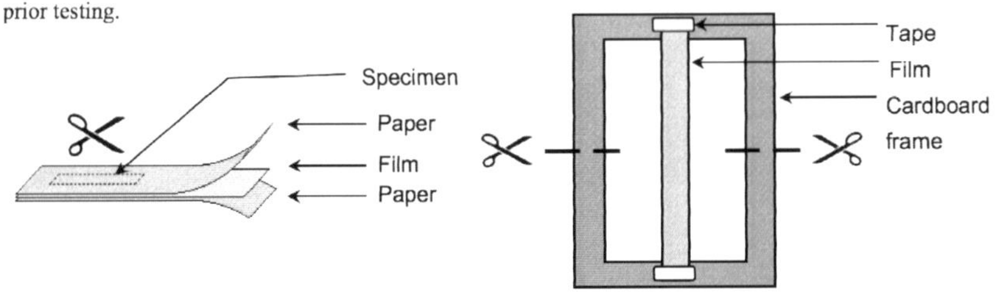

Figure 1 *Assembly and cutting of test specimens*

• Characterization:

Mechanical testings were carried out on a MTS tensile testing machine. The cardboard frame holding the specimen was set into the testing equipment in order to avoid any pre stretching or stressing of the specimen. The frame was cut after the proper tightening of the grips prior starting the measurement.

Tensile properties were performed according to ASTM D882 standard. The presented properties were calculated out of 5 parallel measurements. Both machine and manual films were tested in longitudinal and transverse direction.

Relaxation tests were performed according to ISO 2285 standard and using pre-straining levels of 4, 10, 16, 100, 200 and 300% of the initial length. The presented results were calculated out of 5 parallel measurements. Residual stresses were calculated using the curve fitting program Fityk. Residual stresses were considered as reached when the difference between the measured value and the calculated residual stress value was below 0,05 MPa.

4. Results and conclusions

• Tensile properties:

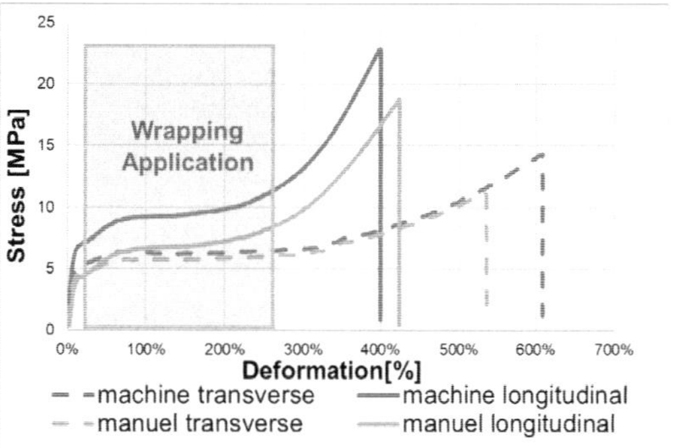

Figure 2 *Traction curve of two types of stretch film in both directions*

Figure 2 shows the stress-strain curves of the LLDPE films in longitudinal and transverse directions. It is clearly visible that both machine and manual films had anisotropic properties. However, no significant difference was measured between manual and machine films. Longitudinal tensile moduli and tensile strength were higher than transverse tensile strengths and moduli. The elongation at break was however higher in the transverse direction. The elastic field was found to end at strain levels around 20%. Commonly used straining levels for wrapping processing are known to be from 80% to 250% according to the internal report of Metropack with the parameters of the wrapping machine. As a result, the films behaviors during wrapping applications correspond to the plastic field behaviors.

• Stress Relaxation:

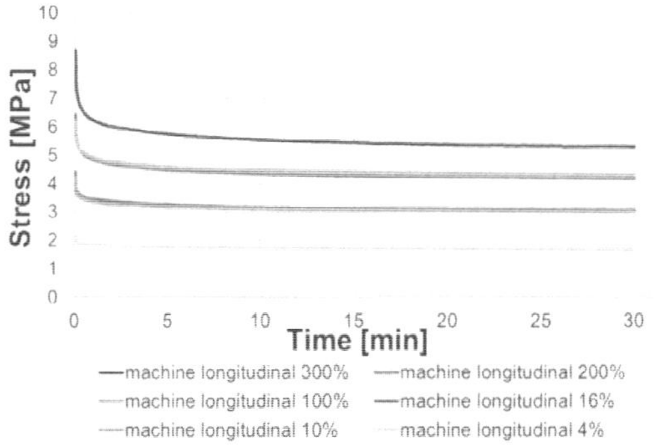

Figure 3 *Effect of strain level*

Figure 3 presents relaxation curves of longitudinal machine films. As expected, initial and residual stresses were increasing with the pre-straining level. It is noticeable that only 15 minutes were enough for reaching the residual stresses levels, even for high pre-straining levels. It is reasonable to admit that a wrapped palet would wait at least 15 minutes prior starting its transportation. Therefore, the residual stresses levels would be achieved prior transportation.

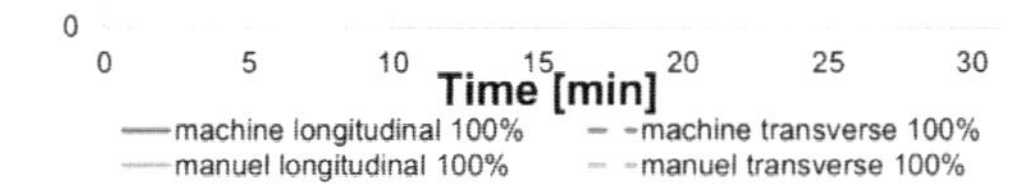

Figure 4 *Effect of film application system*

Figure 4 shows the stress relaxation curve of specimen cut in longitudinal and transverse direction for both machine and manual film pre-strained at 100%. For the different films in one direction, no significant difference between machine and manual films.

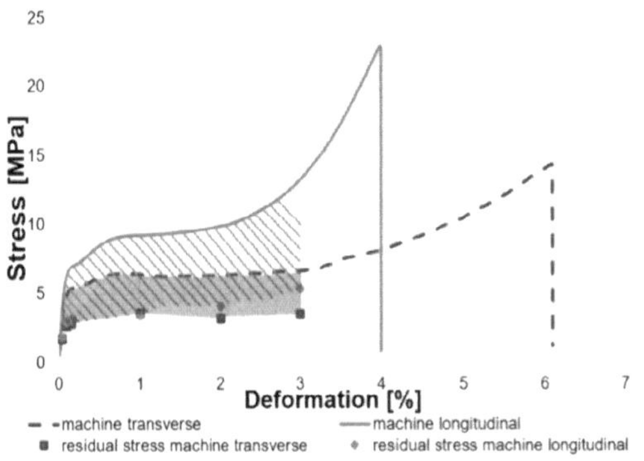

Figure 5 *Residual stress compared with tensile properties*

Figure 5 presents the residual stresses at the different pre-straining levels compared with the stress-strain curved obtained during tensile testing. For both directions, it was noticeable that only about half of the initial stress remained after relaxation. This means that one must not ignore relaxation when considering load stability during transportation.

• **Conclusion:**

Mechanical properties of machine and manual wrapping films were measured and both films showed similar and anisotropic properties. The residual stress during relaxation was found to be achieved after 15 minutes only. The residual stress value was found to depend on film direction and pre-straining level. Stress levels were found to decreased dramatically because of relaxation. Relaxation was therefore considered as an important phenomenon for the understanding of wrapping materials behaviors during transportation.

5. Future Research

The present study was focused on the behavior of the films after wrapping conditions. However, transportation will create dynamic stresses to the material, each transportation mean having specific frequencies. It would therefore be interesting to measure the effect of such dynamic stresses on the material properties.

Assuring load stability means understanding the different problems occurring during transportation. Creating a library of defects on wrapping films during transportation would be a first step for it. Then, a further understanding of wrapping parameters would allow to propose optimal wrapping of palets depending on the load transported and the transportation mean.

6. References

[1] G. M. Mcnally and al - The Effect of Polymer Properties on the Mechanical Behavior and Morphological Characteristics of Cast Polyethylene Film for Stretch and Cling Film Applications - Journal of Plastic Film and Sheeting, 2005, 21.

[2] J. V. Bisha, "Correlation of the Elastic Properties of Stretch Film on Unit Load Containment", Ph.D. thesis, Virginia Polytechnic Institute and State University, 2012.

[3] Klein, Daniel & Stommel, Markus & Zimmer, Johannes, "Influence of the stretch wrapping process on the mechanical behavior of a stretch film", AIP Conference Proceedings, 2018.

[4] Park, Jonghun & Horvath, Laszlo & White, Marshall & Araman, Philip & Bush, Robert, "The influence of stretch wrap containment force on load bridging in unit loads", Packaging Technology and Science, 2018.

Study on adhesion properties of superhydrophobic coatings on aluminum substrates [51]

Ruomei Wu *1, Shuai Wu 2 ,Zigong Chang 3, Haiyun Jiang3 2, Zhiqing Yuan3 3, Qinghua Chen3 4
1 College of Packaging and Materials Engineering, Hunan University of Technology, Zhuzhou, China
2 Zhuzhou Lupo New Materials Company Limited.

Abstract: The adhesion of the layer includes the adhesion of the organic coating and the metal surface of the substrate and the cohesion of the organic coating itself. Low adhesion will cause the coating to fall off the surface of the matrix;The coating with poor cohesion tends to crack and lose its effect. Only by increasing the adhesion of the organic coating to the metal surface and the cohesion of the coating itself can the metal be provided with good protection. In order to improve the quality of superhydrophobic aluminum alloy, the effects of Micro-nano structures of different shapes on aluminum surface were studied. the aluminum alloy surface with step, needle, ellipsoid, triangle shape and columnar micro-nano structure was constructed by using acid etching, anodic oxidation process, chromate-phosphate, and process template method, and the superhydrophobic properties of the aluminum alloy were endowed by stearic acid modification. The contact angle between all samples and water is greater than 150°. Scanning elect ron microscopy (SEM, HITACHIS-3000N) was used to characterize the surface structure and morphology. Film adhesion tester (QFZ-II) and grid method was used to analyze the adhension between film and aluminum matrix. The results show that the surface of aluminum alloy with needle microstructure prepared by anodic oxidation has the best properties.The surface of aluminum is dense; and the contact angle with water is 154.7±1.8°. The shedding area of the film only accounts for 35%, and the adhesion level of the film is 2B.

Keywords: superhydrophobic film; aluminum; adhension.

*Correspondence to: Ruomei Wu. E-Mail:476844203@qq.com

1. Introduction

Superhydrophobic is a common phenomenon in natural plants such as salvinia and rose petals. The most well-known example is lotus leaf with self-cleaning and anti-water properties. Until 1990s, Barthlott et al. investigated the reason of superhydrophobic phenomenon on lotus leaf surface though electron microscope,and found the surface of lotus leaf was covered by mocro-structure and hydrophobic waxes.Later,Jiang lei et al. future studied the structure of the lotus leaf and determined that the nano-structure on the mocro-structure made the lotus leaf surface have the ability.

The preparation of metal superhydrophobic surface has been paid more attention in recent years because the construction of superhydrophobic surface on metal matrix can greatly improve the protection ability of metal. The preparation of superhydrophobic surface of aluminum alloy is one of the hotspots in this field. One of the keys to the construction of superhydrophobic surface is to rough the surface of the material to facilitate the construction of microstructure and improve the surface coating performance.

In this work, five different micro-nano structures are constructed on the surface of aluminum alloy by several simple processes, and superhydrophobic properties of aluminum alloy are endowed after being modified by stearic acid. The effect of these aluminum alloys with different micro and nano-structures on the adhesion of superhydrophobic film was studied.

2. Methods

2.1 Materials

Alunimun alloy (Honghui chemicals corporation of Changsha) with a chemical composition (wt.%) of Al-1.23Mn-0.51Fe-0.14Si-0.08Cu-0.05Zn-Mg0.008. was used in this study.All samples were 2cm×2cm×1 mm. The absolute ethyl alcohol,hydrochloric, sulfuric acid, sodium fluoride and,chromium trioxide were obtained from Chemical Industry Research Institute of Zhuzhou. The analytical pure stearic acid, and NaCl were obtained from KeMiO chemicals corporation of Tianjin.The polydimethylsiloxane was purchased from Maoming petrochemical industry of China. All the reagents in this experiment without further purification.

2.2. Preparation of micro-nanostructures

The aluminum alloy plates were polished by sandpaper of 600#, 800# and 1200# respectively to remove surface defects and oxide film. Then, the aluminum alloy plates were washed with deionized water and dried at 80-100 °C. Micro-nano structures can be constructed on the surface of aluminum alloy by different treatment methods.

Acid etching method: The aluminum alloy plates were immersed in 3mol/L hydrochloric acid solution for 15min. The aluminum alloy plates were immersed in 0.5mol/L potassium permanganate solution for 1 hour after thorough cleaning with deionized water, then the aluminum alloy plates were dried at the furnace temperature of 80-100 °C.

Aanodic oxidation method: The aluninum alloy sheets (2cm×2cm×0.5cm) were polished to remove the oxides,and dried after rinsing with deionized water. Then the aluminum alloy sheet as anode and graphite as cathode were uesd to react in solution of NaCl(15g/L),sulfuric acid(150g/L),and oxalic acid(15g/L).The current dentisy in this experiment was 1.5A/dm2 and the reaction time was 30min.Then,the reacted aluminum alloy sample was dried after cleaning. Chromate-phosphate process: The aluminum sheets were treated with a mixture of 0.653mol/L phosphoric acid, 0.119mol/L sodium fluoride and 0.1mol/L chromium trioxide for 15 minutes. Then the aluminum sheet was washed with distilled water and dried at 80-100 °C for 0.5 ~ 1.5 hours.

Template method: The natural lotus leaf and commeline communis after cleaning with ultrasonic wave was used as the template, then the prepolymer of PDMS, ethyl orthosilicate and tin dibutyl dilaurate were mixed and stirred evenly according to the mass ratio of 10:3:1. After vacuuming, the product was poured on the cleaned leaf surface. After 24h of curing, the porous PDMS template was obtained by peeling off the leaf surface. Then, the cleaned aluminum sheet was coated on the hydrochloric acid-wetted PDMS template, and the pressure of 3.0kN/m^2 was applied. After pressing for 24 hours, the aluminum sheet was taken out, and the surface of the aluminum sheet was similar to the micro-nano structure on the surface of lotus leaf.

2.3 Preparation superhydrophobic surface

The above pretreated aluninum alloy sheets were immersed in solution of alcohol stearate solution(The mass fraction of solution is 1%) for 30 min,the superhydrophobic surface was obtained after drying at room temperature for 24h.

2.4 Characterization of samples

The morphology and microstructures of samples were analyzed by using a scanning electron microscopy (SEM, HITACHI S-3000N, Netherlands) at 30kV. Water contact angle (CA) was measured with contact angle measurement system at room temperature.The average values were obtained by measuring five different positions for each sample.

The adhension between film and surface of aluminum was analyzed by adhesive strength testing instrument(QFZ-II, China).

***Figure 1** Contact angle and micro morphologies of superhydrophobic aluminum alloy (a)step-shaped(b) needle-shaped(c) ellipsoid(d) columnar (e) triangle*

3. Results and Discussion

3.1 The microstructure and contact angle of aluminum surface

It can be seen from the figure 1 that the contact angle between the surface of aluminum alloy and the water drop after the film coating is greater than 150°. All the samples have superhydrophobic property. The contact angle of superhydrophobic aluminum alloy surface is close, which indicates that the microstructure of superhydrophobic aluminum alloy surface has little influence on wettability at room temperature.

3.2 The adhension between film and aluminum

The adhesion performance analysis results of different microstructure on superhydrophobic aluminum alloy surfaces are showen in Table 1. As can be seen from the Table 1, the superhydrophobic surface with needle-like microscopic appearance prepared by anodic oxidation method has the best adhesion, the lowest film shedding area (only 35%), and the shedding area of other samples exceeds 50%.Therefore, the aluminum matrix with needle-like surface micro morphology has better bonding performance to the superhydrophobic film layer.

The surface roughness of needle structure is high. The effective contact area between stearic acid and aluminum alloy was greatly increased when the solution molecules penetrated into the micropore. Therefore, the bonding strength between aluminum alloy surface and stearic acid coating is improved. The surface roughness of other samples is low, so the bonding performance between coating and aluminum matrix is the worst.

Table 1 *The adhesion performance analysis results of different microstructure on superhydrophobic aluminum alloy surfaces*

method	microstructure	The rate of coating spallation area	adhesion level
Acid etching method	step-shaped	82%	0B
Aanodic oxidation method	needle-shaped	35%	2B
Chromate-phosphate method	ellipsoid	56%	1B
Lotus leaf template method	triangle	52%	1B
commeline communis template method	columnar	62%	1B

4. Conclusions

1) At room temperature, the surface microscopic shape of superhydrophobic aluminum alloy has little effect on wettability.

2) The surface of aluminum alloy with needle-like microstructure prepared by anodic oxidation method has the best bonding property with the film layer. The rate of coating spallation area of this sample is 35%, and the film adhesion level is 2B. This shows that the microstructure of the surface of aluminum alloy has a great influence on the bonding force between the superhydrophobic film layer and the aluminum alloy matrix.

5. Acknowledgements

This work was supported by Hunan Provincial Natural Science Foundation of China (No: 2019JJ60057)

And special word of thanks for Ms. Chao Guanghua for the many valued discussions related to this work.

6. References

[1] Y.B. Park, H. Im, M. Im, Y.K. Choi, J. Mater. Chem. 21 (2011) 633–636.

[2] Han Jinping, Han Jinguo, Han Jintai, Han Jinan. The History of Canned Food-200-Year Commenoration of the Invention of Canning. Packaging Journal 2010; 2(4).pp.1-4

[3] Mengnan Qu, Shanshan Liu, Jinmei He, Juan Feng, Yali Yao, Lingang Hou, Xuerui Ma.Bioinspired durable superhydrophobic materials with antiwear property fabricated from quartz sands and organosilane. J Mater Sci (2016);51:8718–8727

[4] Pietschmann N, Stengl K, Hoesselbarth B. Investigations into vinylic addition reaction of modified polyester resin. Progress in Organic Coatings 1999; 36(1-2), pp.64-69.

[5] Wu RM, Liang SQ, Pan AQ, Yuan ZQ, Tang Y, Tan XP, et al. Fabrication of nanostructured super-hydrophobic film on aluminum by controllable immersing method. Appl Surf Sci 2012;258:5933–5.

[6] Youfa Zhang, Dengteng Ge, Shu Yang. Spray-coating of superhydrophobic aluminum alloys with enhancedmechanical robustness. Journal of Colloid and Interface Science 2014;101–107.

[7] Dziczkowski J, Soucek M D. A new class of acrylated alkyds. Journal of coatings technology and research 2010; 7(5), pp.587-602.

[8] Zuxin She, Qing Li, Zhongwei Wang, Cui Tan, Juncen Zhou, Longqin Li. Highly anticorrosion, self-cleaning superhydrophobic Ni-Co surfacefabricated on AZ91D magnesium alloy. Surface & CoatingsTechnology2014;7–14.

[9] Linghao Kong, Xinhua Chen, Guangbin Yang, Laigui Yu, Pingyu Zhang. Preparation and characterization of slice-like Cu2(OH)3NO3 superhydrophobicstructure on copper foil. Applied Surface Science 2008;7255–7258.

[10] Xianming Hou, Lixia Wang, Feng Zhou, Liqing Li. Fabrication of ZnO submicrorod films with water repellency by surface etching andhydrophobic modification. Thin Solid Films 2011;7813–7816.

[11] Teng-Yuan Lo, Yi-Chia Huang, Yi-Nan Hsiao, Chuen-Guang Chao, Wha-Tzong Whang. Preparation of superhydrophobic polyimide films modified withorganosilicasol as effective anticorrosion coatings. Surface & Coatings Technology 2014;310–319.

[12] Junlu Sheng,Min Zhang,Yue Xu,Jianyong Yu, Bin Ding. Tailoring Water-Resistant and Breathable Performance of Polyacrylonitrile Nanofibrous Membranes Modified by Polydimethylsiloxan[J]. ACS Appl. Mater. Interfaces. 2016(8)27218–27226.

[13] Zheng-Bai Zhao, Da-Ming Zhang, Yi-Fan Meng, Li Tai, Yong Jiangn. One-pot fabrication of fluoride-silica@ silica raspberry-like nanoparticles for superhydrophobic coating[J]. Ceramics International,2016.

[14] Deepak Patil, S. Aravindan. Fast Fabrication of Superhydrophobic Titanium Alloy as Antibacterial Surface Using Nanosecond Laser Texturing[J]. Transactions of the ASME,2018.

[15] DegangXie,Wen Lia,.A Novel simple approach to preparation of superhydrophobic surfaces of aluminum alloys[J]. Applied Surface Science, 2011 (258) 1004–1007.

[16] Lee J. W., Hwang W. Exploiting the silicon content of aluminum alloys to create a superhydrophobic surface using the sol-gel process[J]. Materials Letters, 2016, 168:83-85.

[17] Zeng R C, Liu Z G, Zhang F, et al. Corrosion resistance of in-situ Mg–Al hydrotalcite conversion film on AZ31 magnesium alloy by one-step formation[J]. Transactions of Nonferrous Metals Society of China, 2015, 25(6): 1917-1925.

[18] Zhao H Y, Jin J, Tian W J, et al. Three-dimensional superhydrophobic surface-enhanced Raman spectroscopy substrate for sensitive detection of pollutants in real environments[J]. Journal of Materials Chemistry A, 2015, 3(8): 4330-4337.

[19] Zeng R C,Zhang F,Lan Z D,et al.Corrosion resistance of calcium-modified zinc Phosphate conversion coatings on magnesium-aluminium alloys[J].Corrosion Science, 2014, 88(6): 452-459.

[20] Ishizaki T,Kamiyama N,Watanabe K,et al. Corrosion resistance of Mg(OH)2/Mg–Al layered double hydroxide composite film formed directly on combustion-resistant magnesium alloy AMCa602 by steam coating[J]. Corrosion Science, 2015, 92: 76-84.

[21] Cheng Y,Lu S,Xu W, et al.Controllable fabrication of superhydrophobic alloys surface on copper substrate for self-cleaning, anti-icing, anti-corrosion and anti-wear performance[J].Surface & Coatings Technology, 2017, 333:1-36.

[22] Liu Y, Li X, Yan Y, et al.Anti-icing performance of superhydrophobic aluminum alloy surface and its rebounding mechanism of droplet under super-cold conditions[J]. Surface & Coatings Technology, 2017, 331:7-14. [23]Tuo Y, Chen W,Zhang H,et al. One-step hydrothermal method to fabricate drag reduction superhydrophobic surface on aluminum foil[J]. Applied Surface Science, 2018, 446:230-235.

Flexible recyclable packaging materials for the food industry [62]

Juliana Chalá Ortega [1], Carlos A. Diaz [*2]
1 Universidad de Monterrey, NL, México,
2 Packaging Science, Rochester Institute of Technology, Rochester NY, USA

Abstract: The pollution caused by plastics in the environment is making us aware of its impact and has forced our society to think about how current practices are not sustainable.

Flexible packaging is a technology of laminated plastics that protect and preserve the product and additionally are functional for the consumer. It has given us the possibility of transporting food in a lighter, safer and more compact way. Additionally, it has improved the shelf life of food, making it possible to reach many populations. However, these flexible packages are generally made with multiple layers, which limits their recyclability and sometimes, due to mishandling it, ends up polluting our ecosystems. This scenario has caused governments, NGOs and multinational companies to begin evaluating and reformulating their market policies.

Our goal is to analyze through industry examples, and particularly Nestle, the impact on the circular economy of these new developments coming from the converter level. This case study is a fusion between the desire to understand the dynamics of the application of industrial processes and the leverage of driving trends within the largest CPGs (Consumer Packaged Goods companies). Nestlé, for example, seeks the recovery of the credibility in the marketplace based on a strategy to strengthen the company's image by means of environmental focus to improve processes within the company. In addition, the company is working on fostering the circular economy in the communities surrounding production factories.

Through literature and experience at Nestlé, we seek to compare innovations in the field of flexible packaging that encourage recyclability, and other sustainable practices (e.g., compostable packaging). This work seeks to establish which innovations (materials, structures) can be applied in single-use packaging and if their performance is viable for the implementation of these processes in new market launches.

Keywords: sustainability, packaging, materials

***Correspondence to:** Carlos A. Diaz, Department of Packaging Science, Rochester Institute of Technology, 29 Lomb Memorial Drive, Rochester NY 14823, USA. E-mail: cdamet@rit.edu

CHAPTER V

Active & intelligent packaging

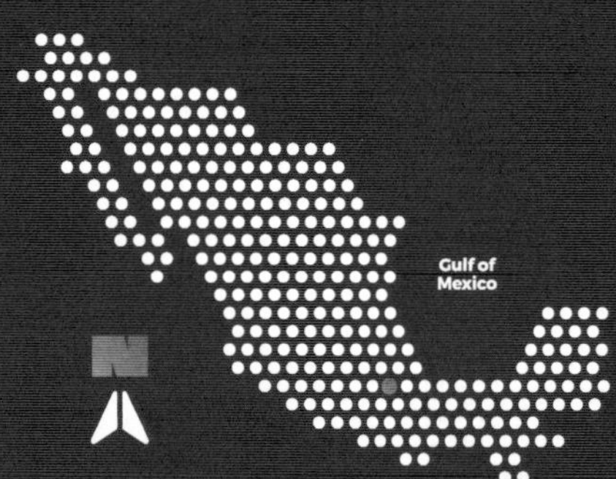

Author:
Marcosecastillo - Freepik.com

Location:
Puebla, PUEBLA

Description:
Few dishes are as complex to prepare as "mole poblano". Even though its origin is unknown (some historians say that it goes back to Aztec times, while others say it is from the Colonial times), its impactful flavor and perfect balance of sweet and savory is a perfect representation of Mexico: feisty yet welcoming and always present in a good celebration.

Implementation of Cellulose-Based Antimicrobial Packaging with Enhanced Barrier Performance [53]

Alexander Bardenstein *1, Birgit Groth Storgaard1, Stanislav Landa 1, Mark Holm Olsen 1, Kiril Andreev Kirilov2, Helle Allermann1, Kenneth Kisbye1, and Steffen Lynge Jørgensen1
1 Danish Technological Institute, Gregersensvej 1, 2630 Taastrup, Denmark
2 Leaf Packaging ApS, Lejrvej 23D, 3500 Værløse, Denmark

Abstract: A solution for implementation of antimicrobial packaging based on surface processing of moulded cellulose and impregnation of essential oils has been developed. Moulded paper trays were coated by a layer of a water-soluble biodegradable polymer and a stratified plasma (PECVD) barrier coating. The synthesized plasma coating comprised two hard layers with low barrier penetrability of $scCO_2$ interleaved with highly penetrable soft polymer-like layers. Thereupon, the trays were impregnated from inside with controlled amounts of thymol using $scCO_2$. The impregnation neither caused any physical damage nor unacceptable degradation of barrier performance of the packaging that was adequately low in order to meet the requirements of a number of food packaging applications.

Keywords: antimicrobial packaging, moulded cellulose packaging, PECVD coating, thymol, $scCO_2$ impregnation

***Correspondence to:** Alexander Bardenstein. E-mail: alb@dti.dk

1. Introduction

Food packaging needs continuous innovation in materials that try to meet societal challenges with improved food safety and quality, food waste reduction, convenience, sustainability, reusability, stability, etc. This cannot be achieved with packaging solutions designed only to be passive barriers that delay the detrimental effects of the environment on the food product. The appropriate solution is a global commercial use of active packaging, especially antimicrobial packaging, which plays a dynamic role in extending food shelf life. Active packaging must also comply with the requirements of the circular economy and the EU's Plastics Strategy, i.e. be recyclable and/or biodegradable to reduce packaging waste.

Numerous antimicrobial packaging solutions have been developed and even commercialized over the past decade. They mostly use essential oils, which are either impregnated in conventional plastic packaging films using high temperature and pressure or placed inside the plastic packaging in sachets containing a plastic granulate impregnated with the functional substances. Supercritical carbon dioxide ($scCO_2$) is often used to impregnate LDPE, PP or PLA films or laminates with antimicrobial substances. The impregnation results in loss of mechanical strength and barrier properties of the plastic films. This deterioration has been attempted reduced by using reinforcing additive masterbatches, for example nano-clay og natural fibres like nano- cellulose, but this makes packaging impossible to recycle as pure plastic. As for the sachets comprising impregnated plastic granules, consumers do not widely accept them in food packaging, and this solution significantly increases the costs of packaging.

Thus, no manufacturing process has been established for industrial implementation of recyclable and biodegradable antimicrobial packaging. In this study we attempt to develop such a process on a pilot scale using moulding of cellulose, deposition of liquid and plasma barrier coatings, and $scCO_2$-impregnation with antimicrobial compounds.

2. Manufacturing of moulded cellulose trays

A solution for implementation of antimicrobial packaging based on surface processing of moulded cellulose and impregnation of essential oils has been developed in our study. It was clear from the beginning that paper-based packaging was the natural choice, since only paper packaging is both bio-based, unconditionally biodegradable and recycled almost anywhere in the world. We mould paper packaging using our Mini Paper Factory [1] shown in Figure 1. Paper trays can be moulded in various grades, compositions, sizes and shapes, see Figure 2.

Figure 1 *Finished moulding cycle in the Mini Paper Factory, where the trays are seen on the drying mould before blow-out.*

Figure 2 *Moulded cellulose trays of different cellulose compositions (from left to right: unbleached kraft cellulose fibres, bleached fibres, 50:50 mixture of the two).*

This manufacturing process results in trays with a surface so smooth and tight that a 10-20 g/m2 liquid barrier coating like polyvinyl alcohol (PVOH) or plasticized and cross-linked starch will decrease the oxygen and moisture transmission rates (OTR and WVTR) of the container to 10 ml/(m2·day) and 100 g/(m2·day), respectively, at 23°C and 50% RH. The scanning electron microscopy (SEM) image of the surface of the moulded cellulose is shown in Figure 3.

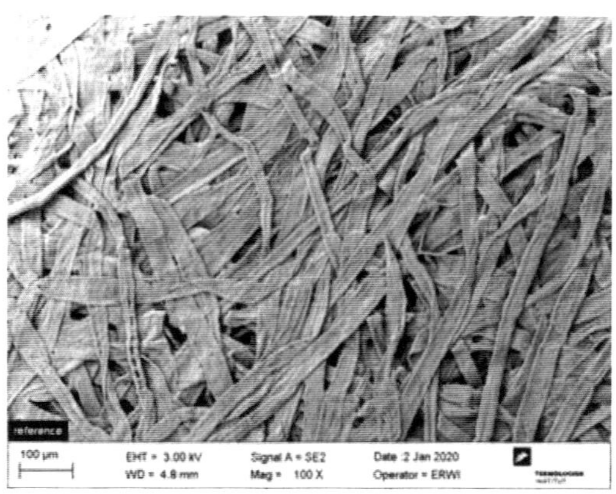

Figure 3 *SEM image of the moulded cellulose surface.*

3. Deposition of barrier coatings

There are various methods for providing paper with the necessary barrier properties; we have implemented one that is selected for its full biodegradability. It combines a biodegradable water- based polymer film with inorganic nanoscale coatings made with a plasma deposition method (PECVD). The water-based polymer coatings have good barrier properties but are naturally water-soluble. Our PECVD process uses a silicon-containing chemistry and provides a coating that improves both waterproofness, as well as oxygen and moisture barriers. Therefore, it has become possible to obtain oxygen and moisture penetration sufficiently low for food packaging by combining the two methods.

In this study we used a commercially available water-soluble biodegradable polymer that is a high performance modified PVOH (water-soluble EVOH) HR-3010 with viscosity of 12-16 mPa·s. The liquid coating film was applied by either spray coating or immersing the moulded paper objects in the solution. The SEM image of the coating can be seen in Figure 4.

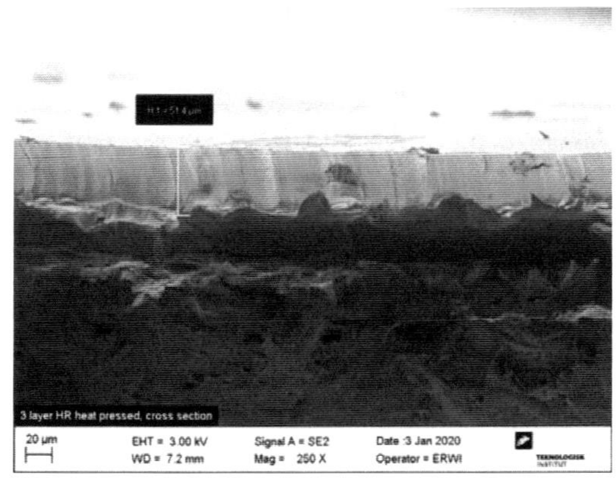

Figure 4 *SEM cross-sectional image of a 50 µm-thick primary liquid coating on the moulded paper substrate.*

The coating has an exceptionally fast biodegradation rate comparative to cellulose, and a perfect oxygen barrier of 380 ml·µm/(m²·day). Unfortunately, since this material is water-soluble, it loses its oxygen barrier by increasing humidity, and its moisture barrier is not sufficient for most food packaging applications.

In order to improve barrier performance and protect the primary liquid coating, pre-coated paper trays were additionally coated by a stratified 100-500-nm-thick plasma (PECVD) coating. PECVD coating was obtained in a laboratory vacuum chamber at a pressure of less than 10-1 mbar using a 13.56 MHz RF plasma of 50-300 W. The PECVD process is optimized for deposition of silica-related films. Hexamethyldisiloxane (HMDSO) has been used as a precursor gas. Plasma chemical conversion of HMDSO should theoretically follow the reaction for full degradation and oxidation of HMDSO, leading to the formation of a coating of pure (glass-like) silica:

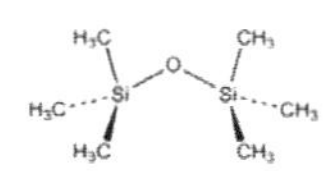
$$+12O_2 \rightarrow 2SiO_2+6CO_2+9H_2O$$

Hexamethyldisiloxane
HMDSO

However, the reaction products are affected by oxygen concentration in the plasma chamber.

An excess concentration of oxygen leads to a (glass-like) coating of silica without any remaining carbon atoms. Lack of oxygen leads to the formation of a silicone-like (polymer) coating containing a significant amount of carbon atoms. This is illustrated in Figure 5.

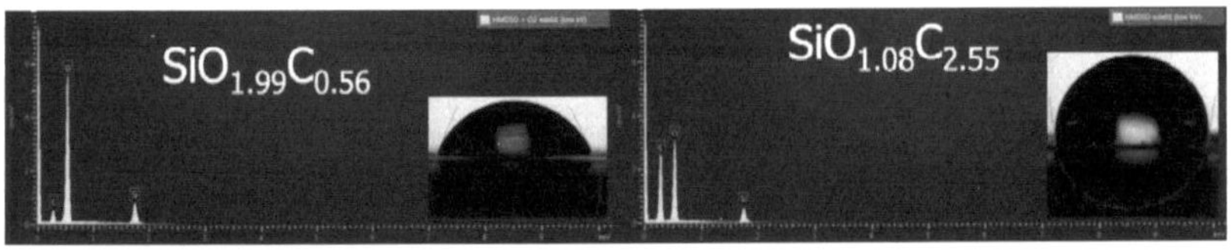

Material	Water	n-hexadecane
PP	96 ± 1	35 ± 2
$SiO_{1.08}C_{2.55}$	98 ± 2	29 ± 2
$SiO_{1.99}C_{0.56}$	65 ± 1	11 ± 2

Figure 5 *The results of XPS (X-ray photoelectron spectroscopy) and EDX (energy dispersive X-ray spectroscopy) analyses of the coatings (top) combined with measurements of water contact angle measured in degrees and compared to polypropylene (PP) (bottom).*

SiO_2 / $SiO_xC_yH_z$ coatings (x = 0.5 → 1.99, y = 4.0 → 0.5)	
x < 1.5	1.5 < x < 1.99
Polymer (silicone)-like	Glass (silica)-like
Poly(dimethylsiloxane) (PDMS)	Silicon dioxide (SiO_2)
Soft and elastic	Hard and brittle
Hydrophobic	Hydrophilic
Reduces oxygen permeation	Reduces both moisture and oxygen permeation

Figure 6 *Physical properties of the two kinds of plasma coating.*

Depending on the stoichiometry of the coating, the physical properties are almost opposite to each other, as shown in the table in Figure 6. Their barrier properties are also very different from one another: the polymer-like coatings reduce oxygen permeability, while the glass-like coatings improve both oxygen and moisture barriers as the enhancements are more than an order of magnitude compared to pre-coated molded cellulose samples.

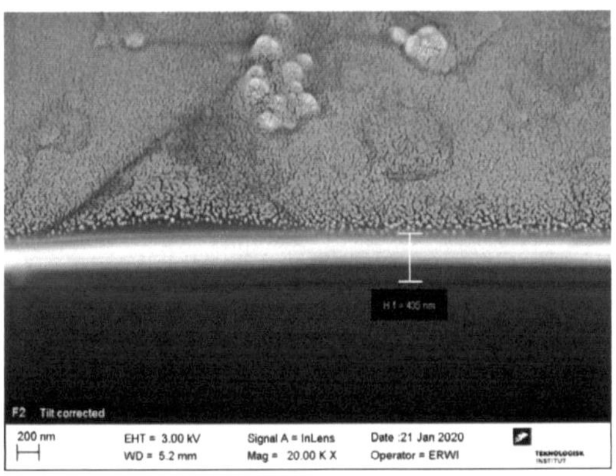

Figure 7 *4-layered sandwich-like PECVD barrier coating.*

The synthesized plasma coating used in this study comprised two hard (silica-like) layers with low barrier penetrability of $scCO_2$ interleaved with highly penetrable soft (silicone-like) layers. The structure of this coating is shown in Figure 7 in an SEM image obtained after profiling of the surface by focused ion beam sputtering.

The OTR and WVTR of the trays with deposited liquid and plasma coating was measured by Mocon OX-tran 2/22 and Mocon Permatran W 3/34. The measurement setup is shown in Figure 8.

The OTR was measured to be 0.08-0.09 ml/(m^2·day) and the WVTR to be 0.2 g/(m^2·day), both at 23°C and 50% RH. These values are far lower than the requirements for almost any food product by a factor of 100 for oxygen and a factor of at least 10 for moisture. This leaves a large margin for deterioration during $scCO_2$ impregnation of antimicrobial compounds into the tray, where the coatings still would provide an adequate barrier post-processing.

Figure 8 *Mocon OX-tran in the process of measuring permeation rates of coated trays.*

4. Impregnation with an antimicrobial compound

We chose thyme oil as an active antimicrobial agent, which contains the active substance thymol. This was to be impregnated into the coated trays using the supercritical CO_2 system shown in Figure 9. A beaker containing different amounts of thymol was initially lowered into the pressure chamber and a simple net was placed above it to prevent direct contact of the oil with the trays, which were then lowered into the chamber (Figure 9, right). Thereupon, the trays were impregnated with controlled amounts of thymol in the range of 1.5-40 mg/cm^2. The coated cellulose trays have a very high absorption capacity.

The impregnation did not cause any physical damage to the trays, judged by visual inspection. As for the degradation of the barrier performance of the packaging due to the high-pressure impregnation process, it was assessed by OTR and WVTR that followed it. These measurements showed that the OTR was increased to 10-15 ml/(m2·day) and the WVTR to 5-10 g/(m2·day), both at 23°C and 50% RH (Figure 10). Thus, the increase in amount of thymol impregnated into the trays causes a more pronounced degradation of the barrier towards oxygen than to water vapour.

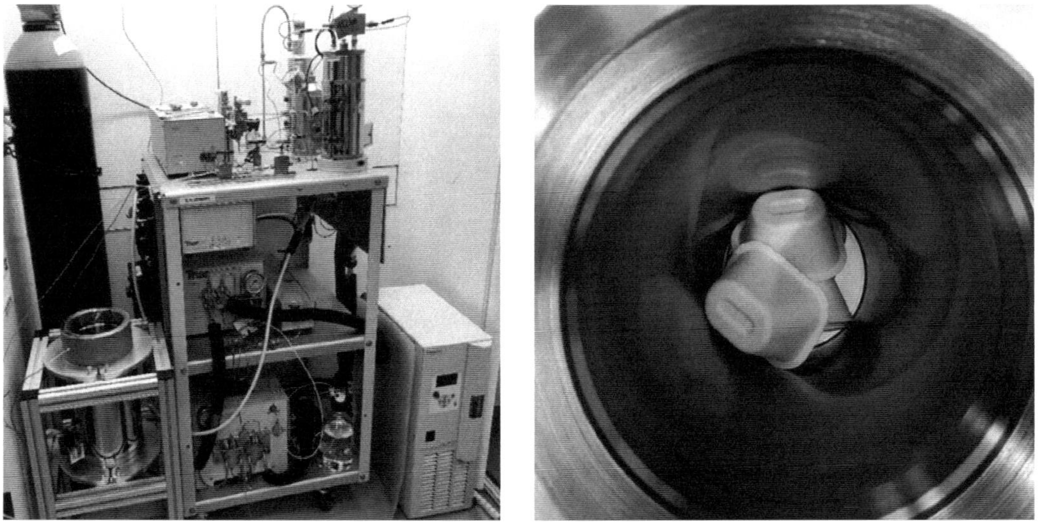

Figure 9 Left, $scCO_2$ setup with pressure chamber seen in top right corner. Right, top view into the pressure chamber with trays visible.

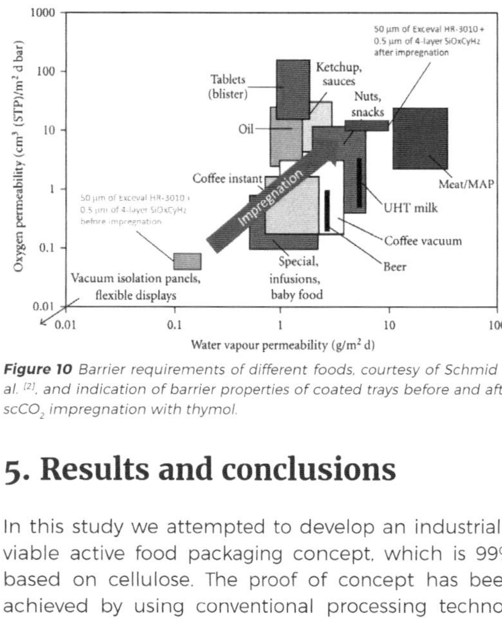

Figure 10 Barrier requirements of different foods, courtesy of Schmid et al. [2], and indication of barrier properties of coated trays before and after $scCO_2$ impregnation with thymol.

5. Results and conclusions

In this study we attempted to develop an industrially viable active food packaging concept, which is 99% based on cellulose. The proof of concept has been achieved by using conventional processing technologies: wet-moulding of cellulose, deposition of liquid and plasma barrier coatings, and impregnation with volatile species by using supercritical CO^2.

It was shown that the barrier performance of a composition of liquid and plasma coatings is so high (Figure 10) that even after high-pressure impregnation treatment they remain adequately low for use in packaging of such barrier-requiring products as fresh and processed meat, cheese, etc.

The achieved impregnated amounts of antimicrobial species were at the same time adequately high to provide for the necessary activity of the packaging against both yeast and mycelial fungi.

Experiments are ongoing to test the antimicrobial effect of the packaging on perishable products such as pâté, sliced sausage, cheese in shredded and block formats, and refrigerated ready-meals. The results will be reported elsewhere.

Acknowledgements

This study was supported by grants from Danish Technological Institute's performance contracts 2019-2020

- B4 (High-value plastic - Recycling and sustainable substitution)
- F2 (Food quality and convenience - Value for money)
- G2 (Bio-based business - Valorization of biomass)

entered with the Danish Agency for Institutions and Educational Grants under The Ministry of Higher Education and Science of Denmark.

References

[1] Kirilov K, Bardenstein A, Landa S, Petersen J, Delagoutte T and Mas O. 2019. Flexible Low-Batch Size Manufacturing of Molded Paper Packaging with Barrier. Proceedings of 29th IAPRI Symposium on Packaging.

[2] Schmid M, Dallman K, Bugnicourt E et al. 2012. Properties of Whey-Protein-Coated Films and Laminates as Novel Recyclable Food Packaging Materials with Excellent Barrier Properties. Intern. J. Polymer Sci. ID 562381, doi:10.1155/2012/562381.

Evaluation of two intelligent packaging prototypes with a pH indicator to determine spoilage of cow milk [75]

Ana Romero *, Kay Cooksey *
Clemson University, Clemson, SC

Abstract:
Introduction: Intelligent packaging utilizes chemical sensors to identify the quality and determine the safety of packaged cow milk for consumers. In the future, such intelligent packaging will reduce food waste and assist in reducing foodborne illnesses related to spoiled cow milk.

Purpose: To evaluate cow milk packaged in two different prototypes of intelligent packaging during the cow milk's shelf life based on volatile compounds, pH, color change, and sensory characteristics.

Methods: For this evaluation, two intelligent packaging prototypes (high-density polyethylene with a color indicator based on the pH) were filled with cow milk (Grade A, whole). The whole cow milk samples from the intelligent packages were prepared in triplicates. Measurements and sensory panels were performed during the shelf life of the cow milk samples, over four separate days. For the cow milk samples, Gas Chromatography-Mass Spectometry was used to identify and quantify the volatile compounds (n=36) and the pH was determined by a pH meter (n=36). The color change of the bottle was measured using the Minolta L*a*b* colorimeter (n=36). Thirty-two panelists from Clemson University (18 males and 14 females between 18 and 42 years of age) evaluated the samples.

Results: The color change of the intelligent packages was expected to activate upon change in pH level. There were significant differences ($p < 0.05$) in pH levels and color change. The panelists of the sensory panel preferred the cow milk that was packaged in one of intelligent packages to the other, due to a significant difference ($p < 0.05$) in color and appearance, aroma, and overall acceptability. The volatile compounds were analyzed over the four different days of experimentation during shelf life.

Significance: Intelligent packaging systems provide consumers with reliable and accurate information concerning the conditions of the food they are consuming (e.g. food spoilage), reduce food waste, and can prevent foodborne illnesses.

Keywords: intelligent packaging, smart packaging, food packaging, milk packaging
Packaging, spoilage indicator, food waste, food safety

***Correspondence to:** Ana Romero, Kay Cooksey. E-Mail: acromer@g.clemson.edu, kcookse@clemson.edu

Encapsulation Efficiency of Hexanal in Cyclodextrin Metal-Organic Framework for Active Packaging [79]

Ajay Kathuria *1, Travis Lang 2, Trevor Harding 2
1 Industrial Technology and Packaging, California Polytechnic State University, San Luis Obispo, CA, USA
2 Materials Engineering, California Polytechnic State University, San Luis Obispo, CA, USA

Abstract: Aliphatic acids, aldehydes, alcohols and ethers have been widely studied for antifungal and antimicrobial activity. Acids and aldehydes have been as most active groups. Various researchers studied the structure-antimicrobial activity relationship of such active species. It was observed that the order of antimicrobial activity follows the order of aldehydes>ketones>alcohols. Hexanal; an antimicrobial C6 aldehyde; is generally regarded as safe (GRAS) low molecular weight fruity flavor, however it has cytotoxic potential at elevated concentrations.

Porous materials have been widely studied for encapulation and release of active species for packaging application. This study is examining the encapsulation efficiency of hexanal in γ-cyclodextrin metal organic frameworks (γ-CDMOFs) as a mechanism for potential active packaging applications. γ-CDMOFs were synthesized by vapor diffusion process. Hexanal was encapsulated within the γ-CDMOFs using vapor diffusion process. The synthesized γ-CDMOFs were characterized both before and after the encapsulation of hexanal using x-ray diffraction (XRD), scanning electron microscopy (SEM), and thermogravimetric analysis (TGA). XRD characterization results matched literature values which confirmed uniform γ-CDMOF crystallinity and a successful synthesis. SEM images were used as an additional confirmation of the γ-CDMOF crystallinity which matched those of previous γ-CDMOF structures. TGA characterization results revealed an encapsulation efficiency of about 5%.

Keywords: active packaging, hexanal, encapsulation, metal-organic framework.

***Correspondence to:** Ajay Kathuria. E-Mail: akathuri@calpoly.edu

1. Introduction

Plants release volatile compounds as a natural defense mechanism under abiotic or biotic stress. Aliphatic acids, aldehydes, alcohols and ethers have been widely studied for antifungal activity [1-4]. Acids and aldehydes have been as most active groups [2]. Hexanal; an antimicrobial natural C6 aldehyde; is generally regarded as safe (GRAS) low molecular weight compound with fruity flavor and it is an approved flavor enhancer. Hexanal has been applied to various climacteric fruits to pre-harvesting and post-harvest to enhance freshness and to reduce post-harvest losses respectively. As observed with other aldehydes hexanal can oxidize to hexanoic acid.

Encapsulation of these volatile compoiunds into porous material is well estabished techchnquie to stabilize them, in addition it provides extended relase essential for commercialization of such molecules in packaging industry.Pore size and pore distribution of the porous materials play important role in payload capacity and controlling the release kinetics. Larger pore size molecules release the encapsulated species at faster rate than smaller molecules. As compared to CD, higher payload, sustained release kinetics.

2. Research Goals / Objectives

The goals of this project are to synthesize and confirm a successful synthesis of γ-cyclodextrin metal organic frameworks (γ-CDMOFs) through vapor diffusion as well as to investigate the encapsulation potential of hexanal in γ-CDMOFs. The purpose of the encapsulation of hexanal in γ-CDMOFs is for potential active packaging applications as a method to extend the shelf life of fruits and vegetables.

3. Research Method

γ-CDMOF crystals were synthesized using vapor diffusion of methanol into a solution of γ-CD and KOH. The γ-CDMOF crystals were activated in a low temperature oven to remove residual methanol and water as well as to open up the pores of the γ-CDMOF prior to encapsulation. XRD and SEM were used to characterize the γ-CDMOF crystallinity which was compared against literature results. After activation, hexanal was encapsulated within the γ-CDMOF crystals for 48 hours and characterized using TGA and XRD to determine the encapsulation efficiency.

4. Results and conclusions

Figure 1 shows the XRD diffractogram produced by the hexanal encapsulated γ-CDMOFs. The peaks observed from the previous diffractogram of the γ-CDMOFs prior to hexanal encapsulation were significantly decreased which suggests the possibility interference by the hexanal molecules with the diffreaction of X-rays.

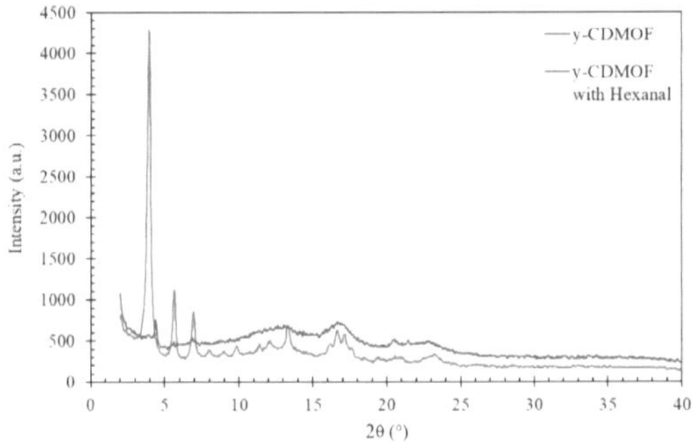

Figure 1 *XRD diffractograms of γ-CDMOFs before and after encapsulation of hexanal.*

Figure 2 shows the SEM micrograph produced by the γ-CDMOFs prior to encapsulation of hexanal. The image was used to evaluate the crystallinity of the γ-CDMOFs to confirm the results of XRD and that a successful synthesis had taken place. The size, shape, and physical appearance of the γ-CDMOFs were comparable to micrographs found in previous literature.

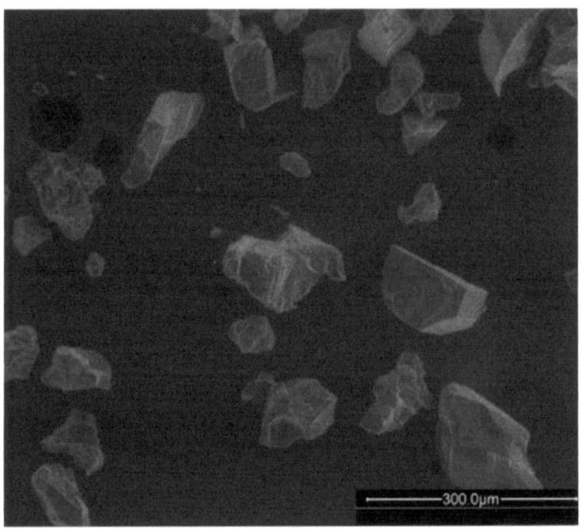

Figure 2 *SEM micrograph of γ-CDMOFs prior to encapsulation of hexanal.*

Figure 3 shows the TGA thermograms of the γ-CDMOFs before and after the encapsulation of hexanal.

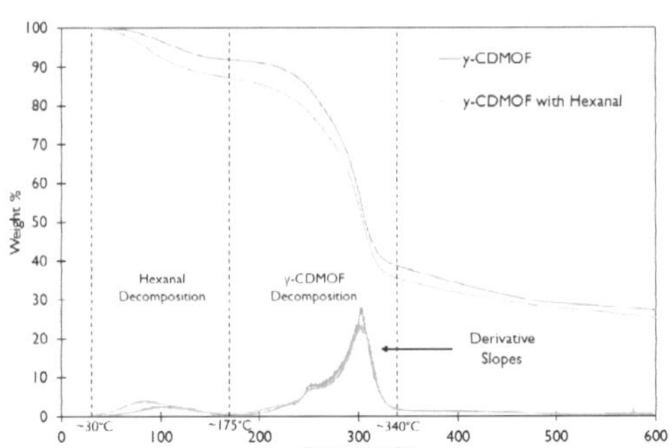

Figure 3 *TGA thermograms of γ-CDMOFs before and after encapsulation of hexanal.*

Using the weight % of the thermogram curves, based on the difference in weight % of the curves, that the hexanal had an encapsulation efficiency in the γ-CDMOFs of about 5%.

5. Future Research

To evaluative the release kinetics of Hexanal and study the shelf-life extension of various fresh commodities/produce.

6. References

[1] AndersenR.A., Hamilton-Kemp T. R., Hildebrand D.F., McCracken C. T, Collins R.W., Fleming P.D. Structure-Antifungal Activity Relationships Among Volatile C6 and C9 Aliphatic Aldehydes, Ketones and Alcohols. Journal of Agricultural Food Chemistry 1994; 42: 1563-1568.

[2] Maruzzella J.C., Chiaramonte J.S., Garofalo M. Effects of Vapors of Aromatic Chemicals on Fungi. Journal of Pharmaceutical Sciences 1961 50 (8); 665-668.

[3] Shantini D., Nainggolan I., Nasution T. I., Derman M. N., Mustaffa R, Wahab N.Z.A. Hexanal Gas Detection using Chitosan Biopolymer as Sensing Material at Room Temperature. Journal of Sensors 2016, 8539169(1-7).

[4] Sahidi F and Pegg R.B. Hexanal as an indicator of the flavor deterioration of meat and meat products.

Incorporation of orange blossom essential oil (Citrus aurantium) in polyethylene films to fabricate antimicrobial active packaging for corn tortillas [81]

Ibarra-Valenzuela, A. P.; Islas-Rubio, A. R.; López-Ortiz, D.; Peralta, E.; Silva-Espinoza, B. A.; Soto-Valdez *, H; Troncoso-Rojas, R.

Research Center for Food and Development
Centro de Investigación en Alimentación y Desarrollo, A.C. (CIAD)
Hermosillo, Sonora, México.

Abstract: During the extrusion processing of plastic antimicrobial active packaging, degradation of the active compounds is unavoidable due to the heat applied to soften the polymer and additives. The coating process is an alternative that diminish this loss. In this work, the effect of the coating and extrusion processes on the preservation of the main component (linalool) of an orange blossom essential oil (Citrus aurantium) extract, incorporated to a polyethylene film, was evaluated. The films were tested in corn tortilla, a staple and perishable food in Mexico. Films were blown extruded with addition of the essential oil (E film) and the remaining linalool was quantified. Control film was produced by the same process with no addition of the essential oil (C film). A batch of the control film was varnished with a solution of essential oil (V film) and the remaining linalool was quantified. After the extrusion, only 22.7% of the linalool remained in the E film. Otherwise, after the coating, 64.2% of the linalool remained in the V film. To assess the antimicrobial effect, a second lot of E and V films was produced adding the exact concentration of the essential oil in order to obtain a similar final concentration of linalool in both active films. Tortillas were packed (triplicates) in E, V and C films and stored for 30 days at 5 °C. The total count of aerobic mesophyll bacteria and molds/yeasts in the tortilla in the active films was significantly reduced compared to that in the C films. The shelf life was extended by 53 and 66% in the E and V films, compared to the C films. The essential oil added to the V films was about a half of that added to the E films, confirming the feasibility of the coating process.

Keywords: antimicrobial active packaging, orange blossom essential oil, corn tortillas, shelf life.

***Correspondence to:** Herlinda Soto-Valdez. E-Mail: hsoto@ciad.mx

Evaluation of the Potential of Functionalised Calcium Carbonate as Carrier for Essential Oils with regard to Antimicrobial Packaging Applications [90]

Nadine Rüegg [1], Barbara Maria Beck [1], Fabien Wilhelm Monnard [2], Florentine Marianne Hilty [2], Aurore Wicht [2], Joachim Schoelkopf [2], Selçuk Yildirim [1]

1 Life Sciences and Facility Management, Zurich University of Applied Sciences, Campus Reidbach, 8820 Waedenswil, Switzerland
2 Omya International AG, Baslerstrasse, 4665 Oftringen, Switzerland

Abstract: To Functionalised calcium carbonates (FCCs) are inorganic mineral-based particles with a high porosity and extended surface area consisting of hydroxyapatite and calcium carbonate crystal structures. Therefore, FCCs have a high potential to be used as a carrier for active substances such as essential oils (EOs), which are well known for their antimicrobial activities, and control their release in antimicrobial packaging applications. In this study different EOs were loaded on FCCs and their antimicrobial activities were studied against L. innocua in in-vitro tests and in food tests using sliced cooked chicken breast. FCCs loaded with thyme or oregano EO (10 wt%) showed the highest reduction in microbial load in in-vitro tests at 37°C (≥ 8.6 log cfu/ filter) as well as at 7°C after 6 days (≥ 7.0 log cfu/ filter for thyme EO and 6.5 log cfu/ filter for oregano EO). However, in food tests FCC loaded with either EO did not show any significant antimicrobial activity. FCCs loaded with cinnamon or rosemary EO (10 wt%) did not show any significant antimicrobial activity in in-vitro tests. On the other hand, they showed a significant reduction in microbial load (1.7 log cfu/g for cinnamon and 2 log cfu/g for rosemary) in food tests. Differences in antimicrobial activities in in-vitro and food tests are probably due to the interaction of the components of the EOs and the components of the food such as fat and proteins.

Keywords: functionalised calcium carbonate, essential oils, active packaging, antimicrobial packaging, sliced cooked chicken breast

PTS Special Edition: https://onlinelibrary.wiley.com/doi/full/10.1002/pts.2508

*Correspondence to: Nadine Rüegg, Life Sciences and Facility Management, Zurich University of Applied Sciences, Campus Reidbach, 8820 Waedenswil, Switzerland. E-mail: renk@zhaw.ch

SANTIAGO PUEBLO MAGICO
502
3

CHAPTER VI
Packaging design & innovations

Author:
Turismo NL/OCV MONTERREY

Location:
Villa de Santiago, NUEVO LEÓN

Description:
Going to Villa de Santiago on the weekend is a way of stepping back in time. Everything is more relaxing, more charming... the food reminds us of our grandma's cooking and the crafts market that sets up outside the church makes us appreciate how inventive and creative people can be.

Development of a Heuristic Guide for Packaging Design [70]

Javier de la Fuente *1, Sonia Ibarreche Domínguez 2, Irene Carbonell 1
1 Industrial Technology and Packaging, California Polytechnic State University, California, USA
2 Universidad de Monterrey, NL, Mexico

Abstract: A heuristic evaluation is a type of inspection technique utilized to analyze and assess a product using a heuristic guide. It involves a small set of expert evaluators who examine the product and evaluate its compliance with recognized design principles (i.e., heuristics). Heuristic evaluations are a cost-efficient method to help identify problems before evaluations with users.

A review of the literature reveals the lack of heuristic guides for new packaging development projects and the evaluation of existing packaged products. This study's objective was to fill this knowledge gap by developing a comprehensive heuristic guide that individuals could use, regardless of their level of packaging expertise.

The study was divided into two phases: guide design and testing. The guide design phase involved identifying design characteristics of packages and refining their description to make them focused, easily understandable, and universally applicable. It required several iterations of refining and grouping. The second phase consisted of testing the heuristics with two panels of evaluators. The heuristic guide was converted into a 5-point Likert scale questionnaire. A group of ten packaging professionals with three levels of expertise (i.e., novice, intermediate, expert) used the evaluation guide to evaluate six packaged products. Qualitative feedback from the evaluators was used to improve the guide. Quantitative data from the questionnaire was used to determine if the evaluator's experience had an impact on the evaluations. A second round of testing was conducted using a panel of nine industry professionals and a new set of packaged products. Again, qualitative information was collected to improve the guide.

The resulting heuristic guide has 50 design characteristics grouped into three main areas, one for each packaging function: protection (three sub-areas, 17 heuristics), utility (three sub-areas, 19 heuristics), and communication (four sub-areas, 14 heuristics). Results from the questionnaires did not show significant differences based on the level of evaluator expertise. Qualitative feedback allowed researchers to refine design characteristics and their wording. Industry professionals expressed interest in this innovative tool.

Keywords: Packaging engineering, packaging development, heuristic guide, heuristic evaluation, innovation

***Correspondence to:** Javier de la Fuente, Industrial Technology and Packaging, California Polytechnic State University, California, USA. E-mail: jdelafue@calpoly.edu

1. Introduction

The origin of the term "heuristic" is connected to the ancient Greek word heúriskein (εὑρισκειν) which mean "to find" or "to discover." [1] It is used to describe both the approach to learning by "trial-by-error" and the use of the general knowledge gained by experience, sometimes expressed as "using a rule-of-thumb." The interjection Eureka!, which means "I have found it!," has the same etymology. The Greek term heúrēka (εὑρηκα) is attributed to Archimedes and used to celebrate a discovery or an invention.

According to Pearl (1984), heuristic refers to the strategies that use current, limited information to guide the search of solutions in problem-solving situations.[2] Newell and Simon (1972) pioneered the use of the concept in the field of cognitive psychology to describe simple processes that replace complex algorithms.[3] More recently, Shah and Oppenheimer (2008) proposed that a heuristic works as an effort-reduction principle that allows people to make judgments fast and efficiently by considering less information while performing a task. [4] Although heuristics are quite helpful and practical in many situations, they may also cause cognitive biases as a result of simplifying information processing. [5]

In the field of user experience and design, a heuristic evaluation is a type of inspection technique used to analyze and assess a particular design using a heuristic guide.[6] An evaluator is guided by an empirically derived list of design guidelines (i.e., the heuristics) asking how well each of these rules of thumb is followed in the product being evaluated. Heuristic evaluations are inexpensive, intuitive, and easy to encourage professionals to do. They are especially useful early in the design process [7], [8] and for analyzing products already in the marketplace.

Nielsen conceived this type of inspections for usability evaluations of computer interfaces before the Internet became ubiquitous (i.e., software). [9] Molich and Nielsen (1990) proposed the first set of heuristics for computer interfaces in the early nineties. [10], [11] Subsequently, Nielsen (1994) used factor analysis and a large database of usability problems to derive a new and improved set of heuristics that are being used today for user interface design in general. [12], [13] They are as follows:

· Visibility of system status
· Match between system and the real world
· User control and freedom
· Consistency and standards
· Error prevention
· Recognition rather than recall
· Flexibility and efficiency of use
· Aesthetic and minimalist design
· Help users recognize, diagnose, and recover from errors
· Help and documentation

The flexibility and wide-ranging characteristics of Nielsen's guidelines have enabled their application to web design and mobile application design. However, researchers have argued recently that the mobile paradigm requires new heuristics. [14], [15] Given the popularization of smart mobile devices and the importance of usability in mobile software applications, researchers have proposed a set of heuristics for mobile applications by considering three usability theory pillars: user, task, and context of use. [14]

Heuristic evaluation's origins are closely related to usability evaluations. However, they can be used for evaluating any product on different dimensions, not just usability. An evaluator just needs the right heuristic guide to do it and basic domain-specific knowledge (e.g., web, mobile, appliances, furniture, vehicles, packaging, etc.).

The main goal of this study was to develop a comprehensive heuristic guide that could be used by packaging professionals and students, regardless of their level of expertise, to analyze existing packaging systems and create new packaging concepts. [16] In either case, the guide would help packaging professionals and students to discover areas of opportunities and for improvement.

2. Materials and Methods

The development of the packaging heuristic guide was divided into two phases:

· Phase I: Guide design
· Phase II: Guide testing

2.1 Phase I: Guide Design

The guide design phase involved identifying a general framework for packaging and packaging design characteristics. Next, design characteristics were translated into brief heuristic items. Heuristics' descriptions were refined to make them focused, easily understandable, and universally applicable. The process required several iterations of refining and grouping.

Packaging Functions Framework

The first challenge was to find a way to categorize heuristics in an organized whole that would make sense. Different frameworks for organizing and classifying the most typical packaging functions were reviewed.

Lockhart (1997) recommended a radical simplification of the packaging functions consisting of three broad categories: protection, utility, and communication. [17] Cervera Fantoni (2003) highlights six areas: product containment, presentation and identification, protection, preservation, transportation, and added-value. [18] Smith and Taylor (2004) proposed three primary functions of packaging: protect (and contain), offer convenience, and communicate. [19] Soroka (2009) lists four packaging functions in his classic book on packaging technology, namely, contain, protect/preserve, transport, and inform/sell. [20] On two separate chapters about food packaging applications, Yam [21] (2009) and Robertson [22] (2012) compromised on four functions: containment, protection, convenience, and communication. Surprisingly, these two authors claim to explain Lockhart's model, but they add a containment function, which Lockhart explicitly classified under the utility function.

As can be seen, defining packaging functions may look trivial and obvious, but it entails important technical and semantic considerations. Good classifications have categories that are clearly defined, exhaustive, and mutually exclusive.

Lockhart's paradigm has several hidden innovations. In his model, protection goes both ways. It is not only about physical protection of the contents but also about protecting the environment from the product and the package system. Under this classification, preservation, a critical function needed for some foods, beverages, and drugs, can be thought of as a type of protection.

Lockhart's utility function encompasses a diverse array of basic functions such as containment, and other added-value features, for example allowing aseptic presentation in medical device packaging. [23] Although some authors consider containment a separate function, we argue that containment is a utilitarian function not always present in packaging systems. In fact, there are many examples of packaging systems that do not contain a product, but rather hold or keep an item or several of them together (i.e., socks, scissors, tools). Considering containment a separate packaging function creates an unbalanced classification, were containment rests narrow-focused and non-mutually exclusive to utility. This is a semantic discussion, but it is critical for a comprehensive model and forward-thinking view of packaging system.

Lockhart's communication function is remarkable, as well. It can include the usual suspects (i.e., promoting and selling the product), any printed information, and the often-forgotten aspects of communication for functionality (i.e., affordances) [24] and product identification.

Lockhart's model is strikingly simple, yet the most powerful of all reviewed. It works for present applications, but it is open to future innovations, concepts, and needs. Lockhart's model is robust, flexible, and, most importantly, comprehensive. It can be adapted to any industry by listing subordinated areas under the three main areas. Since the packaging heuristic guide needed flexibility and future adaptability, we chose Lockhart's framework for organizing the heuristic items.

Packaging Design Considerations

For each of the three functional areas (i.e., protection, utility, and communication), a series of general design considerations were listed. Design considerations allowed researchers to create sub-areas within each functional area and to identify individual heuristics.

A. Protection Area

• Physical and chemical properties of the contents
The physical and chemical properties of the contents dictate which barrier properties are needed in the packaging material to keep the contents in optimal condition during a reasonable period (i.e., shelf-life).

• Durability and hazards during distribution and shipping
Materials should ensure the durability of the package system throughout the distribution chain (from its manufacture, distribution center, point of sale, e-commerce, until it reaches the consumer) the product will go through once packaged, to determine possible hazards. Risks may include shock from impacts, vibrations, abrasion, crushing, gas permeation (e.g., oxygen, carbon dioxide, ethylene oxide), water vapor permeation, odors, temperature, and content/material migration.

• Security during distribution
The package system may need to provide anti-counterfeiting and tamper-evident features for the end consumer and other stakeholders.

• Environmental protection
The package system should protect the environment from the contents and the package system itself.

B. Utility

• Packaging line operations
Each component and the assembled package system should run smoothly in the packaging line. Packaging operations may include cleaning, labeling, filling, sealing, palletizing, loading, and so on.

• Distribution
The package system should provide good containment/holding of the contents. Each component and the assembled package system should have configurations, shapes, dimensions, and weights that optimize cube efficiency and minimize transportation costs per unit.

• Support user tasks physically
The packaging system should support the physical aspect of typical user tasks by allowing most of the users to perform those tasks with ease. Tasks may include purchasing, carrying, handling, stacking, counting, opening, reclosing, gripping, and dispensing.

• Easy open and reclosing
The packaging system should be easy to open and reclose for most of the population.

• Logical sequence for operation
The packaging system should be easy to use for most people by having a simple logical sequence of operations.

C. Communication

• Support user tasks cognitively
The packaging system should support the cognitive aspect of typical user tasks for most of the population by communicating its functionality with clear affordances.

• Differentiation and branding
The package system should differentiate itself from the competition by communicating the brand's positioning and brand's value uniquely. When applicable, the package should have the ability to be memorable for the consumer.

• Product identification
The package system should enable easy product identification (e.g., product type, product variety, size, model). This applies to different contexts of use, such as retail stores, the product library of a hospital, a pharmacy, or a warehouse.

• Clear and accurate information
The package system should provide clear and accurate information for different purposes, such as product identification, net weight, nutritional/drug facts, ingredients, directions, lot number, expiry date, and barcodes.

• Disposal information
The package system should provide information about materials and how to dispose of each component properly.

Design Heuristics

Design characteristics were translated into brief, more focused, heuristic items.

A. Protection Area

The protection area had 17 heuristics and was divided into three sub-areas:
A.1. Protection of the contents (five heuristics)
A.2. Protection during distribution (seven heuristics)
A.3. Protection of the environment (five heuristics)

"Protection of the contents" focuses on the protective characteristics of the product inside the package system. It includes heuristics related to preserving the contents and protection from a diversity of agents such as light, gases (e.g., oxygen, carbon dioxide), moisture, and microorganisms.

"Protection during distribution" focuses on the protection of the contents during distribution. Includes heuristics related to contents shifting, scratching and abrasion, shocks and drops, vibrations, crushing, temperature, and tampering.

"Protection of the environment" focuses on the potential end-of-life scenarios of the package system, such as composting, recycling, and re-using. It also contains items for ease of component separation and post-consumer recycled (PCR) content.

B. Utility Area

The utility area had 19 heuristics classified in three sub-areas:
B.1. Utility at the packaging line (four heuristics)
B.2. Utility during distribution (six heuristics)
B.3. Utility during usage (nine heuristics)

The first sub-area comprises requirements needed for basic packaging operations such as filling, closing/sealing, and labeling, and the ability of the packaging system to run through packaging machinery such as conveyor belts, cleaners, case erectors, fillers, cappers, sealers, labelers, and so on.

"Utility during distribution" contains heuristics to optimize shape, dimensions, and weight during the supply chain operations happening between the moment that the package system leaves the packager's plant until it reaches the consumer. It also includes the ability to stack the package system and transport its components in ways that reduce volume such as nesting and flattening.

Finally, the sub-area named "utility during usage" includes a series of inclusive design heuristics to ensure that most of the population will use the package with ease. These are the physical aspects of packaging ergonomics during product usage. It includes specific heuristics for typical tasks such as opening, reclosing, gripping, carrying, handling, and dispensing. [24] It also considers optimal dimensions, shape, and combined weight of package and contents. The combination of these heuristics provides flexible means to assess specific functional characteristics of packages such as providing child-resistance for hazardous products and drugs [25] or allowing aseptic presentation for medical device packaging that requires it. [16]

For heuristics related to ergonomics design considerations, their written language reminds the evaluator about being inclusive by considering the broadest segments of the population and recognizing their diversity regarding cognitive and physical abilities. Terms such as "anyone" and "minimal effort" have that role in the wording of those heuristics.

C. Communication Area

The communication area had 14 heuristics organized in four sub-areas:
C.1. Brand identity (three heuristics)
C.2. Product identification (three heuristics)
C.3. Embedded information (four heuristics)
C.4. Functional communication (four heuristics)

The first communication sub-area deals with two key "brand identity" elements (e.g., brand positioning and the brand's values) and differentiation from competing products.

The second sub-area focuses on "product identification" requirements such as communicating the type of product it contains and its variety or flavor, being able to be found easily at the point of sale (i.e., shopability), and the ability of the package system to show the contents without opening it.

The third communication area deals with "embedded information". This sub-area refers to information printed or molded on the packaging system's components. It encompasses legible and understandable information for most of the population (e.g., net weight, count, nutrition facts, drug facts, directions), having readable codes (e.g., barcodes, QR codes, radio frequency identification tags, near field communication tags), and providing information related to materials and their disposal on each package component. For example, by adding molded marks with material identifiers in the package's components and/or adding information in the label such as the How2Recycle [26] smart label system in the United States.

Lastly, "functional communication" focuses primarily on the cognitive aspects of ergonomics during product usage. This includes understanding where and how to open the package system, how to use it, and how to manipulate it properly.

Results: Phase I

The main outcome of phase I was a comprehensive heuristic guide with 50 heuristics classified by functional areas and sub-areas (see Table 1).

Table 1 *Full list of heuristic items classified by areas and sub-areas. PS stands for packaging system.*

Area	Sub-Area	Heuristic Items
A. Protection	A.1. Protection of the contents	A.1.1. PS preserves the contents optimally
		A.1.2. PS protects contents from light
		A.1.3. PS protects contents from specific gases
		A.1.4. PS protects contents from moisture
		A.1.5. PS protects contents from microorganisms
	A.2. Protection during distribution	A.2.1. PS prevents contents from shifting
		A.2.2. PS protects contents from scuffing and abrasion
		A.2.3. PS protects contents from shocks and drops
		A.2.4. PS protects contents from vibrations
		A.2.5. PS protects contents from crushing
		A.2.6. PS keeps contents at the adequate temperature
		A.2.7. PS indicates if it has been tampered with
	A.3 Protection of the environment	A.3.1. PS is made with compostable materials
		A.3.2. PS is made with recyclable materials
		A.3.3. PS is made with recycled materials
		A.3.4. PS can be reused
		A.3.5. PS allows easy separation of components
B. Utility	B.1. Utility for the packaging line	B.1.1. PS can be filled easily
		B.1.2. PS runs with ease through the packaging line
		B.1.3. PS can be closed/sealed easily
		B.1.4. PS can be labeled easily
	B.2. Utility during distribution	B.2.1. PS' contains/holds the contents optimally
		B.2.2. PS' shape optimizes space utilization
		B.2.3. PS and contents' weights have been minimized
		B.2.4. PS' dimensions optimize space utilization
		B.2.5. PS can be stacked
		B.2.6. PS' components can be transported in compact configurations
	B.3. Utility during usage	B.3.1. PS can be opened by anyone with minimal effort
		B.3.2. PS can be reclosed by anyone with minimal effort
		B.3.3. PS can be gripped by anyone with minimal effort
		B.3.4. PS can be carried by anyone with minimal effort
		B.3.5. PS can be handled by anyone with minimal effort
		B.3.6. PS can be dispensed by anyone with minimal effort
		B.3.7. PS' shape is optimal for its intended use
		B.3.8. PS' dimensions are optimal for its intended use
		B.3.9. PS and contents' weights are optimal for its intended use
C. Communication	C.1. Brand identity	C.1.1. PS communicates brand positioning clearly
		C.1.2. PS differentiates itself from its competitors
		C.1.3. PS conveys the brand's values
	C.2. Product Identification	C.2.1. PS communicates the type of product that it contains/holds
		C.2.2. PS allows for easy identification of variety or flavor
		C.2.3. PS allows seeing the contents without opening it
	C.3. Embedded information	C.3.1. PS' printed information is legible for anyone
		C.3.2. PS' printed information is understandable for anyone
		C.3.3. PS' codes can be scanned easily
		C.3.4. PS' components indicate its material type and how to dispose it
	C.4. Functional communication	C.4.1. Anyone can understand from where to open the PS easily
		C.4.2. Anyone can understand how to open the PS easily
		C.4.3. Anyone can understand how to use the PS easily
		C.4.4. Anyone can understand how to manipulate the PS easily

2.2 Phase II: Guide Testing

The second phase consisted of testing the heuristics with two panels of evaluators (i.e., panel I and II). Panel I was used primarily to determine the effect of the evaluator's level of experience on the package's assessments. Panel II was used to gather input and feedback to improve the heuristic guide.

Evaluation Guide

The list of heuristic items was converted into an evaluation guide that was administered as a digital questionnaire (Google Forms by Google Inc., Mountain View, California, USA). [27] The same evaluation guide was used for both evaluator panels. In the evaluation guide, each heuristic item had a 5-point Likert scale (1 = strongly disagree, 2 = disagree, 3 = neutral, 4 = agree, 5 = strongly agree), space for comments, and a "not applicable" option. The guide had an introduction in which the evaluator was asked to indicate her/his level of agreement with each statement (i.e., the heuristics). After each package evaluation, there were two open-ended questions. One question asked if the evaluator thought that the evaluation guide missed any aspect of the package. The second question solicited if there was something that she/he would like to change and why. The questionnaire ended with questions about gender, age, job title, and years of experience in the packaging industry.

Participants: Panel I

A panel of ten packaging professionals with three levels of expertise (i.e., novice, intermediate, expert) used the evaluation guide to assess six packaged products (see Table 2). Novice was defined as having up to three years of packaging experience, having between three and ten years of experience was considered intermediate level, and expert level more than ten years of experience. Three novice (m = 1.5 years of experience, sd = 1.3 years) packaging professionals (all female, m = 25.0 years old, sd = 2.6 years old), four intermediate (m = 6.8 years of experience, sd = 2.5 years) packaging professionals (2 females, 2 males, m = 32.8 years old, sd = 3.5 years old), and three expert (m = 22.7 years of experience, sd = 2.1 years) professionals (all males, m = 48.7 years old, sd = 4.2 years old).

Table 2 *Characteristics of evaluators in panel I.*

Experience Level	ID	Experience (Years)	Gender	Age (Years)	Job Title
Novice	1	0.5	F	24	Product Designer
	2	3	F	28	Structural and Graphic Designer
	3	1	F	23	Packaging Engineer
Intermediate	4	7	M	31	Designer
	5	4	M	34	Professor
	6	6	F	29	Project Manager
	7	10	F	37	Packaging Engineer
Expert	8	22	M	50	Commercial Manager
	9	21	M	44	Director
	10	25	M	52	Packaging Engineer

Packages: Panel I

Six primary packages were selected from supermarkets located in Mexico City. Table 3 and Figure 1 summarize their characteristics. Each evaluator received a kit with the six products so that they could evaluate and experience them physically.

Table 3 *Characteristic of six packages provided to the evaluators in panel I.*

ID	Product Name	Brand	Size	Description
a	X Layers Menta	Trident	13.3 g (7 count)	- Chewing gum, mint flavor - Folding carton with paper and aluminum individual wraps
b	Crema S	Pond's	100 g (3.5 oz)	- Moisturizing cream - Plastic container with continuous threaded plastic lid
c	Leche de Magnesia	Normex by Perrigo	60 mL (2 fl oz)	- Milk of magnesia (8.5 g magnesium hydroxide suspension) - HDPE extrusion-blow-molded bottle with flip-top PP closure
d	Sal de ajo	Soriana	100 g (3.5 oz)	- Garlic salt - LDPE bag with paperboard header
e	Pinol Aromas	Pinol	828 mL (28 fl oz)	- Multipurpose cleaner - PET injection-blow molded bottle with continuous threaded PP closure
f	Agua	Mia by Jumex	1 L (33.8 fl oz)	- Water - PET injection-blow-molded bottle with continuous threaded PP closure

LDPE = Low density polyethylene, HDPE= High density polyethylene, PP = Polypropylene, PET = Polyethylene terephthalate

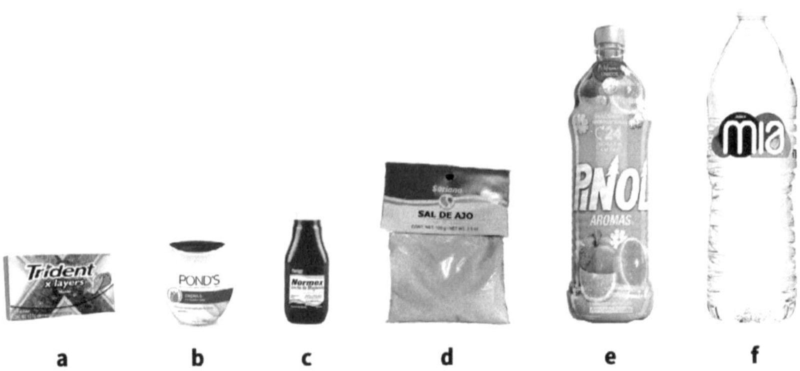

Figure 1 *Packages provided to the evaluators in panel I: a) Chewing gum, b) Moisturizing cream, c) Milk of magnesia, d) Garlic salt, e) Multipurpose cleaner, f) Water.*

Results: Panel I

Qualitative and quantitative data from 60 evaluations (i.e., ten evaluators, six packages) was analyzed to determine the effect of the evaluator's experience and effectiveness of the guide to find improvement opportunities.

Qualitative feedback from the evaluators was used to determine the guide's effectiveness to detect strengths and weaknesses. Table 4 summarizes the number of strengths and weaknesses found for each package (see Appendix A for specific details).

Table 4 *Number of strengths and weaknesses found by evaluators for each package.*

ID	Product Name	Brand	Description	Number of Strengths	Number of Weaknesses
a	X Layers Menta	Trident	Chewing gum	3	5
b	Crema S	Pond's	Moisturizing cream	7	2
c	Leche de Magnesia	Normex by Perrigo	Milk of magnesia	6	4
d	Sal de ajo	Soriana	Garlic salt	0	7
e	Pinol Aromas	Pinol	Multipurpose cleaner	6	2
f	Agua	Mia by Jumex	Water	3	7
Total				**25**	**27**

Quantitative data from the questionnaire was used to determine if the evaluator's experience had an impact on the evaluations. Responses were translated into a 1 to 5 scale, and a mean score for each area and each experience level was calculated (Figure 2). Data were analyzed with Prism version 8.4.3 (GraphPad Software LLC, San Diego, California, USA). Analyses of variance (ANOVA) were conducted to investigate whether and how the evaluator's experience related to package assessment. All comparisons were found not significant, suggesting that, on average, evaluators agreed on their assessment regardless of their expertise.

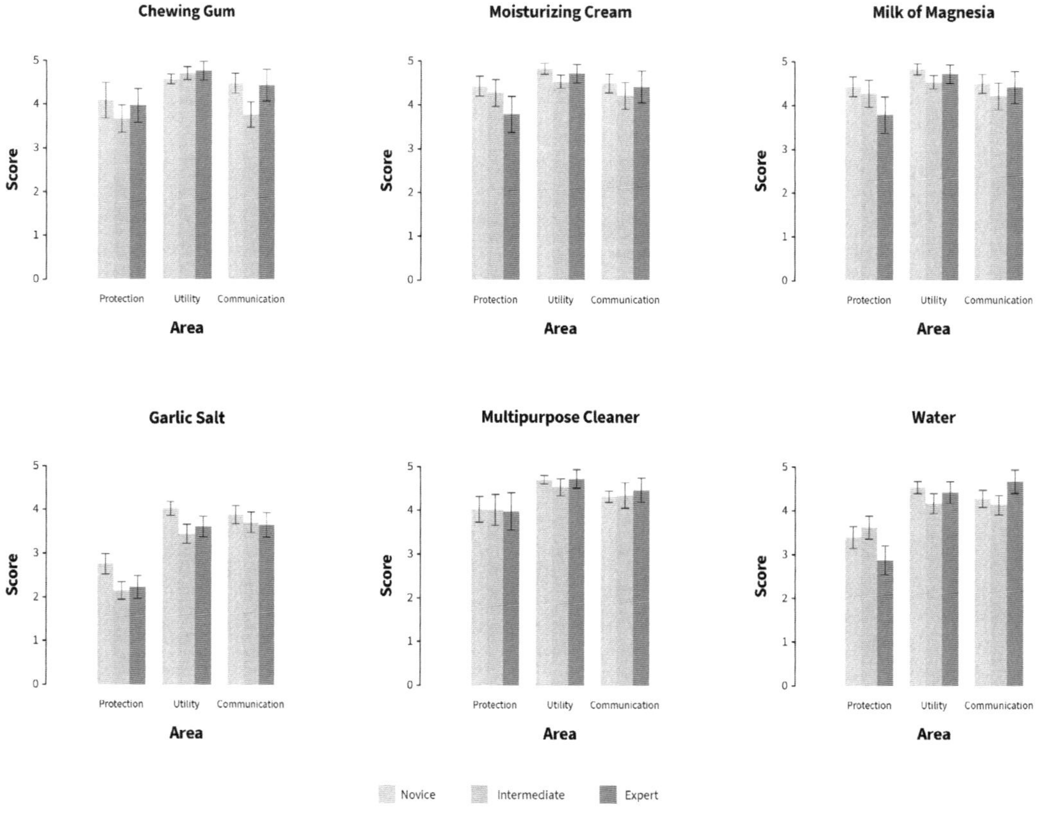

Figure 2 *Mean scores by area and level of evaluator expertise for each package evaluated. Error bars represent the standard error.*

Participants: Panel II

The second round of testing was conducted using a panel of nine industry professionals with intermediate and expert levels. Five packaging professionals (2 females, 3 males, m = 38.6 years old, sd = 5.9 years old) with intermediate experience (m = 8.0 years of experience, sd = 2.8 years) and four expert (m = 29.0 years of experience, sd = 8.8 years) professionals (2 females, 2 males, m = 50.0 years old, sd = 9.4 years old). This panel used the same heuristic guide as the first panel to evaluate a package system of their like. Table 5 summarizes the information for evaluators and package systems chosen.

Table 5 *Evaluators and packages in panel II.*

Experience Level	ID	Experience (Years)	Gender	Age (Years)	Job Title	Company	Package Evaluated
Intermediate	1	4	M	33	Designer	Quala	Amper energy drink (473 mL aluminum can)
	2	6	F	33	Packaging Engineer	Qualtia Alimentos	Ham leg (3 kg)
	3	10	F	43	Designer	Cittacreativos	Just herbal bath essence (50 mL plastic bottle)
	4	10	M	46	Plant Manager	Ampacet	Chocolate bar (120 g plastic pouch)
	5	10	M	38	Innovation & New Product Development Manager	Grupomar	Tuna in water (75 g retortable pouch)
Expert	6	21	F	46	Executive Manager of Technical Area	Grupo Herdez	Mayonnaise (105 g glass jar)
	7	22	M	47	Packaging Engineer	Grupo Bimbo	Cacao Mini Muffin (108 g plastic pouch)
	8	25	F	58	Professor	UDEM	Trident chewing gum (13 g folding carton)
	9	39	M	61	Research & Development Manager	Amcor	Mayonnaise (320 g plastic jar)

Results: Panel II

Qualitative information was collected for improving the guide. The comments and recommendations for the packaging heuristics guide by this group of evaluators were as follows:

· Add an item to evaluate where the product is going to be exhibited, that is, if it is going to be hung or going to be on a shelf.

· If the package is going to have lot number and expiry date printed on it, make sure that there is dedicated space for it. Some containers do not have a defined area for this, and the information is printed on top of the artwork making it difficult to find.

· It would be nice to have items related to evaluation of technical data such as water vapor transmission rate (WVTR), oxygen transmission rate (OTR), coefficient of frictions, permeability, etc.

· If the product is for export, the country's labeling conditions and a more in-depth analysis of transport protection.

· When trying to determine the type of packaging, ask yourself, what do you want to protect the product from? light, oxidation, loss of aroma, volume, volatility? In the case of food, how many days of shelf life are desired.

· Lack of manufacturing efficiency, waste of packaging material during manufacturing (sustainability).

· Focus more on product features. What flaws have you previously presented? What attributes can be improved? Can they be modified to generate greater savings in another container?

· Suggests breaking down the questionnaire into blocks that are less time consuming for the evaluators. This would encourage more thorough answers.

· If the product is part of a product system, it is easily identified and recognized as part of the same system.

· I thought that the evaluation would give me a result as an example recommendation: Proper packaging or Inappropriate packaging, as well as recommendations: change packaging.

· This questionnaire is good to reflect on various things about the packaging, such as a list or checklist.

3. Conclusions and Discussion

The main goal of this study was to develop a comprehensive heuristic guide that could be used by professionals and students, regardless of their level of packaging expertise, to analyze existing packaging systems and create new packaging concepts.

The resulting heuristic guide is organized using Lockhart's paradigm based on three pillars (e.g., protection, utility, and communication). Fifty heuristic items were derived from general packaging design considerations and grouped into ten sub-areas. The full list of heuristic items was then converted into a questionnaire and administered to two evaluators' panels to gather qualitative and quantitative data.

Initial results suggest that the evaluators' level of experience did not have a significant effect on the assessment of the packaging systems. This is encouraging because the guide could be used by packaging students learning how to make correct design decisions.

The guide did an excellent job of helping evaluators reveal weaknesses and strengths of commercially existing packaged products. This is also promising as commercial products have passed several hurdles and design iterations. The results should be even more meaningful for new packaging development.

After testing the guide, based on feedback from evaluators and a more in-depth analysis, some additional heuristics could be added, for example:

· A.3.6. The packaging system minimizes the amount of material used (sub-area: protection of the environment)

· A.3.7. The packaging system minimizes the variety of materials used (sub-area: protection of the environment)

· B.2.7. The packaging system offers different alternatives for enhancing its display (sub-area: utility during distribution)

· C.1.4. The packaging system can be recalled easily (sub-area: brand identity)

· C.2.4. The packaging system can be found easily at the point of sale (sub-area: product identification)

Some evaluators suggested developing a shorter guide. Further research efforts will focus on this issue. One alternative could be grouping heuristics using a common theme or focus such as ergonomics, user experience, sustainability, the first moment of truth, and the second moment of truth, to name a few possibilities. Another strategy could be prioritizing heuristics and having short and extended versions of the guide. In general, packaging professionals welcomed the idea of having a comprehensive checklist for assessing their packaging systems.

Appendix A: Strengths and Weaknesses

Trident chewing gum

Experience Level	ID	Experience (Years)	Gender	Age (Years)	Job Title	Company	Package Evaluated
Intermediate	1	4	M	33	Designer	Quala	Amper energy drink (473 mL aluminum can)
	2	6	F	33	Packaging Engineer	Qualtia Alimentos	Ham leg (3 kg)
	3	10	F	43	Designer	Cittacreativos	Just herbal bath essence (50 mL plastic bottle)
	4	10	M	46	Plant Manager	Ampacet	Chocolate bar (120 g plastic pouch)
	5	10	M	38	Innovation & New Product Development Manager	Grupomar	Tuna in water (75 g retortable pouch)
Expert	6	21	F	46	Executive Manager of Technical Area	Grupo Herdez	Mayonnaise (105 g glass jar)
	7	22	M	47	Packaging Engineer	Grupo Bimbo	Cacao Mini Muffin (108 g plastic pouch)
	8	25	F	58	Professor	UDEM	Trident chewing gum (13 g folding carton)
	9	39	M	61	Research & Development Manager	Amcor	Mayonnaise (320 g plastic jar)

Pond's moisturizing cream

Strengths (7)	Weaknesses (2)
1) The container preserves the content in optimal conditions. 2) Package has tamper-evident features. 3) The container can be reused. 4) The shape of the container is optimal for use. 5) The package visually differentiates itself from its competitors. 6) The package is easy to remember and expresses the brand's values. 7) Anyone can easily understand how the container is to be used.	1) Anyone cannot easily read what is in the package. 2) Each component of the package does not indicate the material from which it is made.

Normex milk of magnesia

Strengths (6)	Weaknesses (4)
1) The package contains the product inside it safely. 2) The package can be reused. 3) The shape of the container optimizes its distribution. 4) Anyone can carry the package with minimal effort. 5) The package visually differentiates itself from its competitors 6) The package is easy to remember.	1) Anyone cannot dose the content with this container. 2) The shape of the container is not optimal for use. 3) Anyone cannot easily read what is in the package. 4) Anyone cannot easily understand how the container is used.

Soriana garlic salt

Strengths (0)	Weaknesses (7)
None	1) The packaging does not protect the content from light, oxidation, humidity, or microorganisms. 2) The packaging does not protect the content from shocks, bumps, or crushing. 3) The packaging is not optimized for its distribution. 4) The container does not fill or close easily on the packaging line. 5) The packaging does not communicate the brand's positioning. 6) The package does not visually differentiate itself from its competitors. 7) Anyone cannot easily understand how the container is used or how the container is handled.

Pinol multipurpose cleaner

Strengths (6)	Weaknesses (2)
1) The container preserves the content in optimal conditions protects the content from scratches, abrasion, shocks, shocks, vibrations and crushing.	1) Not everyone can dose the contents.
2) The packaging indicates if it has been previously opened.	2) Not everyone can easily read the information on the package.
3) The container can be reused.	
4) The dimensions of the container are optimal for use.	
5) The packaging visually differentiates itself from its competitors and allows its variety or flavor to be easily identified.	
6) Each component of the package indicates the material from which it is made.	

Mia water

Strengths (6)	Weaknesses (7)
1) The packaging indicates if it has been previously opened.	1) The container does not protect the content from crushing; therefore it does not allow stacking or stowing.
2) The container fills, circulates, and closes easily on the packaging line.	2) The shape of the container is not optimal for use.
3) The packaging is easily labeled on the packaging line.	3) The packaging does not communicate the brand's positioning
	4) The package does not visually differentiate itself from its competitors
	5) The package does not express the brand's values.
	6) The appearance is not easy to remember.
	7) Each component of the package does not indicate the material from which it is made.

4. Referenses

[1] Chambers Concise Dictionary. Chambers Harrap Pub Ltd., 2010.

[2] Pearl J. Heuristics: Intelligent Search Strategies for Computer Problem Solving. Addison-Wesley Publishing Company, 1984.

[3] Newell A and HA Simon. Human Problem Solving. Prentice-Hall, 1972.

[4] Shah AK and DM Oppenheimer. Heuristics Made Easy: An Effort-Reduction Framework. Psychol. Bull., vol. 134, no. 2, pp. 207–222, 2008.

[5] Tversky A and D Kahneman. Judgment Under Uncertainty: Heuristics and Biases, Science, vol. 185, no. 4157, pp. 1124–1131, 1974.

[6] Hartson R and P Pyla. Analytic UX Evaluation Methods: Data Collection Methods and Techniques, in The UX Book: Agile UX Design for a Quality User Experience, Cambridge, MA, USA: Elsevier, Inc., 2019.

[7] Nielsen J. Finding Usability Problems Through Heuristic Evaluation, in Proceedings of CHI '92 Conference on Human Factors in Computing Systems, 1992, pp. 373–380.

[8] Nielsen J and R Molich. Heuristic Evaluation of User Interfaces, in Proceedings of CHI '90: Proceedings of the SIGCHI Conference on Human Factors in Computing Systems, 1990, pp. 249–256.

[9] Nielsen J. Usability Inspection Methods, in Proceedings of CHI '94 Conference on Human Factors in Computing Systems, 1994, pp. 413–414.

[10] Molich R and J Nielsen. Improving a Human-Computer Dialogue, Commun. ACM, vol. 33, no. 3, pp. 338–348, 1990.

[11] Nielsen J. Traditional Dialogue Design Applied to Moder User Interfaces, Commun. ACM, vol. 33, no. 10, pp. 109–119, 1990.

[12] Nielsen J. Enhancing the Explanatory Power of Usability Heuristics, in Proceedings of CHI '94 Conference on Human Factors in Computing Systems, 1994, pp. 152–158.

[13] Nielsen Norman Group. 10 Usability Heuristics for User Interface Design. [Online]. Available: www.nngroup.com/articles/ten-usability-heuristics/. [Accessed: 01-Jun- 2020].

[14] Parente da Costa R and E Dias Canedo, A Set of Usability Heuristics for Mobile Applications, in Human-Computer Interaction. Perspectives on Design. HCII 2019. Lecture Notes in Computer Science, vol. 11566, M. Kurosu, Ed. Springer, Cham, 2019, pp. 180–193.

[15] Durães Dourado MA and E Dias Canedo, Usability Heuristics for Mobile Applications: A Systematic Review, in Proceedings of ICEIS 2018 - 20th International Conference on Enterprise Information Systems, 2018, vol. 2, pp. 483–494.

[16] Bix L, J de la Fuente, RP Sundar, and H Lockhart, Packaging Design and Development, in The Wiley Encyclopedia of Packaging Technology, 3rd ed., K. Lam, Ed. Hoboken, NJ, USA: John Wiley & Sons, Inc., 2009, pp. 859-866.

[17] Lockhart HE, A Paradigm for Packaging, Packag. Technol. Sci., vol. 10, no. 5, pp. 237- 252, 1997.

[18] Cervera Fantoni ÁL, Introducción al Mundo del Envase, in Envase y Embalaje, Madrid,
Spain: Escuela Superior de Gestión Comercial y Marketing (ESIC), 2003, pp. 19-36.

[19] Smith PR and J Taylor, The Three Basic Functions of Packaging, in Marketing Communications: An Integrated Approach, 4th ed., London, United Kingdom: Kogan Page Business Books, 2004.

[20] Soroka W, Packaging Functions, in Fundamentals of Packaging Technology, 4th ed., Naperville, IL, USA: Institute of Packaging Professionals (IoPP), 2009, pp. 29-48.

[21] Yam KL, Packaging Functions and Environments, in The Wiley Encyclopedia of Packaging Technology, 3rd ed., Hoboken, NJ, USA: John Wiley & Sons Inc., 2009, pp. 869–871.

[22] Robertson GL, Introduction to Food Packaging, in Food Packaging, 3rd ed., Boca Raton, FL, USA: Taylor & Francis Group LLC, 2012, pp. 1–8.

[23] Bix L and J de la Fuente, Medical Device Packaging, in The Wiley Encyclopedia of Packaging Technology, 3rd ed., K. Yam, Ed. Hoboken, NJ, USA: John Wiley & Sons, Inc., 2009, pp. 713–727.

[24] de la Fuente J, S Gustafson, C Twomey, and L Bix, An Affordance-Based Methodology for Package Design, Packag. Technol. Sci., vol. 28, no. 2, pp. 157–171, Feb. 2015.

[25] de la Fuente J and L Bix, User-pack Interaction: Insights for Designing Inclusive Child- resistant packaging, in Designing Inclusive Interactions: Inclusive Interactions Between People and Products in Their Contexts of Use, 2010.

[26] Green Blue Institute, How2Recycle, 2020. [Online]. Available: www.how2recycle.info. [Accessed: 01-Jun-2020].

[27] Google Inc., Google Forms. Mountain View, CA, USA, 2020.

[28] GraphPad Software LLC, Prism v8.4.3. San Diego, CA, USA, 2020.

Design Heuristics for Innovative Packaging Ideation [71]

Javier de la Fuente *, Irene Carbonell, Autumn Lopez
Industrial Technology and Packaging, California Polytechnic State University, California, USA

Abstract: Concept ideation can be facilitated by using techniques such as design heuristics to stimulate divergent thinking. Heuristics are general design principles extracted from existing solutions that can help designers create novel solutions. While extensive research has been done on design heuristics when applied to product design, there are no reports of their application to innovative packaging design.

The objective of this study was to assess the effects of design heuristics on the level of innovation of packaging concepts. Fifty-five undergraduate students were randomly assigned to three groups. Participants in the control group generated ideas without the help of design heuristics (i.e., group A). Participants in group B ideated with the help of existing product design heuristics. Participants in group C created ideas using design heuristics tailored specifically to packaging design.

A total of 293 packaging concepts were rated using three 5-point Likert scales for morphological, technological, and functional innovations. An overall level of innovation was calculated by adding the three scores. Participants who used design heuristic cards (i.e., experimental conditions B and C) created on average more than one additional idea than participants who ideated without heuristic help (i.e., control group). Idea generation using packaging-specific design heuristics yielded more innovative ideas than idea generation using product design heuristics. Forty-nine percent of the ideas in group C had significantly higher levels of innovation compared to 35% of the ideas in group B (χ^2 (1) = 4.023, p = .045) and 32% in the control group (χ^2 (1) = 5.996, p = .014).

Product design heuristics can be extremely useful to make ideation processes more efficient and productive. However, this study provides evidence that there needs to be a match between heuristic description, examples of application of the heuristics, and the target domain (i.e., the type of product being created). Findings suggest a significant and positive effect of using field-specific heuristics for early ideation sessions of novice students with minimal design background.

Keywords: package design, design heuristics, innovation, engineering, ideation

***Correspondence to:** Javier de la Fuente, Industrial Technology and Packaging, California Polytechnic State University, California, USA. E-mail: jdelafue@calpoly.edu

1. Introduction

Ideation is a complex and critical activity of any new packaging development process. [1] Early ideation activities occur during the concept design phase and typically continue throughout the entire development process with different focus areas. Early ideas tend to be exploratory and are the embryonic seeds for more refined ideas and final breakthroughs.

Packaging concept ideation requires both domain-specific knowledge (e.g., packaging technology, materials, manufacturing processes) to produce feasible solutions and design thinking skills (e.g., empathy, problem framing, systematic exploration, teamwork) to create innovative solutions. [2]

Recent cognitive psychology experiments suggest that coming up with new ideas requires memory retrieval (e.g., a person's knowledge about something).[3] It could be argued that design creativity happens when a designer makes unexpected brain connections between relevant memories systematically. A process that is typically referred as to divergent thinking. An ability that allows humans to explore as many different options as possible to create the new and unusual. For ideation, it becomes crucial to find those relevant memories that help the designer solve the problem at hand.

Concept ideation can be challenging for anyone, but creative processes can be facilitated by creating the right environment and by using techniques that stimulate divergent thinking. Some examples of such techniques include the ubiquitous brainstorming, [4] the Synectics problem- solving method, [5] the Theory of Inventive Problem Solving (TRIZ), [6] morphological analysis, [7] the SCAMPER technique, [8] and several techniques based on inspiration cards focusing on different characteristics such as building empathy with stakeholders (IDEO method cards), [9] biomimicry principles, [10] and design heuristics. [11]

Design heuristics are general design principles extracted from existing products that can help designers in creating novel solutions. [12] These principles act as cognitive shortcuts and can help designers become unstuck and overcome idea fixation, the tendency to fixate on initial design ideas and fail to fully explore the solution space. [12], [13] Empirical research conducted with industrial design, [12] mechanical engineering, [14], [15] and biomedical engineering [16] students show that students who use design heuristics produce ideas that are considered more creative than those who do not use them.

Yilmaz et. al developed and compiled 77 design heuristics suitable for product design. [17] These heuristics were derived from studies of expert designers and award-winning products. This set of design heuristics are available as a system of printed cards that can be used for brainstorming sessions. [11] Each card contains information about one design heuristics. On one side, the card has a short, written description and a sketch of the concept. On the other side, each card has two examples of how the heuristic is used in existing products.

While extensive research has been done on design heuristics when applied to product design, there are no reports of their application to innovative packaging design. The authors of this study have noticed that, despite being applicable, some existing product design heuristics have a degree of abstraction that may be difficult to decode for a non-design-major student or even a novice student. Interpreting a heuristic may require extensive training. Also, the conceptual idea behind the examples in existing product design heuristic cards may be difficult to translate into other domains or types of products (e.g., packaging).

The purpose of this study was to determine the effect of using different types of design heuristics in ideation for packaging design applications. It is hypothesized that:

• **H1:** Idea generation without the assistance of design heuristics will yield fewer innovative ideas.

• **H2:** Idea generation using product design heuristics will yield more innovative ideas than not using heuristic help at all.

• **H3:** Idea generation using packaging design heuristics will yield more innovative ideas than using product design heuristics.

2. Materials and Methods

2.1 Experimental Design

In order to test these hypotheses, three groups were used to assess the effects of design heuristics on the level of innovation of packaging concepts (see Table 1). A group of undergraduate students was randomly assigned to a group. The three groups met for a 30-minute brainstorming session in which participants explored design ideas for the primary packaging of a specific consumer packaged good (i.e., pasta).

Table 1 *Summary of the experimental design.*

Characteristic	Group		
	Control	B	C
Design Heuristics	• None	• Four existing product design heuristic cards were provided one at a time in the following order: – Use repurposed or recycled materials – Add natural features – Use packaging as functional component – Create system	• Four new packaging design heuristic cards were provided one at a time in the following order: – Use sustainable packaging materials – Use nature as inspiration – Provide additional utilitarian value – Create a system
Procedure	• Participants were asked to create as many novel ideas as possible in 7 minutes. • After each 7-minute period, participants were asked to take a 10-second break.	• Participants were asked to create as many novel ideas as possible in 7 minutes. • After each 7-minute period, participants were asked to use the next design heuristic card.	• Participants were asked to create as many novel ideas as possible in 7 minutes. • After each 7-minute period, participants were asked to use the next design heuristic card.
Participants	• Randomly assigned undergraduate students. • Major, class standing, and packaging experience were balanced among groups.		
Design Task	• Create ideas for primary packaging for pasta		

2.2 Design Heuristics

Four design heuristics were selected from a set of 77 design heuristics commercialized by Design Heuristics LLC. [11], [17] The selection was based on the following criteria:

· The total duration of the brainstorming sessions (i.e., about 30 minutes) with short ideation periods of seven minutes determined the need for four heuristics.

· The ability of the heuristic to support early conceptualization, instead of supporting ideation of details or components.

· The ability of the heuristic to support packaging themes.

· The ability of the heuristic to support ideation for form, technology, and functionality.

The selected design heuristics were:

· Card #3: Add natural features.
· Card #29: Create system.
· Card #73: Use packaging as functional component.
· Card #74: Use repurposed or recycled materials.

The four selected cards were then refined for packaging development applications. The heuristic intent of the original cards was adjusted to make sense in the packaging domain. The look-and- feel of the original cards were kept consistent in the modified cards as much as possible. The names of the original cards were adjusted to prompt students to think of packaging designs rather than product designs. Explanations on the front of the cards were changed to provide packaging- specific instructions.

For example, references to "product" were changed to "package" and guidelines that did not translate well to packaging were changed. Product design examples on the backs of the original cards were replaced with examples of packaging designs that fit the given heuristic. See Figure 1 for a comparison of an existing card to the packaging-specific version. See Appendix A for details and images of all eight cards. Titles of the packaging-specific cards were use sustainable packaging materials, use nature as inspiration, provide additional utilitarian value, and create a system.

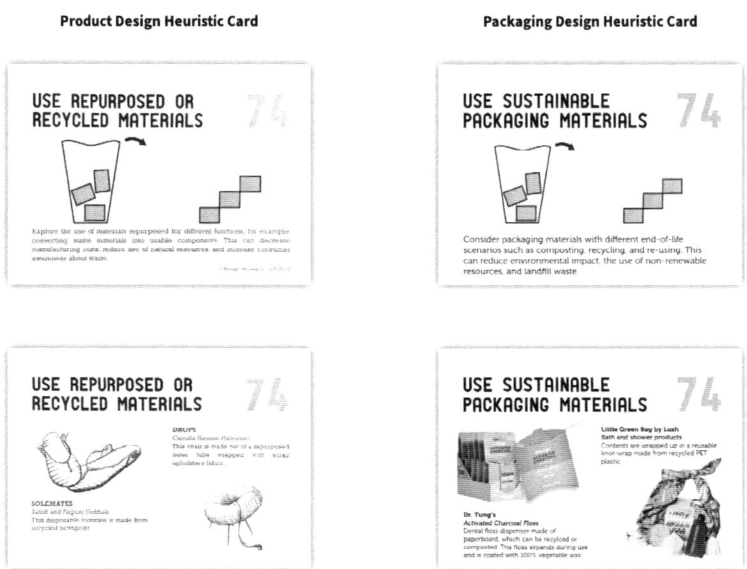

Figure 1 *Example of existing product design heuristic card and the equivalent packaging design heuristic card.*

2.3 Procedure

The brainstorming sessions took place during class laboratories and were conducted using a video conferencing software (Zoom® by Zoom Video Communications Inc., San Jose, California, USA). [2] Before the class meeting, participants were told they would be participating in a brainstorming activity. They were instructed to prepare a pen or pencil and white letter-size paper or a tablet and stylus. The assignment handouts were posted on the Canvas Learning Management System (Canvas LMS by Instructure Inc., Salt Lake City, Utah, USA), [19] and each participant was assigned the handout corresponding to their group. Once the class meeting started, participants were guided through the process of navigating to Canvas and finding the handout but were asked not to open the handout until instructed to do so. Participants were then provided instructions regarding the nature of the assignment, including the design task, time limits, and an overview of the information present in the handouts. Participants were asked to turn their cameras on and were instructed to ask any questions during the assignment via private chat to the instructor.

Participants were instructed to open the handout to page one and were given five minutes to read over page one. Participants were then given seven minutes to create and draw as many novel ideas as possible utilizing each prompt. The instructor kept time and instructed participants on when to turn the page. Each brainstorming session took a total of 33 minutes. After the assignment was completed, participants were asked to photograph and upload their drawings to the Canvas LMS. Students were also asked to fill out a survey providing their gender, age, expected year of graduation, and whether they consented to have their ideas published in a research paper.

2.4 Participants

Undergraduate students enrolled in a 300-level packaging fundamentals course during spring quarter 2020 at a Californian university were randomly assigned to one of the three groups. Students participated individually in a brainstorming session as part of their classwork and received course credit in exchange for their involvement.

2.5 Design Task

Instructions were provided to students in the form of a five-page PDF file handout. The first page of the handout consisted of introductory instructions, which were the same for each of the three treatments. Participants were asked to imagine that they were working as a package designer for a company and were given a design assignment to create design ideas for a primary packaging for pasta. Participants were asked to consider aesthetics, functionality, where and how the package would be used, who would use it, how it would be discarded, what type of material would be used, and how the package would be manufactured. They were instructed to create as many novel ideas as they could and were reminded that the exercise has no right or wrong answer.

Participants were asked to use letter-size white paper sheets, to draw only one idea per page, and to number each idea. They were reminded not to write their name on the sheets. Lastly, they were informed that the handout consisted of four activities (one per page, seven minutes per activity) and that the instructor would be keeping time and letting them know when to turn the page.

The last four pages of the handout were specific to the experimental condition. Participants in the control group received a "Reboot" prompt in which they were told to take a 10-second break to reboot their brain. Experimental condition B received one unaltered product design heuristic card per page along with the message, "You may use the following design heuristic card for inspiration." Experimental condition C received the same message alongside packaging design heuristic cards. All pages included a message reminding the participant that they had seven minutes to create as many novel ideas as possible and that the instructor would let them know when they could turn the page.

2.6 Data Management

Photographs of participants' drawings were downloaded from the Canvas LMS and were converted to JPG format. An image-editing software (Adobe Photoshop Lightroom® v3.3 by Adobe Inc., San Jose, California, USA) [3] was used to standardize images, including adjustments to brightness, contrast, and color balance. In addition, any information written on the submissions that could allow a judge to identify the treatment condition was removed.

All photos were subsequently renamed using a coding system to identify the treatment group, experiment, class, class section, participant number, and idea number. For example, the code A-1-330-02-07-06 would indicate a participant in group A performing brainstorming exercise one. The participant is a student in ITP 330 class, section 2, and she/he is the seventh student on the roster. This is their sixth idea.

For rating the innovation level of each idea, photo files were given a random four-digit number between 0001 and 0999 as the filename. Each code, described in the previous paragraph, was assigned a random number, and a copy of the coded files was renamed with the random numbers. This copy of the files was passed on to the rater.

2.7 Levels of Innovation Assessment

Based on the product concept definition by Ulrich, Eppinger, and Yang, [4] a packaging concept can be defined as the combined description of the form, technology, and working principles of a packaging system. [1] Therefore, the level of innovation of a packaging concept can be established by assessing three areas, namely, morphology, technology, and functionality.

Morphology includes all the visuals characteristics of the structure (e.g., tri-dimensional shape, configuration, colors, materials) and graphics (e.g., two-dimensional shapes, layout, colors, patterns, images, illustrations) of the packaging concept. Technology comprises manufacturing and packaging processes and material choices. Functionality refers to any utilitarian value provided through the three packaging functions (i.e., protection, utility, and communication). [22]

Three 5-point Likert scales were developed to measure the degree of novelty of the three dimensions. To operationalize their rating, scoring rubrics and criteria definitions were developed (See Table 2). An overall innovation score was calculated by adding the morphological, technological, and functional scores.

Table 2 *Scales for assessing morphological, technological, and functional innovations.*

Morphological Innovation					
Description (Level)	**Not at all Innovative** (1)	**Slightly Innovative** (2)	**Moderately Innovative** (3)	**Mostly Innovative** (4)	**Very Innovative** (5)
Short Definition	• Common morphology.	• Common morphology. • New small features. • Clear intention.	• New morphology.	• New morphology. • Clear intention.	• New morphology. • Clear intention. • Morphology is logically connected to manufacturing and materials.
Criteria	Morphology is commonly used in the product category being explored.	Morphology is commonly used in the product category being explored, but it incorporates additional features (graphical or structural) with a clear intention.	Morphology is not commonly used for the product category being explored, but has an arbitrary shape with no apparent intention.	Morphology is not commonly used in the product category and has a clear intention, but the shape is not logically connected to manufacturing or material of choice.	Morphology is not commonly used in the product category. The shape has a clear intention and is connected to manufacturing or material of choice.
Technological Innovation					
Description (Level)	**Not at all Innovative** (1)	**Slightly Innovative** (2)	**Moderately Innovative** (3)	**Mostly Innovative** (4)	**Very Innovative** (5)
Short Definition	• Common technology.	• Common technology. • Novel application.	• Uncommon technology.	• Uncommon technology. • Novel application.	• Novel technology. • Novel application.
Criteria	Manufacturing processes and/or materials are commonly used in the product category being explored.	Manufacturing processes and/or materials are commonly used in the product category being explored, but the application is novel.	Manufacturing processes and/or materials are uncommon for packaging applications in the product category being explored.	Manufacturing processes and/or materials are uncommon for packaging applications in general, and the application is novel.	Manufacturing processes and/or materials and their application are novel.
Functional Innovation					
Description (Level)	**Not at all Innovative** (1)	**Slightly Innovative** (2)	**Moderately Innovative** (3)	**Mostly Innovative** (4)	**Very Innovative** (5)
Short Definition	• Common functions.	• Basic fucntional improvement of one feature.	• Moderate functional improvement of one or more features.	• Advanced functional improvement for one feature.	• Advanced functional improvement for more than one feature.
Criteria	Functionality is limited to the containment and protection of the contents.	Functionality is limited to a basic improvement of one characteristic of the package.	Functionality has been moderately improved for one or more characterisics of the package.	Functionality includes advanced improvements for one characterisic of the package.	Functionality includes advanced improvements for more than one characterisic of the package.

2.8 Data Analysis

Data were analyzed with Prism version 8.4.3 (GraphPad Software LLC, San Diego, California, USA). [5] Chi-square tests of independence and analysis of variance (ANOVA) were calculated to investigate whether and how the type of design heuristics utilized in individual brainstorming sessions are related to the level of innovation of the packaging concepts created with them.

3. Results and Discussion

3.1 Participants

A total of 55 undergraduate students in three sections of a 300-level packaging fundamentals course at a Californian university participated in the brainstorming exercises. Students were randomly assigned to a group. Since the class is taken by students of different majors (i.e., Business, Industrial Technology and Packaging, Graphic Communication, Food Science) and to ensure balanced representation, class standing, major, and previous packaging experience were also considered for assigning participant to a group. Students who had taken one or more packaging-related classes were classified as having previous packaging experience and were distributed throughout the three groups (See Table 3).

Table 3 *Summary of participants' information for each group.*

Characteristics		Group		
		Control	**B**	**C**
Age	Average (*SD*)	22.1 (*7.5*)	21.2 (*3.5*)	20.4 (*0.9*)
Gender	Female (%)	32	39	39
	Male (%)	68	61	61
Class Year	Freshman	0	0	0
	Sophomore	2	2	1
	Junior	5	5	6
	Senior	12	11	11
Major	Business	10	10	11
	Food Science	2	1	1
	Graphic Communication	2	2	1
	Industrial Technology and Packaging	5	4	5
	Other	0	1	0
Total		**19**	**18**	**18**

3.2 Packaging Concepts

A total of 293 packaging concepts were generated. Participants in the control group created 84 ideas, an average of 4.4 ideas per participant. Participants in group B generated 106 ideas (a 26% more than group A) with an average of 5.9 ideas per participant. Participants in group C created a total of 103 ideas (23% more than the control group) with an average of 5.7 ideas per participant.

3.3 Levels of Innovation

A packaging engineer with nine years of packaging development experience scored each idea using the morphological, technological, and functional scales (see Table 2). Table 4 summarizes the distribution of the scores along the three dimensions for all groups.

Table 4 *Percentage of ideas for each level of innovation for the three dimensions for all groups.*

Dimension	Group	Level of Innovation (%)				
		1	**2**	**3**	**4**	**5**
Morphology	Control Group	43	11	29	8	8
	B	45	11	26	7	11
	C	27	15	28	13	17
Technology	Control Group	38	26	30	1	4
	B	38	16	31	11	4
	C	31	18	33	14	4
Functionality	Control Group	28	47	18	2	5
	B	38	43	11	4	4
	C	23	42	24	4	6

For each of the three dimensions, the percentage of ideas considered to be not innovative (i.e., level 1, not at all innovative) was compared with the percentage of ideas with some degree of innovation (i.e., levels 2-5, from slightly innovative to very innovative). These comparisons are shown in Figure 2. Contingency tables and chi-square tests of independence were employed to explore significant relationships between the percentage of innovative and not innovative ideas for the control group and the two experimental conditions.

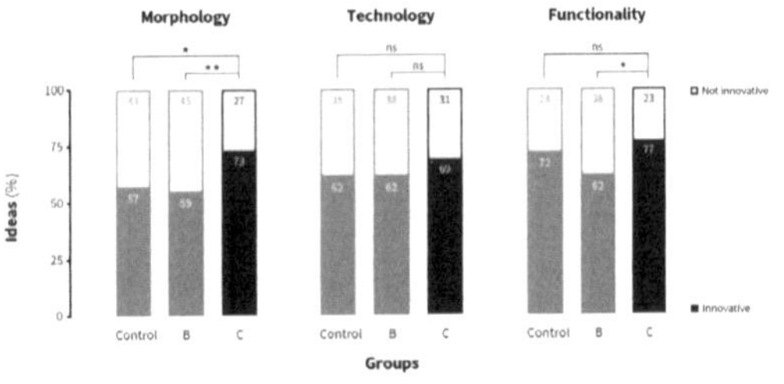

Figure 2 *Percentage of ideas rated as innovative and not innovative along three dimensions (morphology, technology and functionality) for the three groups. Statistical significance: ns = $p \geq .05$, * = $p < .05$, ** = $p < .01$.*

Morphological Innovation

A significant interaction was found for morphological innovation. Participants in experimental condition C were more likely to create a morphologically innovative solution (73%) than participants in the control group (57%) (χ^2 (1) = 5.626, p = .018). Participants in group C were also more likely to create an innovative solution than participants in the experimental condition B (55%) (χ^2 (1) = 7.031, p = .008).

Technological Innovation

Although participants in group C also tended to generate more technologically innovative ideas (69%) than participants in the control group (62%) and in group B (62%), no significant statistical relationships were found for technological innovation (χ^2 (1) = 1.084, p = .298).

Functional Innovation

Another significant interaction was found for functional innovation. Participants in experimental condition C were more likely to create a functionally innovative solution (77%) than participants in the experimental condition B (62%) χ^2 (1) = 2.304, p = .021). Participants in group C created more innovative solution than participants in the control group (72%), but this relationship was found not significant (χ^2 (1) = 0.658, p = .471).

Overall Innovation

An overall innovation score was calculated for all ideas with scores for the three dimensions (n = 240) by adding the morphological, technological, and functional scores. Consequently, the overall innovation score ranged from 1 through 15. A one-way ANOVA was calculated comparing the overall innovation score of each complete idea for all experimental conditions. A significant difference was found (F (2, 237) = 3.721, p = .026). Tukey's HSD was used to compare experimental conditions B and C against the control group and determine the nature of the differences. This analysis revealed that ideas created by participants in group

C were more likely to have a higher overall innovation score (m = 7.46, sd = 3.04, SEM = 0.344) than ideas created by the control group (m = 6.38, sd = 2.50, SEM = 0.299). The effect size for this comparison (d = .39) was found to exceed Cohen's convention for a medium effect (d = .30). [24] The level of innovation of ideas created by group B (m = 6.46, sd = 2.76, SEM = 0.286) were not significantly different from those of the control group (see Figure 3). A closer look at the overall innovation scores revealed significant differences in their distribution (See Table 5). Group C created more ideas (49%) with an overall innovation score equal or greater than 7.5 (i.e., the midpoint of the scale) than the control group (32%) (χ^2 (1) = 5.996, p = .014) and group B (35%) (χ^2 (1) = 4.023, p = .045).

Table 5 *Percentage of ideas categorized based on the overall innovation scale midpoint (i.e., 7.5).*

Group	Ideas (%)	
	Less Innovative (Overall innovation score < 7.5)	More Innovative (Overall innovation score ≥ 7.5)
Control Group	68	32
B	65	35
C	51	49

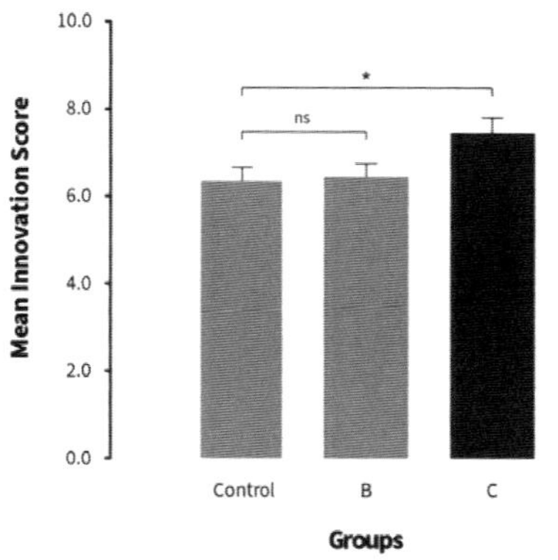

Figure 3 *Mean innovation score for the three groups. Error bars represent one standard error of mean (SEM). Statistical significance: ns = $p \geq .05$, * = $p < .05$.*

The distribution of all innovation scores is shown in Figure 4 as violin graphs. It is interesting to observe how the shape of the three density plots is different. For the control group, the shape of the distribution has a "lower belly," indicating more ideas with a low level of innovation. The shape of the distribution for group B is a bit more rectangular with more ideas in the middle of the innovation scale and a few ideas scoring high. Finally, for group C, the distribution is wider just above the midpoint of the scale with considerably many more ideas at the top of the innovation scale. Initial ideas are the critical seeds of innovation-driven projects. These seeds typically evolve and change towards more innovative and feasible solutions. The more ideas at the top of these distributions, the larger the chances of developing innovative final solutions.

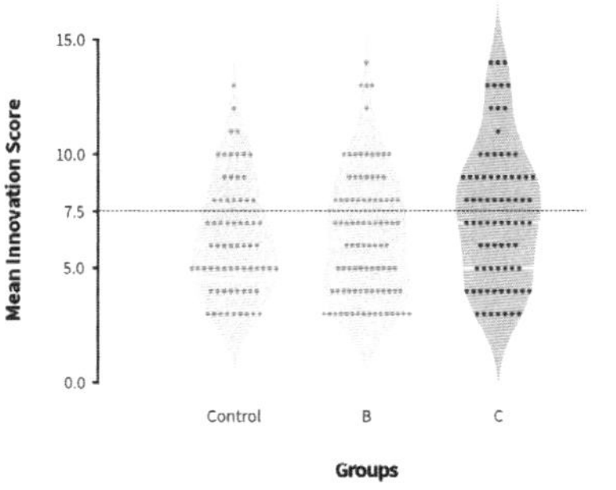

Figure 4 *Distribution of all innovation scores for the three experimental conditions.*

4. Conclusions

The purpose of this study was to determine the effect of using two types of design heuristics in ideation for packaging applications. After analyzing 293 packaging concepts for primary packaging for pasta created under three experimental conditions, the findings can be summarized as follows:

· Participants who used design heuristic cards (i.e., experimental conditions B and C) created on average more than one additional idea than participants who brainstormed without heuristic help (i.e., control group). This is significant for an experimental setup that tends to constraint the creative pace for all groups. This also confirms something that previous studies have found for other disciplines. [12], [14]-[16]

• **H1:** Idea generation without the assistance of design heuristics will yield fewer innovative ideas. Hypothesis one was partially supported. As it can be seen in Figure 4 and Table 5, 68% of the ideas in the group without heuristic inspiration had lower levels of innovation compared to 51% of the ideas in group C. However, group B had a 65% of the ideas scoring in the lower part of the innovation spectrum. Both differences were statistically significant at p < 0.05. This may be signaling a problem with the type of help provided by product design heuristics.

• **H2:** Idea generation using product design heuristics will yield more innovative ideas than not using heuristic help at all. Hypothesis two was not supported. The group of participants using product design heuristics (i.e., group B) created ideas with comparable levels of innovation to the control group, who did not use any heuristic help. This is shown in Figure 3. In terms of percentage of innovative ideas (see Figure 2), group B created fewer innovative ideas for the morphology and functionality dimensions than the control group and the same percentage of ideas for the technology dimension.

• **H3:** Idea generation using packaging design heuristics will yield more innovative ideas than using product design heuristics. Hypothesis three was supported. The group of participants using packaging design heuristics (i.e., group C) was more likely to create packaging concepts with higher levels of innovation than the control group and the group using product design heuristics (i.e., group B). The difference was statistically significant at $p < 0.05$ (see Figures 3 and 4). The shape of the innovation scores distribution shown in Figure 4 illustrates this effect. It can also be seen in Figure 3 that the use of packaging-specific design heuristics had a significant effect on morphological and functional innovation dimensions when compared to the use of product design heuristics. The effect was also present for technological innovation, but the difference was not significant.

Product design heuristics can be extremely useful to make ideation processes more efficient and productive. However, this study provides evidence that there needs to be a match between heuristic description, examples of application of the heuristics, and the target domain (i.e., the type of product being created). Findings suggest a significant and positive effect of using field-specific heuristics for early ideation sessions of novice students with minimal design background.

Appendix A: Design Heuristics

Card #3: The heuristic intent is to encourage the designer to look at nature for inspiration.

	Product Design Heuristic Card	Packaging Design Heuristic Card
Name	Add natural features	Use nature as inspiration
Explanation	Explore relationships between the product and nature. This can help achieve the product's function or improve aesthetics.	Establish metaphors between the package and natural elements. For example, consider the shape and texture of ingredients, working principles observed in nature, natural materials, etc.
Example 1	**Flower Offering** *Satyendra Pakhale* This chair is made of ceramic pottery, allowing the user to put plants or flowers in the backrest.	**Mighty Nuts** *Pistachios* Working principle and shape are inspired by the pistachio. The outer part separates and becomes a tray for the shells.
Example 2	**Wooden Memory Sticks** *Ooms* These USB flash memory sticks are encased in handpicked branches.	**La Habra** *Avocado Oil* Molded fiber shells give structure to an internal pouch with a closure fitment. Its general shape and texture are a reference to the main ingredient.

Front

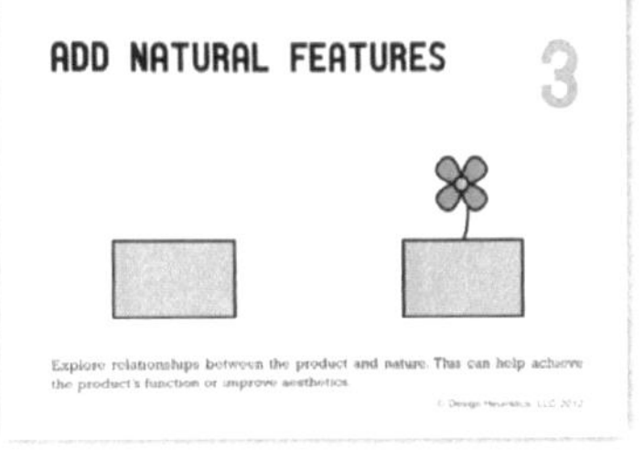

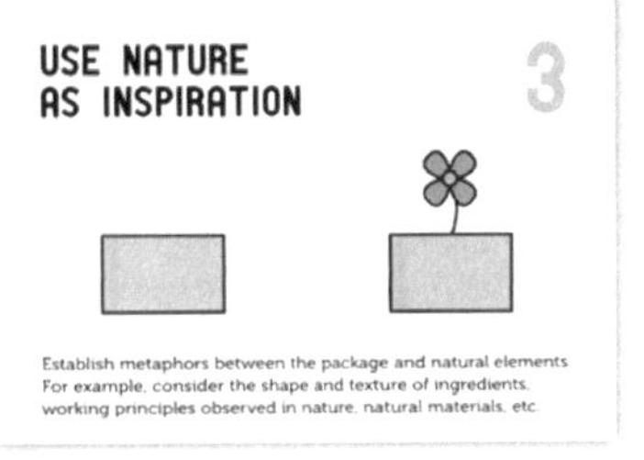

Back

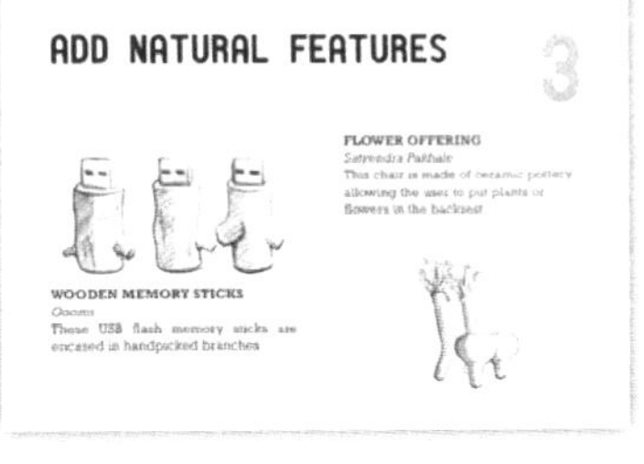

Card #29: The heuristic intent is to stimulate creation of a system which may lead to company and consumer benefits as well as reduced material usage.

	Product Design Heuristic Card	Packaging Design Heuristic Card
Name	Create system	Create a system
Explanation	Identify the core product functions and define a multi-stage process to achieve the overall goal. Separate the stages to organize functional steps, build a complex function, and increase efficiency.	Explore opportunities in which your package is a system. Consider opportunities in which your package is part of a more extensive system. Consider the main functions and components needed to achieve these functions.
Example 1	**Flatpack** *Sarah Paculdo* This chair is built through a system where the user molds the chair from a flat shape, and sets it by applying water to a resin coating.	**Truman's** *Household cleaning products* A system of non-toxic spray cleaners offering concentrated refill cartridges and dispenser containers.
Example 2	**Wet Jet** *Swiffer* This floor cleaner system dispenses cleaning fluid onto a disposable cloth while in use, making mopping easier for the user.	**Loop** *Multi-product* A system with multiple types of reusable containers. Returnable and refillable packages are made from stainless steel and plastics to minimize waste.

Front

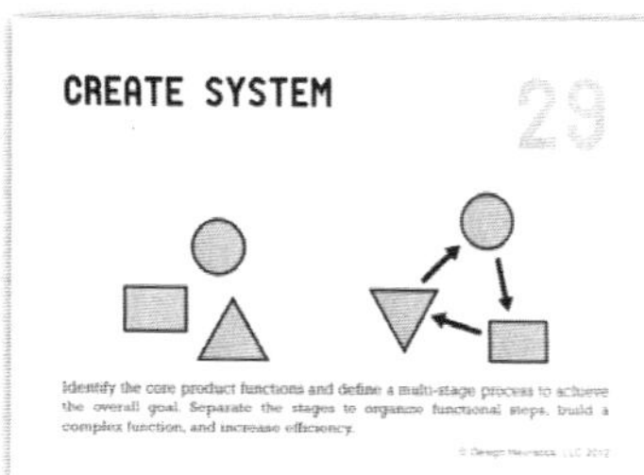

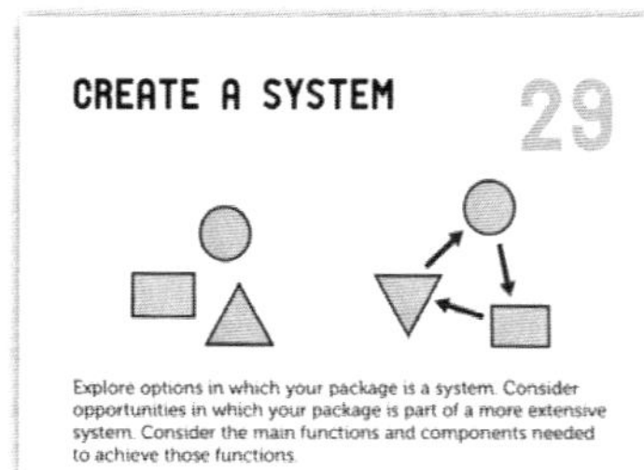

Back

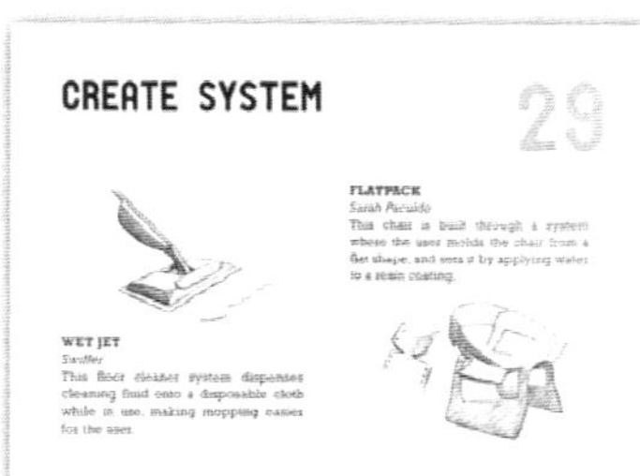

Card #73: The heuristic intent is to encourage the use of packaging as a key component to product use, extending the useful life of the package and reducing wasted material.

	Product Design Heuristic Card	Packaging Design Heuristic Card
Name	Use packaging as functional component	Provide additional utilitarian value
Explanation	Instead of disposable packaging, incorporate packaging within the product to perform a supportive function. This can reduce waste and provide a storage or organizational option.	Explore options in which your package has additional functions beyond product protection and storage. Consider assigning additional functions to some of the packaging components.
Example 1	**Wheeled Cube** *Heinz Julen* This chair can be folded into a wooden box with wheels when not in use, protecting interior cushions.	**Duracell EasyTab™** *Hearing Aid Batteries* Package empowers consumers with poor eyesight and reduced dexterity to change their batteries.
Example 2	**Flipbox Pencil Case** *Faber Castell* This set of colored pencils comes inside a package that also serves as a stand during use.	**Twist & Pour® Dutch Boy** *Paint* Its integrated handle facilitates carrying and handling. Its screw-on lid makes it easy to open. Its built-in spout allows for pouring paint easily while minimizing spills.

Front

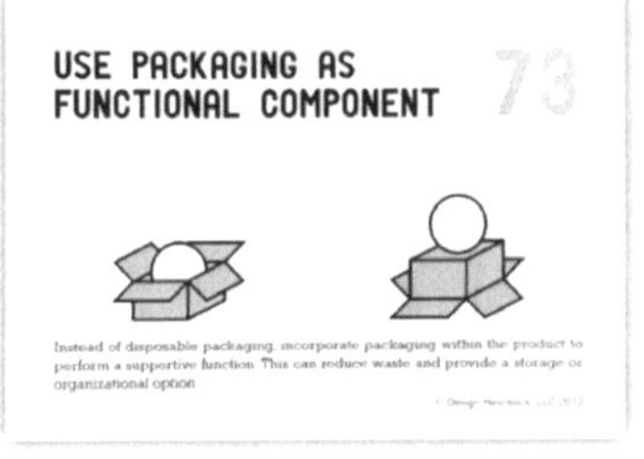

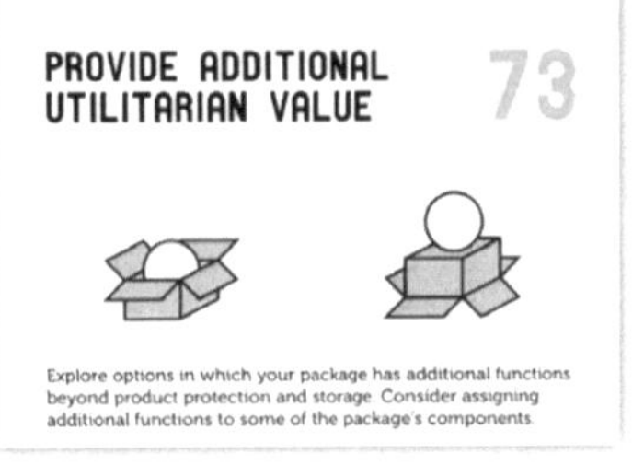

Back

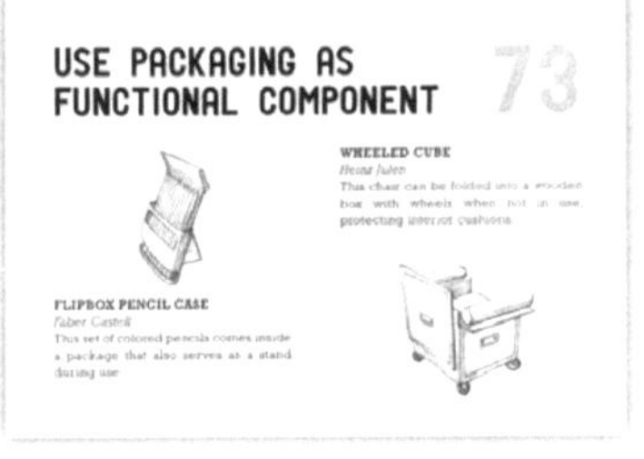

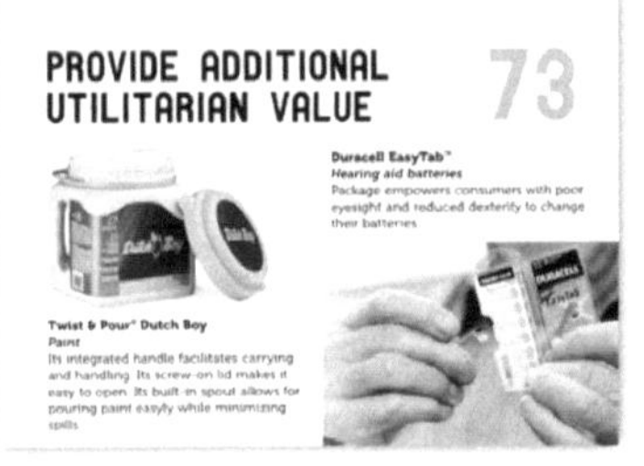

Card #74: The heuristic intent is to stimulate the use of more sustainable materials by considering different end-of-life scenarios.

	Product Design Heuristic Card	Packaging Design Heuristic Card
Name	Use repurposed or recycled materials	Use sustainable packaging materials
Explanation	Explore the use of materials repurposed for different functions: for example, converting waste materials into usable components. This can decrease manufacturing costs, reduce use of natural resources, and increase consumer awareness about waste.	Consider packaging materials with different end-of-life scenarios such as composting, recycling, and re-suing. This can reduce environmental impact, the use of non-renewable resources, and landfill waste.
Example 1	**Drops** *Camilla Hounsel Halvorsen* This chair is made out of a repurposed inner tube wrapped with scrap upholstery fabric.	**Little Green Bag by Lush** *Bath and shower products* Contents are wrapped up in a reusable knot-wrap made from recycled PET plastic.
Example 2	**Solemates** *Satish and Falguni Gokhale* This disposable footware is made from recycled newsprint.	**Dr. Tung's** *Activated charcoal Floss* Dental floss dispenser made of paperboard, which can be recycled or composted. The floss expands during use an is coated with 100% vegetable wax.

Front

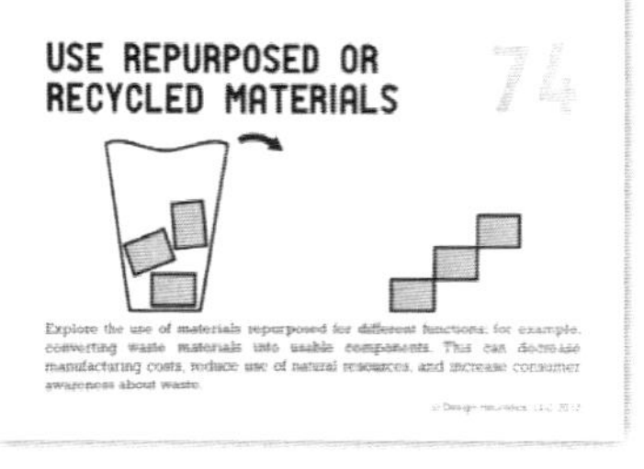

Back

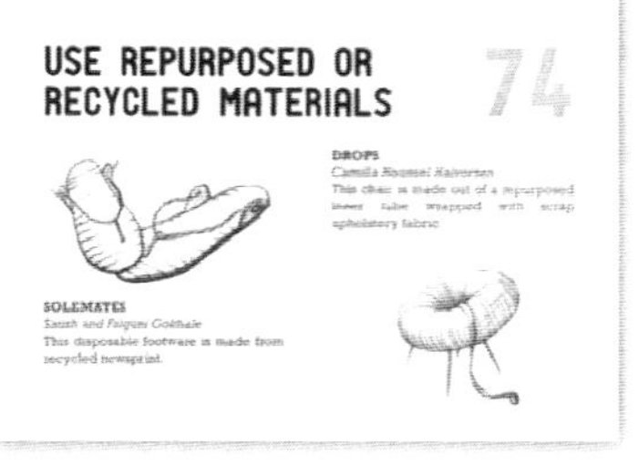

5. References

[1] Bix L, J de la Fuente, RP Sundar, and H Lockhart, Packaging Design and Development, in The Wiley Encyclopedia of Packaging Technology, 3rd ed., K. Lam, Ed. Hoboken, NJ, USA: John Wiley & Sons, Inc., 2009, pp. 859–866.

[2] de la Fuente J, I Carbonell, and M LaPorte, Design Thinking as a Framework for Teaching Packaging Innovation, J. Appl. Packag. Res., vol. 11, no. 1, pp. 39–69, 2019.

[3] Madore KP, DR Addis, and DL Schacter, Creativity and Memory: Effects of an Episodic-Specificity Induction on Divergent Thinking, Psychol. Sci., vol. 26, no. 9, pp. 1461–1468, 2015.

[4] Osborn AF, Applied Imagination: Principles and Procedures of Creative Thinking, 1st ed. New York City, NY, USA, 1953.

[5] Gordon WJJ, Synectics: The Development of Creative Capacity. New York City, NY, USA: Harper and Row, 1961.

[6] Altshuller G, L Shulyak, and S Rodman, 40 Principles: TRIZ Keys to Technical Innovation, 1st ed. Worcester, MA, USA: Technical Innovation Center, Inc., 1998.

[7] Allen MS, Morphological Creativity: The Miracle of Your Hidden Brain Power. Englewood Cliffs, NJ, USA: Prentice-Hall, 1962.

[8] Eberle R, Scamper: Games for Imagination Development. Waco, TX, USA: Prufrock Press, 1996.

[9] IDEO, Method Cards, 2020. [Online]. Available: https://www.ideo.com/post/method-cards. [Accessed: 18- Jun-2020].

[10] Biomimicry 3.8, Biomimicry Resource Cards. [Online]. Available: https://biomimicry.net/product/resource- cards/. [Accessed: 18-Jun-2020].

[11] Design Heuristics LLC, Design Heuristics, 2020. [Online]. Available: https://www.designheuristics.com/. [Accessed: 18-Jun-2020].

[12] Yilmaz S, JL Christian, SR Daly, C Seifert, and R Gonzalez, How Do Design Heuristics Affects Outcomes?, in Proceedings of DESIGN 2012, the International Design Conference, 2012, vol. DS 70, pp. 1195-1204.

[13] Leahy K, C Seifert, S Daly, and S McKilligan, Overcoming Design Fixation in Idea Generation, in Proceedings of the Design Research Society 2018: Design as a catalyst for change, 2018, vol. 7, no. Section 24, pp. 2764–2775.

[14] Yilmaz S, SR Daly, and CM Seifert, Design Heuristics: An Evidence-Based tool to Improve Innovation, in Proceedings of the 121st ASEE Annual Conference and Exposition, 2014.

[15] Jablokow K, W Teerlink, S Yilmaz, S Daly, E Silk, and C Wehr, Ideation Variety in Mechanical Design: Examining the Effects of Cognitive Cognitive Style and Design Heuristics, in Proceedings of the ASME 2015 International Design Engineering Technical Conferences & Computers and Information in Engineering Conference - IDETC/CIE 2015, 2015, pp. 1–10.

[16] Ostrowski AK, JW Lee, SR Daly, A Huang-Saad, and CM Seifert, Design in Biomedical Engineering: Student Applications of Design Heuristics as a Tool for Idea Generation, in Proceedings of the 124th ASEE Annual Conference and Exposition, 2017.

[17] Yilmaz S, SR Daly, CM Seifert, and R Gonzalez, Evidence-Based Design Heuristics for Idea Generation, Des. Stud., vol. 46, pp. 95–124, 2016.

[18] Zoom Video Communications Inc., Zoom v5.0.4. San Jose, CA, USA, 2020.

[19] Instructure Inc., Canvas LMS. Salt Lake City, UT, USA, 2020.

[20] Adobe Inc., Adobe Photoshop Lightroom v3.3. San Jose, CA, USA, 2020.

[21] Ulrich K, S Eppinger, and M Yang, Concept Generation, in Product Design and Development, 7th ed., McGraw Hill, 2019, pp. 117–142.

[22] Lockhart HE, A Paradigm for Packaging, Packag. Technol. Sci., vol. 10, no. 5, pp. 237–252, 1997.

[23] GraphPad Software LLC, Prism v8.4.3. San Diego, CA, USA, 2020.

[24] Cohen J, Statistical Power Analysis for the Behavioral Sciences, 2nd ed. Hillsdale, NJ, USA: Lawrence Erlbaum Associates Inc., 1988.

Application of a Database Management System to Improve the Efficiency of Eye-tracking Package Design Testing [86]

Mengmeng Zhao, PhD, R. Andrew Hurley, PhD *,

Department of Food, Nutrition and Packaging Sciences,
223 Poole Agricultural Center
Clemson University
Clemson, SC 29634-0316, USA

Abstract: In recent years, more than two hundred studies have occurred in developing eye-tracking methodologies for quantifying consumer attention on packaging design preference. Due to time and expense, most research analyzes consumer attention for a relatively small number of products within a specific planogram. Answers to larger questions concerning category trends and insights are difficult using common, one-off studies. Broad data aggregation and analysis are crucial for understanding packaging design within product categories in order to comprehend category-wide design trends and insights. Considering the amount of effort required for manual processing, a method that can improve efficiency and data aggregation would benefit all researchers. A relational database management system (DBMS) fits this need. This paper describes the development of a DBMS and compares it to traditional file-based methods; analysis of this system included eye-tracking procedures, data management, and data analysis methodology. A relational database with a web portal was designed and created to aggregate, store, access, share, and analyze eye-tracking data based on studies in a retail environment. The database was utilized across fourteen eye-tracking projects involving 34 planograms and 421 consumer goods. Statistical analysis included t-tests and ANOVA which were integrated by using PHP/JavaScript to determine data significance ($p<0.05$). The DBMS system reduced overall time working on the project by 48%. Using computerized data collection, storage, and analysis provides logic for development and is an expense justified with savings, not only in the amount of time needed to conduct the study but in the reduction of human labor as well. was observed for the positive total stretch of the general-performance film. No differences were observed in the percent loss when comparing the total stretch scenario at the two storage conditions for either film type. These results indicate that although there was a loss in containment force due to storage conditions, the total stretch scenario of the film applied to the simulated load had no effect on the percent loss.

Keywords: packaging; eye-tracking methodology; consumer attention; DBMS.

***Correspondence to:** Dr. R. Andrew Hurley, Department of Food, Nutrition and Packaging Sciences, 223 Poole Agricultural Center, Clemson University, Clemson, SC 29634-0316, USA. E-mail: ruperth@clemson.edu

1. Introduction

Packaging design performs a key function in a market economy, from consumer and competitive perspectives, to its role in differentiation and segmentation, all while supporting rivalry, commercialization, and innovation. [1] Despite this, packaging design is often involved in the later stages of product development, which are relatively short, to match the product launching timeline. [2] A rising number of consumer behavior researchers have focused on packaging design and related branding strategies, providing actionable insight and attempting to ensure business success. [3]

Eye-tracking is a technique that enables researchers to measure a consumer's point of view. It is a widely used method to quantitatively evaluate the effectiveness of package design. [3] By utilizing eye-tracking devices in a retail environment, researchers are able to capture the eye movements of participants in order to determine how their packaging design performs among the competitive array.

There are many examples of how eye-tracking technology can be used to obtain information on consumer behavior for specific items within retail planograms. One researcher investigated the effect of display trays in a simulated retail environment on consumer preference. [4] Another study analyzed carbonated soft drinks in reusable shells by using eye-tracking technology to test the role of secondary packaging on brand awareness [5].

Even though package analysis studies that offer insight on specific products are more commonplace, the larger questions concerning category trends and insights are difficult to answer within common, one-off studies. A broad data aggregation and analysis is crucial for understanding packaging design per product category in order to understand category-wide design trends and insights. The timeline for a new product launch can be tight. Statistical analysis of the product design is crucial, but the amount of time and effort it takes to manually retrieve that data can create scheduling conflicts. If feedback could be provided faster, the next round of packaging design modifications could be conducted sooner in order to speed up the product launch phase. A method that leverages a database management system (DBMS) to improve efficiency in data collection and aggregation would benefit all researchers studying consumer behavior in relevant product categories.

A DBMS is software designed to assist in maintaining and utilizing large amounts of data, making analysis tasks easier. [6] By storing eye-tracking data in a DBMS rather than as a collection of operating system files, the DBMS's features can be used to manage the data in a more robust and efficient manner. [7] The DBMS built for this paper was built on MySQL, a popular and widely-used database program that is also equipped with a web portal for easy access to data. It is aimed at providing a wide range of marketing data in aggregate for the food packaging sector. Every step of the eye-tracking process can be conducted in a single place and all the data is saved in the database, including mixed methods surveys and raw data. A refined and logical data analysis section is designed for generating final reports automatically from the raw data exported directly from the eye-tracking device. With this tool, researchers will be able to better understand how a packaging design performs in the marketplace by making the data analysis portion accurate and efficient. This DBMS was populated with fourteen recent eye-tracking projects collected at CUshopTM Consumer Experience Laboratory (Figure 1), involving 34 planograms and 421 consumer goods. The consumer goods industry will overarchingly benefit from this tool by being able to gather consumer feedback on new products faster, which in turn will shorten the launching phase for new products.

Figure 1. *CUshop™ Consumer Experience Laboratory*

2. Methods

2.1 DBMS Design

The database design was divided into three phases (Figure 2). In the first phase, Requirements Analysis was conducted to determine the necessary functions of the database. This process involved interviews with user groups to identify the functionality required from the database, the data that needed to be processed, and the most frequently performed operations. In the second phase, a Conceptual Database Design was created to construct a model of the information used. In the third phase, the Logical Database Design was used to construct a model of information used based on a specific data model.

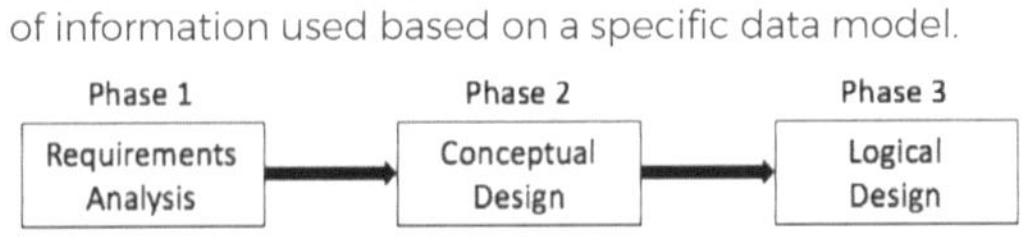

Figure 2 *Three phases of database design*

Eye-tracking key metrics, participants, projects, planograms, products, and user accounts were stored in the database as the key entities used in running studies and analyzing results. The relationship of these entities was developed in the database and shown in Figure 3.

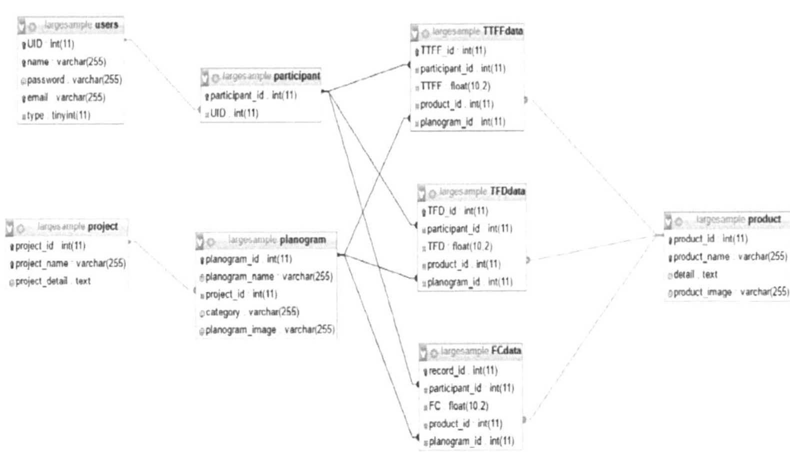

Figure 3. *Relationship of key entities in database design*

2.2 Web Portal Design

By having data structured in a database, eye tracking results can be retrieved and managed through SQL queries. Database operations require sufficient knowledge on database management and SQL programming. A user-friendly web portal (Figure 4) for managing and accessing the database was built on top of the database. In this research, the management system was built based on a relational database by using PHP, HTML, JavaScript, and CSS, along with SQL queries for data retrieval from the database. Users of the web portal are able to conduct operations for the eye tracking data import, aggregation, retrieval, and report generation.

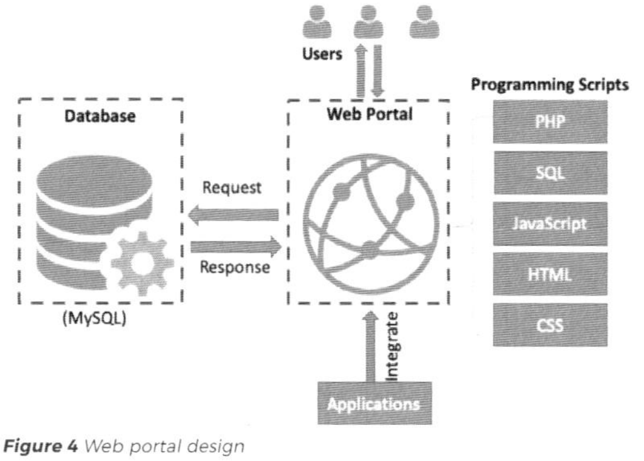

Figure 4 *Web portal design*

2.3 Data Collection Workflow

TobiiTM Pro Eye Tracking 2 Glasses (Figure 5) were used to record the participants' eye movements. These glasses are binocular video-based pupil and corneal reflection glasses, which sample at a rate of 50Hz.[8] A TobiiTM Recording Controller gathers the eye-tracking data and guides the researcher through the calibration process, indicating successful calibration for each new participant.

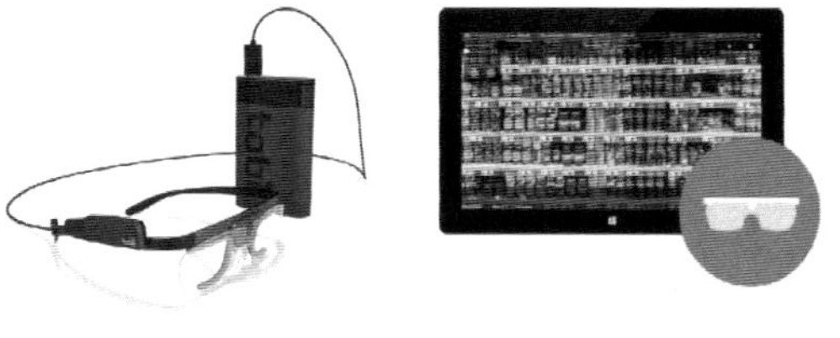

Figure 5 *Tobii ™ Pro eye tracking package [8]*

For each eye-tracking study, the participants were asked to wear the eye-tracking glasses and shop in a grocery environment, which had been set up as specific planograms per individual study requirements. Once the calibration was complete, the participant was provided a clipboard with a shopping list; the list was identified only by the participant number. The participants were instructed to shop for each product on the list as they normally would in a grocery store, writing down the number corresponding to the product they selected for each item on the list. Areas of Interest (AOI's), areas of analysis used in the eye-tracking software to collect fixation data, were designed for the stimuli and used to determine three measured metrics of eye movement:

Time to First Fixation (TTFF) is the time in seconds from the point at which a product first enters a participant's field of view until they fixate on it. The lower the number, the better the package performed.

Total Fixation Duration (TFD) is the average time, in seconds, participants fixated on an item. The higher the number, the better the package performed.

Fixation Count (FC) is the total number of times a participant's scan of the planogram crossed into a particular area of interest.

2.4 Data Analysis

The Tobii ™ Pro Glasses Analyzer was used to collect raw eye-tracking data. To obtain statistical analysis results, three steps were required: data uploading, data analysis, and report generation. By uploading raw data, defining the report type, and specifying the products for comparison, an automatic report was able to be generated. As shown in Figure 6, the specified products were first sorted by categories or planograms. An Analysis of Variance (t-test, ANOVA) was then conducted by PHP/JavaScript Library (Math-php and jStat v 1.7.1) to measure if the data was significantly different ($p<0.05$). Mean, standard deviation, and standard error of eye-tracking key metrics (TTFF, TFD, FC) were also calculated.

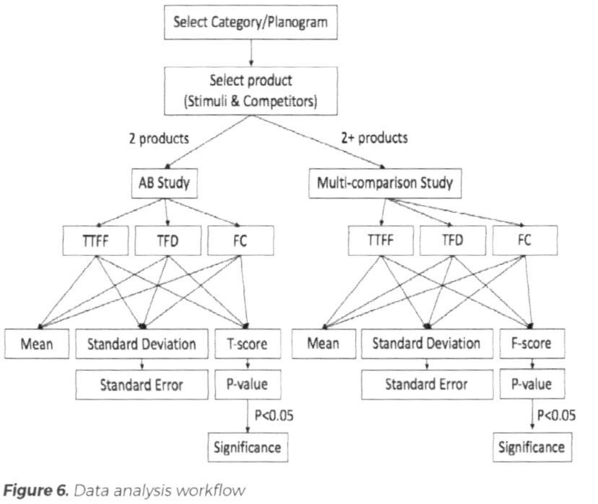

Figure 6. *Data analysis workflow*

3. Results and Discussion

3.1 Results of Data Retrieval at the Planogram Level

The study level data can be retrieved by selecting a planogram name. The result in Figure 7 showed a set of eye tracking data collected in a single study using a coffee planogram. Within the planogram, eleven coffee products were tested. When those results were retrieved by specifying the planogram name, the planogram-wide result is shown for the eye-tracking key metrics of TTFF mean, TFD mean, and FC mean.

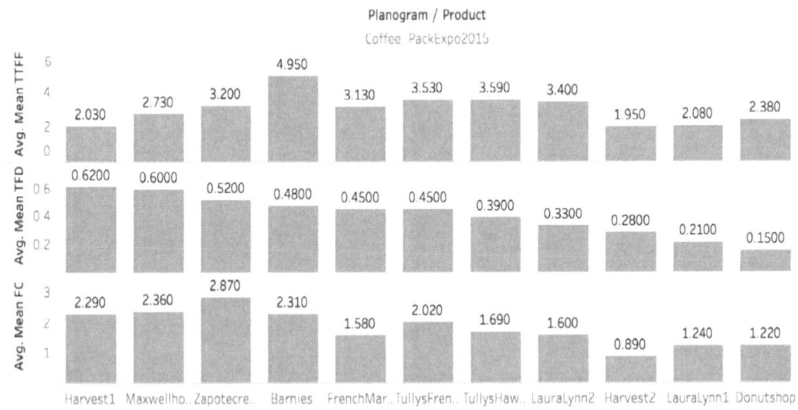

Figure 7 *Eye-tracking results retrieved at the planogram level*

3.2 Results of Data Retrieval at the Category Level

The results of data retrieval at category level shows the broader results of the research program aggregate. In Figure 8, forty-seven products within a category have been retrieved by specifying the category name. A category-wide result is shown for the eye-tracking key metrics of TTFF mean, TFD mean, and FC mean.

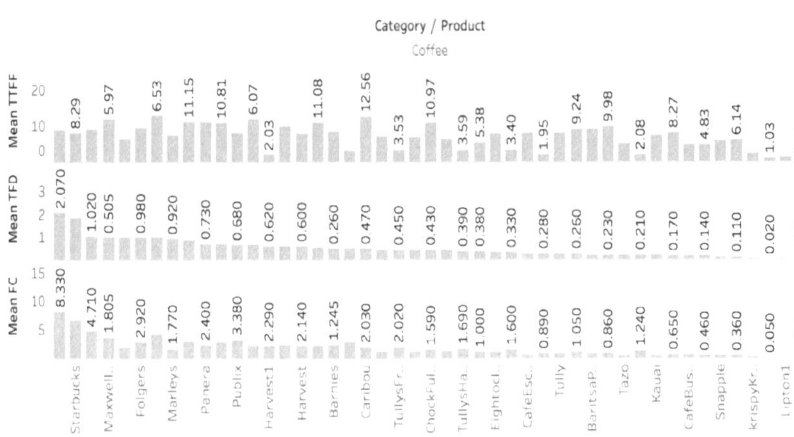

Figure 8 *Eye-tracking results retrieved at the category level*

3.3 Efficiency Analysis

A comparison demonstrating the average time, in hours, it takes to generate a complete eye-tracking study analysis between a file-based method versus a DBMS method is shown in Figure 9. This was calculated by interviewing experienced researchers. The reduction of time that the DBMS method allows compared to the file-based method is also illustrated. In terms of time, it was found that the entire process takes 48% less time when using the DBMS system. The time needed for the individual pre-survey, report writing, and statistical analysis processes was also significantly decreased.

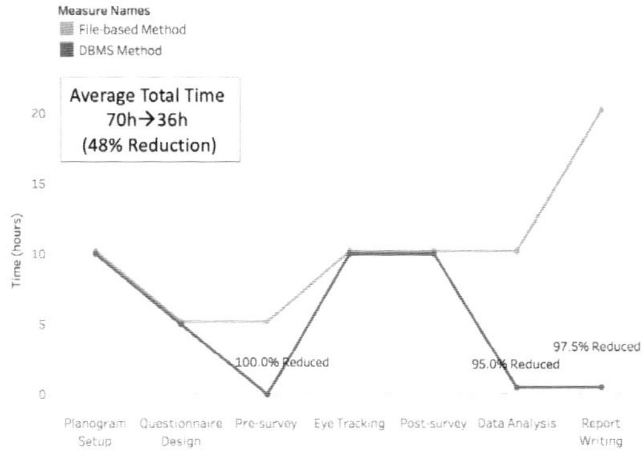

Figure 9 *Time comparison of file-based method and DBMS method*

The DBMS eliminated the need to repeat the participant pre-survey for each eye-tracking study. As long as the participants were invited from the pre-screened participant pool, the background investigation of each participant had been completed before each study occurred and responses were saved in the database, creating a 100% decrease in time to complete, since the pre-survey was replaced by direct data retrieval from stored data.

For report writing, which typically encompasses the most time to complete, at 20 hours, the DBMS's ability for auto-reporting decreased time consumption by 97.5%. The DBMS method associated with analysis programming has a significant positive effect on data access and processing times. A customized template of a study report was designed and utilized in the linked web portal, providing various ways for users to generate reports according to the different study types.

Statistical analysis has been considered the most crucial and time-consuming step of all the key procedures. This portion of work does not only require knowledge of statistical analysis but also the need to maintain accuracy while working with a large set of quantitative (e.g., eye-tracking key metrics) and qualitative (e.g., survey responses) results. Human errors are more likely when using a file-based method, with higher workloads potentially lending itself to a number of errors. By using a DBMS method, time needed to compile a report was reduced by 95%, and human errors were avoided by the use of direct data retrieval from the data source.

4. Conclusion

By using a relational database system, eye-tracking data collected and added to the database becomes more accessible and easier to integrate. This, in turn, provides convenience for further statistical analysis and reporting, which significantly improves the efficiency of the body of research. Managing information by using a database allows researchers to have a more strategic method to manipulate various data analysis-required operations. Data aggregation of eye-tracking studies using a DBMS can provide a greater wide-range comparison and analysis of packaging design compared to the conventional one-off study methods. These findings are crucial for the future of packaging science, specifically the design aspect, in order to provide the packaging industry a more comprehensive method of consumer behavior research that can help improve the success of product launches.

5. References

[1] Dobson PW, Yadav A. Packaging in a market economy: The economic and commercial role of packaging communication. 2012. https://ueaeprints.uea.ac.uk/id/eprint/41228/.

[2] Tonkin C, Ouzts AD, Duchowski. AT: NGCA '11: Proceedings of the 1st Conference on Novel Gaze-Controlled Applications. Eye-tracking within the packaging design workflow: interaction with physical and virtual shelves; 2011:1-8. doi:https://doi.org/10.1145/1983302.1983305

[3] Hurley RA, Rice JC, Conlon G, Tonkin CE, O'Hara L. The impact of simulated kraft substrates on consumer attention at the point of sale. Journal of Applied Packaging Research. 2015;7(1):4. doi:DOI: 10.14448/japr.03.0004

[4] Snyder E, Hurley RA, Tonkin CE, Cooksey K, Rice JC. An eye-tracking methodology for testing consumer preference of display trays in a simulated retail environment. Journal of Applied Packaging Research. 2015;7(1):6.

[5] Hurley RA, Rice JC, Koefelda J, Congdon J, Ouzts A. The role of secondary packaging on brand awareness: analysis of 2-L carbonated soft drinks in reusable shells using eye-tracking technology. Packaging Technology and Science. 2017;30(11):711-722. doi:https://doi.org/10.1002/pts.2316

[6] Wells DL, Blakeley JA, Thompson CW. Architecture of an open object-oriented database management system. Computer. 1992;25(10):74-82. doi:https://doi.org/10.1109/2.161282

[7] Dix A. Human-computer interaction. In: Encyclopedia of Database Systems. New York, NY: Springer Science Business Media; 2009:1327-1331.

[8] Tobii Pro Glasses 2. https://www.tobiipro.com/product-listing/tobii-pro-glasses-2/#Features. Accessed October 13, 2017.

CHAPTER VII

Food packaging, barrier properties & migration

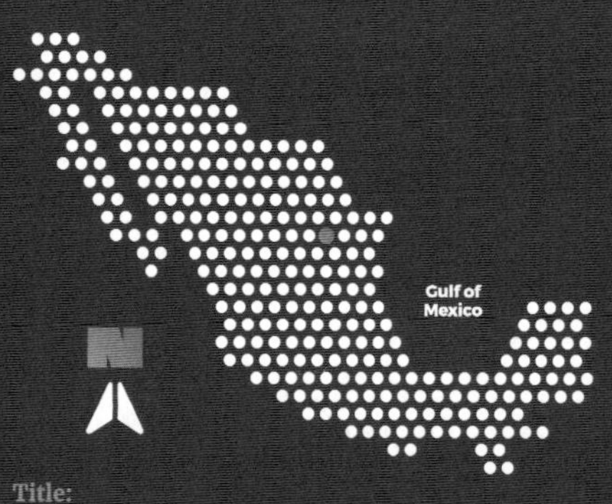

Title:
Pan Comido

Author:
Sarai Cuello Gutiérrez

Technique:
Digital photography

Location:
Monterrey, NUEVO LEÓN

Description:
Nothing beats a good cup of coffee and a delicious freshly-baked piece of bread. Pancomido is a bakery located in Monterrey's downtown, where they bake daily delicious sweet treats that will definitley bring a smile to your face as you smell it and enjoy it.

Influence of relative humidity and temperature on water vapor transmission rate of metallized paper [13]

Yves Wyser *, Alexey Vishtal
Nestlé Institute of Packaging Sciences, Société des Produits Nestlé,
Lausanne Switzerlan

Abstract: Plastic packaging waste is one of the biggest sustainability issues the world is facing. Many players in the packaging value chain have taken commitments towards a reduction of their contribution to the issue. Fiber-based packaging materials such as paper, that provide the food protection requirements while remaining recyclable in the existing mixed paper recycling stream, is one of the potential solutions to reduce packaging waste load on environment.

Paper is lacking barrier properties and specifically, due to hydrophilic nature of cellulosic fibres barrier towards water vapor. Barrier functionality can be brought to paper by applying polymer coatings of various nature and physical vapor deposition of aluminum.

Typically barrier properties of packaging materials are assessed at 23 °C and 50% Relative Humidity (RH) for Oxygen Transmission Rate (OTR) and at 38°C and 90 % RH for Water Vapor Transmission Rate (WVTR). The conditions used for WVTR may alter structure of material by inducing dimensional expansion of the paper which in own turn may disrupt polymeric and/or inorganic barrier coatings.

This study looks at the influence of temperature and RH during WVTR testing on the obtained results, demonstrating that the exposition to high water vapor pressure during testing may generate barrier losses. In the case of a high barrier paper, it is shown that testing at 38°C and 90% RH yields a WVTR close to 10 times higher than when testing at 23 °C and 85 % RH, displaying non-linear dependence of barrier performance on partial water vapour pressure.

The study concludes with a recommendation of optimized conditions to test WVTR of barrier paper.

Keywords: water vapor transmission rate, testing methods, barrier paper packaging

***Correspondence to:** Yves Wyser, Nestlé Institute of Packaging Sciences, Société des Produits Nestlé, Lausanne Switzerland. E-mail: yves.wyser@rd.nestle.com

1. Introduction

Paper-based materials are used in packaging applications since the beginning of industrial era. They possess key attributes essential to packaging such as mechanical strength and ability to be printed and converted into a variety of different formats. Recently paper regained a strong development focus as a route to decrease the use of fossil-based materials. However, paper materials lack other key packaging attributes such as barrier properties required to protect food from degradation due to moisture, in the case of dry foods, or oxygen, in the case of food sensitive to oxidation1. Figure 1 gives approximate order of magnitudes of the requirements of different long shelf life food categories in terms of packaging barrier properties. These properties can be achieved by using modern multi-layer laminates, often composed of various polymers and barrier materials or coatings 2. However, this renders recycling of such flexible paper packaging multimaterials close to impossible.

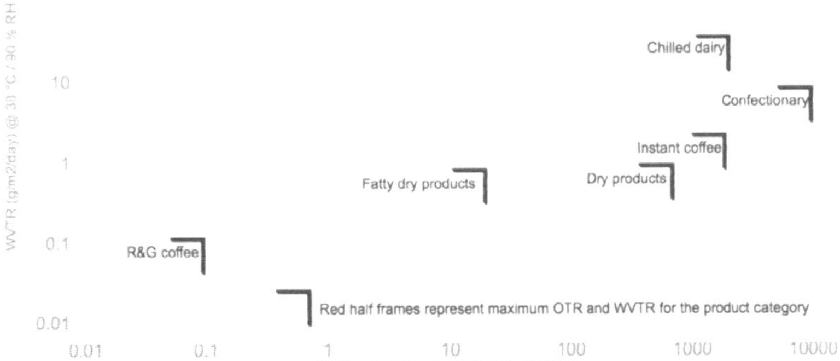

***Figure 1** Barrier requirement estimates for different product categories, adapted from [3]*

In the meantime, plastic packaging waste has become one of the biggest sustainability issues the world is facing [4]. This is partly triggered by the complexity of modern flexible packaging materials, which often end up as litter or in landfill, due to the absence of effective recycling infrastructures. Many players in the food value chain have taken commitments towards a reduction of their contribution to the issue, by, among other actions, using packaging materials that are more readily recyclable [5-9]. Paper-based packaging materials, that provide the food protection requirements while remaining recyclable in the existing mixed paper recycling stream, is one of the promising routes followed. These materials are referred to as "barrier papers" or "functional papers".

Typically, structure of such barrier paper is composed of one or several layers of polymeric coatings with an overall thickness of less than 10 μm which are applied as water-based polymer dispersions on paper in online or offline coating process. To further improve barrier properties, these coatings can be combined with vacuum deposited inorganic layers, such as aluminium or silicon oxide [10].

Key advantage of these materials is that the barrier performance range achieved is comparable to that of multilayer plastic laminates while remaining recyclable in a classic paper recycling stream. Recyclability is maintained via controlling adhesion of coatings to paper and their respective mechanical strength allowing faster disintegration in repulping and higher accept yields in comparison with the conventional paper-plastic laminated structures [11].

On the other hand, one of the key limitations of such thin coatings is their insufficient mechanical strength, especially when loaded in tension. This can happen during the converting process of the paper or the food packing process, potentially inducing loss of barrier performance [12,13]. The barrier loss linked to stress induced rupture in the coatings is especially severe when deposited on substrates with low to absent barrier properties, such as paper.

Paper is a hygroscopic material capable of absorbing significant amounts of water, depending on the temperature and the relative humidity (RH) of the environment it is exposed to, changing its geometrical and volumetric dimensions [14-16]. In accordance with the type of the fiber, extent of the refining and drying method, the dimensional changes in paper, also referred as hygro-expansive strain maybe more or less profound [17].

A positive hygro-expansive strain of the paper will generate tensile stresses on the thin coating, which might induce cracking of the coating and therefore barrier performance degradation [13].

This poses a challenge to overcome when we consider the methodologies used to measure the water vapor transmission rate (WVTR) and might induce misleading results. Indeed, water vapor properties of packaging materials are typically measured by applying a water vapor pressure gradient on both sides of the material, by applying humid air on one side of the material, and dry air on the other.

The gravimetric dish method [18] uses silica gel or another desiccant to absorb the moisture passing through the packaging material, generating a close to perfectly dry environment inside an aluminium dish placed in a humid environment. The moisture absorption by the desiccant is measured by weighing the dish on a precision scale at different time intervals during a certain period.

Other methods use moist air on one side of the sample and a flow of dry air on the other side. The moisture picked up by the dry air is determined by modulated infra-red sensor [19] or by electrolytic detection sensors [20].

In all cases, the obtained value of transmission rate depends on the temperature and on the water vapor pressure gradient applied to the materials, the conditions in which the tests are performed are therefore standardized in order to enable easy comparison between materials.

ISO 2528 [18] suggests 5 different testing conditions at which water vapor transmission rates should be performed, namely 25 °C and 90 % RH, 38 °C and 90 % RH, 25 °C and 75 % RH, 23 °C and 85 % RH, or 20 °C and 85 % RH.

With the occurrence of high barrier materials, the most aggressive conditions, i.e. 38 °C and 90 % RH, have become the common standard used in industry, in order to reduce testing time. There was no issue when considering dimensionally stable materials like plastic and laminates, but when including the recently developed barrier paper, a better understanding seems necessary.

Considering the previous considerations on hygro-expansive strain, it is however to be expected that using such humid conditions might artificially degrade the measured properties of barrier paper. Up to our knowledge, no other research study have tried to clarify this point.

This study aims at verifying this hypothesis and proposing new testing conditions more adapted to these new high barrier paper. The water vapor transmission rate of a high barrier paper with a brittle and thin inorganic layer (i.e. metallized paper) will be measured in different conditions to evaluate the effect of using classical testing conditions on an undesirable degradation of barrier properties during testing.

2. Materials and methods

Materials

A high barrier metallized paper with basis weight 65 g/m^2 was used in this study. The paper was coated with a heat-seal layer on the side opposite the metallization. The metallized side was printed, and an over print varnish deposited.

The deposit layers were thin (less than 4 g/m²) and sensitive to crack despite varnishes. Before any use the samples were stored at 23°C and 50% HR at least 24 hours.

Methods

WVTR measurement

Water vapor transmission rate was determined gravimetrically by applying ISO 2528 [18].

Samples were sealed at room temperature on dishes containing silica gel (Silica gel with indicator (orange gel, Supelco, Darmstadt, Germany) using a mix between wax (60 % w/w, Sasolwax 7835, Sasol Wax GmbH, Hamburg, Germany) and paraffin (40% w/w, Parrafin Wax, Sigma Aldrich, Darmstadt, Germany). The exposed surface area was 50 cm2. In some instances, the samples were oriented to have the printed metallization towards the moist side (Figure 2, Left), and in other instance towards the dry side (Figure 2, Right).

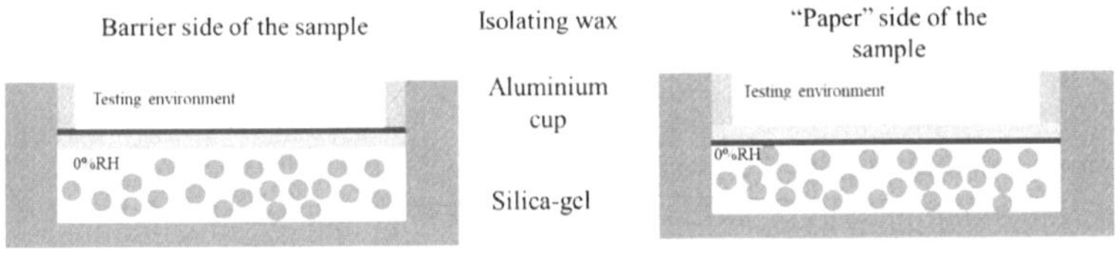

Figure 2 *Schematic representation of the WVTR dishes with sample mounted with metallization towards moist side (left) and towards dry side (right)*

A sample prepared identically but containing no silica gel was used as blank, to compensate for moisture uptake by the sample itself and buoyancy effects linked to atmospheric pressure changes.

The samples were stored in climatic cabinets set at the desired temperature and relative humidity. The samples were weighed at regular intervals (1-4 days) until equilibrium was reached in the blank sample and linear water uptake was achieved. The samples were taken out of the climatic cabinet approximately 15 minutes before weighing and were reintroduced directly after.

The water vapor transmission rate (WVTR, g/m2/day) was determined by the slope of the weight uptake versus time curve, corrected for weight changes in the blank specimen, divided by the exposed surface area of paper. In some instances, for comparison purposes, the WVTR is divided by the water vapor pressure gradient applied to the sample. All the samples are identical with same thickness and taken from the same production batch.

Samples were tested at 38°C / 90 % RH (corresponding to a water vapor pressure of 60 mbar) and 23 °C / 85 % RH (corresponding to a water vapor pressure of 24 mbar).

In some instance, samples were pre-conditioned, unrestrained, at 38 °C and 90 % RH and 30 °C and 70 % RH during 2 weeks prior to measurement of WVTR and Optical density.

Optical density

The optical density of a metalized material corresponds to the logarithm of the inverse of the light transmission (T) through the sample:

$$D_T = log\frac{1}{T} = log\left(\frac{I_0}{I}\right)$$

Where I_0 is the intensity of the incident light and I the intensity of the transmitted light.

The optical density is an indirect measure of the quality and homogeneity of metallization.

The optical density of the samples was measured before and after the WVTR tests and after pre- conditioning using a Gretag Macbeth TR-524 densitometer. 5 measurements were taken over the exposed 50 cm² surface of samples used to determine WVTR. The blank sample was not included in the measurements. The values are reported as the average value of 5 measurements per specimen, performed on 6 specimens.

3. Results and Discussion

Table 1 lists the WVTR of the material as obtained in the various conditions as well as the Dt of the samples after the various tests. The optical density of the material prior to any testing was determined as 4.83 ± 0.06.

Table 1 *WVTR and Optical density results of the metalized paper after testing and pre- conditioning in various climatic conditions*

Sample code	Testing conditions	Water vapor pressure	Pre-conditioning	Sample exposition	WVTR	Dt
	°C / % RH	mbar	-	Metallization towards	g/m²/day	-
M24/N	23 / 85	24	None	Moist side	0.13 ± 0.04	4.87 ± 0.03
D24/N	23 / 85	24	None	Dry side	0.42 ± 0.09	4.79 ± 0.09
M60/N	38 / 90	60	None	Moist side	1.1 ± 0.1	4.66 ± 0.04
D60/N	38 / 90	60	None	Dry side	12 ± 3	4.48 ± 0.16
M24/60	23 / 85	24	38 °C /90 % RH (60 mbar)	Moist side	1.9 ± 0.6	4.33 ± 0.10
M24/30	23 / 85	24	30 °C /70 % RH (30 mbar)	Moist side	0.10 ± 0.03	4.87 ± 0.04

Those results show that the orientation of the sample with respect to exposure to moisture has a significant effect on the measured WVTR, both at 23 °C and 85 % RH (M24/N vs D24/N) and at 38°C and 90 % RH (M60/N vs D60/N), the effect in the latter conditions being more pronounced.

As mentioned in the introduction, this difference is due to a difference in the hygro-expansion of the samples linked to its moisture content which create cracks in the thin barrier layers. Indeed, when the metalized layer is facing the moisture, the paper is in contact with the dry side of the setup, which is close to 0% RH. The paper is therefore in slight compression compared to the usual standard conditions of 23°C and 50 % RH, which shall not cause any significant change in the dimensions of paper. On the contrary, when the metallization is facing the dry side, the paper faces the high relative humidity, inducing moisture content increase in the paper and therefore positive hygro-expansive strain. This strain then induces cracks in the metalized layer (as shown by the decrease of the optical density) which induce barrier performance loss.

Changes in the tension/compression of the testing specimens can also be observed visually after 48 hours of sample exposure to high RH environment. These changes are shown in Figure 3. As can be seen in the cases when "paper" component of the barrier paper was allowed to pick up moisture upon conditioning it appears somewhat "wavy" which is a consequence of a tension loss. It is evident in both cases when paper is exposed directly to high RH (Fig 3 middle) and when there is no dehydrating silica-gel present inside of the cup (case of blank sample, Fig 3 right).

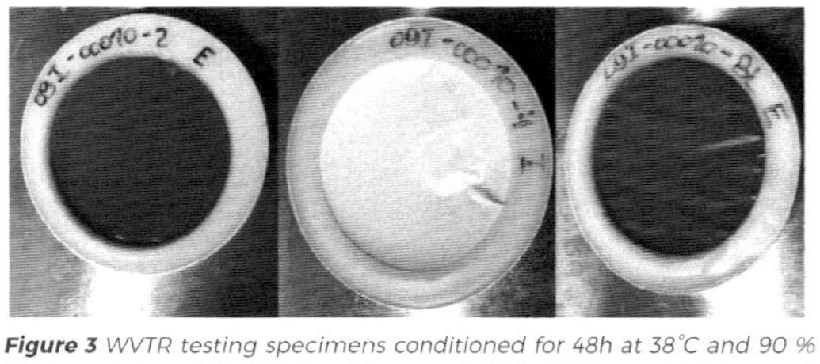

Figure 3 *WVTR testing specimens conditioned for 48h at 38°C and 90 % RH, from left to right: Barrier side towards high RH, "paper side" towards high RH, Barrier side towards high RH-blank sample*

When considering the permeation, gradient in partial pressure and temperature are the main parameters affecting the rate at which moisture permeates through a material.

In the case of Fickian diffusion, the effect of the water vapor pressure gradient can be considered as mostly linear and the WVTR of laminates is therefore sometimes normalized by the water vapor gradient across the sample. Table 2 lists the normalized WVTR results for the different conditions.

A very strong increase in permeability can be observed when changing the testing temperature.

Table 2 *Normalized WVTR results of the metalized paper in various climatic conditions*

Sample code	Testing conditions	Water vapor pressure	Sample exposition	Normalized WVTR
	°C / % RH	mbar	Metallization towards	10^{-3} g/m²/day/mbar
M24/N	23 / 85	24	Moist side	5.5 ± 1.7
D24/N	23 / 85	24	Dry side	18 ± 4
M60/N	38 / 90	60	Moist side	19 ± 1
D60/N	38 / 90	60	Dry side	190 ± 40

Although temperature does have a significant effect on the permeability of materials, it seems clear the acceleration factors observed for a 15 °C increase (3.5 and more than 10) cannot solely attributed to temperature increase. It is to be expected that other mechanisms come into play, such as hygro-expansive strain-induced cracking of the metalized layer, and potentially changes in the supporting polymeric structures caused by increased temperature.

In order to decouple the effects of hygro-expansive strain on barrier loss from the effects of testing conditions, samples where pre-conditioned at 38°C and 90 % RH for 2 weeks (M24/60), prior to testing at 23 °C and 85 % RH. During this pre-conditioning, the samples are exposed to identical water vapor pressure and temperature conditions as sample D60/N, with the paper side in direct contact with humid air.

The results obtained show 15 times increase in WVTR compared to M24/N, suggesting that storage at such aggressive conditions induce irreversible barrier loss and supporting the hypothesis of hygro-expansive strain.

Comparing the normalized WVTR of M24/60 and D60/N, i.e. 79 10^{-3} g/m²/day/mbar and 190 10^{-3} g/m²/day/mbar, respectively, one can observe an acceleration factor due to temperature of 2.4, more inline with what would be expected for such a temperature increase.

The optical density between those two samples, i.e. 4.33 ± 0.10 for M24/60 and 4.48 ± 0.16 for D60/N are not significantly different, suggesting a similar level of defects in the metalized layer.

Effect of realistic tropical conditions

Since determining the WVTR of metalized papers at 38°C and 90 % RH clearly strongly affects the integrity of the barrier layer, determination of whether such a detrimental effect would occur in tropical environmental conditions is essential. Aforementioned conditions are primarily used to accelerate testing and increase throughput of testing equipment and do not simulate actual climatic conditions in any part of the world. Following an unpublished study on data of numerous climatic stations of the world [21], tropical climatic conditions are approximated by 30°C and 70 % RH as a standard within Nestlé.

Samples were pre-conditioned at 30°C and 70 % RH for 2 weeks, prior to testing at 23 °C and 85 % RH (M24/30).

The results given in Table 1 clearly show that exposing paper to these conditions does not significantly affect the barrier properties and optical density, suggesting tropical climatic conditions are not a hurdle for the application of barrier papers worldwide. This assumption requires further validation as in real life conditions, temperature/humidity variations are cyclic in nature which may bring additional stress on paper-based materials.

4. Conclusion

The study presented in this paper aimed at determining whether water vapor transmission rate testing conditions commonly applied to high barrier materials were directly applicable to barrier paper, more specifically to high barrier polymer dispersion coated paper.

The study clearly demonstrated that applying harsh climatic conditions induced irreversible deterioration of the barrier properties of the materials, probably linked to the hygro-expansive strain induced by the high moisture pickup of water in these humid conditions, which potentially disrupts the vacuum deposited metallized layer and/or the polymeric layer on paper. This suggest that testing barrier paper at 38 °C and 90 % RH is not adapted to barrier paper and that other standard conditions, as proposed in ISO 2528 18 should be preferred. The results obtained in the present study suggest that testing barrier paper at 23 °C and 85 % RH, corresponding to condition D of Annex B of ISO 2528 [18], presents a good compromise between testing speed (i.e. relatively high water vapor pressure) and barrier retention.

It further showed that the exposition of the paper has a significant effect on the testing results and that it should therefore be taken into consideration according to the final application and reported as an additional parameter usually absent from reports for classical packaging materials. It is recommended that barrier paper shall be stored in conditioned warehouses prior to conversion into finished packs.

Finally, the study demonstrated that exposing barrier paper to environmental conditions simulating averaged tropical climate does not significantly affect its barrier properties, opening its application as an alternative to plastic packaging even in countries with elevated levels of temperature and relative humidity.

5. Acknowledgement

The authors would like to acknowledge Chantal Pelletier, Maria Isabelle Giardiello and Frédéric Deantoni for their support in performing testing.

6 References

[1] Söremark C and Tryding J, Packaging, in Paper Products Physics and Technology, Ek M, Gellerstedt G, Henriksson G, Eds, Walter de Gruyter GmbH & Co. KG, Berlin Germany, 2009

[2] Lange, J.; Wyser, Y. Recent Innovations in Barrier Technologies for Plastic Packaging - A Review. Packaging Technology and Science 2003, 16 (4), 149.

[3] Wyser, Y.; Shires, D. Increasing the quality and impact of manuscripts in the field of new materials. Packaging Technology and Science 2019, 32 (1), 3.

[4] European commission, DG -ENV "Plastic waste in the environment," 2011, https://ec.europa.eu/environment/waste/studies/pdf/plastics.pdf (accessed 19.05.2019)

[5] The Coca-Cola Company, Sustainable packaging, https://www.coca-colacompany.com/sustainable-business/packaging-sustainability. (accessed 19.05.2019)

[6] Dow, 2025 sustainability goals, https://corporate.dow.com/en-us/science-and-sustainability/2025-goals.html. (accessed 19.05.2019)

[7] Mars, Plans To Rethink Our Packaging, https://www.mars.com/sustainability-plan/healthy-planet/sustainable-packaging (accessed 19.05.2019)

[8] Nestlé, Nestlé aiming at 100% recyclable or reusable packaging by 2025 https://www.nestle.com/media/pressreleases/allpressreleases/nestle-recyclable-reusable-packaging-by-2025. (accessed 19.05.2019)

[9] PepsiCo, Circular future for packaging, https://www.pepsico.com/sustainability/sustainable-food-system/packaging (accessed 19.05.2019)

[10] Field, R., Metallized C1S paper with moisture barrier: The ultimate in sustainabilitv. in Proceeding of PaperCon 2010, Atlanta (Ga), USA, 2010

[11] Lee, T. J.; Yoon, C.; Ryu, J. Y. A new potential paper resource; Recyclability of paper cups coated with water-soluble polyacrylate-based polymer. Nordic Pulp and Paper Research Journal 2017, 32 (1).

[12] Hertlein, J. Untersuchungen über Veränderungen der Barriereeigenschaften metallisierter Kunststoffolien beim maschinellen Verarbeiten; Utz Verlag: Munich, Germany, 1997.

[13] Leterrier, Y.; Wyser, Y.; Manson, J. A. E.; Hilborn, J. A Method to Measure the Adhesion of Thin Glass Coatings on Polymer Films. The Journal of Adhesion 1994, 44 (3), 213.

[14] Uesaka, T. General formula for hygroexpansion of paper. Journal of Materials Science 1994, 29 (9), 2373.

[15] Parker ME, Bronlund JE and Mawson AJ, Moisture Sorption Isotherms for Paper and Paperboard in Food Chain Conditions, Packag. Technol. Sci. 2006; 19, 193

[16] Fellers C, The Interaction of Paper with Water Vapour in Paper Products Physics and Technology, Ek M, Gellerstedt G, Henriksson G, Eds, Walter de Gruyter GmbH & Co. KG, Berlin Germany, 2009

[17] Lindner, M. Factors affecting the hygroexpansion of paper. Journal of Materials Science 2018, 53 (1).

[18] International Organization for Standardization., Sheet materials — Determination of water vapour transmission rate (WVTR) — Gravimetric (dish) method; (ISO 2528-2017) ISO: Geneva, 2017.

[19] American Society for Testing Materials (2013), Standard Test Method for Water Vapor Transmission Rate Through Plastic Film and Sheeting Using a Modulated Infrared Sensor. (ASTM F1249-13) ASTM: West Conshohocken, PA, 2013.

[20] American Society for Testing Materials (2013), Standard Test Method for Water Vapor Transmission Rate Through Plastic Film and Sheeting Using an Electrolytic Detection Sensor (Coulometric P2O5 Sensor). (ASTM F3299-18) ASTM: West Conshohocken, PA, 2018.

[21] Muller, M. J.; Baltes, K.; Werle, D. Handbuch ausgewahlter Klimastationen der Erde.; 4th edition.; University of Trier: Trier, Germany, 1987.

The Effect of Polymer Structure and Temperature on Permeability of Key Aroma Compound in Fresh-Cut Durian [35]

Nuttapong Atipalungkool [1], Pattarin Leelaphiwat [*1], Charinee Winotapun [2]
1 Department of Packaging and Materials Technology, Faculty of Agro-Industry, Kasetsart University, Bangkok, Thailand
2 National Metal and Materials Technology Center, National Science and Technology Development Agency, Thailand Science Park, Pathumthani, Thailand

Abstract: Durian is an economic fruit of tropical countries in Southeast Asia and it has a specific and strong smell. A strong odor from aroma compound of packaged fresh-cut durian caused the problems during storage and transportation. This research aims to study the permeability of the key aromatic compound in fresh-cut durian through the multilayer of polylactic acid (PLA) and low-density polyethylene (LDPE) films comparing to the single layer of those films at 5 and 25°C, which are the temperature for storage and transportation condition of fresh-cut durian. The aroma profile of fresh-cut durian was analyzed by using gas chromatography-mass spectrometry (GC-MS) machine. Film properties were characterized by differential scanning calorimetry (DSC) and scanning electron microscope (SEM). The permeation of key aroma compound mass was analyzed using a gas chromatograph with a flame ionization detector (GC-FID) at the interval time while the extraction method was used to extract the sorbed compound from the film samples by dichloromethane at the equilibrium time. Diffusion, solubility and permeability coefficients of a key aroma compound through the packaging films were determined by modeling the aroma compounds permeation kinetics. The results showed that 2-ethyl-1-hexanol is the one of key aroma compounds in fresh-cut durian. The permeability coefficient of 2-ethyl- 1-hexanol through the packaging films could not be determined at 5° C whereas the permeability coefficient of 2-ethyl-1-hexanol through the packaging films was highest in PLA film, followed by PE/60PLA40PE/PE film and PE/30PLA70PE/PE film at 25° C, respectively. The results supported that permeability is primarily affected by the polymer structure and temperature. The study of these factors is useful to design the polymer matrix and select the condition during the storage and transportation of fresh-cut durian.

Keywords: 2-Ethyl-1-hexanol; Fresh-cut durian; Permeability; Multi-layer films; Temperature.

***Correspondence to:** Pattarin Leelaphiwat, Department of Packaging and Materials Technology, Faculty of Agro-Industry, Kasetsart University, Bangkok, Thailand. E-mail: Pattarin.le @ ku.ac.th

1. Introduction

Durian (Durio zibethinus) is one of the most important export fruits, which is grown in tropical countries, especially Southeast Asia such as Thailand, Indonesia, Philippines and Malaysia. 'Monthong' is the most popular from several varieties of durian fruit because it has a light yellow pulp, creamy texture, mild taste and unique strong odor [1-8,10,14]. There are many exotic volatiles in the ripe durian for example diethyl sulfide, ethyl propanoate, etc. one of the key aroma compounds is '2-ethyl-1-hexanol' [5-6,14], which has been detected in large amount of mix aroma compounds [1,3,6,10]. Moreover, minimally processed durian (MPD) or fresh-cut durian has been consumed and popular because the durian fruit is covered with inedible thick husk and sharp spikes which make it difficult to peel for a consumer [1,3,5,7-8,14]. Nowadays, the packed fresh-cut durian has been requiring for the market. Polypropylene (PP) containers with sealing film or PP containers with shrink wrap were used for both of retail and transportation of fresh-cut durian [9]. However, package of fresh-cut durian is not allowed in some public places and transportation areas because it bring unpleasant odor to other people.

Polylactic acid (PLA) was reported as a good aroma sorption material as well as good aroma barrier for ethyl acetate and d-limonene compounds [19]. On the other hand, low density polyethylene (LDPE) is the low barrier material for the strong odor but it has many important properties for packaging applications due to transparency, low cost, good flexibility and useful gas transmission rates for low to medium respiring fresh produce. These properties of them are suitable for apply to produce the fresh-cut durian packages [14]. There are many important parameters of polymer characteristics affecting the aroma permeability including, morphology, crystallinity, glass transition temperature (Tg) and polarity. Moreover, permeant is a key role in permeation schematic which involves with molecular size, functional group, partition coefficient, saturated vapor pressure and boiling point of aroma compound along with main external factor such as temperature [18].

Permeability coefficient (P) can be a parameter to determine the aroma barrier properties of polymeric films, which relates to diffusion coefficients (D) and solubility coefficients (S). Although, various methods could be used to measure gas permeability, but aroma permeability measurements had no standard procedure [16,18].

Quasi-isostatic method is one of the solution to determine P, D and S values which has one side providing the constant permeant concentration on the high partial pressure and another side has no concentration on low partial pressure and afterwards, the permeant will accumulate on the low partial pressure side. This method appropriate to the high barrier property and homogenous material. Gas chromatograph with a flame ionization detector (GC-FID) is a regular technique to analyze the quantity of aroma compounds which permeates through the polymeric film. In addition, it also requires many mass transfer equations to predict the P, D and S values of aroma compounds through and sorbed in the polymeric films [18].

The aim of this study was investigated transportation coefficients of key aroma compound (2- ethyl-1-hexanol) in fresh-cut durian through blend multilayer of PLA and LDPE comparing to single layer of them at 5 and 25 °C [4-9]. Furthermore, morphology and thermal properties of polymeric films were studied to support transportation coefficients for explaining the mass transfer phenomenon in this system obviously.

2. Materials and methods

2.1 Film and aroma compound

The polymeric films used in this study were multilayer of PLA and LDPE (PE/30PLA70PE/PE and PE/60PLA40PE) and the single layer of PLA and LDPE (obtained from the National Metal and Materials Technology Center in Pathumthani, Thailand). The key aroma compound of durian used in this study was 2-ethyl-1-hexanol. The key aroma compound was obtained from SIGMA- ALDRICH, Co., (Germany) with purity of 99% (GC). Dichloromethane with a purity of 99.5% was obtained from QRëC (New Zealand) used as the extraction solvent.

2.2 Film characterization

2.1.1 Thermal properties and degree of crystallinity

Thermal properties of film samples were observed using Modulate Differential Scanning Calorimetry, MDSC (DSC, Mettle Toledo, Canada). Samples of about 8 mg were tested under N2 flow. A period of 60 s, a modulation amplitude of 1 ∞C, and a heating rate of 1 ∞C /min were employed. The cold crystallization and melting of PLA and LDPE, Degree of crystallinity in percentage was calculated using the following Eqn:

$$X_c = \frac{\Delta H_m - H_{cc}}{\Delta H^{\circ}_m} \times \frac{100}{w} \quad (1)$$

$$W_{PE\ in\ multilayer\ film} = \frac{2}{3} \times \frac{w_{PE\ in\ core\ layer}}{3} \quad (2)$$

$$W_{PLA\ in\ multilayer\ film} = \frac{w_{PLA\ in\ core\ layer}}{3} \quad (3)$$

where X_2 is the percentage of crystallinity, ΔH_m and ΔH_{cc} are the measured heat fusion and enthalpy of cold crystallization from experiment (J/g), and ΔH°_m is the enthalpy of fusion crystalline polymer (287 J/g for LDPE and 93 J/g for PLA), and W is the weight fraction of polymer in the multilayer film. A minimum of three samples were tested. The average values and standard deviations were reported.

2.2.2 Scanning Electron Microscope (SEM)

The images of the cross-sectional view of film samples were observed for microstructure of blend multilayer and pure single layer of PLA and LDPE using a scanning electron microscope, SEM (SU5000, Hitachi, Japan) operated at an accelerating voltage of 5 kV. The samples were cryogenically fractured in liquid nitrogen to minimize any possibility of phase deformation and coated with gold to prevent charging. The average scales of the images were determined using ImageJ software.

2.2.3 Thickness of films

The film thickness was determined by using a handheld micrometer caliper (Mitutoyo Corporation, Kanagawa, Japan). The measurement was used in average of five replications with random across the surface of film samples.

2.3 Aroma compound permeation experiments

2.3.1 Aroma mass transport measurement

A quasi-isostatic system was used to determine the aroma permeation through the packaging films. This method has been used for many aroma permeation tests by Leelaphiwat et al. The film samples were cut in size 1.1 cm × 1.1 cm and placed on the top of a small vial (4 mL) containing the pure aroma compound and then covered with the cap with the exposed film area 0.785 cm^2. The small vial was placed in a bigger vial (40 mL) which was closed with a Mininert ™ valve screw cap used as the permeation cell. The cell was retained at 5 and 25 °C. The 500 µL of gas sample of 2-ethyl-1-hexanol which permeated through the film was collected and injected into an Agilent model 6890 gas chromatograph (GC) (Agilent Technologies, USA) with a flame ionization detector at regular time intervals. The condition of GC was the helium flow rate at 1 mL min^{-1} and the oven temperature was increased from 100 to 160 °C at a rate of 10 °C min^{-1}. The column used to detect the key compound was a 30 m long fused silica column (i.d. 0.32 mm) with a film thickness of 0.25 mm (DB-WAX) (Agilent Technologies). The experiments were performed in triplicate.

2.3.2 Aroma sorption measurement

Sample films (1.1 cm × 1.1 cm) with the sorbed 2-ethyl-1-hexanol from the permeation experiments were extracted using dichloromethane. After the aroma concentration in the headspace above the small vial reached equilibrium, the film samples were removed from the cell and then rinsed with distilled water for 2 minutes and dried. Film samples were placed in vial with 5 mL of dichloromethane sealed with Teflon/silicone rubber septum and screw cap maintained at room temperature for 24h. Extraction yield was determined by placing a known amount of compound into the films. The extracted liquid sample from film (1 µL) was injected to the GC-FID using the conditions as same as vapour permeation measurement. These were performed in three replications.

2.3.3 Determination of diffusion coefficients

The diffusion coefficients were identified by using data-fitting Eqn (4) for the sorption of a penetrant by a film sample which was described by Crank:

$$\frac{M_t}{M_\infty} = 1 - \frac{8}{\pi^2}\sum_{n=0}^{\infty}\frac{1}{(2n+1)^2}\cdot \exp\left[-\frac{(2n+10)^2\pi^2}{4L^2}D\cdot t\right] \quad (4)$$

The experimental diffusivity data was obtained from aroma mass transport measurements under different conditions. Where M_t and M_∞ are the amount of penetrant sorbed by the film sample at time t and the equilibrium sorption after infinite time, respectively. D is the diffusion coefficient (m^2 s^{-1}), t is the time required to maintain M_t and L is the thickness of film. For each experimental run, the substance penetrate sorbed of 2-ethyl-1-hexanol by the film sample was monitored for an additional 24h until reaching equilibrium. The prediction curve was compared with the experimental sorption data for calculation root mean square error (RMSE), which used to estimate the good of model fitting.

2.3.4 Determination of solubility coefficients

The solubility coefficients were obtained from the aroma vapour sorption measurements. S was determined using Eqn (5):

$$S = \frac{M_\infty}{V\Delta p} \quad (5)$$

Where S is the solubility coefficient (kg m^{-3} Pa^{-1}). M_∞ is the mass of aroma compound extracted at steady state (kg). V is the volume of the film sample (m^3) and Δp is the partial pressure of the aroma vapour in contact with the film sample (Pa) determined by the perfect gas law at 25 °C.

2.3.5 Determination of permeability coefficients

The permeability coefficients relate to D and S values. P was determined using Eqn (6):

$$P = DS \quad (6)$$

Where P is permeability coefficient (kg m m^{-2} s^{-1} Pa^{-1}). D is the diffusion coefficient (m^2 s^{-1}) and S is the solubility coefficient (kg m^{-3} Pa^{-1}).

3. Results and Discussion

3.1 Film and key aroma compound characteristics

Table 1 shows the film thickness, glass transition temperature (T_g), melting temperature (T_m) and the crystallinity of the films determined by MDSC. The range of thickness was 29 to 34 µm. The thickness of multilayer films was less than that of the single layer films. Although, The T_g of LDPE could not be determined but it has been reported in the reference at -80 °C [18-19]. The T_g of blend multilayer films between LDPE and PLA was close to the T_g of PLA whereas the degree of crystallinity for LDPE and PLA in the multilayer films decreased comparing to the single layer film.

Table 1 *Thickness and thermal properties of the polymer films*

Polymeric film	Thickness[a] (µm)	T_g (°C)	T_m (°C)	Crystallinity[a] (%)
PE/30PLA70PE/PE	29 ± 1	57	T_m, LDPE = 111, T_m, PLA = 155	%X_c, LDPE = 22.79 ± 7.2, %X_c, PLA = 6.45 ± 1.3
PE/60PLA40PE/PE	29 ± 2	57	T_m, LDPE = 111, T_m, PLA = 155	%X_c, LDPE = 22.22 ± 5.6, %X_c, PLA = 8.19 ± 0.9
PLA	33 ± 1	61	154	9.26 ± 1.5
LDPE	34 ± 1	N/D	111	36.00 ± 0

[a]The values are reported as mean ± standard deviation

N/D: Values could not be determined because the method did not appropriate for sample.

Table 2 *Physico-chemical properties of the key aroma compound studied*

Aroma compound	Molecular structure	Molecular weight (g.mol^{-1})	Boiling point (°C)	P_{vs} [a] at 25 °C (Pa)	Log P [b]
2-Ethyl-1-hexanol	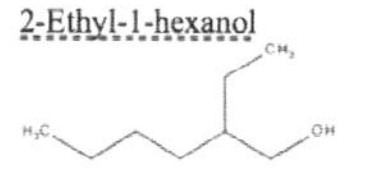	130.231	184.6	18.1	2.73

[a] P_{vs}: saturated vapor pressure at 25°C

[b] Log$P$: octanol-water partition coefficient

Table 2 shows the physico-chemical properties of 2-ethyl-1-hexanol consisting of molecular structure, molecular weight, boiling point, P_{vs} at 25 °C and LogP.

3.2 Film morphology

Figure 1 shows SEM images of the cross-sectional area of multilayer and single layer films along TD and MD. The single layer film with PLA and LDPE showed homogenous structure and smooth surface both of along MD and TD. The morphologies of multilayer films were observed at LDPE skin layers, which had a smooth surface and no disperse phase. For the middle layer of PE/30PLA70PE/PE, PLA was deformed to the fiber or ribbon-like structure and small void was clearly seen. In the case of PE/60PLA40PE/PE, PLA complex structure with an expansion of ribbon-like structure to layer-like structures which was tight compacted [11-14]. It also showed clearly separation of each layers for PE/60PLA40PE/PE.

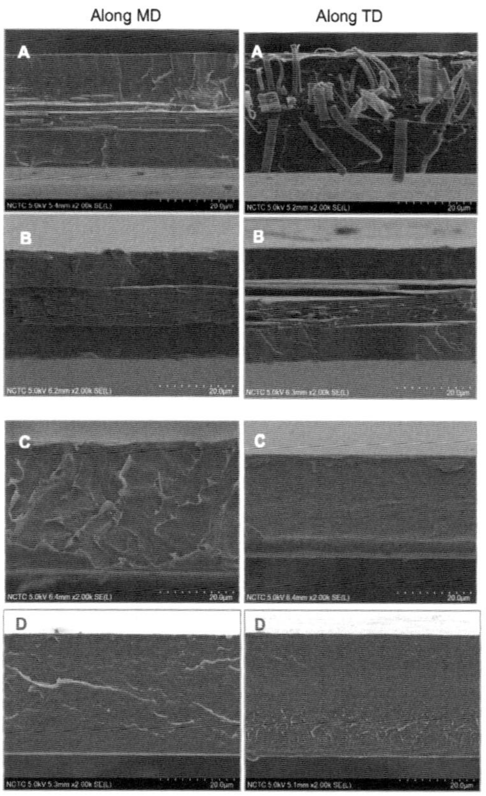

Figure 1 *SEM micrographs of fractured surfaces (fracture direction along MD and TD) of multilayer films: (A): PE/30PLA70PE/PE, (B): PE/60PLA40PE/PE and single layer films: (C): PLA, (D): LDPE (magnification of 2000×)*

3.3 Diffusion coefficients

Diffusion coefficients were evaluated from permeation kinetic for initially indication of these values. D values for 2-ethyl-1-hexanol was calculated from Eqn (4) described by Crank [16]. It was estimated by fitting the concentration of 2-ethyl-1-hexanol permeating through the films into the headspace air versus time. The results showed that the model fitted well with the experimental data (Figure 2) and the diffusion coefficients were determined.

Diffusion coefficients of PE/30PLA70PE/PE, PE/60PLA40PE/PE and PLA increased with increasing temperature whereas LDPE had the higher D values at 5 °C than that at 25 °C (Figure 3). It might be due to the lower T_g value of LDPE. Moreover, 2-ethyl-1-hexanol had a low saturated vapor pressure and high boiling point; therefore, it was not affected by temperature. At 5 °C, the diffusion coefficients were highest in LDPE, followed by PLA, PE/60PLA40PE/PE and PE/30PLA70PE/PE, respectively. The transport of aroma compounds occurred in the rubbery state follows Fick's law as the T_g values of LDPE was lower than the storage temperature while T_g values of multilayer films and PLA were higher than the storage temperature. In addition, the multilayer films showed low D values due to the middle layer of microstructure, which have been developed to the barrier layer (Figure 1).

At 25 °C, The D values was highest in PLA close to D value of LDPE followed by PE/60PLA40PE/PE and PE/30PLA70PE/PE, respectively. For the D value of PLA, the 2-ethyl- 1-hexanol might played an important role as a penetrant plasticizer, which occurred the plasticizing effect. Therefore, D value of PLA increased when the temperature was increased from 5 to 25 °C.

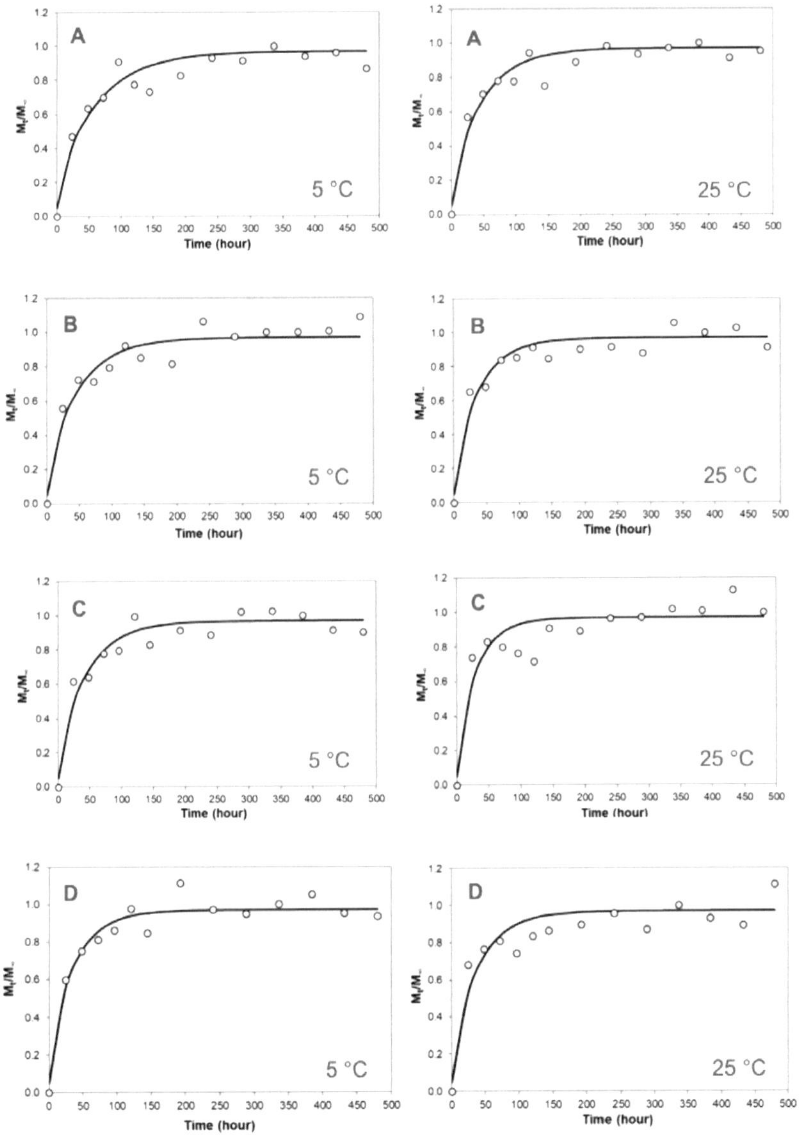

Figure 2 *2-Ethyl-1-hexanol permeation kinetics through multilayer films: (A): PE/30PLA70PE/PE, (B): PE/60PLA40PE/PE and single layer films: (C): PLA, (D): LDPE in a quasi-isostatic system at 5 and 25 °C respectively. Experimental data are plotted with symbol, the fitted curve using line.*

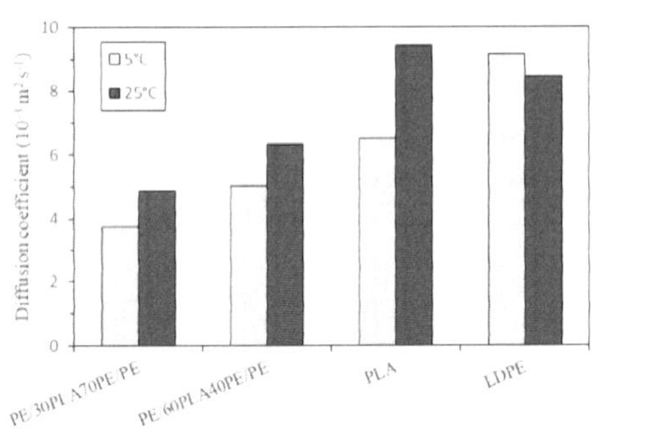

Figure 3 *Apparent diffusion coefficients (D) of 2-ethyl-1-hexanol in multilayer films and single layer films at 5 °C and 25 °C. The ordinate is discontinuous as indicated to present all small values.*

3.4 Solubility coefficients

The solubility coefficients were determined by calculating the mass of the aroma sorbed in the films at equilibrium as an initially estimate from Eqn (5). Figure 4 represents the values of 2- ethyl-1-hexanol sorption in PE/30PLA70PE/PE, PE/60PLA70PE/PE, LDPE and PLA films at 5 and 25 °C. The S values for 2-ethyl-1-hexanol through all of films at 5 °C could not be detected.

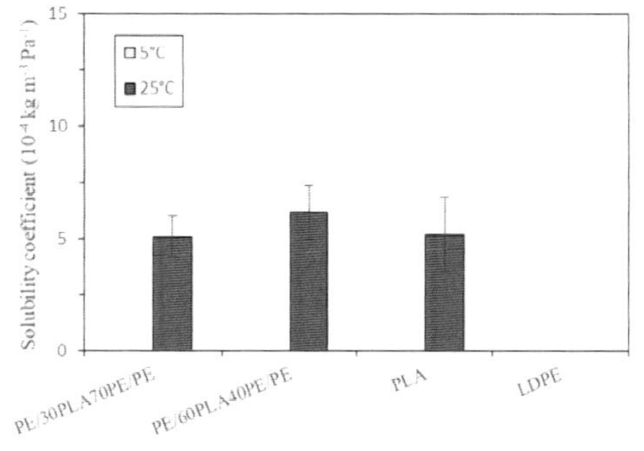

Figure 4 *Apparent solubility coefficients (S) of 2-ethyl-1-hexanol in multi-layer films and single layer films at 5 °C and 25 °C. The ordinate is discontinuous as indicated to present all small values.*

At 25 °C, almost all of films showed the S values except for LDPE. The S values of PE/30PLA70PE/PE, PE/60PLA40PE and PLA affected from the high temperature. Moreover, one of the important factors was the plasticizing effect. The plasticization of films by aroma compounds could be explained due to high concentration of aroma compound. The plasticization could induce an increase the polymer mobility and consequently on the sorption site accessibility [15-18]. Although, The LDPE has shown hydrophobicity and the LogP value (octanol- water partition coefficient) of 2-ethyl-1-hexanol also indicates that it has the similar polarity but the plasticizing effect in the polymer matrix of LDPE may not occur due to the huge degree of crystallinity of LDPE (Table 1). In accordance with the eucalyptol permeation study, The S value of eucalyptol in LDPE film was lower than that in PLA films and LogP value of 2-ethyl-1- hexanol and eucalyptol is similar [18]. On the other hand, the S values of PE/30PLA70PE/PE, PE/60PLA40PE/PE and PLA increased as the temperature increased that according to the Arrhenius theory.

3.5 Permeability coefficients

The P values were calculated by using Eqn (6). Permeability coefficients for 2-ethyl-1-hexanol was highest in PLA, followed by PE/60PLA40PE/PE and PE/30PLA70PE/PE, respectively. The P value of LDPE for both temperatures could not be calculated and the P values of the films at 5 °C could not be determined because the solubility coefficients could not be detected. The results showed that the permeability coefficients depend on the diffusion coefficients which have a higher value whereas the S values of the films at 25 °C was in the same range. The results indicated the effect of polymer structure and temperature obviously. As the P values was lowest for multilayer films at high temperature (Table 3).

Table 3 *Diffusion (D), solubility (S) and permeability coefficients (P) for 2-ethyl-1-hexanol in the multilayer films: PE/30PLA70PE/PE, PE/60PLA40PE/PE and single layer films: PLA, LDPE at 5 ∞C and 25 ∞C*

	Diffusion coefficient; D ($m^2 s^{-1}$)				Solubility coefficient; S ($kg\ m^{-3} Pa^{-1}$)		Permeability coefficient; P ($kg\ m\ m^{-2} s^{-1} Pa^{-1}$)	
Polymeric film	5 °C	RMSE	25 °C	RMSE	5 °C	25 °C	5 °C	25 °C
PE/30PLA70PE/PE	3.74E-16	0.078	4.88E-16	0.075	N/D	5.01E-04	N/D	2.44E-19
PE/60PLA40PE/PE	5.01E-16	0.075	6.31E-16	0.063	N/D	6.16E-04	N/D	3.89E-19
PLA	6.50E-16	0.073	9.42E-16	0.112	N/D	5.19E-04	N/D	4.89E-19
LDPE	9.14E-16	0.066	8.44E-16	0.086	N/D	N/D	N/D	N/D

N/D: Values could not be determined because the system did not meet the assumption

4. Conclusion

The diffusion, solubility and permeability coefficients of a key aroma compound of durian were determined. The results showed that 2-ethyl-1-hexanol is the one of key aroma compounds in fresh-cut durian. The permeability coefficient of 2-ethyl-1-hexanol through the packaging films could not be determined at 5 °C whereas the permeability coefficient of 2-ethyl-1-hexanol through the packaging films was highest in PLA film, followed by PE/60PLA40PE/PE film and PE/30PLA70PE/PE film at 25 °C, respectively. Moreover, the results supported that permeability is primarily affected by the polymer structure and temperature. The study of these factors is useful to design the polymer matrix and select the storage condition for storage and transportation of fresh-cut durian.

5. Acknowledgements

The authors are thankful to Department of Packaging and Materials Technology, Faculty of Agro Industry, Kasetsart University and the National Metal and Materials Technology (MTEC) for their support.

6. References

[1] Jiang J, Choo SY, Omar N, Ahamad N. GC-MS analysis of volatile compounds in durian (Durio zibethinus Murr). Developments in Food Science 1998; 40, pp. 345-352.

[2] Chin ST, Nazimah SAH, Quek SY, Che Man YB, Abdul Rahman R, Mat Hashim D. Analysis of volatile compounds from Malaysian durians (Durio zibethinus) using headspace SPME coupled to fast GC-MS. Journal of Food Composition and Analysis 2007; 20(1), pp. 31-44.

[3] Li JX, Schieberle P, Steinhaus M. Characterization of the Major Odor-Active Compounds in Thai Durian (Durio zibethinus L. 'Monthong') by Aroma Extract Dilution Analysis and Headspace Gas Chromatography–Olfactometry. Journal of agricultural and food chemistry 2012; 60(45), pp. 11253–11262.

[4] Amornputti S, Ketsa S, Van Doorn WG. Effect of 1-methylcyclopropene (1-MCP) on storage life of durian fruit. Postharvest Biology and Technology 2014; 97, pp. 111–114.

[5] Niponsak A, Laohakunjit N, Kerdchoechuen O. Contribution to Volatile Fingerprinting and Physico-chemical Qualities of Minimally Processed Durian cv. 'Monthong' During Storage: Identification of a Novel Chemical Ripeness Marker. Food Bioprocess Technology 2015; 8, pp. 1229–1243.

[6] Niponsak A, Laohakunjit N, Kerdchoechuen O, Wongsawadee P, Uthairatanakij A. Novel ripeness label based on starch/chitosan incorporated with pH dye for indicating eating quality of fresh-cut durian. Food Control 2020; 107, pp. 106785.

[7] Voon YY, Sheikh Abdul Hamid N, Rusul G, Osman A, Quek SY. Physicochemical, microbial and sensory changes of minimally processed durian (Durio zibethinus cv. D24) during storage at 4 and 28 °C. Postharvest Biology and Technology 2006; 42(2), pp. 168–175.

[8] Voon YY, Sheikh Abdul Hamid N, Rusul G, Osman A, Quek SY. Volatile flavour compounds and sensory properties of minimally processed durian (Durio zibethinus cv. D24) fruit during storage at 4 °C. Postharvest Biology and Technology 2007; 46(1), pp. 76–85.

[9] Nur Azlin R, Latifah MN, Siti Aisyah A, Pauziah M, Zaipun MZ, Nurul Adibah M, Zainab MY, Hairiyah M, Habsah M, Razali M, Zaulia O, Nur Syafini G, Joanna CLY, Nur Alisha O. Simulation studies for export of minimally processed durian by air shipment to Hong Kong. Acta Horticulturae 2016; 1141, pp. 283-288.

[10] Jaswir I, Che Man YB, Selamat J, Ahmad F, Sugisawa H. Retention of volatile components of durian fruit leather during processing and storage. Journal of Food Processing and Preservation 2008; 32(5), pp. 740–750.

[11] Trongsatitkul T, Chaiwong S. In situ fibre-reinforced composite films of poly(lactic acid)/low-density polyethylene blends: effects of composition on morphology, transport and mechanical properties. Polymer International 2017; 66(11), pp.1456-1462.

[12] Singh G, Bhunia H, Rajor A, Choudhary V. Thermal properties and degradation characteristics of polylactide, linear low density polyethylene, and their blends. Polymer bulletin 2011; 66, pp.939-953.

[13] Vrsaljko D, Macut D, Kovačević V. Potential Role of Nanofillers as Compatibilizers in Immiscible PLA/LDPE Blends. Journal of Applied Polymer Science 2015; 132(6), pp.41414.

[14] Winotapun C, Phattarateera S, Aontee A, Junsook N, Daud W, Kerddonfag N, Chinsirikul W. Development of multilayer films with improved aroma barrier properties for durian packaging application. Packaging Technology and Science 2019; 32(8), pp. 405–418.

[15] Colomines G, Ducruet V, Courgneau C, Guinault A, Domenek S. Barrier properties of poly(lactic acid) and its morphological changes induced by aroma compound sorption. Polymer International 2010; 59(6), pp. 818- 826.

[16] Peychès-Bach A, Moutounet M, Peyron S, Chalier P. Factors determining the transport coefficients of aroma compounds through polyethylene films. Journal of Food Engineering 2009; 95(1), pp. 45–53.

[17] Salazar R, Domenek S, Courgneau C, Ducruet V. Plasticization of poly(lactide) by sorption of volatile organic compounds at low concentration. Polymer Degradation and Stability 2012; 97(10), pp. 1871-1880.

[18] Leelaphiwat P, Auras RA , Burgess GJ, Harte JB, Chonhenchob V. Preliminary quantification of the permeability, solubility and diffusion coefficients of major aroma compounds present in herbs through various plastic packaging materials. Journal of the Science of Food and Agriculture 2018; 98, pp. 1545–1553.

[19] Auras R, Harte B, Selke S. Sorption of ethyl acetate and d-limonene in poly(lactide) polymers. Journal of the Science of Food and Agriculture 2006; 86(4), pp. 648-656.

Inhibitory Effect of Visible Light on Sitophilus oryzae in Rice Packaging [36]

Naipaporn Korbsakulkarn, Amporn Sane, Vanee Chonhenchob, Pattarin Leelaphiwat *
Department of Packaging and Materials Technology, Kasetsart University, Bangkok, Thailand

Abstract: Rice is an economic crop in Thailand. Consumption of rice has increased amount every year and it has been exported to many countries. Rice may be subjected to insect infestations leading to loss the appearance quality and economical value. The effect of visible light against the rice weevil (Sitophilus oryzae) infestation was studied and the color packaging films based on the visible light effect were developed. The extrusion blown film was used to process LLDPE films containing masterbatch colors in different wavelengths. The properties of developed films were characterized by using a UV-Vis spectrophotometer, colorimeter, and tensile testing machine. Five hundred grams of rice was packed in the developed films in the bag form and stored at 25°C for 2 months after that the number of rice weevil and gas composition in bags were investigated. The result showed that the wavelength of LEDs affected rice weevil based on the phototactic behaviors of agricultural insects. Blue of wavelengths 455 nm to 465 nm was more attractive to the rice weevil than green and red (wavelengths 620-630 nm). Moreover, the transmittance decreased with the increasing concentration of pigments leading to the lower number of the rice weevil in the red bag compared to the blue bag. In addition, the concentrations of oxygen and carbon dioxide were observed. It can be concluded that packaging materials combined with color pigment present the inhibition of rice weevil in packaged rice. This information can be used to develop the packaging for quality preservation of packaged rice from an insect infestation instead of using the chemical fumigation method.

Keywords: Visible light, Rice, Packaging film, Sitophilus oryzae, LLDPE

***Correspondence to:** Pattarin Leelaphiwat, Department of Packaging and Materials Technology, Faculty of Agro-Industry, Kasetsart University, Bangkok, Thailand. E-mail: pattarin.le@ ku.ac.th

1. Introduction

Rice is popular consumption in Thailand and it is one of Thailand's main exports. Therefore, packaging and transportation are very important for rice product but the consumers often find rice weevils in the rice bags. Rice weevil is the mainly insect which was found in rice. The life cycle of rice weevil as an egg, larvae, and pupae occurring within the kernel of whole grain during storage until it reaches the adult stage [1-2]. An egg of rice weevil is very small and it is difficult to be observed and separated from rice before filling in the package leading to the quality loss of rice product. Therefore, the chemical fumigation was commonly applied to inhibit the rice weevil infestation before packaging by using methyl bromide and phosphine but these chemical substances may affect the health of humans and environment [3-4]. Visible light has a wavelength from 400 nm to 700 nm which is the wavelength between UV radiation (<400 nm.) and infrared radiation (>700 nm.). There are many reports about the effect of this visible light on the life of living organisms. The source of visible light from LEDs has been popularly used for various grain storage because LEDs lamps are generally low power consumption, long life, low maintenance, and lightweight. In addition, LEDs are easily adjusted the concentration and wavelength of light with high luminous efficiency and low temperature [5]. Light from LEDs affected the phototactic response of insects as blue light of wavelength 450 nm was the most attractive to the rice weevil, followed by green light of wavelength 520 nm and red light of wavelength 660 nm, respectively [6]. Similarly, Katsuki et al [7] reported UV and blue were more attractive color than green, yellow and red colors to the rice weevil. Contrastingly, It was found that the blue color was less attractive to the rice weevil and sweet potatoes weevil than red and green colors [8, 9]. For other insects, the near UV ray of wavelength 390 nm was the most attractive radiation to the red flour beetle [10] and to apple blossom weevil, especially for the male weevils [11]. Pigment has been widely used in polymer applications for coloring plastic materials. LDPE was mixed with different additives and pigments to make the green packaging material for preservation the quality of dairy products. The packaging was used to block out the visible light regions between 400-450 and 600-650 nm because it had an effect on the product deterioration [12]. In addition, Chonhenchob et al [13] reported that the different light transmittance bags showed the different effects on the fruit quality, especially for mangoes. LDPE was mixed with various pigments)yellow, red, blue/violet and blue(compared to kraft paper. The blue/violet and violet films were suitable for mangoes storage with the best fruit development and diseases resistance. The purpose of this study was to observe the visible light against the rice weevil (Sitophilus oryzae) and study the inhibitory effect of visible light on the rice weevil in rice packaging.

2. Materials and methods

2.1 Rice

Organic rice (Oryza sativa L.) cv. Hom Pratum was obtained from Bangkuwat Organic Agricultural Community Enterprise (Pathum Thani province, Thailand).

2.2 Insects

The cultures of rice weevil were supported by Bangkuwat Organic Agricultural Community Enterprise (Thailand). The insects were reared in plastic rearing containers (21 cm ×15 cm × 8 cm) at 25°C, 60% RH in the laboratory room. The adult weevils were chosen for behavioral tests.

2.3 Light source

The 20mA LEDs (Luechai Welding, Thailand) were used as followed: red (634 nm, V= 2.2volts), green (557 nm, V=2. 2volts), and blue (455 nm, V=3.2 volts). These three circuit broads (200 mm × 200 mm) were installed because three colors affected the phototactic response.

2.4 Light box

The phototactic response of rice weevils was investigated by using a modified light box designed by Katsuki et al. (2013). Light box was made from an opaque plastic and cover with the transparent plastic on the top. Three macro-holes were punched on the top and LEDs circuit boards were placed in the holes. LEDs were connected with a battery on top of the target area and this area was opposite with the insect release area. (Figure 1). Thirty rice weevils were released into light box at the released area, then open LEDs by varying light durations 15, 30, 60 and 120 minutes. The number of rice weevils in the target area was recorded. In addition, the effect of attraction of each wavelength was investigated. Storage temperature of light box was 25°C. The experiment was performed in triplicate.

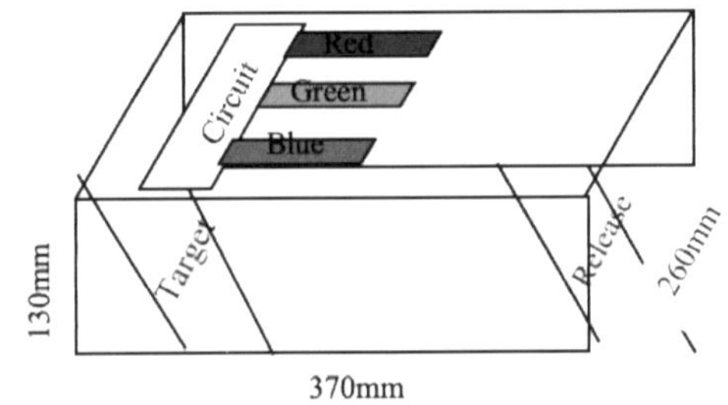

Figure 1 *Modified LEDs box for phototactic response testing of rice weevils*

2.5 Film samples preparation

2.5.1 Material

Linear low density polyethylene (LLDPE) pellets were supplied by Liack Seng Trading Co., Ltd., Thailand. Red and blue masterbatch colors (Salee Colour Public Co., Ltd., Thailand) had been selected according to the wavelength of LEDs light. The concentration of pigments used in this study was presented in Table 1.

2.5.2 Compounding process

LLDPE pellets were mixed by twin screw extruder (Labtech Engineering Co., Ltd., Thailand) and the barrel temperature profile was maintain at: 95/105/120/125/130/135/145/145/150/155 and screw speed adjust to be 180 rpm. The formulations was presented in Table 1. The control film (LL) was prepared using the same method without adding pigment color.

Table 1 *Formula compositions of sample bags*

Materi al	Color	Concentration (%)	Formulati on
LLDPE	Colorless	0	LL
	Red	1	LL1R
	Red	2	LL2R
	Blue	1	LL1B
	Blue	2	LL2B

2.5.3 Blown film extrusion

Compounded samples were blown into a films by using a single screw extruder (Labtech Engineering Co., Ltd., Thailand) with the barrel temperature profile which was maintained at: 140/150/160/165/165/165/165. Screw and nip roll speed were adjusted to 65 rpm and 2.5 rpm, respectively. The film thickness was measured by a digital micrometer.

2.6 Film characterization

2.6.1 UV-Visible spectrophotometry

Light transmittance and wavelength of the film were measured at the wavelength ranges from 400-700 nm by using a UV-Visible spectrophotometer (Evolution 300, Thermo Scientific, US).

2.6.2 Color measurement

Color of the samples films were determinate by using colorimeter (CQXE, Color Global Co., Ltd., Thailand) and evaluated for Hunter L^*, a^*, b^* value.

2.6.3 Mechanical properties

Tensile properties of the sample films were tested using a 5965 universal testing machine (Instron, USA) according to the standard method ASTM D882-12 with a modified storage conditions. Sample were cut into size 2.5 cm × 10 cm. Ten specimens were tested for each sample.

2.7 Rice packaging

All film samples were cut into 24 cm × 18 cm then sealed by sealing machine (DZ-280 Brother, China). Five hundred grams of rice sample were filled in bags and stored at 25 °C, 60%RH for 2 months. Samples were measured in triplicate. The headspace gas compositions (oxygen and carbon dioxide) in the bags was measured by using a gas analyzer (CheckPoint 3 Premium, Mocon Dansensor, Denmark).

3. Results and Discussion

3.1 Effect of visible light on the rice weevil

The result of visible light on rice weevils on the phototactic system in LEDs box showed that blue light (634 nm) was the most attractive wavelength of about 30% to rice weevil, followed by green (557 nm) and red (455 nm) about 20 and 10%, respectively (Table 2). The duration time (15, 30, 60, and 120 min) did not significantly affect rice weevils. The result was in accordance with Joen et al. [6] who found that blue light (450 nm) was the most attractive wavelength to rice weevil (Coleoptera : Curculionidae) about 84.3%, followed by green (520 nm), red (660 nm), ultraviolet (365 nm), and infrared (730 nm) about 74.3, 64.3, 63.3, and 48.7%, respectively. Katsuki et al. [7] reported that ultraviolet (375 nm) and blue light (470 nm) were more attractive to cigarette beetle (Coleoptera : Anobiidae) than green (520 nm), yellow (560 nm), and red (640 nm). While, Nakamoto and Kuba [9] reported that green light (536 nm) was the most attractive to sweet potato weevil (Coleoptera: Curculionidae), followed by blue (536 nm), yellow (536 nm) and red (536 nm), respectively. Hausmann et al. [11] also reported that apple blossom female weevil (Coleoptera: Curculionidae) chose ultraviolet, green, and blue over black. In contrast with other result, male weevil only chose UV over black because of the trichromatic visual system with UV, blue, green receptors. And, Lin [14] reported that the phototactic system of Coccinella septempunctata (Coleoptera: Coccinellidae) were composed of 3 photoreceptors which have ultraviolet (360 nm), blue (420 nm), and green (520 nm) light. Therefore, no response was detected in the wavelength shorter than 310 nm or longer than 600 nm. The total 39 recording cells which had 25 cells were recorded green receptor, 8 cells were recorded blue receptor and 6 cells were recorded an ultraviolet receptor.

Table 2 *Effect of visible light on the rice weevil*

Time (min)	Blue (%)	Green (%)	Red (%)	%SUM
15	32.22 ± 0.58^{Ab}	24.44 ± 2.31^{Ab}	10.00 ± 0.00^{Aa}	66.67
30	31.11 ± 0.58^{Ac}	20.56 ± 1.26^{Ab}	10.00 ± 0.00^{Aa}	61.67
60	32.22 ± 1.53^{Ac}	20.56 ± 1.26^{Ab}	5.56 ± 1.15^{Aa}	58.33
120	30.00 ± 1.00^{Ab}	17.78 ± 0.58^{Aa}	10.00 ± 1.73^{Aa}	57.78

The data is reported as mean ± SD, n=3. Capital letters compare treatments duration time in the same column, and lowercase letters compare color light treatments in the same row. The different letter indicate significant difference at p<0.05.

3.2 UV-Vis spectrophotometry

Wavelength and light transmittance of red and blue films were shown in Figure 2. Red and blue film samples had wavelengths around 620-630 and 455-465 nm, respectively. The wavelength values of film samples were closed with red LEDs wavelength (634 nm) and blue LEDs wavelength (455 nm). Since pigment color was dispersed in the polymer matrix and had higher particle size so this could obstruct the light and affect the light transmittance. However, the LL1% sample for both colors were higher light transmittance than LL2%. Intawiwat et al. [12] reported that light transmittance depending on the pigment. When the intensity of green and yellow pigment was increased from 0.8 and 1.0% to 1.5 and 3%, the light transmittance was decreased because of the good pigment dispersion in the matrix resulting in the light blocking.

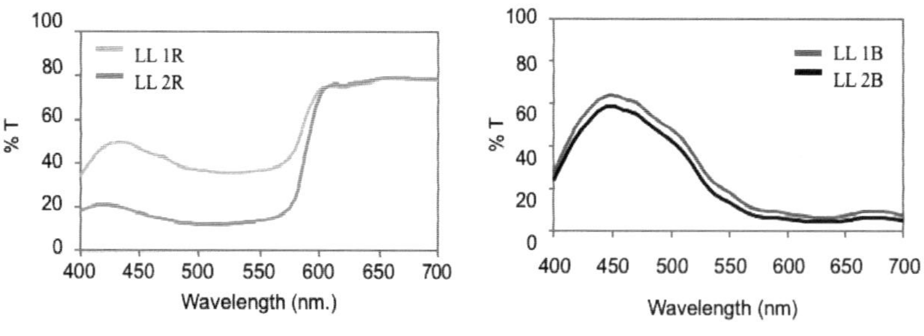

Figure 2 *Wavelength and light transmittance of red and blue films*

3.3 Color of films samples

From the result, the pigment concentration of LL1% was higher than LL2% in L* value but the pigment concentration of 1% was lower than 2% in a* and b* values because the pigment concentration in 2% had higher color intensity than 1% (Table 3). Ge et al. [15] reported that LDPE with red composite was produced from bio-filler dye loaded shell powder additive instead of calcium carbonate so a* and b* values were directly changed with color intensity. However, L* value was inversely changed with the color intensity. None additive, L* a* and b* values were 43.86, 0.48, and -0.90 but when adding 2% additive, L* a* and b* values became 31.89, 4.71 and 1.07, respectively.

***Table 3** L*, a* and b* values of the film samples*

Sample	L*	a*	b*
LL1% red	73.04 ± 0.84	27.43 ± 1.12	11.95 ± 0.54
LL2% red	62.86 ± 0.78	44.77 ± 1.26	21.97 ± 0.96
LL1% blue	55.33 ± 1.88	-17.07 ± 0.61	-40.91 ± 1.26
LL2% blue	42.24 ± 1.88	-9.31 ± 1.56	-42.32 ± 0.76

3.4 Mechanical properties

Tensile strength and elongation at break of the machine direction (MD) and cross machine direction (CD) of sample films were shown in Figure 3. Tensile strength and elongation of MD were higher than that of CD in all film samples. Tensile strength and elongation of the control sample in MD, and CD were 14.20 MPa, 11.87 MPa, 575.56 %, and 419.07%, respectively. Hong and Rhim [16] reported that tensile strength of LLDPE blown film in MD was higher than CD around 5.6 MPa. Although 2 types of nanoparticles were added to the polymer matrix, also yield stress of MD is higher than CD. These might be the effect of the interlamellar region and axis orientation. The tensile strength of film samples was decreased after masterbatch color was added into the polymer matrix. Tensile strengths of LL1R and LL1B films were decreased to 12.49 MPa and 12.86 MPa, respectively because the wax was a major component of red and blue masterbatch color, especially in red. This color was produced by wax and calcium carbonate. However, Tensile strengths of LL2R and LL2B were increased to 13.32 MPa and 13.66 MPa, respectively because of the crosslinking between masterbatch and polymer matrix. Also, elongation at break was increased, especially in blue because of the wax component. Siročić et al. [17] explained that the elongation and tensile strength of LDPE composites containing 3% of calcium carbonate filler were moderately reduced about 20 and 10%, respectively because the filler might reduce the cross-section of the polymer resisting deformation.

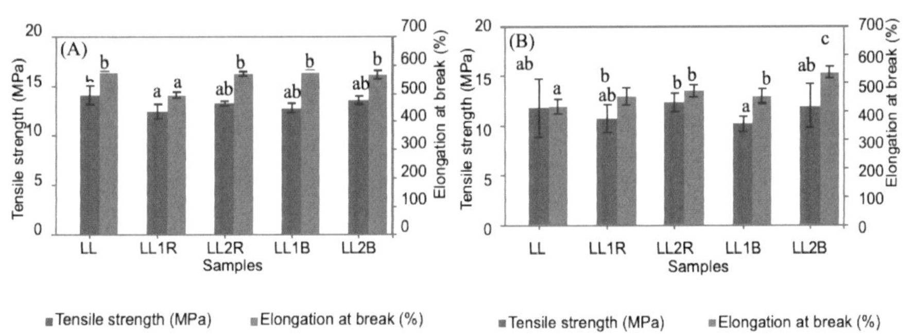

***Figure 3** Tensile strength and elongation at break of film samples: (A) MD side (B) CD side*

3.5 Number of insects in rice packaging

Color and concentration were the main factors and non-significantly affected but tended to decrease the number of insects in packaging. The result showed that (Table 4) LL2R had the lowest number of insects than other samples because coleoptera had 3 receptors: ultraviolet, blue, and green in the phototactic system. Blue light was the most attractive to rice weevil from the result of the effect of visible light, therefore; blue film samples had more insect number than the red film sample. Jeon et al. [6] reported the attractive effect of red LEDs that when the light intensity was increased from 25, 55 and 100 lux the number of weevils decreased about 15, 13 and 9, respectively. These might be related to the illumination equation, $E=I/R^2$.

Table 4 *The data is reported as mean ± SD, n=3. Lowercase letters compare number of insect between treatments in the same column. The different letter indicate significant difference at p<0.05*

Sample	Number of insect	Sample	Number of insect
LL	8.00 ± 1.00^{a}	LL	8.00 ± 1.00^{a}
LL1R	8.00 ± 1.00^{a}	LL1B	8.33 ± 2.31^{a}
LL2R	7.00 ± 1.00^{a}	LL2B	7.33 ± 1.53^{a}

3.6 Gas compositions in rice packaging

Gas compositions inside the packaging slightly changed (Table 5). Oxygen concentration was significantly the lowest in LL1R and LL2B packages while carbon dioxide concentration was significantly the highest. This means that rice weevils were used gas compositions for breathing. Normally, LLDPE film was a good tear and moisture resistance but only fair gas barrier properties. However, another material package showed an obvious effect of change of gas composition inside the packaging. Njoroge et al. [18] reported that the more amount of rice weevils were kept in hermitic storage jar increased, oxygen concentration inside the package decreased rapidly because of the high population of rice weevils.

Table 5 *The data is reported as mean ± SD, n=3. Lowercase letters compare oxygen and carbon dioxide between treatments in the same column. The different letter indicate significant difference at p<0.05.*

Sample	Oxygen	Carbon dioxide	Sample	Oxygen	Carbon dioxide
LL	20.30 ± 0.10^{b}	0.30 ± 0.06^{a}	LL	20.30 ± 0.10^{b}	0.30 ± 0.06^{a}
LL1R	20.00 ± 0.20^{a}	0.60 ± 0.07^{b}	LL1B	20.30 ± 0.05^{b}	0.23 ± 0.06^{a}
LL2R	20.20 ± 0.02^{ab}	0.33 ± 0.06^{a}	LL2B	20.00 ± 0.50^{a}	0.60 ± 0.10^{b}

4. Conclusion

Blue LEDs light color was the most attractive to rice weevil on the phototactic system followed by green and red, respectively. Wavelength and color intensity of packaging were main factors that could inhibit rice weevils. Red film sample which had a wavelength of about 620-630 nm with optimum color intensity tended to inhibit rice weevil more than blue and colorless. Thus, these results can be used to develop the packaging for quality preservation of rice packaging from an insect infestation instead of using the chemical fumigation method.

5 References

[1] Arthur F.H, James E.T. Efficacy of diatomaceous earth to control internal infestations of rice weevil and maize weevil (Coleoptera: Curculionidae). Journal of economic entomology 2003; 96(2), pp. 510-518.

[2] Plarre R. Three-dimensional distribution of Sitophilus granaries (L.) (Coleoptera: Curculionidae) in wheat influenced by the synthetic aggregation pheromone. Journal of stored products research 1996; 32(3), pp. 275-283.

[3] Athanassiou C.G, Papagregoriou A.S, Buchelos C.Th. Insecticidal and residual effect of three pyrethroids against Sitophilus oryzae (L.) (Coleoptera: Curculionidae) on stored wheat. Journal of stored products research 2004; 40, pp. 289-297.

[4] Michaelraj S, Sharma R. K. Fumigant toxicity of neem formulations against Sitophilus oryzae and Rhyzopertha dominica. Journal of agricultural technology 2006; 2(1), pp. 1-16.

[5] Yeh N, Chung J-P. High-brightness LEDs—Energy efficient lighting sources and their potential in indoor plant cultivation. Renewable and Sustainable Energy Reviews 2009; 13(8), pp. 2175-2180.

[6] Jeon J-H, Oh M-S, Cho K-S, Lee H-S. Phototactic response of the rice weevil, Sitophilus oryzae linnaeus (Coleoptera: Curculionidae), to light-emitting diodes. Journal of the Korean Society for Applied Biological Chemistry 2012; 55(1), pp. 35-39.

[7] Katsuki M, Arikawa K, Wakakuwa M, Omae Y, Okada K, Sasaki R, Shinoda K, Miyatake T. Which wavelength does the cigarette beetle, Lasioderma serricorne (Coleoptera: Anobiidae), prefer? Electrophysiological and behavioral studies using light-emitting diodes (LEDs). Applied Entomology and Zoology 2013; 48(4), pp. 547-551.

[8] De Groote H, De Groote B, Bruce A.Y, Marangu C, Tefera T. Maize storage insects (Sitophilus zeamais and Prostephanus truncatus) prefer to feed on smaller maize grains and grains with color, especially green. Journal of Stored Products Research 2017; 71, pp. 72-80.

[9] Nakamoto Y, Kuba H. The effectiveness of a green light emitting diode (LED) trap at capturing the West Indian sweet potato weevil, Euscepes postfasciatus (Fairmaire) (Coleoptera: Curculionidae) in a sweet potato field. Applied Entomology and Zoology 2004; 39(3), pp. 491-495.

[10] Duehl A.J, Cohnstaedt L.W, Arbogast R.T, Teal P.E.A. Evaluating Light Attraction to Increase Trap Efficiency for Tribolium castaneum (Coleoptera: Tenebrionidae). Journal of Economic Entomology 2011; 104(4), pp. 1430-1435.

[11] Hausmann C, Samietz J, Dorn S. Visual Orientation of Overwintered Anthonomus pomorum(Coleoptera: Curculionidae). Environmental Entomology 2004; 33(5), 1410-1415.

[12] Intawiwat N, Myhre E, Øysaed H, Jamtvedt S.H, Pettersen M.K. Packaging materials with tailor made light transmission properties for food protection. Polymer Engineering & Science 2012; 52(9), pp. 2015-2024.

[13] Chonhenchob V, Kamhangwong D, Kruenate J, Khongrat K, Tangchantra N, Wichai U, Singh S.P. Preharvest bagging with wavelength-selective materials enhances development and quality of mango (Mangifera indica L.) cv. Nam Dok Mai #4. Journal of the Science of Food and Agricultural 2011; 91, pp. 664-671.

[14] Lin J-T. Identification of photoreceptor locations in the compound eye of Coccinella septempunctata Linnaeus. Journal of Insect Physiology 1993; 39(7), pp. 555-562.

[15] Ge L, Yang W, Lv H, Xia M, Ji X, Yao Z. Colorating and mechanical performance of low-density polyethylene (LDPE)/dye-loaded shell powder (DPSP) composites. Fibers and Polymers 2015; 16(6), pp. 1294-1302.

[16] Hong S-I, Rhim J-W. Preparation and properties of melt-intercalated linear low density polyethylene/clay nanocomposite films prepared by blow extrusion. LWT - Food Science and Technology 2012; 48(1), pp. 43- 51.

[17] Siročić A.P, Rešček A, Ščetar M, Krehula L.K, Hrnjak-Murgić Z. Development of low density polyethylene nanocomposites films for packaging. Polymer Bulletin 2013; 71(3), 705-717.

[18] Njoroge A.W, Mankin R.W, Smith B.W, Baributsa D. Effects of Hermetic Storage on Adult Sitophilus oryzae L. (Coleoptera: Curculionidae) Acoustic Activity Patterns and Mortality. J Econ Entomol 2017; 110(6), pp. 2707-2715.

Inverse method for estimating diffusion coefficient of oxygen in different polymeric packaging materials [38]

Anbuhkani Muniandy [1], Ferhan Ozadali [1,2], Patnarin Benyathiar [3], Dharmendra K. Mishra [*1]

1 Department of Food Science, Purdue University, West Lafayette, IN 47907

2 Mead Johnson Nutrition, Reckitt Benckiser Health, Evansville, IN 47712

3 Islander Consulting and Engineering, West Lafayette, IN 47907

Abstract: Oxygen diffusion across polymeric packages is an important parameter needed for different research and commercial applications. This is particularly important for the food industry because excessive diffusion of oxygen can be detrimental to the quality of food. The reaction of oxygen with food can change the sensory quality and degrade the nutrients present in the food. Hence, understanding diffusion of oxygen under various circumstance is crucial. The aim of this study was to study the diffusion coefficient of oxygen in High Impact Polystyrene (HIPS) and High-Density Polyethylene (HDPE) packaging materials under heat and pressure. Both HIPS and HDPE containers were filled with water and flushed with nitrogen to keep oxygen level below 2%. Samples were kept at three different conditions, 1) room temperature, 2) 40° C, and 3) at 40° C under oxygen pressure. The changes in the headspace oxygen over time was monitored using OxySense 520i. The diffusion coefficient was estimated based on Fick's 2nd Law using inverse problems approach. After 20 day, the headspace oxygen level in samples kept at room condition did not change. For HIPS, the headspace oxygen level reached 2.77% at 40∞C and 14.47 % at 40° C at 5 psig pressure in 20 days. Similarly, in HPDE the headspace level was at 3.2 % and 12.57 % at 40∞C in 20 days and 40° C with 20 psig pressure in 15days, respectively. The diffusion coefficient for HIPS with and without pressure at 40° C is 1.01 x10-14 m2/s and 6.56 x10-15 m2/s, respectively. For HDPE the diffusion coefficient was slightly higher, 1.26 x10-13 m2/s and 8.46 x10-14 m2/s for with and without pressure, respectively. The use of higher temperature coupled with pressure increased the diffusivity of oxygen through polymeric packaging materials. The results are helpful for food industry in determining product shelf life at different distribution and storage conditions.

Keywords: diffusion coefficient, oxygen, temperature, pressure

***Correspondence to:** Dharmendra K. Mishra. E-Mail: mishradh@purdue.edu

Overall and specific migration of phthalates from cling films available on the Mexican market [82]

Yubia Berenice De Anda-Flores, Alberto González-León, Ana Isabel Valenzuela-Quintanar, Elizabeth Peralta and Herlinda Soto-Valdez *

Research Center for Food and Development
Centro de Investigación en Alimentación y Desarrollo, A.C. (CIAD)
Hermosillo, Sonora, México.

Abstract: Phthalates are plasticizers used in the polyvinyl chloride (PVC) industry to produce cling films which are often used as food packaging. Chronic exposure to bis (2-ethylhexyl) phthalate (DEHP) has shown harmful effects on human health. Consequently, the European Union (EU) regulations and Food and Drugs Administration in USA (FDA) have established limit concentrations in food contact materials as 0.1% and 5.0%, respectively. Additionally, EU regulation has a specific migration limit of 1.5 mg/kg of DEHP in food/food simulants. Despite the regulations, the presence of DEHP in cling films has recently been reported in different countries. The objective of this study was to determine the migration of phthalates from PVC cling films acquired from the Mexican market. Fifteen films were bought from the retail market. Five of them were positive to DEHP and three to Bis (2-ethylhexyl) terephthalate (DEHT). Three films resulted to contain levels of DEHP higher than 17% (films A and B) and DEHT higher than 16% (film C). Overall migration (OM) was determined to the films that were positive to both, DEHP and DEHT, in aqueous, acidic and fatty food simulants at 5 and 40°C. The results showed that the OM in aqueous and acid food simulants complied with the EU regulation; but the results obtained in the fatty food simulant were over the limit in all the tested films (60 mg/kg) at 5 and 40°C. The specific migration of DEHP was positive only in the films that showed high percentage of the plasticizer (A and B) in contact with the fatty food simulant at 5 and 40°C. The levels of migration were well above the limit established by the EU regulation (1.5 mg/kg). Regarding the specific migration of DEHT, it was positive in only one film (C) at levels below the EU limit (60 mg/kg).

Keywords: DEHP, phthalates, cling film, migration

***Correspondence to:** Herlinda Soto-Valdez. E-Mail: hsoto@ciad.mx

CHAPTER VIII
Packaging logistics

Title:
Blue Agave Wagon Closeup

Author:
Jess Kraft (jkraft5)

Location:
Tequila, JALISCO

Description:
Tequila. Name of a town, of a beverage, of a hill and of a song as well. One of the most characteristic liquors from Mexico, its origin is the blue agave plant. If life gives you lemons... break out the salt and the tequila bottle the salt and enjoy.

Analysis to develop a packaging engineering model for e-commerce in the grocery market [32]

Roland ten Klooster *1, Bjorn de Koeijer1, Corné Huijben 2

1 Department of Design, Production and Management, Faculty of Engineering Technology, University of Twente, Drienerlolaan 5, Enschede, The Netherlands
2 NVC Netherlands Packaging Center, Stationsplein 9a, Gouda, The Netherlands

Abstract: E-commerce in the grocery market is a new retail environment. Products are picked on base of consumer orders and delivered in cardboard boxes or plastic crates and are transported with special trucks or by use of postal service delivery in special crates. The retailer remains responsible for the products until delivery to the consumer. To become more efficient, inefficiency and damages that occur in the chain have to be known. The insights can be used to optimize the design or the way of packing and handling.

Delivery of products of four retailers has been analyzed from fulfillment center up to the last mile. Complaints and broken packages are analyzed, drop tests of filled cartons and crates are executed, and transport loggers are used. The visits to the retailers lead to flow charts of the way of handling. Complaints and broken packages gave insight in the causes of damages.

Transport loggers gave insight in the vibrations and shocks that occur during delivery. Drop test results are used as reference.We can conclude that the process of order picking can be optimized by using retail-ready packaging without foil and by placing products in the carton with the barcode to the front. During delivery the filling grade of the cardboard boxes and crates, the combination of type of packs and the way of filling are important causes of failure. Damage also occurs during the last meters, from delivery truck to front door.

The existing ISTA 6OB test method for e-commerce is based on parcel sending and is too severe for retailer delivery service as seen in this study. At the researched transport 7.2 G and 0.8 m/s in x-axis direction and 10.4 G and 0.3 m/s in the z-axis direction are measured.

The developed packaging design model for e-commerce consists of a checklist which should guide and inform the packaging designer through the new processes and the fillers during packing. In this study, the diffusion coefficients of 13 kinds of small molecules with molecular weights ranging from 32 to 339 $g.mol^{-1}$ in amorphous PET are calculated based on molecular dynamics (MD) simulation. The results suggest that diffusion coefficient of migrant depends not only the molecular weight but also the shape of migrant molecules. Further, the free volume of polymer matrix is calculated using Connolly surface method. The results show that some small free volume cavities conjoin together and form the larger cavities which facilitate the diffusion of migrant molecules in polymer matrix. The diffusion trajectories suggest that the molecules in first class move actively, but the molecules in class third class move limitedly and the movement mobility of molecules in second class is between that of first class and third class. The diffusion trajectories of small molecules strongly depend on the shape and molecular weight of migrant molecules, which is consistent with the diffusion coefficients.

Keywords: distribution, e-commerce, last mile, engineering design model, packaging design

***Correspondence to:** Roland ten Klooster, Department of Design, Production and Management, Faculty of Engineering Technology, University of Twente, Drienerlolaan 5, Enschede, The Netherlands. E-Mail: r.tenklooster@utwente.nl

1. Introduction

E-commerce in the grocery market is a new retail environment. Products are picked on base of consumer orders and are delivered packed in cardboard boxes or plastic crates and are transported with special trucks or by use of postal service delivery. The retailer remains responsible for the products until delivery to the consumer. To become more efficient, inefficiency and damages that occur in the chain have to be known. The insights can be used to optimize the design of the primary packaging or the way of packing and handling of the cardboard boxes or crates with the articles for one client used for transport.

E-commerce of grocery articles has grown fast and retailers do not want to miss market share. They started delivery of articles in a short time without much preparation, mostly on base of improvising and the business is becoming more professional over time also meaning that changes in the way of packing and delivering are introduced all the time. Four Dutch retailers have been chosen to get insight in the developments and state of art: Albert Heijn, Jumbo, Picnic and Stockon. With these four retailers more than 90% of the market share of home delivery of grocery articles is covered (situated 2018/2019). They use different transport means and work in different ways.

To get insight in the way products are delivered several activities are executed:

- Analysis of market development to get insight in the figures;

- Visits are executed to three retailers to see and analyze the way of order picking and the way of packing the cardboard boxes and crates that are send to the consumer;

- Semi-structured discussions with key internal stakeholders about development, failures, complaints, etc.;

- The filled transport packaging is followed from distribution center to the customer, as far as possible. Parcel sending could not be followed;

- A data logger is used to analyze the shocks and vibrations that occur during transport;

- Drop tests with filled boxes and crates with a mix of articles are executed to get insight in possible damages.

All findings are collected and used to define a design model for e-commerce to be used in design packaging projects for primary and secondary packaging.

2. Analysis of market development

E-commerce is the upcoming trend and also reached the grocery market. Different sources show growing numbers in the growth of e-commerce, as well the market share online retailers are claiming in the FMCG market. The market shares in 2016 are low in the Netherlands with a percentage of 1.2% of the total FMCG market (Kantar, 2016), but doubled in 2017 to a market share of 2.6% (Kantar, 2017). The speed of development is currently high with annual growth rates between 30-40% and will grow to 13%-22% in 2023 (De Weerd, 2018). In other countries e-commerce is growing as well but in different rates. The UK and France are currently leading in e-commerce with the biggest market shares. In Germany discount shops have a high market share in the retail environment (~45%) and e-commerce is growing slower than in the earlier mentioned countries. With e-commerce growing globally, the expectation is that e-commerce will grow until 2025 to a market share of 10% of the total FMCG market (Kantar, 2017).

2.1. Different players in e-commerce

Due to e-commerce, the retail environment is changing driven by multiple new business ideas. In the end, they have to fulfil the needs and the consumer drivers have to be taken into account to make it a success. Currently, three main participators in the market of e-commerce can be distinguished: traditional brick-and-mortar retailers, pure online retailers and companies who use e-commerce as a category expansion (Syndy, 2015). A classification can also be used to distinguish parties in the market like a mono channel retailer that uses only one channel to sell and market its services, a multi-channel retailer and that uses multiple channels but has separate marketing and logistics for each channel and cross-omnichannel sellers that integrate the different sales channels in logistics and marketing. The level of integration makes the difference between cross- and omnichannel retailer.

2.2 Traditional retailer

The traditional retailer has already a network of brick-and-mortar stores and uses e-commerce to provide its customers with a different distribution channel. This is also the category which focuses on the omnichannel offering. The traditional retailer has to maintain its online platform as the stores. This can cause problems due to the fact they provide more options to a similar group of customers. This can cannibalize their own sales in store. New business innovations are already tested to give a new purpose to the physical store for that reason, like an "eatery" (Smit, 2018, Syndy, 2015).

2.3 Pure online retailer

The pure online retailer only has a digital shelf to provide its customers. Between the pure online players, two different categories can be seen which are relevant for the current retail environment.

The first one is the retailer pure online player, who is similar to the traditional retailer but has no physical stores. It has its own delivery service to serve its customers and the supply chain from the retailers' distribution center to the customer is their responsibility. Also, the quality of the product is their responsibility during those processes.

The second online retailer is using a third party to deliver groceries to the customer. This is mostly done by an existing postal deliverer.

2.4 Category expansion

Next to the existing retailers, e-commerce offers also opportunities for other companies who are no specialist in retailing. Those companies who expand a category have similarities with some aspects of e-commerce. Those companies use their knowledge of their current business to enter the e-commerce market. Examples of those companies are Alibaba (China) and PostNL (Netherlands) which have a mature distribution network and are able to use this in e-commerce (Syndy, 2015).

The difference in the way products are sold is shown in figure 1. Especially changes in the so called first and last mile can be noticed.

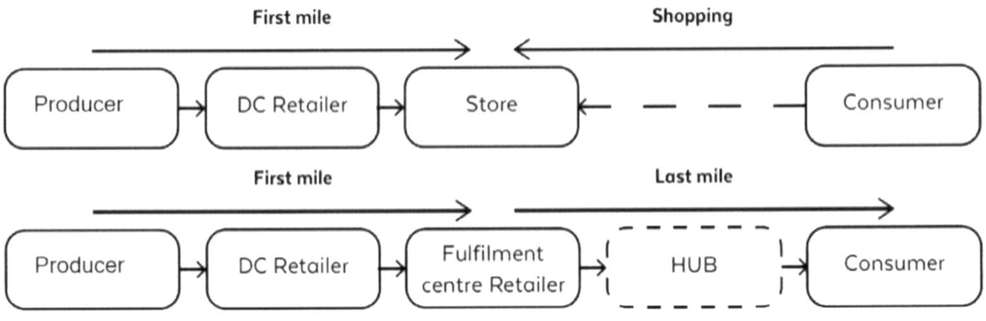

Figure 1 *Changes in the distribution channel of groceries, the above row shows brick and mortar shops, the bottom row shows e-commerce.*

2.5 The first mile

The packaging used in the first mile can be separated into two different parts. From the supplier to the distribution centers mostly pallets are used as tertiary packaging. The requirements of the tertiary packaging are dependent on the requirements of the distribution chain and the distribution center (DC). DC requirements may differ due to the level of automatization. Most automatic DCs have stricter standards to fit the machines. However, the developments in DCs will influence both products for online and offline markets. The second part concerns the transport packaging, like cardboard boxes, trays, shrink films or plastic crates.

2.6 The last mile

The part in the supply chain which is only for e-commerce products is the last mile. From the fulfilment center where the process starts, the orders have to be delivered to the customer via one of the channels. After the orders are collected in the fulfilment center, the customer can be reached in different ways. In this situation, the products are collected by the retailer and brought to the customer. In the traditional supply chain, the responsibility for the product ends for the retailer after the consumer paid for the groceries at the cash register. In the new environment, the retailer is also responsible for the transport to the consumer and for the collection of the products.

According to the Syndy report, to fulfil the needs of the consumer, multiple ways of delivering the groceries are available (Syndy, 2015). The options can vary from home delivery to a pick-up point. The option which is most popular differs per country. In the Netherlands and the UK, home delivery is the most popular option, while in France pick and collect wins in popularity. In 2014 there were more pick-up points than hypermarkets in France and the second largest online retailer did not even offer home delivery. The popular business model is based on the geography and grocery culture of the specific country.

In e-commerce the delivery options can be divided into four categories; In-store pick-up points, standalone pick-up points, home delivery and home delivery by a third party (Syndy, 2015). In practice, some retailers make use of multiple channels at the same time to reach as many as their consumers.

2.7 In-store pick-up points

In case of in-store pick-up points, the store gets a double function. Next to the original function, stores give the possibility to pick-up groceries at the store itself. Within in-store pick-up points, the fulfilment can be done differently. Instead of picking the orders in the fulfilment center the order will be collected in the store. In theory, this has the advantages of low initial investments, no duplicate stock keeping and low floor space required. In the other hand, the double workload for replenishment, possible faster out of stock and in-store congestion, make it not easy profitable. Therefore this fulfilment option is not seen often, but the option to pick it up in-store is. If it only functions as pick-up point, the order will be collected in the fulfilment center. In some cases, products with really low rotation speed, like care products, are added to the online container in-store.

2.8 Standalone pick-up points

Next to the in-store pick-up points, there are standalone pick-up points. Those can be placed next to commuting areas, like stations or highways to make it easier for the consumer. Also for areas with a lower density of population, where home delivery is not possible, pick-up points can be the solution. It is relatively easier for the retailer, while a larger group can be reached with relatively low effort.

Next to the pick-up points of the retailer, third parties can help them out as well. With collaborations between retailers and other companies already existing networks can be used for distributing the orders.

2.9 Home delivery

In the Netherlands home delivery is the most dominant option and also the one which requires the most effort by the retailer. The orders do not only have to be brought to a few central places, but to all individual addresses of the consumers. The supply chain is the longest and most complex compared to other options. If a package fails before reaching the address, products can be rejected and compensations have to be taken in place. However, most retailers have solutions for compensation. Nevertheless, the missing products can lead to frustrations for the consumer.

In the traditional supply chain, the route of the products did not end in the store and had to be taken home too. However the consumer is responsible for the products and if there are damages, the consumer knows it is his/herself to blame. In the new situation, the expectations have to be set again. The question is if consumers still expect a product in perfect condition or if imperfections are excepted and if so, to what extent.

2.10 Home delivery by a third party

Another option to reach the customer with home delivery, but without an own delivery service, is to use a third party for transport. Some retailers use postal delivery services to deliver their orders. The responsibility for the sent orders becomes more important if third parties are being used. The terms and conditions of PostNL (the Dutch postal delivery service)state that if the package is missing or has been damaged during transport the responsibility is for the consumer (PostNL, 2019). In this case, the risk will be for the retailer to not incur any image damage.

With all these options the supply chain gets more complex. In the traditional supply chain, the store was the only option for the retailer to maintain. With the introduction of e-commerce and the availability of multiple options, the total supply chain gets more complex than before. In Figure 2 from Colliers International (Colliers, 2015), the complexity of the e-commerce supply chain is represented.

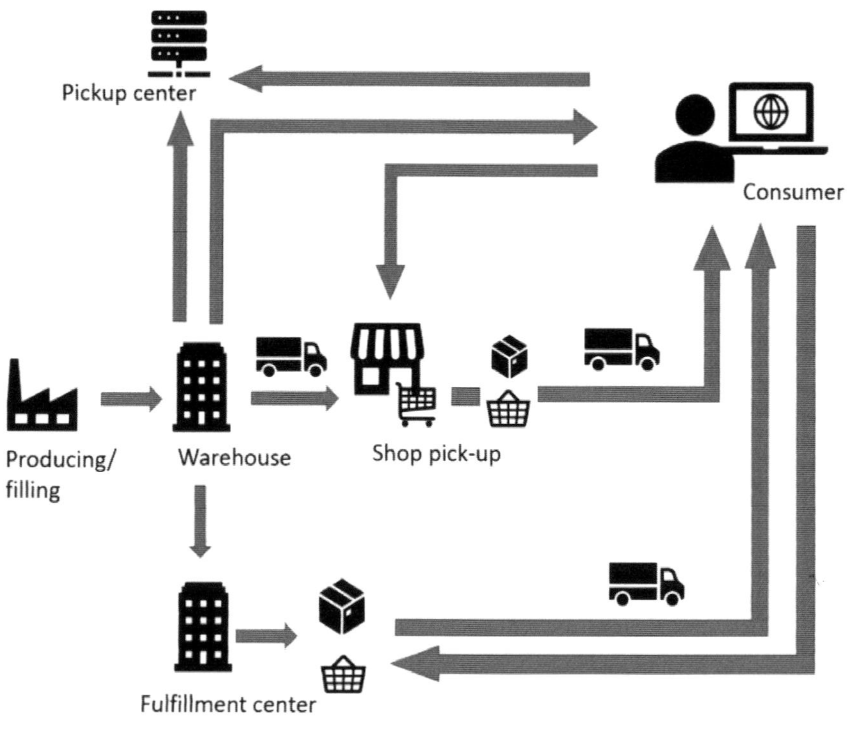

Figure2 *Last mile options (free after Colliers, 2015)*

3. Research

Four Dutch retailers have been taken into account in this research; Albert Heijn, Jumbo, Picnic and Stockon. They all work according a channel option as represented in the presented models in Figure 2. They represent over 90% of the online retail market of the Netherlands, as shown in Table 1.

Table 1 *The four researched e-commerce retailers and their market share in the Netherlands in 2018*

Albert Heijn Traditional retailer	**Jumbo** Traditional retailer	**Picnic** Pure e-commerce retailer	**Stockon** Categories expansion
ah	JUMBO	PIC NIC	STO CK ON Nooit meer zonder.
Online Market share: 53% (Distrifood, 2018b)	Online Market share: 26% (Distrifood, 2018b)	Online Market share: 12% (Distrifood, 2018b)	Online Market share: <1% (estimated market share, only one small warehouse)

To understand the way of working of these retailers, information is gathered with interviews, visits to fulfilment centers and information from their websites. Furthermore, tests are executed to understand the processes in the fulfilment center and the last mile, as shown in Table 2. Information is not gathered in even amounts due to differences in the level of participation by the retailers, nevertheless the information was good enough to create a realistic view of the current approach of these four retailers in the Netherlands and the consequences for the packaging due to the developments in e-commerce.

Table 2 *Overview of research activities*

Albert Heijn	**Jumbo**	**Picnic**	**Stockon**
Interview with supply chain department	Interview with supply chain department	Interviews with supply chain department, marketing and order picker	Interviews with owners and order picker
Visit Fulfillment center De Meern		Visit Fulfillment center Amsterdam and Eindhoven	Visit Fulfillment center Oud-Gastel
		Observation and testing in the fulfillment center	Observation and testing in the fulfilment center
		Observation and testing of the last mile	Testing of the last mile

3.2 Albert Heijn

Albert Heijn offers its portfolio both online and offline, with some extra products specifically for e-commerce. Albert Heijn made the choice to offer e-commerce directly to all of their customers and cover 86% of the Netherlands by home delivery. The other parts of the Netherlands, which are mostly less densely populated areas, only have access to a number of pick-up points. By offering multiple ways to buy groceries, the choice is made differently by the consumer than in the past. The sales volumes in the brick-and-mortar stores declined with 0.3% in 2018, while the online market is growing fast (Distrifood, 2018a). They expect the upcoming years a growth of 20-30% in turnover in e-commerce. Currently, they already have about 100.000 orders a week.

3.2 Jumbo

Jumbo is another traditional retailer who participates in e-commerce. In many ways, Jumbo has the same approach as Albert Heijn. Also jumbo offer the same portfolio as their normal shop and has multiple ways to deliver the groceries to the consumer. Although there are similarities between Albert Heijn and Jumbo, the main difference is the distribution to the customer. Instead of using hubs to be closer to the customer, centralized stores are used as a hub. In a city such as Veghel, one Jumbo location is chosen to be the distribution point for a certain area.

The choice of using stores instead of hubs also affects the supply chain in other ways. The slow movers, for example, can be added in-store and not be brought with an extra crate. Jumbo only works with three different crates and will transport more product types together. The crates Jumbo is using are divided on base of the type of product: ambient, chilled or frozen.

3.3 Picnic

Picnic is a pure online retailer and only offers its services via their app. In contrast to the traditional retailers, Picnic did not have any loyal consumers from the start. This also gave them the opportunity to slowly build up their distribution network. They only deliver in a certain area when there are enough consumers and a hub or fulfilment center is close by. This efficiency in transport is important to make e-commerce profitable. With their business believes; easy to order, free to deliver for a low amount (25 euro) and everything with a smile, they want to persuade the consumer.

Furthermore, they only offer 6000 SKUs, which is a low amount compared with Albert Heijn. Following their vision, two or three brands per product are enough to fulfil the needs of the consumer, mostly the brand leader and a private label. Due to the limited amount of SKUs the floor space needed in the fulfilment centers is smaller than Albert Heijn's and Jumbo's. After delivering the groceries, Picnic also returns other packages from e-commerce. Packages ordered at the webstore of Wehkamp, one of the biggest players in non-food e-commerce, can be returned via the delivery service of Picnic. This service should offer the consumer even more convenience.

Picnic buys their products from the wholesaler Boni, which supplies the fulfilment centers directly. In general, smaller retailers use a wholesaler to supply the fulfilment centers. Just as Jumbo, Picnic uses three types of secondary packaging: for ambient, chilled and frozen products.

Next to the distribution, the ownership of the products is a bit different in this case. Because a wholesaler is in place, the ownership of the products for Picnic starts after checking the incoming goods at the fulfilment center. Picnic has the ownership untill the delivery at the consumer.

3.4 Stockon

Stockon is a start-up from PostNL, a category extension. Their strategy is to start retailing in e-commerce with the knowledge and infrastructure of the postal delivery service. Their network already covers the whole of the Netherlands (except the islands in the North of the Netherlands). No full trucks are needed because the groceries will be transported next to other packages sent by PostNL. Only home delivery is possible.

Stockon is focusing on pantry products, which are most times the heavy and more bulky products of the shopping list. Stockon is also using wholesaler Boni as the supplier of their fulfilment center. Only this process is fully owned by Stockon, although they are owned 50% by PostNL, the logistical networks are used like another retailer. In this way, similar retailers can be compared better too. The products will be received in dollies and are till this process similar to the other retailers. After they picked the orders, the crate is put on a dolly again to be sent in the supply chain of PostNL. This crate is special for Stockon not similar to the competitors. If something breaks in the last-mile, it is still the responsibility of Stockon, because the transporter is only responsible for the transport from A to B (PostNL, 2019).

In 2019 Stockon decided to stop their business in this field, they did not acquire enough customers.

4. Secondary packaging used for e-commerce

The secondary packaging that is used to deliver the products to the fulfillment center is removed during the order picking process and is replaced by the container (secondary packaging) of the specific e-commerce party. The business approach has its consequences for the secondary packaging the retailer uses. For example, Albert Heijn leaves the secondary packaging at the consumers and asks deposit money, while Picnic is giving bags to the consumer and takes back the secondary packaging. Furthermore, the kind of product also has an influence on the container of the retailer.

In general 3 kinds of crates are used for different type of products: ambient, chilled and frozen. The crates for chilled and frozen products are Styrofoam (expanded polystyrene) crates which have cool packs inside to keep the products at the wanted temperature. The main difference between the frozen and chilled containers are the used cool packs. Also, these containers are similar to all retailers and are always returned after delivery. The ambient crate can differ per retailer and is adjusted to the last mile transport. In the table below an overview is given of the used crates by the retailers.

Only Albert Heijn uses more crates. For fresh and really slow movers they have different crates. The design is based on the ambient crate. Fresh products use a crate with one plastic bag and the slow mover crates are divided into two or three compartments for multiple orders and the products are packed in a paper bag which is delivered to the consumer.

Table 3 *Overview of secondary packaging used by the four e-commerce retailers*

	Albert Heijn	Jumbo	Picnic	Stockon
Ambient			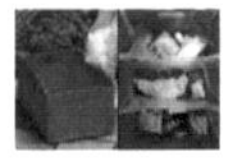	
	Crate without support	Crate without support	Crate plus 3 plastic bags	Crate plus 3 paper bags
Chilled	Styrofoam crate with plastic bags/multiple orders in crate 2 to 4 cool packs	Styrofoam crate with plastic bags/ multiple orders in crate 2 to 4 cool packs	Styrofoam crate with plastic bags/ multiple orders in crate 2 to 4 cool packs	Styrofoam crate with plastic bags/multiple orders in crate
Frozen	Styrofoam crate with plastic bags/multiple orders in crate Special cool packs	Styrofoam crate with plastic bags/multiple orders in crate Special cool packs	Styrofoam crate with plastic bags/multiple orders in crate Special cool packs	No frozen products sold

The reason to put products loose in the crate without a fixed orientation is the efficiency of the order picking process.

4.1 Replenishment process

The replenishment process is one of the two main processes in the fulfilment center. The major difference in work environment with the shelves for picking boxes for shops, is the shelf. At Albert Heijn and Picnic, the shelf has two sides; one side for the replenishment process and the other to pick the products.

This will disrupt the process of replenishment known for the store. In store, the old products have to be brought to the front and new products should be placed at the back (FIFO). Because the shelf has two sides the shelf can be replenished more efficiently. The product only has to be pushed to the order pick side of the shelf, which create FIFO replenishment automatically. See Figure 3.

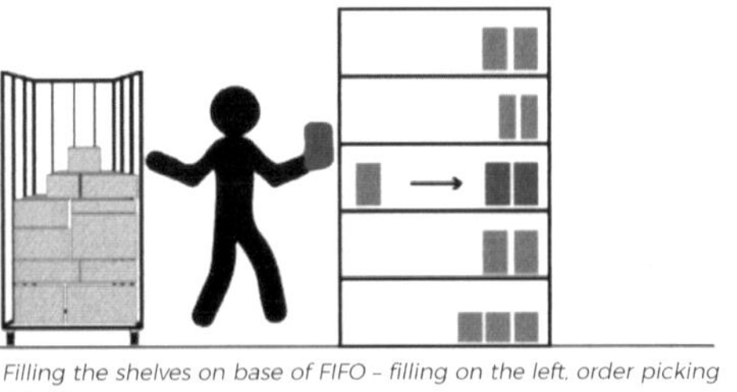

Figure 3 *Filling the shelves on base of FIFO – filling on the left, order picking on the right side*

This logistical process has the interaction with the primary and secondary packaging the packer uses and the tertiary packaging of the retailer. In most cases the dolly is used as tertiary packaging.

Between retailers there are some differences in fulfilling this process. Especially Stockon had a different way of working than Albert Heijn and Picnic. This is caused due the different layout, shortage of space in the fulfilment center and choices they made in the replenishment process. The replenishment process is shown in a flow chart in Figure 4.

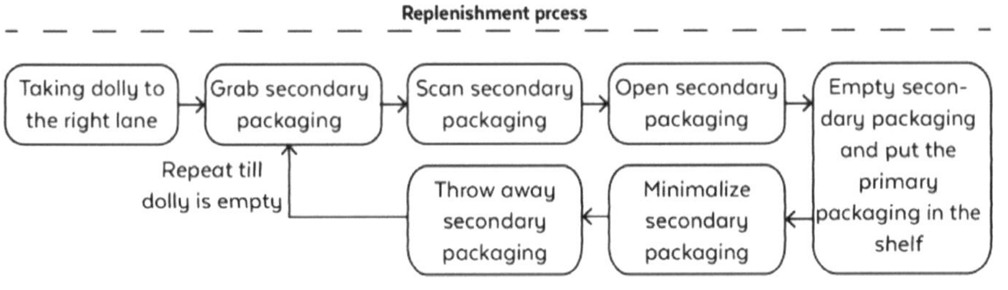

Figure 4 *The replenishment process of Albert Heijn and Picnic*

At Stockon the replenishment process is executed slightly different. In contrast to the other retailers the secondary packaging was placed in the shelf. Spare time was used to unpack secondary packaging, but only seen at some smaller products. Shelf-ready packaging was preferred by Stockon, to save time. Figure 5 shows the replenishment process of Stockon.

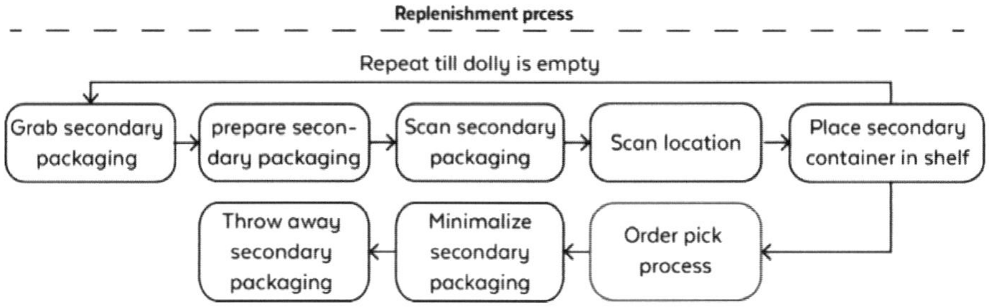

Figure 5 *The replenishment process of Stockon*

4.2 Order pick process

The order pick process is for the retailer the most important process of the fulfilment center, which is supported by the other processes. During the order pick process, the orders of the consumers are collected, as illustrated in Figure 6. The retailers are trying to reach an as high as possible pick rate, and therefore no other tasks should be performed by the order picker.

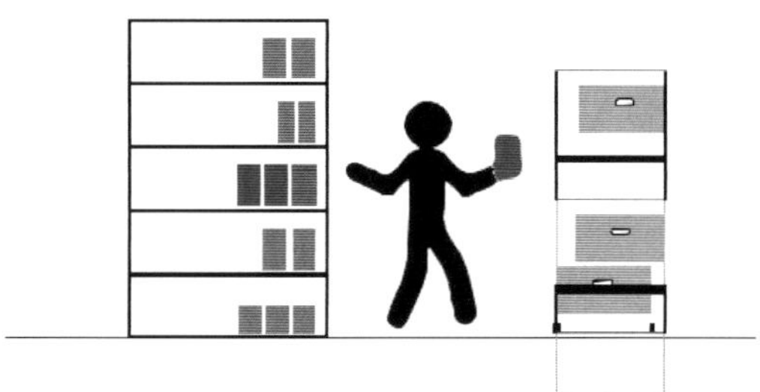

Figure 6 *The order pick process*

The efficiency of this process really differs per retailer. First of all, Stockon only picks one order at the time. Also the randomness of allocation of products, results in more time and efforts to pack the order in a logic way. Albert Heijn and Picnic have a comparable way of order picking. Due to the large amounts of products of Albert Heijn (26.500 SKUs) compared to Picnic (6000 SKUs) the route is longer and therefore more time is spend on transportation between the products. Most products are picked per hour at Picnic, least at Stockon, see Table 4.

Table 4 *Amount of orders per time*

	Albert Heijn	Picnic	Stockon
Products picked per hour	140	180-200	60
Orders per trip	~12	~12	1

The barcode on the packaging is scanned. It is noticed that a lot of products have to be turned around before they can be scanned because the barcode is on the backside.

In the fulfilment centerr the order pick process of Stockon and Picnic is examined. During a test with a product drone, pressure is mapped over time by placing the drone in the crate during the order pick process. The test exists out of three runs, in which the drone is placed to detect the pressure during the order pick process.

Peaks of 8.5 bar were registered because of replacing heavy products in the crate. See Figure 7 for the registered pressure map. The order picker of Stockon takes relatively much time to reorganize the crate in comparison to the Picnic process. In general, products are handled with care and time pressure does not influence the picking process. Dropping of products in a crate has not been observed. It is noticed that at Stockon the allocation of the products is often reorganized during filling.

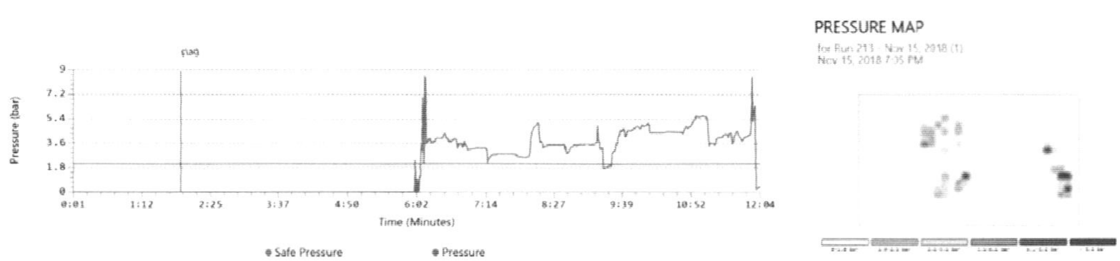

Figure 7 *Pressure map of fulfillment center – peaks up to 8.5 bar were measured*

5. Shipping the orders to the consumer

The traditional retailers Albert Heijn and Jumbo do look alike in the choice of transporting the crates. Picnic has a different dispatch frame than the other two. In the frame of Picnic the crates are the most fixed of the chosen options, as seen in the table below. Stockon is using the vans that are used for parcel sending. PostNL does not fix packages in the vans.

***Table 5** Transport of the last mile of the three retailers*

Retailer	Albert Heijn	Jumbo	Picnic
Delivery van			
Tertiary packaging	 Fixated by frame on sides, but free to move in longitudinal direction	 Fixated by frame on sides, but free to move in longitudinal direction	 Fixated in all orientations
Secondary packaging	Crate without bags	Crate without bags	Crate with 3 bags

To get a better understanding about the impact of the transport on the packaging and the representativeness of the current packaging tests, transport tests are executed. A transport logger is placed in the crates in between the products. The logger that is used is the Lansmont SAVER™ 9X30 shock and vibration field data recorder 127 x 124 x 43 mm, total weight of 1 kg. The logger is not fixed to the crate but is placed in between the products to simulate real product behaviour of products that are not fixed. The first shock that will be recorded is caused by the movement of the van, the next movements are caused by the interaction with other products and the behaviour of the logger itself. The logger of 1 kg can represent a product of 1 kg, like a glass bottle of wine with content of 0.75 liters and a glass weight of 0.4 kg (average weight of wine bottles, in total 1.15 kg) or a bottle of sauce for example (bottle weight of 400 grams with 500 grams content). These articles are regarded as fragile.

To get understanding of transport of mixed groceries in transport packaging, first a parcel is sent with TNT and PostNL, similar to Amazon's ISTA 6OB test. The outcome can be used in the research of the transport processes of the retailers and will show if the ISTA 6OB standard is representative. The parcel is sent from the location of a brand owner to a location in the Netherlands and returned afterwards, with the postal delivery services TNT and PostNL.

The package is packed according the ISTA 6 method. First the products are placed; afterwards packaging material is added to fill the remaining spaces. Instead of air pillows, as used in the ISTA 6OB norm, Styrofoam particles are being used, see Figure 8. Furthermore, products are chosen to represent the packaging formats of one cooperating brand owner with a large grocery portfolio and have a total weight of 12.1 kg. The dimensions of the box are 31x43x26 cm.

Product composition	After adding transport packaging

***Figure 8** Products placed in cardboard box for parcel sending test The packed products are described in Table 6.*

Table 6 Products that are sent as parcel in one box

	Packaging format	Damage	Level of damage
Tomato beans	Can	Can is dented	Major
Soup 500ml	Can	-	-
Tomato beans 500g	Can	-	-
Lentils 500ml	Can	-	-
Syrup	Aluminium can	Leakage in cap, syrup under seal cap	Major
Tagliatelle 500g	Flow pack	Broken product in bag	Major
Potato starch	Folding board	Paper board is damaged/dented	Minor
Soup	Folding board	Paper board is damaged/dented	Minor
Chocolate sprinkles	Folding board	Small damage on paper board	Minor
Bread spread jar 300g	Glass	-	-
Baby food 200g	Glass	-	-
Tomato soup	Pouch	-	-
Soup 570ml pouch	Pouch	--	-
Soup 570ml pouch	Pouch	-	-
Heinz by nature 180g	Pouch	-	-
Condiments 700g	Rigid bottle	-	-
Condiments 460g	Rigid bottle	-	-
Sauce 500g	Rigid cup	-	-
Condiments 500 ml	Rigid bottle	-	-
Soup 1L	Tetra pak	Dented on multiple sides	Minor
Sauce 500ml	Tetra pak	Small dents on top	Minor

An overview of damages is taken up the graph in Figure 9. Shocks as registered are presented in Figure 10.

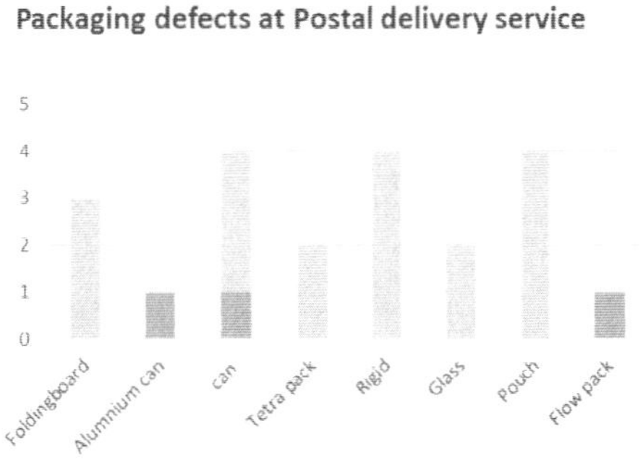

Figure 9 *Overview of damages of the packages during postal delivery service.*

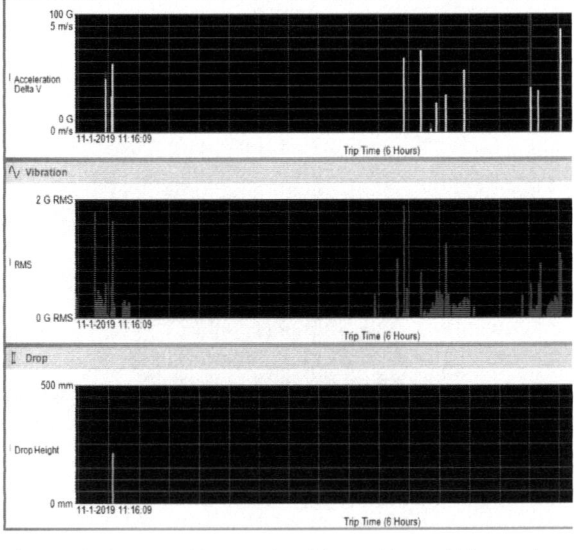

Figure 10 *Shocks registered during sending of the parcel by postal delivery services*

Accelerations and changes in velocity as registered during the transport of the parcels are presented in Table 7.

Table 7 *Measured data of sending parcels filled with grocery articles*

	TNT		PostNL	
Shocks numbered from highest down	**Acceleration (m/s^2)**	**Delta V (m/s)**	**Acceleration (m/s^2)**	**Delta V (m/s)**
1	100	1,90	85,79	2,82
2	51,69	2,28	24,61	0,60
3	47,86	2,75	24,22	1,64
4	40,77	1,40	20,16	0,65
5	38,57	1,83	19,87	0,58
6	33,32	0,76	16,66	0,48
7	31,95	1,38	14,20	0,65
8	23,13	1,54	14,18	1,80
9	18,06	0,87		
10	17,96	0,58		

5.1 Vibrations of the transports

TNT parcel sending: Vibrations are comparable with ISTA 6OB norm. Only the peaks in the ISTA standard are not shown in the transport. However, the higher frequencies (> 150 Hz) are heavier than the ISTA 6OB standard.

PostNL parcel sending: the second part of the trip with PostNL as transporter is similar to the TNT transport. The ISTA 6OB line is really close to the PostNL vibrations, but has heavier vibrations in the peaks. At the other hand the PostNL data shows heavier vibrations between 7 and 12 Hz. Also compared to the TNT transport the vibrations are similar.

5.2 Shocks of the transports

During the transports of the postal delivery services multiple shocks are detected. The highest (based on acceleration) are noted in Table 7. In the diagram shocks of all directions are seen. However, when the strongest shocks are evaluated these are mostly in the z-axis. The timelines show that the packaging has to resist many shocks.

The ISTA 6OB standard can be seen as a test method for postal delivery services, which transport the groceries packed in a corrugated box. The primary packaging showed multiple packaging defects. Therefor the risk on packaging defects is real and primary packaging packed in a box filled with Styrofoam particles is not ready for this kind of transport yet.

5.3 Test with Stockon crate

A transport logger was put in the crate of Stockon and was sent from the fulfilment center in Oud Gastel to Waalre via the distribution network of PostNL. The groceries are packed in the Stockon crate. Although PostNL is a parcel sender, it is expected that the forces will be less strong than when packed in a corrugated box. The registered data is presented in Table 8.

Table 8 *Research data of the executed test with the Stockon crate*

From high to low	Date	Time	Acceleration (G)	Delta V (km/h)	Temperature
1	16-11	15:15	14,83	2,57	10,7
2	16-11	12:38	13,57	8,06	10,2
1	15-11	20:06	11,54	3.13	17,8
4	16-11	20:24	9,84	0,6	12,1
5	15-11	20:06	9,77	5,27	17,8
6	16-11	12:37	8,74	2,39	10,2
7	16-11	12:41	6,72	1,39	10,3
8	16-11	13:05	6,13	1,34	10,7
9	16-11	13:05	5,05	3,5	10,7
10	16-11	12:37	4,86	1,47	10,2
11	16-11	12:37	4,43	1,07	10,2
12	16-11	15:15	4,28	1,66	10,7

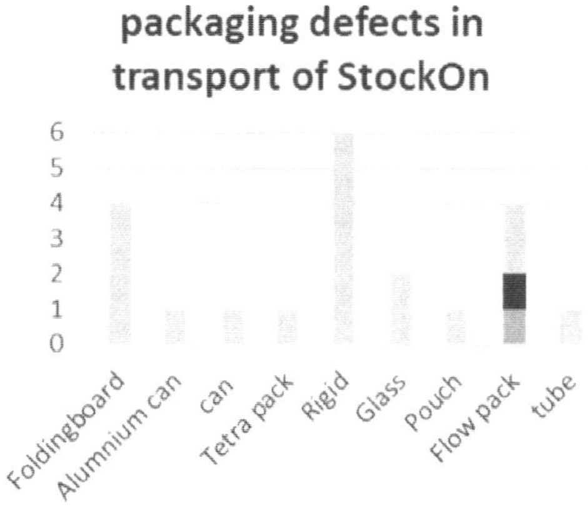

Figure 11 *Packaging defects after transport of the Stockon crate*

The amount of impacts is smaller than with parcel sending in a corrugated box. It look likes the crate of Stockon is handled with more care, but this is based on a single shipment. However the groceries packaging still had defects. This may be caused by the lack of fixation of the products in the crate.

For packaging design it is important to understand the type of loads that can be expected during sending of e-commerce orders.

5.4 Picnic order picking and last mile transport

At Picnic the process of order picking and the last mile are monitored. To monitor the effect of the order picking procedure, a transport logger is placed in the crate beforehand. Two different compositions of ambient products and one composition of chilled products are taken. The compositions are based on the biggest amounts based on Picnic's data. For the ambient products, the crates around 30l/7kg and 45l/17kg are chosen. Furthermore the chilled crate contains a composition of 10l/8Kg. With the three chosen crates the test can represent different situations, with a limited amount of testing.

The order pick test did not show any mentionable impacts during the order pick process.

In interviews with Picnic employees, they mentioned that some packages are harder to open and to replenish than others. Shrink film was one of the major frustrations, especially if no perforations are made in the packaging. Also corrugated boxes can create frustration, the box can be too hard to open or the products are packed too tight. The secondary packaging should support the opening process.

The transport tests of the last-mile transport of Picnic is executed five times. The shipment goes from the fulfilment center to the Picnic hub in a lorry. Here it will be transferred from the lorry to a delivery van, which delivers the order to the customer. The test will contain four ambient transports (twice half full, twice full) and one chilled transport.

The transport logger is put upside down in the middle bag of the crate with the orientations as in Figure 12. Afterwards the crate is placed in the transport shelf. Here it will stay till the delivery van arrives at the destination. The order is taken into an automated system meaning that the place in the transport shelf is based on the location of the system. The locations could not be registered. Heavier crates will be relatively low in the dispatch frame and lighter ones on the top.

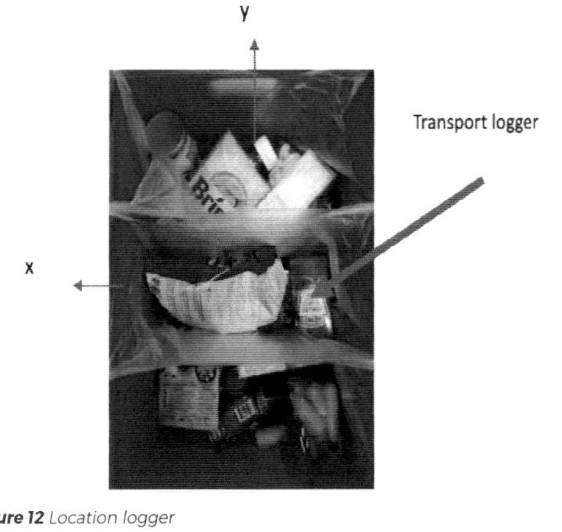

Figure 12 *Location logger*

Hardly any packaging defects were detected. See Figures 13 and 14.

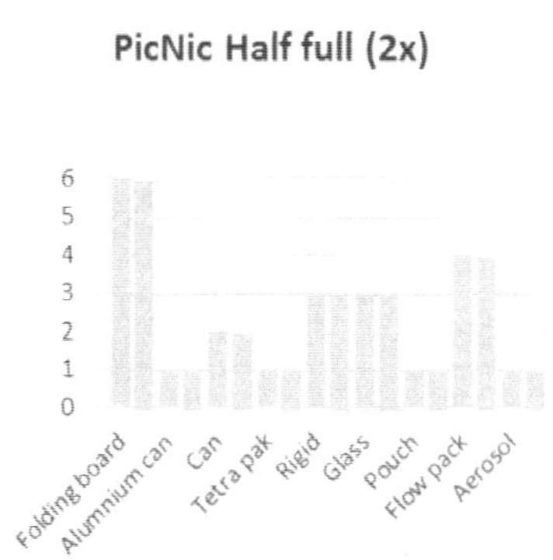

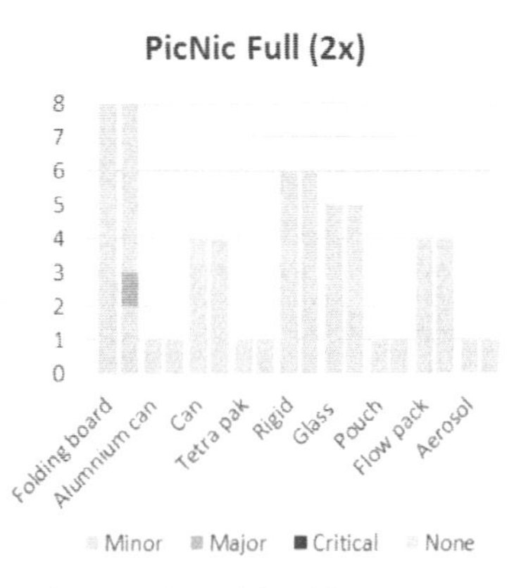

Figure 13 *Packaging defects half full crate*

Figure 14 *Packaging defects full crate*

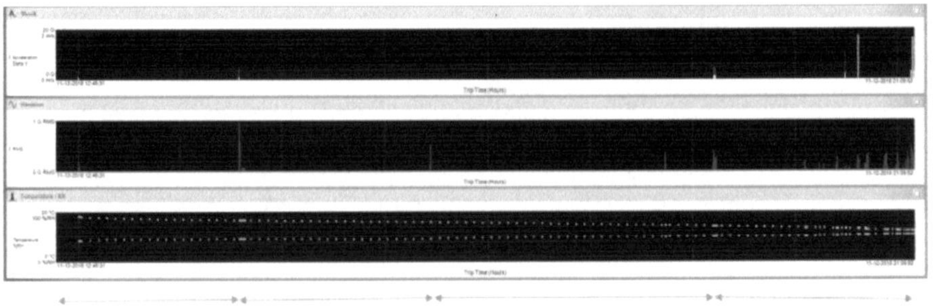

Figure 15 *Registered vibrations of one trip*

In some cases the vibration in the z-axis are touching the ISTA 6OB standard. Also the vibrations between the different levels of content seem to be comparable, although the second transport of full ambient has stronger vibrations than the others. Also the vibrations above 200Hz are higher than the ISTA 6OB standard.

There are a few shocks measured with relative high values in the acceleration, but these accelerations do have a low change in velocity (<1 m/s). The values of the impacts are not always in the z-axis, also forces in the x-direction are measured. Those probably represent corners or roundabouts during transports. During the observation in one of the transports, the vans can lean relatively far, compared to a car. In the end, a few shocks are seen, but not in the amounts or strength of the postal delivery service.

In the transport of Picnic the most vulnerable part for the packaging is the transport in the delivery van. Here are the highest values measured, next to the transfer moments in the supply chain. The interactions by humans, all transfer moments are executed by workers, show the highest interactions. In the end the last mile process is not comparable with the tests of the ISTA 6OB standard. Lower values can be used to test new packaging designs.

However, still packaging defects are seen. Those are only seen at the folding board boxes, which are relatively fragile products and probably caused compression by the other products.

Lastly it is remarkable that the chilled crate shows much more activity in the last mile than the ambient crates. While the ambient transports did not show much shocks during the transport, the chilled transport shows a few.

This test is executed to see how the products behave during the transport. In grocery e-commerce products are not fixed in the secondary packaging

6. Results of the interviews

Interview are hold with supply chain managers and order pickers. The field is in strong development and the way of working is adopted to findings very fast. The rate of parcels ordered via e-commerce is 36% in the Netherlands. For grocery articles the interviewed people mentioned that there is no return option available. If products are damaged they will be taken back directly. The deliverer has to check the content and has to put down the crate carefully. In the beginning when deliverers did not get proper instructions this caused some issues, especially with glass bottles in the crate. Putting them down too fast or small drops was the cause. At one retailer the instruction is to clean the crate if something is broken, at another the whole crate is replaced. When glass is broken the whole crate will be replaced in any case.

It was noted that delivering the products in such a way that the packaging does not have to be turned around, in a retail ready packaging can save time during the fulfillment process.

7. Packaging design model for e-commerce

Based on the findings an overview of aspects that are of concern is made. The checklist is split up after primary and secondary packaging. Steps of the chain like the fulfillment center, the dimensions of transport packaging, the need to open the secondary packaging that is on the shelf etc. are taken up in the model. The model is presented in the next graphs.

The model is tested by looking at several packaging and discussing the needs for redesign. This was a very preliminary test and needs expansion.

7.1 Design model for e-commerce for secondary packaging

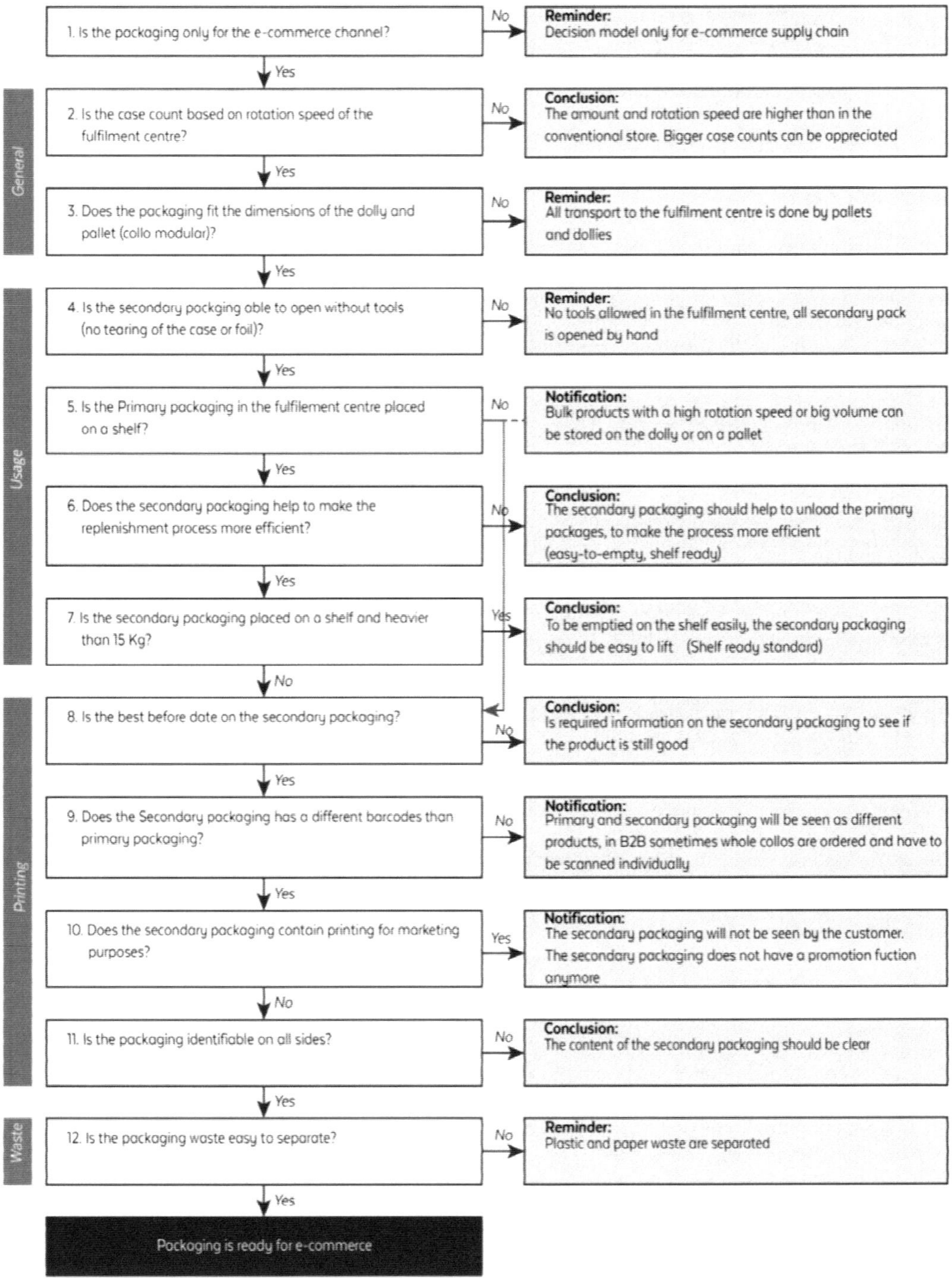

7.2 Design model for e-commerce for primary packaging

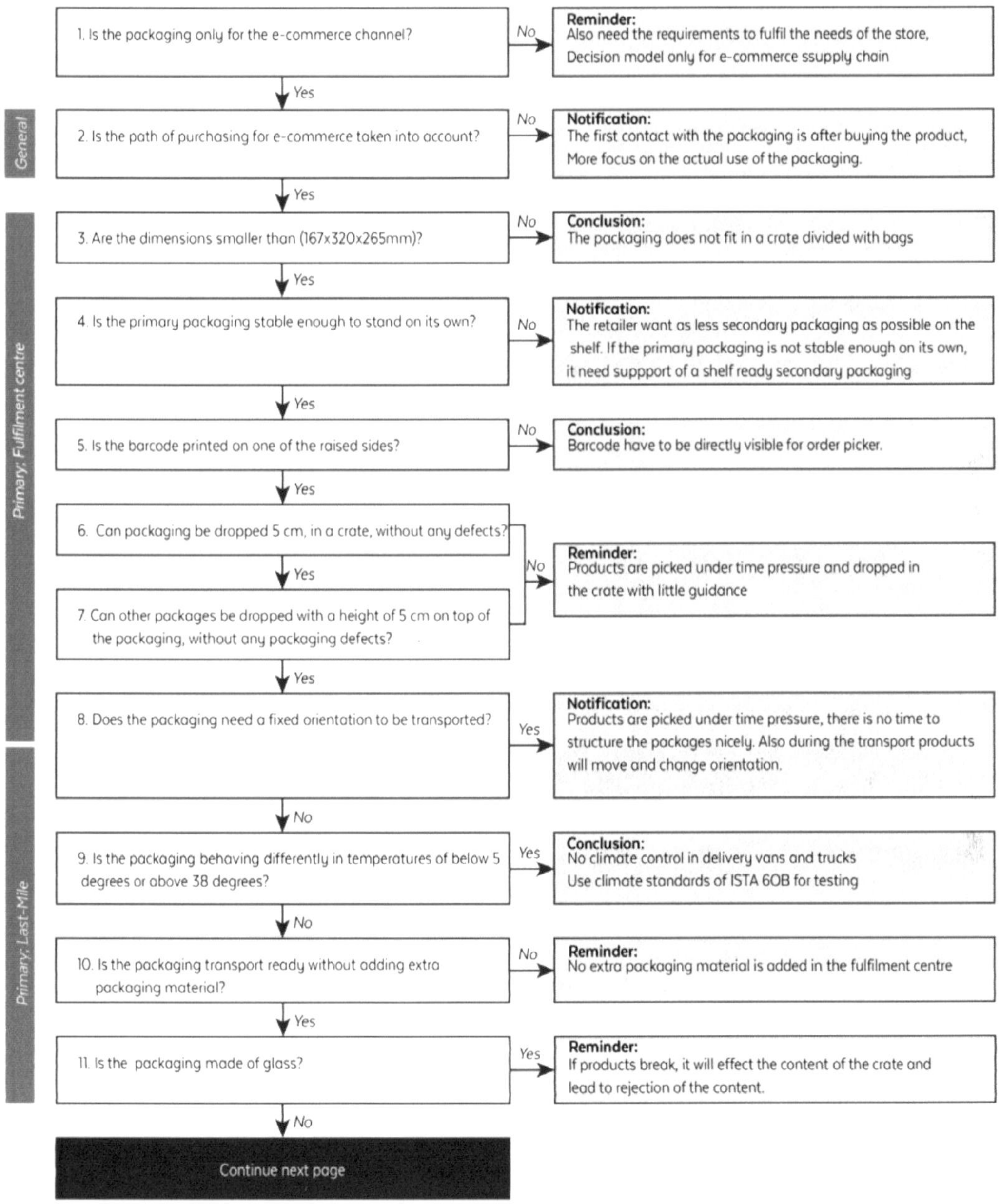

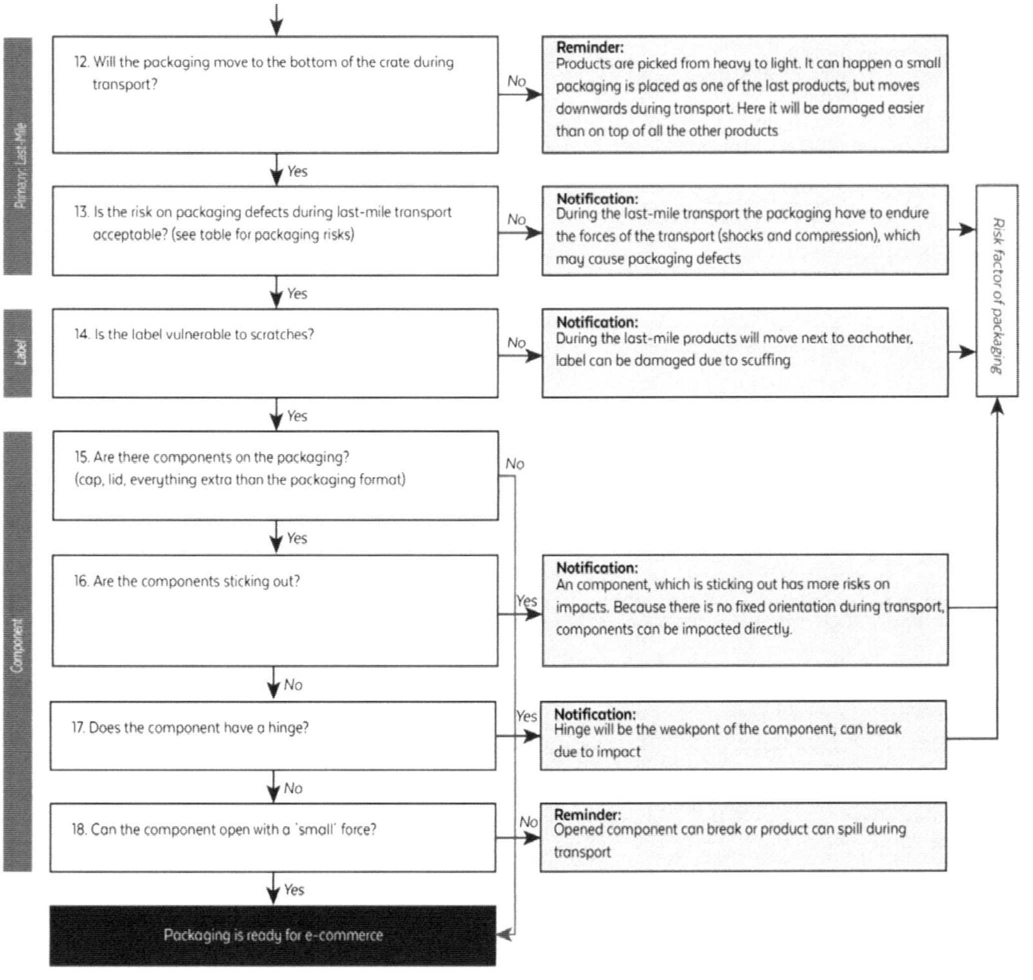

8. Discussion

The research is based on a few measurements to get insight in the loads on packaging in the way they are transported by retailers. Stockon is a unique party in this business because they use the service of parcel sending of PostNL. The design of the crates is specific for them and probably because of instruction of the operators the loads are less. In 2019 Stockon decided to stop their business in this field, they did not acquire enough customers.

As measured the loads in the crates and vans used by the retailers is less than the ISTA 6OB standard based on parcel sending. Still packages get damaged because they are put loose in the crates by two of the three researched retailers. The damages are mostly small like dented folding boxboard, broken products in flowpacks that do not provide any buffer and small dents in cans. Until now this has not lead to serious complaints of the consumers, probably because damages like these also can occur when consumers do their own shopping.

The amount of tests is very small. The expectation was that more damages would be noticed.

To get a reliable image from practice more tests have to be executed. It should be noticed that this way of working is very new and the execution is still in development and changes regularly. It can be expected that a way of filling of the crates is found and/or developed which caused the least damage. Nevertheless, filling crates with such a high variety will not easy lead to a standard although instructions will definitely help. The drivers in the cars to deliver the groceries are only working with one type of products which are still owned by the grocer. This is rather different than normal parcel sending. This will be the reason that the ISTA 6OB standard is too severe.

Putting the data logger in between the grocery articles is questionable because the movements of the van are not registered, but the movement of the data logger itself.

The design model can help in evaluating the product portfolio to reduce damages but has to be tested more extensively, especially in design projects and teams working on structural packaging design as done in practice.

9. Conclusions and recommendations

The process of order picking can be optimized by using retail ready packaging without foil and by placing products in the carton with the barcode to the front. The filling grade of the cartons and crates, the combination of type of packs and the way of filling are important causes of failure, although the failures are small. Damage also occurs during the last meters, from delivery truck to front door.

The existing ISTA 6OB test method for e-commerce is too severe for retailer delivery service as executed in the Netherlands. Measured are 7.2 G and 0.8 m/s in x-axis direction and 10.4 G and 0.3 m/s in the z-axis direction. The packaging design can be structured more by use of the developed model which consists of a checklist and guidelines. The checklist should guide and inform the packaging designer through the new processes and the fillers during packing.

It is recommended to do further research in this field. At first to expend the amount of tests to get more reliable data. At second the design of the secondary packaging can be optimized. dkjfdjf

10. References

[1] Colliers International. From First mile to last mile: Global industrial & Logistics trends, 2015

[2] Distrifood. AH-winkels onder marktgroei in 2019. Retrieved from https://www.distrifood.nl/formules/nieuws/2018/12/ah-winkels-onder-marktgroei-in-2019-101120685, 2018a

[3] Distrifood. Jumbo en Picnic winnen online van AH. Retrieved from https://www.distrifood.nl/branche-bedrijf/nieuws/2018/11/jumbo-en-picnic-winnen-online-van-ah-10112 0059?vakmedianet-approve-cookies=1&_ga=2.203457043.2069599819.1558176392-2143063819.1557 490795, 2018b

[4] Kantar. The future of e-commerce in FMCG. In. 2016

[5] Kantar. The Future of e-commerce in FMCG. In. November 2017.

[6] PostNL Algemene voorwaarden online frankeren en pakket ontvangen. 2016

[7] Smit, R. AH bouwt supermarkten om tot 'eetcentrum' om teruggang te stoppen. Retrieved from https://fd.nl/ondernemen/1281687/ah-bouwt-supermarkten-om-tot-eetcentrum-om-teruggang-te-stoppen #, 2018

[8] Syndy. 2015. THE STATE OF ONLINE GROCERY RETAIL IN EUROPE. In.

[9] De Weerd, P., 2018. E-commerce boodschappen groeit naar 22 procent. Retrieved from https://www.logistiek.nl/supply-chain/nieuws/2018/11/e-commerce-boodschappen-groeit-naar-22-proce nt-101165971

The Effect of Pallet Top Deck Stiffness on the Compression Strength of Asymmetrically Supported Corrugated Boxes [49]

Chandler Quesenberry, Laszlo Horvath *, John Bouldin, Marshall S. White
Virginia Tech, Department of Sustainable Biomaterials,
Virginia Tech 1650 Research Center Dr, Blacksburg VA, USA

Abstract: During unitized shipment, the components of unit loads are interacting with each other. During floor stacking of unit loads, the load on the top of the pallet causes the top deck of the pallet to bend which creates an uneven top deck surface resulting in uneven, or asymmetrical support of the corrugated boxes. This asymmetrical support could significantly affect the strength of the corrugated boxes, and it depends on the top deck stiffness of the pallet. This study is aimed at investigating how the variations of pallet top deck stiffness and the resulting asymmetric support, affects corrugated box compression strength.

The study used a scaled down unit load compression test on quarter scale pallet designs with different deckboard thicknesses using four different corrugated box designs. Pallet top deck stiffness was determined to have a significant effect on box compression strength. There was a 27- 37% increase in box compression strength for boxes supported by high stiffness pallets in comparison to low stiffness pallets. The fact that boxes were weaker on low stiffness pallets could be explained by the uneven pressure distribution between the pallet deck and bottom layer of boxes. Pressure data showed that a higher percentage of total pressure was located under the box sidewalls that were supported on the outside stringers of low stiffness pallets in comparison to high stiffness pallets. This was disproportionately loading one side of the box.

Utilizing the effects of pallet top deck stiffness on box compression performance, a unit load cost analysis is presented showing that a stiffer pallet can be used to carry boxes with less board material; hence, it can reduce the total unit load packaging cost.

Keywords: instant coffee, shelf life, sustainable packaging, flexible packaging

***Correspondence to:** corrugated box, box compression strength, pallet, pallet stiffness, unit load interactions

The effect of storage conditions on stretch film containment force [66]

Kyle Dunno * and Maria Symanski
Department of Packaging Science, Rochester Institute of Technology, Rochester, NY, USA

Abstract: Even in today's fast-paced and dynamic logistics channels, packages are still unitized and stored for various periods of time prior to being transported through the supply chain. While there are several stabilizer options that can be used to unitize packaged products, by far the most common is stretch film. Even with the abundant use of stretch film and its great importance delivering successful shipments, much about how it behaves after application to the load is unknown. Therefore, this study examined the behavior of stretch film performance over time at different storage temperatures, 23°C and 38°C. Two 20.3 micron cast stretch films, general- purpose and high-performance, were selected and applied to a simulated unit load to produce both neutral and positive total stretch scenarios. The simulated unit loads were stored at ambient and elevated storage conditions for a period of thirty days. The containment force, referencing a common ASTM D4649 technique, was utilized to monitor the behavior of the film during the storage period. The measurements were recorded and stretch film relaxation curves were produced for each film type and storage condition. Results from this study showed significant differences in the containment forces measured between the ambient and elevated storage conditions for each film type. The relaxation curves developed from each test indicate the relaxation rate of the films varied based on the storage condition. The high-performance film when applied to produce a neutral total stretch, reported a 23.3% and 40% loss in containment for the ambient and elevated storage conditions respectively. A similar percent loss in containment force was observed for the positive total stretch of the high-performance film. The general-purpose film when applied to produce a neutral total stretch, reported a 25.9% and 43.2% loss in containment for the ambient and elevated storage conditions respectively. Again, a similar percent loss in containment force was observed for the positive total stretch of the general-performance film. No differences were observed in the percent loss when comparing the total stretch scenario at the two storage conditions for either film type. These results indicate that although there was a loss in containment force due to storage conditions, the total stretch scenario of the film applied to the simulated load had no effect on the percent loss.

Keywords: stretch film; containment force; load stability

***Correspondence to:** Kyle D. Dunno, Department of Packaging Science, Rochester Institute of Technology, Rochester, NY, USA. Email: kddipk@rit.edu

1. Introduction

Even in a world where e-commerce is becoming increasingly popular, unitized loads are often used to ship goods. To unitize the packages, stretch film is still the most common load stabilizer because of its cost-effectiveness and a broad range of capabilities to handle a variety of load types [1]. In typical warehouse operations, packaged products are unitized together by stretch film and stored before transport. Warehousing and storage times can vary from hours to several months depending on the product and its intended application [2]. As a result, it is imperative to understand factors affecting a unit load during storage so it can safely survive shipment from the warehouse to the distribution center. A lack of knowledge in this area of packaging could result in excessive damages and could pose a threat to the safety of handlers.

In general, there are two types of stretch film, hand and machine film, used within the packaging industry to secure loads for transport. These films are produced by a blown or cast extrusion process, with cast film accounting for the majority of machine film used in the transport packaging market [3]. Table 1 displays different stretch film attributes comparing film produced through these two processes. Each film extrusion process yields a stretch film providing different mechanical properties. Stretch films are typically selected on the products they are trying to secure, but should also be based on warehousing and shipping environments [4].

***Table 1** General characteristics for cast and blown stretch films [6]*

Film Attribute	Cast Film	Blown Film
Clarity	Clear	Hazy
Noise	Quiet	Loud
Puncture / Tear Resistance	Medium / High	High / Low
Load Containment	Medium	High

The application of stretch film is a function of two types of stretch: primary and secondary stretch. Primary stretch occurs in the carriage of the stretch wrapper equipment. Primary stretch is the pre-stretch ratio set on the stretch wrapper carriage. Secondary stretch occurs between the load and the carriage in the form of tension, revolutions, overlap, etc. Total stretch is the actual stretch percentage after application to the load. The total stretch of the system yields three scenarios based on the relationship between total and primary stretch. These scenarios are negative (primary stretch < total stretch), neutral (primary stretch = total stretch), and positive stretch (primary stretch > total stretch). To create the different total stretch scenarios, the secondary stretch is the factor more commonly altered as the primary stretch is controlled and held constant for most applications. The secondary stretch is largely based on tension but can be influenced by other parameters such as revolutions and percent overlap.

Previous research has been conducted to understand the effects of stretch film application, specifically regarding the importance of wrap patterns and cycles, primary and secondary stretch percentages, and performance differences based on the grade of the stretch film [5-6]. An area needing to be explored further is the wrapping application and storage condition and how they affect the containment force of the stretch film over time.

One way to evaluate stretch film application is through measuring its containment force. Containment force is a common method used to measure the holding force of stretch film after it has been applied to a load of packaged products. This information can be easily obtained by following the protocol described in ASTM D4649 - Standard Guide for Selection and Use of Stretch Wrap Films [7]. In this standard, a force plate and gauge are used to measure the containment force of the unit load. These systems can range from a simple steel plate or fingerstyle tool with a force gauge to a complex system capable of measuring various film properties. Although the containment force values do not indicate or predict the success of the unit load during transport, research has shown it to be a repeatable tool for performing comparative analysis between unit loads having undergone different wrapping applications [5].

The objective of this study is to understand the effects of storage conditions on the performance of the stretch film. The study will focus on the containment force of stretch wrap for a period of 30 days at both elevated and ambient temperatures after being applied to a simulated unit load.

2. Materials and Methods

The containment force of high performance and general purpose stretch films was tested by observing the stress and relaxation of the polymer at elevated and ambient temperatures for an extended storage duration. Containment force refers to the ability of a material to securely hold a load together as defined by ASTM 4649 - Standard Guide for Selection and Use of Stretch Wrap Films [2]. The films used for this study were 20.3 micron cast stretch films. One film is described as being a high performance (HP) stretch film and the other a general performance (GP) grade stretch film. To reduce the bias and influence of the packaging materials on the stretch film, a wood crate was utilized to simulate the unit load (Fig. 1). By using a standard closed crate, the performance of the film could be isolated to determine the effects of the different storage conditions.

Figure 1 *Simulated unit load used for research study*

Equipment to evaluate stretch film

The containment force of the stretch film was measured using a load cell device. The Highlight Industries Portable Film Force System (Highlight Industries, Wyoming, MI USA) was employed to measure the containment force of the stretch film after application. The load cell device was attached to the crate according to the ASTM D4649 standard at a position of 18in from the center and 10in from the top of the load [7]. The load was wrapped once the device was secure and zeroed. The strain gauge was then used to measure the containment force of the material.

Stretch wrap application, storage conditions, and recording parameters

The unit loads were stretch wrapped using a RoboPac RotoPlat 750 stretch wrapper (RoboPac USA, Duluth, GA, USA). This stretch wrap equipment can adjust a variety of parameters to change the total stretch of the system. In this study, the pre-stretch (primary stretch) was held constant at 250%. To adjust the total stretch of the system, the secondary stretch parameters were changed to yield the different scenarios. Neutral and positive total stretch scenarios were used. Table 2 shows the stretch wrapping load parameters applied during testing. The total stretch for each of the unit load scenarios was calculated by performing a cut and weigh analysis using the Highlight Industries Stretch Tools App.

Two storage conditions were selected for this project. After application, the unit loads were either stored at ambient laboratory conditions or stored at elevated conditions inside a climate- controlled chamber. The ambient conditions were laboratory conditions averaging 23°C and 38%RH throughout the duration of the study. The elevated conditions selected for this study were 38°C and 50%RH. For each of the storage conditions, the unit loads were stored for a period of 30 days.

Sample ID	Load LxW (in)	Total Wraps	Film Weight (oz)	Total Stretch (%)	Scenario	Storage Conditions
HP-1	48x40	13	5.55	252	Neutral	Ambient
HP-2	48x40	13	5.35	265	Positive	Ambient
HP-3	48x40	13	5.56	251	Neutral	Elevated
HP-4	48x40	13	5.34	266	Positive	Elevated
GP-1	48x40	15	6.41	251	Neutral	Ambient
GP-2	48x40	15	6.14	267	Positive	Ambient
GP-3	48x40	15	6.44	250	Neutral	Elevated
GP-4	48x40	15	6.18	265	Positive	Elevated

Table 2 *Stretch wrap and unit load parameters*

The containment force was measured periodically for the duration of the experiment to understand the behavior of the stretch wrap for each application type and storage condition. The portable film force system was used to capture the containment force at the following intervals for each scenario: 0h, 3h, 24h, 7d, 21d, 28d, and 30d. From 0h to 3h, the portable film force system was programmed to record the relaxation of the film continuously. From there, the remaining points were collected statically throughout the remainder of the 30-day test.

3. Results and Discussion

Tables 3-4 and Figures 2-4 illustrate the results collected from this research experiment. For each scenario and storage condition, there was a decrease in containment force over time.

Table 3 *Containment force values for High Performance Stretch Film*

Sample ID	0h (lbs.)	30d (lbs.)	Δ Force (lbs.)	Percent Loss (%)	Percent Difference (%)
HP-2	23.5	17.3	6.2	26.3	-38.2
HP-4	22.7	13.6	9.1	40.0	
HP-1	20.6	15.8	4.8	23.3	-48.1
HP-3	19.7	11.9	7.8	39.7	

Table 4 *Containment force values for General Purpose Stretch Film*

Sample ID	0h (lbs.)	30d (lbs.)	Δ Force (lbs.)	Percent Loss (%)	Percent Difference (%)
GP-2	17.8	13.0	4.8	26.9	-39.4
GP-4	17.7	10.6	7.1	40.2	
GP-1	18.1	13.4	4.7	25.9	-48.2
GP-3	17.8	10.1	7.7	43.2	

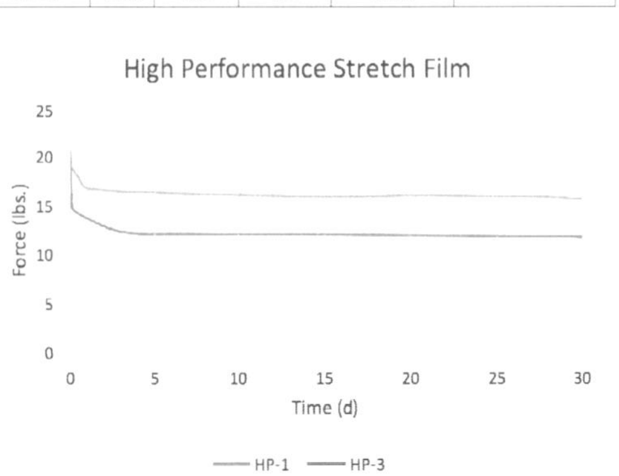

Figure 2 *High Performance stretch film (neutral, compare storage temperature)*

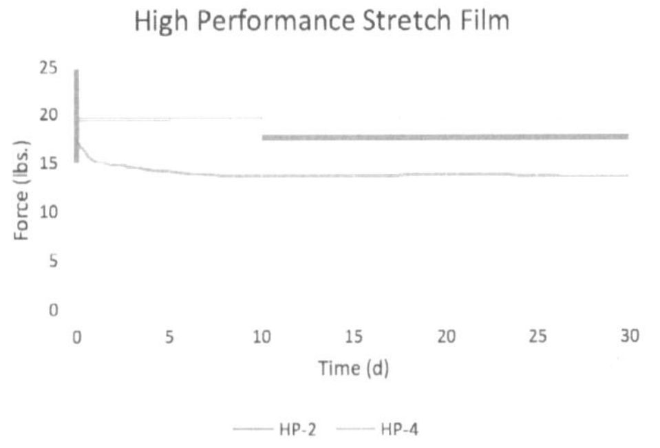

Figure 3 *High Performance stretch film (positive, compare storage temperature)*

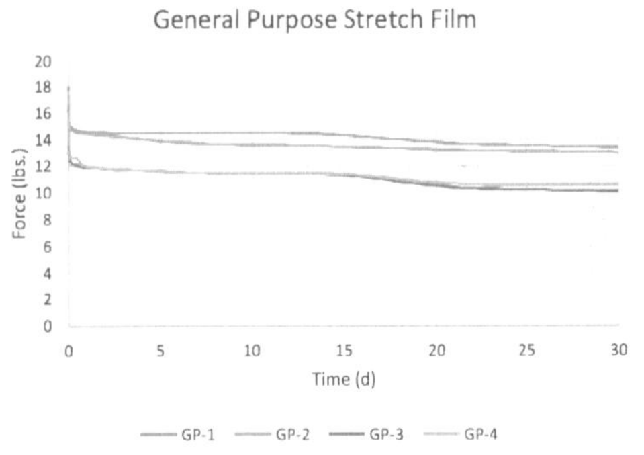

Figure 4 *General Purpose stretch film*

It can be observed from Table 2 and Figures 2-3 there was a loss in containment over time for each of the test parameters. Comparing HP-2 and HP-4, the loss in containment was 26.3% and 40% respectively. This resulted in a percent difference of 38.2% when comparing the positive total stretch at the different storage conditions. These results show the containment force is largely affected by the storage conditions. Although storage conditions affect the loss in containment, when comparing the percent loss of HP-3 and HP-4, the effect of total stretch showed no difference. This indicates that regardless of the total stretch application, both scenarios result in a similar loss in containment. The results were also observed for the neutral and positive total stretch for the loads stored in ambient conditions.

When comparing the two different film types, no differences were observed between total stretch and storage conditions. For this study, these observations showed no improvements were gained with the high-performance stretch film. Although the initial containment forces were greater, the percent loss between all of the parameters (storage and total stretch) were similar.

Previous research has indicated the largest percent change in the containment force occurs within 120 minutes after application [6]. Figure 5 illustrates the high-performance containment loss during the first 3 hours after application. Results from this study showed for the ambient conditions a loss in containment of 13% after 2 h was observed. These results are similar to previous research which stated the decline in containment force was 15% after two hours of testing [6]. For the elevated conditions, again the majority of percent loss occurs during the first 2 h, but the loss in containment was much greater, reporting a loss in containment of 25%. These results show the majority of containment loss occurs within the first 2 h after application to the unit load for both storage conditions.

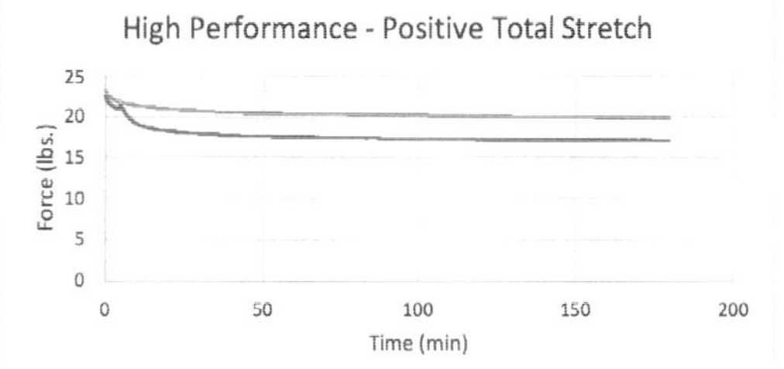

Figure 5. *High Performance stretch film during the first 3h after application*

4. Conclusion

Examined during this study were the effects of storage conditions on the containment force for two 20.3 micron stretch films. Two different categories of stretch film were evaluated; high- performance and general purpose. A simulated unit load was used to complete all tests to isolate the performance of the stretch film while eliminating bias or influence of traditional packages which could be affected by storage conditions. The results from this study showed elevated temperatures greatly reduced the containment force of the stretch film after application, when compared to ambient storage conditions. The containment force was decreased at elevated temperatures, but no differences were observed between neutral and positive total stretch scenarios. The high-performance film resulted in an overall higher containment force as compared to the general-purpose film, but no differences were observed in the percent loss. Additionally, it was determined the majority of containment force loss occurred within the first 2 h of the testing. Although the films continued to lose containment throughout the 30 day examination, the greatest loss occurred within the first 2 h of the test. The observations from this project can be used by the packaging industry to understand how storage conditions can influence the containment force of the stretch film. Understanding the total loss and the percent loss for each test scenario can provide packaging engineers the ability to adjust containment force values to match those desired not just immediately after application, but throughout the supply chain.

5. References

[1] Rogers, L.K. 2011. Keeping it together. Modern Materials Handling, pp.32-35.

[2] Ackerman, Kenneth B. (1990) Practical Handbook of Warehousing. Third Edition. New York: Van Nostrand Reinhold

[3] Robertson, G.L. (2006) Food Packaging: Principle and Practice. CRC Press, Boca Raton, FL

[4] Singh, Paul; Singh, Jay; Antle, John; Topper, Erin; and Grewal, G. (2014) "Load Securement and Packaging Methods to Reduce Risk of Damage and Personal Injury for Cargo Freight in Truck, Container and Intermodal Shipments," Journal of Applied Packaging Research: Vol. 6 : No. 1 , Article 6. DOI: 10.14448/japr.01.0005

[5] Dunno, K. D., Wyns, J., and Cook, J. (2017) Evaluation of Containment Force Variability between Different Grades of Stretch Film. International Journal of Advanced Packaging Technology, Vol. 4, No 1: 216-225. doi: 10.23953/cloud.ijapt.318

[6] Wyns, Jake; Cook, John; and Dunno, Kyle (2018) "Post-wrapping behavior of high-performance stretch film," Journal of Applied Packaging Research: Vol. 10 : No. 3 , Article 1.
Available at: https://scholarworks.rit.edu/japr/vol10/iss3/1

[7] ASTM D4649-03. 2016. Standard Guide for Selection and Use of Stretch Wrap Films. ASTM International, West Conshohocken, PA. Available from: https://www.astm.org/Standards/D4649.htm

Wood Pallet Performance Analysis with Palletized Drums in Distribution and Warehousing [87]

Mary Paz Alvarez [1], Laszlo Horvath [*1], Farhad Shahabi [2]
1 Department of Sustainable Biomaterials, Virginia Tech, Blacksburg, VA, USA
2 National Wooden Pallet and Container Association, Alexandria, VA, USA

Abstract: Wood pallets are an integral part of the modern-day supply chain. There are 2.6 billion pallets used in the U.S. every year. Currently, pallets are designed assuming that a uniformly distributed and flexible load is supported on the pallet. However, the types of products carried by the pallet can cause the load to redistribute unevenly on the pallet. This phenomenon is called load bridging. Load bridging has been extensively studied for corrugated boxes, but the effect has not been characterized for drums. The objective of this study was to gain more understanding about how pallet deflection, and the pressure distribution on top of the pallet, is influenced by drums. The drum's material had a significant effect on the deflection of the pallet. Significant load bridging was observed for metal drum resulting in 46%-81% reduction in pallet deflection when compared to an airbag. Meanwhile, plastic drums created concentrated pressure areas on the pallet that, in most cases, resulted in more pallet deflection than what was measured for the airbag.

Keywords: pallets; load bridging; drums; pressure; sustainability

*Correspondence to: Laszlo Horvath, Department of Sustainable Biomaterials, Virginia Tech. E-mail: lhorvat@vt.edu

1. Introduction

There are three components to the supply chain - the products, the pallet, and the form of transportation that is used to ship [1]. All three of these components interact with each other and can be optimized in order to lower costs and create safer unit loads. Pallets themselves are an essential piece of the puzzle, making small changes to a pallet could lead to high amount of savings and a smaller environmental impact. There were an estimated 508 million wooden pallets created in 2016 [2] so optimizing and creating efficient unit loads can have a large impact on the amount of natural resources that are used for manufacturing wood pallets.

One of the main phenomena that affects the load capacity of pallets is load bridging. Load bridging was first investigated by Fagan [3] using wooden pallets carrying corrugated boxes. It was observed that during pallet deflection (bending), the pressure of the boxes is redistributed to the ends of the pallet instead of being distributed evenly across the pallet's top deck. This pressure redistribution can have a large impact on how much load the pallet can ultimately carry. This can affect the sustainability and potentially the safety of the unit load.

After Fagan's [3] research, load bridging continued to be heavily investigated using corrugated boxes. In 1984, Collie [4] researched load bridging for stringer pallets, specifically looking into how support conditions affect the way that the load is distributed. The effect of box size was investigated by Park [5], Morrisette [6], and Clayton [7], who all studied the effect of box size on load bridging and found the load bridging increases with increasing box size. Molina [8] conducted research on what effect corrugated box stacking patterns have on load bridging and concluded that interlocked boxes increase load bridging and decreases the deflection of the pallet. Park9 found that increasing containment force, using stretch films, increases load bridging and reduces the deflection of the pallet. Despite these extensive investigations using corrugated boxes, there is a lack of information about how other packaging types, such as drums, affect load bridging and consequently the deflection of the pallet. Understanding the effect that drums have on load bridging will allow pallet designers to design more efficient and sustainable pallets.

2. Objectives

The objectives of the project were as follows:

1. Investigate the effect of drums on the pressure distribution and deflection of stringer class wooden pallets using multiple support conditions and pallet designs.

2. Investigate the difference between the load distribution caused by drums and a uniformly distributed load.

3. Investigate the effect of a drum's material on pallet deflection and pressure distribution on the top deck of the pallet.

3. Materials

3.1 Wood Pallets

3.1.1 Component Dimensions

The experiment included four 48 in. x 48 in. stringer class, non-reversible pallet designs: partial four-way, four stringer, winged pallet (D1), two-way, four stringer, flush pallet (D2), two-way, three stringer, flush pallet with 1/2 in. (D3) and 5/8 in. (D4) top deckboards. (Figure 1). All lumber used to construct these pallets was kiln dried to 19% moisture content and had a grade of standard or better.

All of the top and bottom deckboards for these pallets were 5 1/2 in. wide Baltic birch plywood graded at BB/BB and were either 1/2 in. or 5/8 in. thickness based on the design. Seven top and five bottom deckboards were used. All top deckboards were evenly spaced. Bottom deckboards were configured so there were two boards used as end deck boards while the other three were placed more towards the center of the pallet (clustered). The stringers were made from 3 ½ in. x 1 ½ in., kiln-dried to 19% moisture content, standard or better grade southern yellow pine boards. Each deck board was attached using three 2 in. long, #7 type wood screws per connection. The screws were pre-drilled, and once screwed in, the holes were covered with wood putty. The notched pallet had a notch located 6 in. from the end of the stringer, and the notch itself was 9 in. long, 1 ½ in. deep, and had a notch radius of ¾ in. The variations between the four investigated stringer class pallets designs are presented in Table 1.

Table 1 *Specifications of the four investigated stringer class pallets designs.*

Pallet Design	Deck Board Thickness (in.)	No. of Stringers	Entry Type	Wing (in.)
D1	½ in.	4	Partial 4-way	1 ½ in.
D2	½ in.	4	2-way	N/A
D3	5/8 in.	3	2-way	N/A
D4	½ in.	3	2-way	N/A

Figure 1 *Representative views of the three investigated pallet designs: 1) 4-stringer, winged, notched pallet design (D1), 2) 4-stringer, flush pallet design (D2), 3) 3-stringer, flush pallet design (D3 and D4)*

3.2 Drums and Pails

The investigation utilized four, 55-gallon, tight-headed, steel drums (Model: ULINE S-10759) and four, 55-gallon, tight-headed, plastic drums (Model: ULINE S-10757). All drums were obtained from Uline and measured before use (Table 2). The drums were filled with water which resulted a 504 lb. and 489 ½ lb. filled drum weight, respectively, for the two different drum materials.

3.3 Drum Unit Load Construction

When creating the drum unit load, a pressure mat (Tekscan model #7202) was sandwiched between two .06 in. thick polypropylene sheets and a .063 in. EPDM roofing rubber mat was placed on the pallet first (Figure 2). The plastic sheets covered the whole pallet; but, the pressure mat only measured 27.813 in. x 24.844 in. The pressure mat had a 0-125 psi pressure measurement range and contained .14 in x .14 in. measurement sensels. The Tekscan equipment utilized I-scan software which is what was used to record the pressure mat readings for each support condition that the unit load experienced.

Table 2 *Specifications of the investigated drum designs.*

Design	Drum Material	Top Ring Diameter (in.)	Bottom Ring Diameter (in.)	Chime Diameter (in.)	Weight When Filled (lbs.)
D1	Metal	24	24	23 ½	504 ½
D2	Plastic	22	N/A	21 ½	489 ½

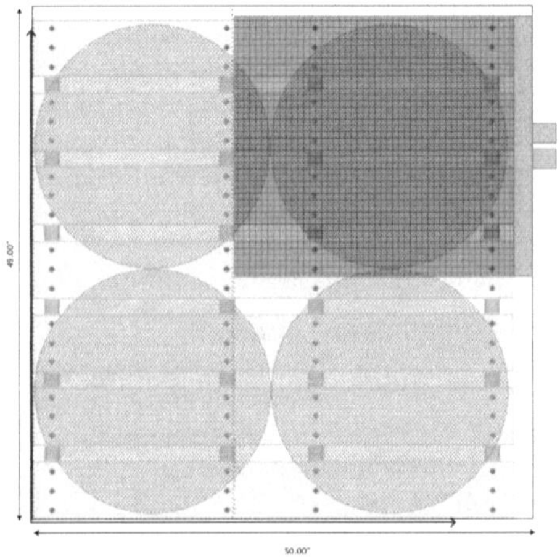

Figure 2 *Pressure mat sleeve placement on the pallet.*

Once the pallet was prepared with the rubber mat and the two plastic sheets with the pressure mat between them, four drums were loaded onto the pallet. The drums were loaded on individually as close together as they could possibly be without any overhang. There was no containment used on the drums.

4. Methods

4.1 Warehouse Rack Support

The pallet was supported on two 2 in. x 2 in. metal beams positioned to leave a 43 in. span. The deflection of the pallet was measured using three Mituyo dial gauges (Mituyo model #4887S-19) located halfway between the supports - one at each end and one in the middle of the pallet. The pallet was tested in this support condition both across its length and width.

4.2 Single and Double Stacked Unit Loads

The single-stacked unit loads were placed on a level surface. Deflection measurements were then collected using four measurement locations - at the center of the underside of four of the first top deckboards. To simulate double-stacking, a second unit load was placed on the top of the drums. The pressure between the drums and the bottom of the top pallet was measured and the deflection of those bottom deckboards was also measured in four locations. All readings were recorded (Figure 3).

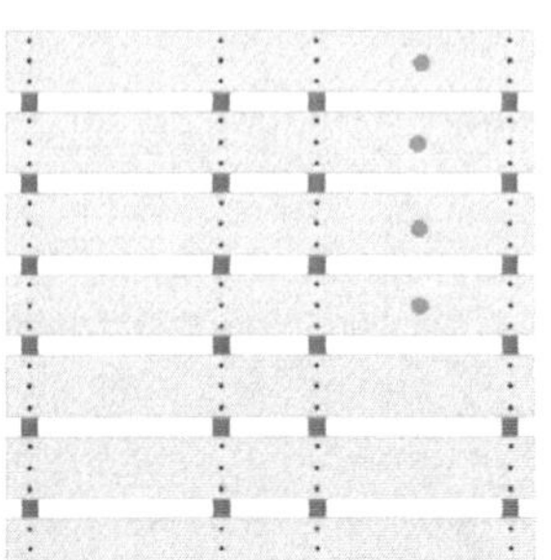

Figure 3 *Stringer pallet deflection reading locations in the single and double-stack conditions.*

4.3 Pallet bending using a flexible airbag

The deflection of the pallet was also measured while carrying a flexible airbag using the same support conditions that were investigated during the drum portion of this study. A Tinius Olson compression tester equipped with four 10,000 lb. load cells was used. The deflection of the pallet was measured using string potentiometers (Standard EP Series, UniMeasure, Corvallis, Oregon, United States). The measurement locations coincided with the locations listed in prior sections. Pallets were loaded with a test load representing the same weight as the four drums for the warehouse racking condition and for the single stacking condition, and the weight of eight drums and a pallet was used for the double-stacked condition. The deflection measurements under these test loads were recorded. Only one measurement was conducted for each pallet design.

4.4 Limitations

The following limitations apply for this study:

- The results only apply for the two drum materials and styles that were investigated.

- The effect of drums was only investigated for pallet deflection; therefore, the observed reduction in deflections should not be attributed to increased load capacity.

- The effect of load stabilizers was not investigated in this study; therefore, the results could significantly change if load stabilizers are used.

- Only one replicate test was conducted for the airbag portion of this study.

- Only three replicate tests were conducted for the unit loads of drums portion of this study.

4.5 Experimental Design

The research's experimental design was based on two different drum materials, four different stringer pallet stiffnesses, and five different support conditions (Table 3). Three repetitions were conducted for each combination of drum material and pallet design. The experiment was conducted in cycles following the same order of steps: single stacked support, double stacked support, warehouse racked support across the width, and then warehouse racked support across the length. At the end of each cycle the drums were unloaded in order to allow the pallet to be consistent between the different cycles and tests. Deflection measurements and pressure mat readings were collected for every support condition. Each pallet experienced three cycles with both drum materials. Pressure mat readings and deflection readings were collected two minutes after the pallet was placed into the appropriate condition.

Table 3 *Specifications of the four investigated stringer class pallets designs.*

		Drum Material	
Pallet Design	**Thickness**	**Plastic Drums**	**Metal Drums**
3-Stringer, two-way, Flush	½ in.	3 cycles	3 cycles
	5/8 in.	3 cycles	3 cycles
4-Stringer, two-way, Flush	½ in.	3 cycles	3 cycles
4-Stringer, partial 4-way, wing	½ in.	3 cycles	3 cycles

5. Results

5.1 Statistic Model

For each of the support conditions, there were three deflection measurements taken at varied locations depending on the support condition itself. The highest deflection was used to create a statistical model to further understand how pallet design, deflection, and drum material interacted with each other. The highest deflection was typically seen in the center of the pallet when placed in the racking condition.

A standard ANOVA test was run for all of the conditions. The deflections measurements were used as the Y variable, the pallet design and drum material were used as model effects along with drum materials and pallet designs that were crossed. The analysis was run separately for each individual support condition. The model itself utilized the following formula:

$$y_{ij} = \mu + D_i + P_j + D_i P_J + \varepsilon_{ij}$$

Where = pallet deflection, μ = overall mean, = drum material with material, = pallet design with number, = interaction effect between drum materials and pallet design and = random error.

A Tukey's HSD multiple comparison analysis was also utilized when analyzing the drum material and the pallet design in order to understand the levels of differences between material and pallet design.

5.2 Stringer Pallets – Racked Across the Length (RAL)

5.2.1 Deflections

The results of the pallet deflection measurements for the investigated drum and pallet designs and the results of the airbag testing are presented in Table 4. The drum material ($p<0.026$) and pallet stiffness ($p<0.0051$) were shown to have a statistically significant effect using a one-way ANOVA test. In addition, a significant interaction was found between the drum material and the pallet design ($p<0.0172$), indicating that the effect of the drum material depends on the pallet design. Further analysis, using Tukey's HSD multiple comparison test, revealed that pallets supporting plastic drums experienced significantly more bending than the metal drums (Table 4).

Although the effect of pallet design was found to be significant, further analysis using Tukey's HSD to compare the pallet designs together, revealed that only the 3-stringer pallet design with the ½ in. top deckboard (D4) was significantly different from the others (Table 5).

When compared to the airbag results, there was a general trend of the pallet's deflection, while under an airbag load, being less than the pallet's deflection while being loaded with either of the two different types of drums (Table 4). This trend was not seen in the 3-stringer, ½ in. deckboard pallets (D4); this pallet bent more while being under a uniformly distributed load. The 4-stringer, winged pallet (D1) with notches displayed the highest amount of deflection under both metal and plastic drums. Notches decrease the overall strength of stringers, and when racked across the length, stringers are one of the most important components of the pallet.

Table 4 *Summary table of average pallet deflections for the investigated pallet designs and drum materials using warehouse rack support across the length.*

	Pallet Deflection (in.)							
	4-Stringer				3-Stringer, Two-way, Flush			
Loading Method	**Winged, Notched, ½ in. deckboard thickness (D1)**		**Flush, ½ in. deckboard thickness (D2)**		**5/8 in. deckboard thickness (D3)**		**½ in. deckboard thickness (D4)**	
Airbag	0.189		0.084		0.128		0.179	
Plastic Drum	0.236 (10%) A	+25%	0.214 (4%) A	+155 %	0.163 (4%) A	+27%	0.160 (2%) A	-10%
Metal Drum	0.189 (13%) B	+0.4 %	0.171 (7%) B	+103 %	0.181 (7%) B	+41%	0.163 (6%) B	-8%

Notes: *Values in parentheses are Coefficient of Variance values.*
The different letters indicate that statistically significantly differences using a = 0.05.
The deflections of the two drum materials were compared to the deflection caused by the airbag.

Table 5 *Results of the Tukey's HSD multiple comparison test for average pallet deflection observed for the individual pallet designs while supported in a warehouse rack support across the length.*

Pallet Design	Tukey's	Least Sq. Means
D1 (4-Stringer, Winged, Notched, ½ in. thickness)	A	0.2127
D2 (4-Stringer, Flush, ½ in. thickness)	A	0.2075
D4 (3-Stringer, Flush, 5/8 in. thickness)	A/B	0.1722
D3 (3-Stringer, Flush, ½ in. thickness)	B	0.1625

Notes: The different letters indicate that statistically significantly differences using a = 0.05

5.2.2 Pressure Mat Readings

Representative pictures of the pressure distributions are presented in Figure 3. Metal drums applied pressure to the pallet through their chimes which created a more concentrated circular pressure distribution (Figure 4). Meanwhile, plastic drums distributed the pressure more evenly towards the handles of the drums themselves (Figure 5). Pallets supporting metal drums experienced more pressure shifted towards the side and middle stringers on lower stiffness pallets while the pressure was distributed more evenly on stiffer pallets. The same phenomenon was not observed for plastic drums.

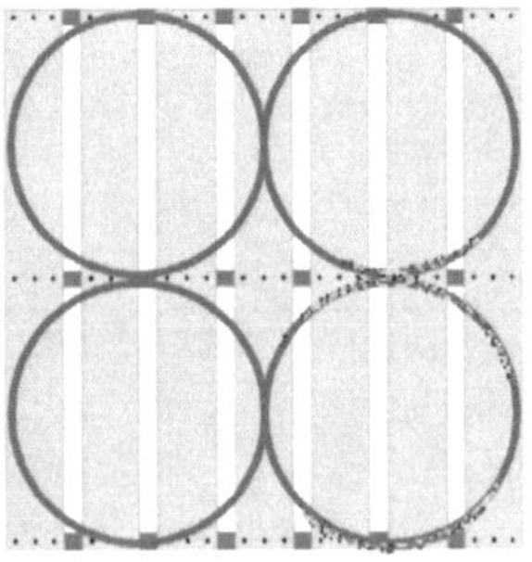

Figure 3 *Pressure distribution on pallets carrying metal drums on the 3-stringer pallet with 5/8 in. thick top deckboards (D3).*

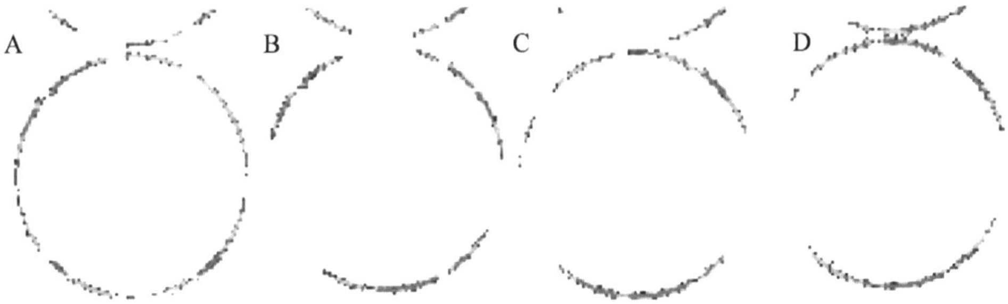

Figure 4 *Pressure distribution on stringer pallets carrying metal drums using warehouse racking across the length. A) D1 pallet design, B) D2 pallet design, C) D3 pallet design, and D) D4 pallet design.*

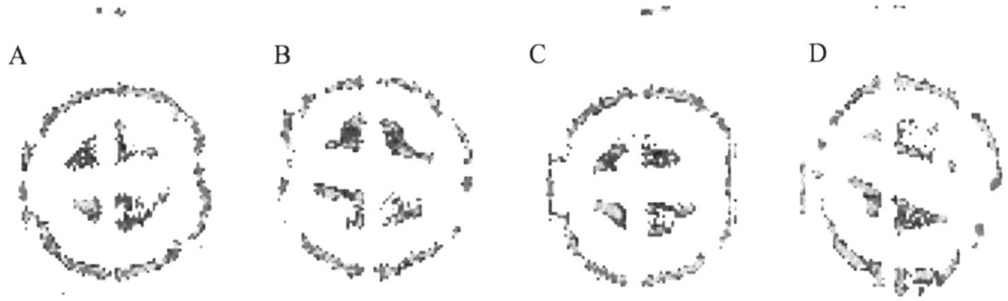

Figure 5 *Pressure distribution on stringer pallets carrying plastic drums using warehouse racking across the length. A) D1 pallet design, B) D2 pallet design, C) D3 pallet design, and D) D4 pallet design.*

5.3 Stringer Pallets – Racked Across the Width (RAW)

5.3.1 Deflections

The results of the pallet deflection measurements for the investigated drum and pallet designs and the results of the airbag tests are presented in Table 6. Only the drum material was found to be significant ($p<0.0003$); the pallet design ($p<0.6528$) and the interaction between pallet design and drum material ($p<0.5346$) were not significant. The deflection of the pallet was highest for the least stiff pallet (D4), and this trend is the same for both the plastic and metal drum (Table 6). The pallet deflection was significantly greater when the pallet supported plastic drums compared to the pallets supporting metal drums, most likely this was because the plastic drums are more flexible and can follow the bending of the pallet more easily.

The largest reduction in deflection was observed for pallet design D2. There was a 34% difference found between the pallet deflection measurements while under the plastic versus the metal drums. When compared to the airbag test results, all drum unit loads had lower deflection meaning that a uniformly distributed load causes the pallet to deflect more when racked cross the width. Both metal and plastic drums exhibited varying amounts of load bridging compared to the airbag.

Table 6 Summary table of average pallet deflections for the investigated pallet designs and drum materials using warehouse rack support across the width.

Loading Method	Pallet Deflection (in.)							
	4-Stringer				3-Stringer, Two-way, Flush			
	Winged, Notched, ½ in. deckboard thickness (D1)		Flush, ½ in. deckboard thickness (D2)		5/8 in. deckboard thickness (D3)		½ in. deckboard thickness (D4)	
Airbag	0.672		0.704		0.684		0.957	
Plastic Drum	0.467 (3%) A	-31%	0.520 (2%) A	-26%	0.533 (2%) A	-22%	0.6 (<1%) A	-37%
Metal Drum	0.272 (5%) B	-60%	0.279 (3%) B	-60%	0.368 (4%) B	-46%	0.362 (1%) B	-62%

Notes: Values in parentheses are Coefficient of Variance values.
The different letters indicate that statistically significantly differences using a = 0.05.
The deflections of the two drum materials were compared to the deflection caused by the airbag.

5.3.2 Pressure Mat Readings

For both drum materials, more pressure was concentrated on the stringers; this explains the observed reduction in pallet deflection compared to the results of the airbag tests (Figure 6). Similarly to the warehouse racking across the length condition, the pallets supporting plastic drums experienced more even pressure distribution than the pallets supporting metal drum (Figure 7). This phenomenon could be explained by the lower stiffness of the plastic drums. In addition, there was more uneven pressure distribution along the chimes that was most likely due to the more extensive bending of the pallet along the width.

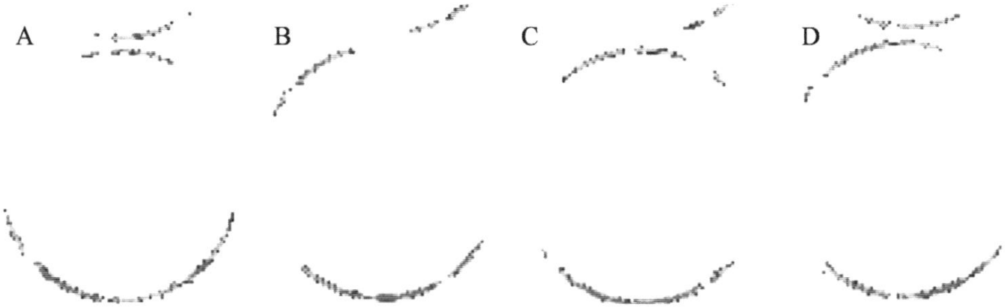

Figure 6 Pressure distribution on stringer pallets carrying metal drums using warehouse racking across the width. A) D1 pallet design, B) D2 pallet design, C) D3 pallet design, D) D4 pallet design.

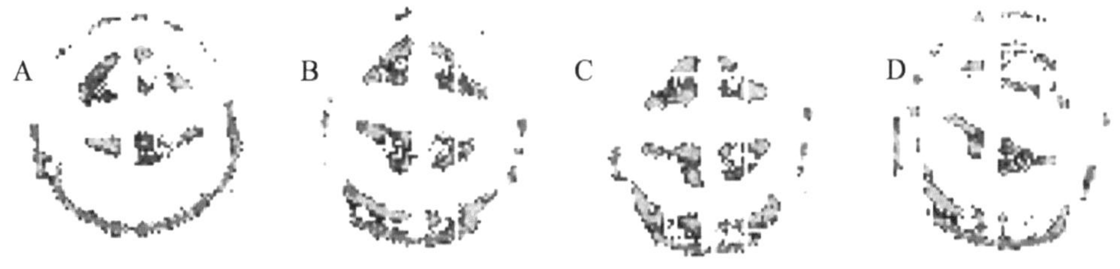

Figure 7 *Pressure distribution on stringer pallets carrying plastic drums using warehouse racking across the width. A) D1 pallet design. B) D2 pallet design. C) D3 pallet design. D) D4 pallet design.*

5.4 Stringer Pallets – Single and Double Stacked

5.4.1 Deflections

The results of the pallet deflection measurements for the investigated drum and pallet designs and the results of the airbag testing are presented in Table 7 for the single stacking condition and Table 9 for the double stacking condition. The ANOVA results revealed that for both the single stack and double stack conditions the pallet design ($p<0.0013$ for single stacking and $p<0.0001$ for double stacking) and the drum material ($p<0.0001$) were proven to be significant. The interactions between the pallet design and the drum material were also significant ($p<0.0001$).

The deflection increases in the double stack condition because of the additional weight placed on the drums. When the pallet designs were compared using a Tukey's HSD multiple comparison test, it was found that only pallet design D3 was statistically different from the other designs for the single stacking condition (Table 8). However, more differences in pallet designs were found for the double stacking condition. There is a significant difference between the stiffest 4-stringer, winged pallet (D1) and both of the 3-stringer pallet designs (D3 and D4). In addition, the two 3-stringer pallets (D3 and D4) with the lower deck stiffness were also statistically different from each other. The overall pallet deflection was higher in the double stack condition which emphasizes the differences in pallet designs.

Similar to the warehouse racking condition, pallets supporting plastic drums deflected significantly more than pallets supporting metal drums. The largest reduction was observed for pallet design D4 where an 85% difference was found between the pallet deflection measurements while under the plastic versus the metal drums. In addition, for plastic drums, the pallet deflection increased as the stiffness of the pallet decreased;; meanwhile, metal drums did not show any deflection trends. This is seen consistently in both the single stack and the double stack conditions.

When compared to the airbag, in the single stack condition, the plastic drums deflected more than the airbag while the metal drums deflected less (Table 7). In the double stack condition, both the pallets carrying the plastic and the metal drums deflected less than the pallets carrying an airbag except when observing pallet design D4 where the plastic drums did deflect more than the airbag (Table 9). The largest difference between materials is seen in pallet design D4 where the difference was 142%.

The differences observed for the behavior of the pallet supporting plastic drums while in both the single and double stacking conditions could be explained by the way the load was distributed onto the pallet. During single stacking, the load is distributed through the bottom of the drums due to the weight of the water. This applied a concentrated force at the bottom of the drum which could have increased the deflection of the deckboards. This could explain why pallets with plastic drums deflected more than pallets loaded with the airbag. Once the pallet was double stacked, the weight of the second unit load is distributed through the side walls of the drums contained in the first/bottom unit load. This could have resulted in the weight of the load being distributed to the stringers and could have been responsible for the reduction in the pallet's deflection when compared to the airbag.

Table 7 *Summary table of average pallet deflection for the investigated pallet designs and drum material using single stacking condition.*

Loading Method	**Pallet Deflection (in.)**							
	4-Stringer,				**3-Stringer, Two-way, Flush**			
	Winged, Notched, ½ in. deckboard thickness (D1)		**Flush, ½ in. deckboard thickness (D2)**		**5/8 in. deckboard thickness (D3)**		**½ in. deckboard thickness (D4)**	
Airbag	0.044		0.081		0.080		0.123	
Plastic Drum	0.062 (9%) A	+38%	0.097 (2%) A	+19%	0.104 (3%) A	+29%	0.156 (2%) A	+27%
Metal Drum	0.018 (12%) B	-59%	0.026 (17%) B	-68%	0.038 (16%) B	-53%	0.023 (23%) B	-81%

Notes: *Values in parentheses are Coefficient of Variance values.*
The different letters indicate that statistically significantly differences using a = 0.05.
The deflections of the two drum materials were compared to the deflection caused by the airbag.

Table 8 Results of the multiple comparison tests for the average pallet deflection observed for the individual pallet designs while supported in single stacking.

Pallet Design	Tukey's	Least Sq. Means
D1 (4-Stringer, Winged, Notched, ½ in. thickness)	B	0.0493
D2 (4-Stringer, Flush, ½ in. thickness)	B	0.0627
D4 (3-Stringer, Flush, 5/8 in. thickness)	A/B	0.0707
D3 (3-Stringer, Flush, ½ in. thickness)	A	0.0882

Notes: The different letters indicate that statistically significantly differences using a = 0.05.

Table 9 Summary table of average pallet deflection for the investigated pallet designs and drum material using double stacking condition.

Loading Method	Pallet Deflection (in.)							
	4-stringer				3-stringer, two-way, flush			
	Winged, notched, ½ in. deckboard thickness (D1)		Flush, ½ in. deckboard thickness (D2)		5/8 in. deckboard thickness (D3)		½ in. deckboard thickness (D4)	
Airbag	0.087		0.142		0.154		0.241	
Plastic Drum	0.085 (6%) A	-2%	0.108 (12%) A	-24%	0.126 (11%) A	-18%	0.264 (2%) A	+9%
Metal Drum	0.034 (28%) B	-61%	0.055 (4%) B	-61%	0.055 (45%) B	-64%	0.035 (10%) B	-85%

Notes: Values in parentheses are Coefficient of Variance values.
The different letters indicate that statistically significantly differences using a = 0.05.
The deflections of the two drum materials were compared to the deflection caused by the airbag.

Table 10 Results of the multiple comparison tests for the average pallet deflection observed for the individual pallet designs while supported in double stacking.

Pallet Design	Tukey's	Least Sq. Means
D1 (4-Stringer, Winged, Notched, ½" thickness)	C	0.0681
D2 (4-Stringer, Flush, ½" thickness)	B/C	0.0818
D4 (3-Stringer, Flush, 5/8" thickness)	B	0.0973
D3 (3-Stringer, Flush, ½" thickness)	A	0.1503

Notes: The different letters indicate that statistically significantly differences using a = 0.05.

5.4.2 Pressure Mat Readings

For the metal drum pressure mat readings, the main difference between the different pallet designs for both the single and double stack support conditions is the amount of contact that the drum chimes made with the pallet; contact area increased with pallet stiffness (Figure 8).

The plastic drums show consistent pressure over the different pallet designs, but in the double stack condition, it is clear (Figure 11-B and Figure 11-D) that the plastic drums can potentially flex with the pallet itself due to the additional pressure. However, the pressure is still focused towards the pallet stringers and drum handles.

When comparing the single stack to the double stack condition for the plastic drums (Figure 10-A and 11-A), we can see that the outer perimeter of the drum is under more pressure. In Figure 10-A, the perimeter is present, but in Figure 11-A, the amount of pressure on the perimeter is higher. This is due to the fact that the second unit load placed on top during the double stack condition has its weight distributed through the drum itself more than through the center of the drum. In metal drums, this is shown in Figure 8-B and 9-B where we can see that the pressure the chimes experience is increased.

5.4.3 Pressure Mat Figures

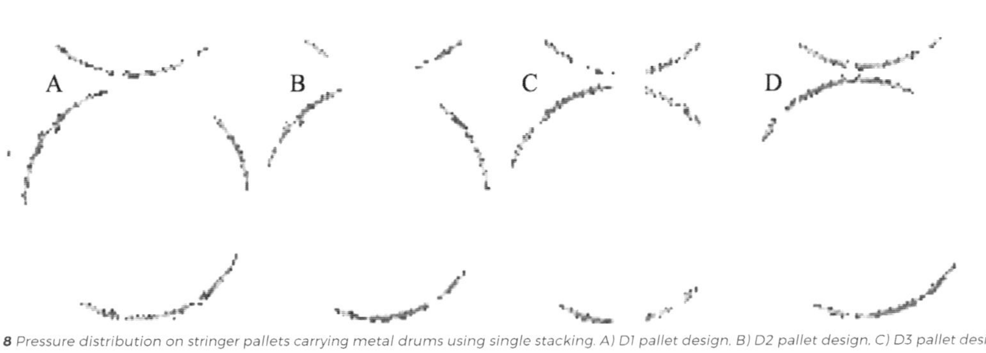

Figure 8 Pressure distribution on stringer pallets carrying metal drums using single stacking. A) D1 pallet design. B) D2 pallet design. C) D3 pallet design. D) D4 pallet design.

Figure 9 *Pressure distribution on stringer pallets carrying metal drums using double stacking. A) D1 pallet design. B) D2 pallet design. C) D3 pallet design. D) D4 pallet design.*

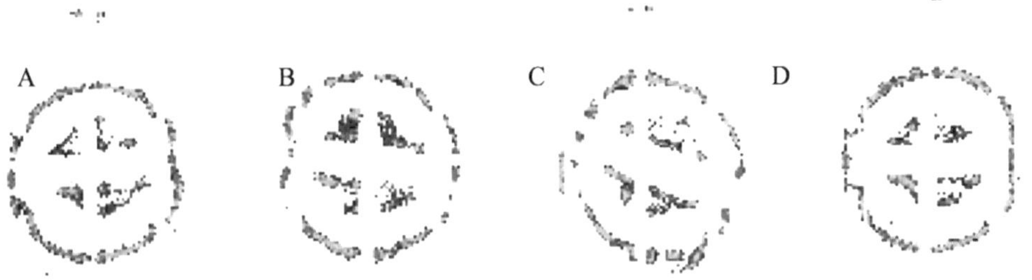

Figure 10 *Pressure distribution on stringer pallets carrying plastic drums using single stacking. A) D1 pallet design. B) D2 pallet design. C) D3 pallet design. D) D4 pallet design.*

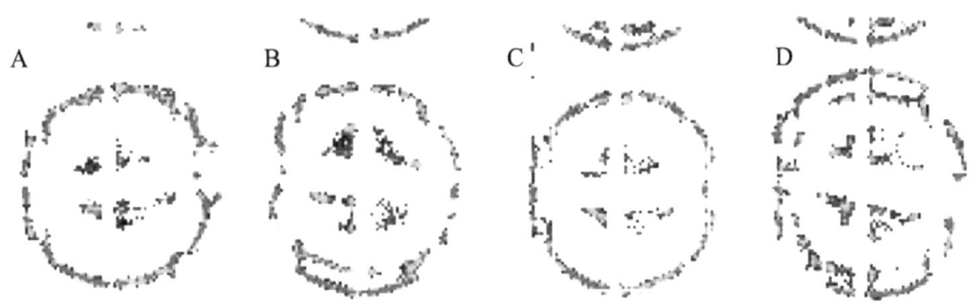

Figure 11 *Pressure distribution on stringer pallets carrying plastic drums using double stacking. A) D1 pallet design. B) D2 pallet design. C) D3 pallet design. D) D4 pallet design.*

6. Conclusions

1. The effect of drum material on pallet deflection is statistically significant for every single investigated support condition. In racked across the length, this difference averaged 23%; in racked across the width, it averaged 29%; in single stack, it averaged 93%; and in the double stack, it averaged 59%. The difference between the behavior of the metal and plastic drums was attributed to their material rigidity. The plastic drums are more flexible than metal drums; therefore, they exhibit lower load bridging because they are able to follow the bending of the pallet more. This was confirmed by measuring the pressure distribution where more even pressure distribution was found for plastic drums while the pressure for metal drums was mainly found under the chimes.

2. Other than the warehouse rack across the width pallet support condition and the double stacked support condition, pallets supporting plastic drums deflected more than the pallets loaded with a flexible airbag. The difference in the most extreme circumstance had the plastic drum unit load bending 115% more than the pallet loaded with the airbag. This increased pallet deflection could be attributed to the bottom structure of the plastic drums. A significant pressure concentration was consistently observed in the middle of the plastic drums; these resulting concentrated forces could be responsible for the increased deflection of the pallet. The single stack plastic drum unit loads compared to the metal drum unit loads displayed the largest differences in deflection measurements; hence, show one of the effects of the materials' differences.

3. Pallet supporting metal drums deflected 46%-81% less than pallets loaded with the flexible airbag. The reduced deflection is attributed to the increased load bridging caused by the aspect ratio and stiffness of the metal drums. It indicates the potential for cost saving opportunities when the load capacity of the pallet is limited by the pallet's deflection.

4. The effect of drum material was dependent on the pallet's stiffness. This interaction was significant for the racked across the length, single, and double stacked support conditions. However, any consistent trend indicating that the effect increases or decreases with changing pallet stiffnesses was not found.

These results indicate cost saving opportunities especially for pallets supporting metal drums in scenarios where the load capacity of the pallet is limited by pallet deflection. However, it was also revealed that there is a significant difference in pallet behavior depending on the type of drum; therefore, the exact drum material and design need to be considered during pallet design.

7. Acknowledgements

This project was funded by the Pallet Foundation of the National Wood Pallet and Container Association.

8. References

[1] White, M. S., & Hamner, P. (2005). Pallets move the world: The case for developing system-based designs for unit loads. Forest Products Journal, 55(3), 8–16.

[2] Gerber, N. (2018). Investigation of New and Recovered Wood Shipping Platforms in the United States [Unpublished master's thesis]. Virginia Polytechnic Institute and State University, Blacksburg, VA, USA. http://hdl.handle.net/10919/83801

[3] Fagan, G. B. (1982). Load-support conditions and computerized test apparatus for wood pallets [Unpublished doctoral dissertation]. Virginia Polytechnic Institute and State University, Blacksburg, VA, USA.

[4] Collie, S. T. (1984). Laboratory verification of pallet design procedures [Unpublished master's thesis]. Virginia Polytechnic Institute and State University, Blacksburg, VA, USA.

[5] Park, J., Horvath, L., White, M. S., Phanthanousy, S., Araman, P., & Bush, R. J. (2017). The influence of package size and flute type of corrugated boxes on load bridging in unit loads. Packaging Technology and Science, 30(1-2), 33–43. https://doi.org/10.1002/pts.2279

[6] Morrissette, S. (2019). Investigation into the load bridging effect for block class pallets as a function of package size and pallet stiffness [Unpublished master's thesis]. Virginia Polytechnic Institute and State University. Retrieved from https://www.unitload.vt.edu/wp-content/uploads/2019/10/Morrisette-Investigation-into-the-load-bridging-effect-for-block-class-pallets-as-a-function-of-package-size-and-stiffness.pdf

[7] Clayton, A. P., Horvath, L., Bouldin, J., & Gething, B. (2019). Investigation of the effect of column stacked corrugated boxes on load bridging using partial four-way stringer class wooden pallets. Packaging Technology and Science, 32(9), 423–439. https://doi.org/10.1002/pts.2438

[8] Molina, E., Horvath, L., & White, M. S. (2018). Investigation of pallet stacking pattern on unit load bridging. Packaging Technology and Science, 31(10), 653–663. https://doi.org/10.1002/pts.2406

[9] Park, J., Horvath, L., White, M. S., Araman, P., & Bush, R. J. (2018). The influence of stretch wrap containment force on load bridging in unit loads. Packaging Technology and Science, 31(11), 701–708. https://doi.org/10.1002/pts.2385

CHAPTER IX
Consumer research & marketing

Title:
Festividades de Oaxaca (Festivities in Oaxaca)

Author:
Rolando Angulo

Location:
Oaxaca, OAXACA

Description:
The festivities in Oaxaca are always framed by colors, joyful music, and pyrotechnics. These type of installations aim to make us be happy for being alive, showing images such as smiling suns, stars, comets... elements that combine the physical and the aethereal realms of our lives.

Packaging Value for the Consumer – Findings of the Finnish LOHAS2020 Study [52]

Virpi M. Korhonen * and Ia M. Ahl
Association of Packaging Technology and Research (PTR), Finland

Abstract: Currently, a massive, heated debate is raging about packaging and its role in the society. Brands are struggling for survival, faced with pressure from increasing legislation, recycling requirements, and consumer demands. Frequently, companies are forced to base their decisions on the voice of the consumer. Do brands ultimately recognize what aspects consumers appreciate in packaging? Does the most vocal crowd represent the views of the entire population? Who feels most critical about packaging? How have perceptions of the role of packaging changed over the last decade?

This paper presents some of the key findings of the Finnish LOHAS2020 survey conducted in February 2020. The aim of the survey (N=1000) was to elicit and deliver updated knowledge on the packaging attitudes and preferences of Finnish consumers. The same study was previously conducted in 2014 (N=1000) and 2011 (N=1967) providing longitudinal data on the subject. The data were analyzed against generic socio-demographic segments, as well as LOHAS segments showing special interest in personal health and well-being, along with sustainable products and lifestyle.

The study showed a significant increase in the size of the LOHAS heavy and medium segments, as well as in the pro-environmental behaviors between 2014 and 2020. The value dimensions gaining most importance in packaging within the time frame were functional value, aesthetic/design value, informational value, price value, and environmental value, respectively. Thus, the results confirm that consumers have become more environmentally aware and started to act accordingly. This change does not only manifest as appreciation for sustainable packaging but increases the demand for other basic packaging functions as well.

Keywords: packaging, value, LOHAS, consumers, survey.

***Correspondence to:** Virpi M. Korhonen, E-Mail: virpi.korhonen@ptr.fi

1. Introduction to Finnish LOHAS consumers

LOHAS (acronym for Lifestyles Of Health And Sustainability) is a global consumer trend that has been spreading from Japan and the USA since the late 1990s. The Cultural Creatives [1] form the basis for the LOHAS segment.

The LOHAS trend represents a kind of consumer activism, containing major drivers for the package sector, such as growing interest in personal health and well-being, as well as in sustainable (i.e. ecological, socially responsible, and ethical) products. Considering the recent environmental debate on packaging, the environmentally conscious and creative LOHAS consumers could be predicted to feel more critical towards packaging.

In 2020, 17% of the Finnish consumers aged 18-75 represent LOHAS heavy consumers (Figure 1), which is 7 percentage points higher than in 2011 and 2014. The LOHAS heavy consumers' values are grounded in modern humanism, and they show a strong interest in social responsibility, aesthetics, as well as ecological and ethical products. They consider themselves creative and are satisfied with their lives and active in social media.

LOHAS medium consumers account for 28% of the population, which is 4 percentage points higher than in 2014. They support both modern and traditional humanism. They are equally interested in climate change and nature conservation. They prefer organic and ethicalproduction and encourage their friends to do so. They consider themselves as ordinary consumers and feel satisfied with their lives.

LOHAS light consumers account for 16 % of the population. They have expressed interest towards the LOHAS lifestyle but have not yet applied it in their consumption behavior. The not-interested group, decreased to 33% from 40%, shows no interest in LOHAS values, but at the same time they do not feel uncomfortable with such selling arguments. The Anti-LOHAS consumers, currently 6%, are unmotivated by LOHAS values and are unwilling to buy products aimed at this market.

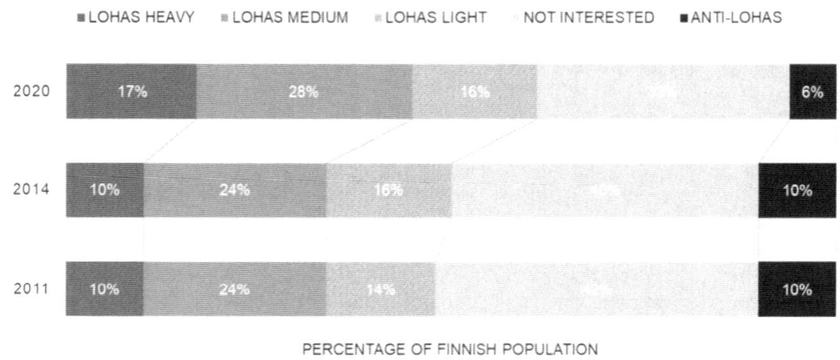

Figure 1 *LOHAS groups in Finland 2020 (N=1000), 2014 (N=1000) and 2011 (N=1967).*

The demographic background of the LOHAS groups is presented in Figures 2-4, showing that a majority (60%) of the LOHAS heavy consumers are women, while in the Anti-LOHAS segment a majority (77%) are men. The age groups 55-64 and 65-75 together constitute 45% of the LOHAS heavy and 41% of the LOHAS medium segments. These generations, often referred to as Baby Boomers (born 1946-1964), have experienced the poverty and scarcity after the Word War II with Finland's war reparations to the Soviet Union. At that time, many families had to be self-sufficient and use all resources as carefully and thoroughly as possible. This might explain the relatively large portion of Boomers in the Finnish LOHAS segments.

More than half of the LOHAS heavy consumers hold a university degree at bachelor's or master's level (Figure 4). In 2020, the Anti-LOHAS segment showed an increase in the education level, which could partly be explained by the strong polarization in the public discussion on the global environmental problems and national political actions needed to be taken.

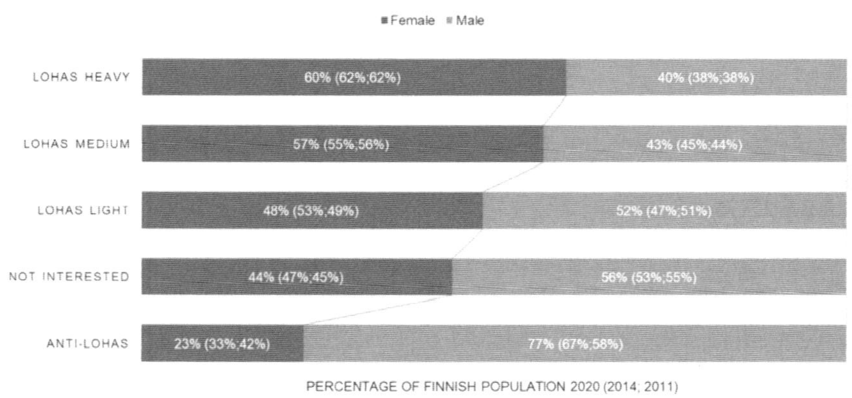

Figure 2 *Finnish LOHAS groups by gender in 2020 (N=1000), 2014 (N=1000) and 2011 (N=1967).*

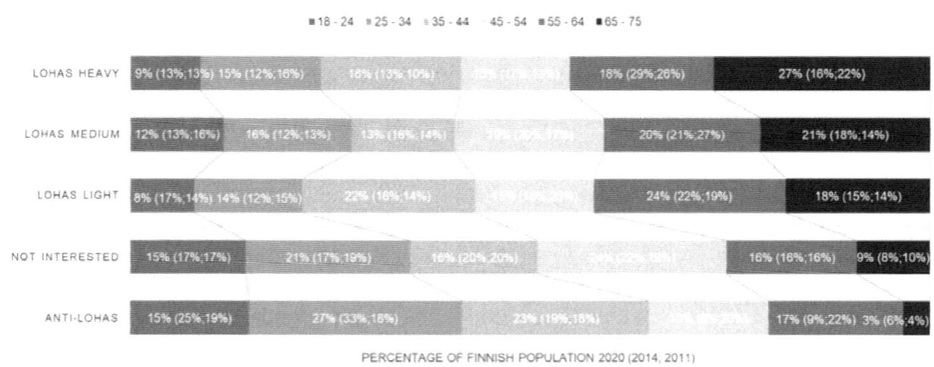

Figure 3 *Finnish LOHAS groups by age in 2020 (N=1000), 2014 (N=1000) and 2011 (N=1967).*

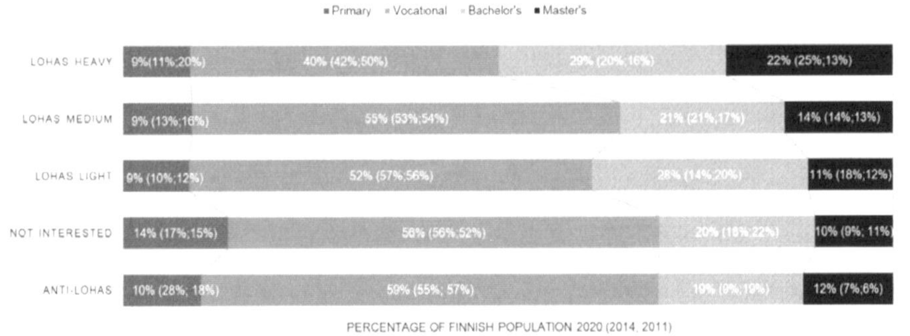

Figure 4 *Finnish LOHAS groups by highest level of education in 2020 (N=1000), 2014 (N=1000) and 2011 (N=1967).*

Figure 5 presents the differences in pro-environmental behaviors in the LOHAS heavy and medium groups compared to the Finnish general population. The behaviors were measured on a 7-point scale (1=does not describe me or my actions at all; 7 = describes me or my actions very well). The full data with mean ratings for each group are presented in Appendix 1. Figure 5 shows the proportion of consumers rating 6 or 7 on the 7-point scale, i.e. expressing very high interest in the listed actions. According to the results, LOHAS heavy consumers are highly more likely to buy eco-friendly or organic products, or purchase products made of reused materials. They are also much more critical towards overpackaging and sort their household waste carefully. The extremely high national recycling activity for bottles and cans can be explained by the comprehensive deposit system for beverage packaging in Finland.

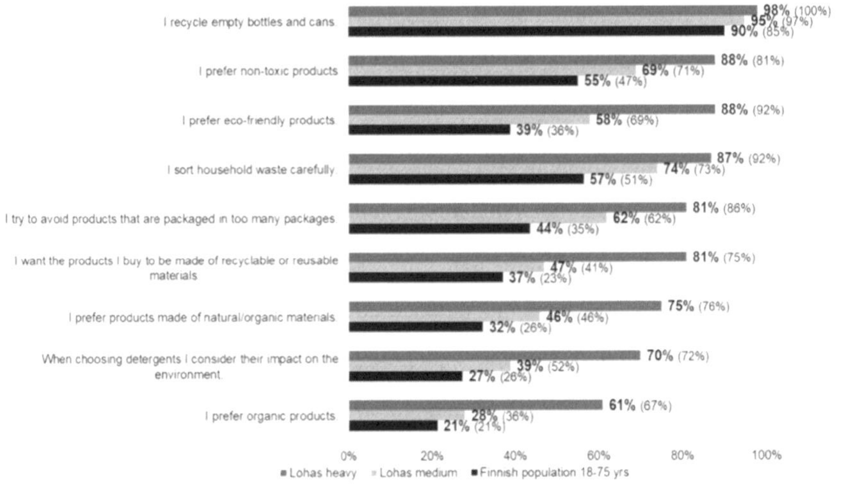

Figure 5 *Pro-environmental behaviors conducted in the LOHAS heavy and medium segments compared to the Finnish population in 2020 (2014), N=1000 (1000) (describes me or my actions well or very well), %.*

The aim of the next section is to elicit and deliver updated knowledge on packaging value for the Finnish consumers, as well as LOHAS segments in 2020 and 2014.

2. Methodology

2.1 Data collection

The research data were collected using an M3 Internet panel in Finland in 2020 and 2014. The data represents the overall demographics of the Finnish population aged 18-75 years. The respondents were divided into five groups based on the LOHAS classification by Tripod Research described in the introduction.

2.2. Value measures

A total of 37 attitude statements were constructed for measuring packaging value (Appendix 2). All items were presented with 7-point bipolar Likert-type rating scales (1 = strongly disagree; 4 = neither agree nor disagree; 7 = strongly agree). The attitude statements were tested and validated in the previous surveys conducted in 2011 and 2014 [2].

The statements were categorized by statistical multivariate analyses. Principal axis factoring with Varimax rotation was employed for analyzing and validating the value dimensions. The reliability of the scales was tested and reported with Cronbach's alpha. The differences in means at LOHAS group or population level were tested with one-way ANOVA and t-tests.

3. Results and discussion

3.1 Package value for LOHAS consumers

The factor analysis yielded eight factors that were labelled according to the highest loadings on each factor (Appendix 2). The factors represented functional, informational, environmental, aesthetic/design, social/expressive, emotional, price and instrumental value experienced from packaging. Figure 6 presents the summated scale means for each value dimension both at LOHAS group as well as at population level. The results are displayed according to the highest means at population level, for which a t-test was applied to test significant changes between 2014 and 2020. The differences tested were significant in all value dimensions except in "social/expressive value" and "instrumental value". The group means displayed in Appendix 2 show that LOHAS heavy and medium groups experience higher value from packaging in all other dimensions except price and instrumental value. LOHAS heavy also shows the highest increases in value ratings between 2014 and 2020, especially in informational and aesthetic/design value.

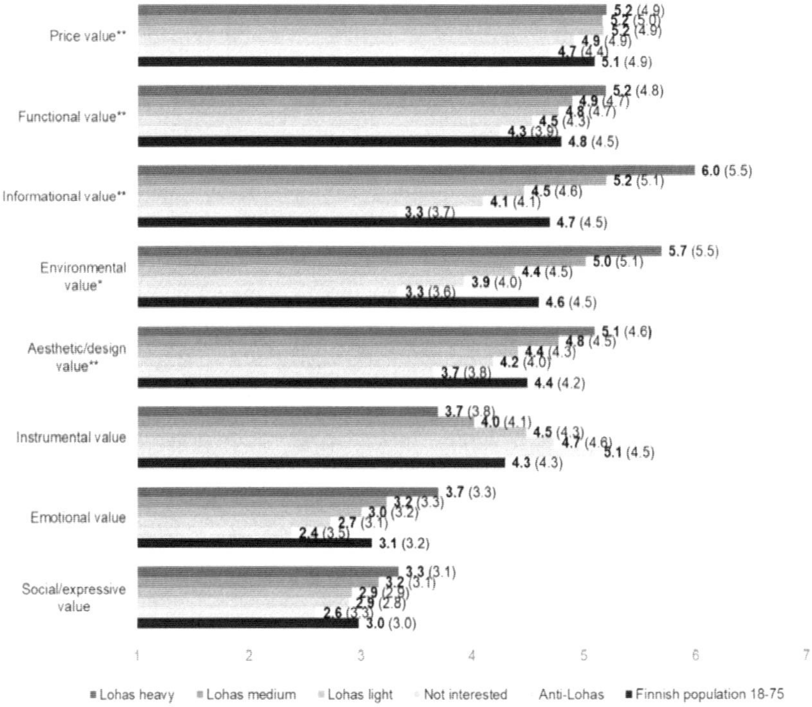

t-test at population level, * $p<0.05$; ** $p<0.01$

Figure 6. *Mean ratings for packaging value dimensions 2020 (2014), N=1000 (1000), (range 1-7, see original data in Appendix 2).*

4. Conclusions

The results show that not only do LOHAS consumers appreciate the environmental aspects in packaging, but they also set high standards for packaging functionality, information, and aesthetics/design. Higher value will emerge if packaging succeeds to deliver several benefits. While the LOHAS heavy and medium segments have gained size, their appreciation for the basic functions of packaging has increased simultaneously. In other words, the ecological debate seems to have contributed to the importance of other packaging functions such as reducing food waste, increasing product safety and information, and enhancing product appeal to consumers. It is highly likely that consumers are unwilling to sacrifice these other properties for sustainability, at least to a great extent. These findings support the notion that packaging is a holistic consumer experience that contributes to the quality impression of the product.

Acknowledgements

The research data presented in this paper from 2011-2014 was collected in the LOHASPACK project funded by Business Finland (former TEKES) and several companies. In 2011-2014, the companies involved in the study were Anton & Anton, Atria, Coveris Rigid Finland, The Environmental Register of Packaging, Finnish Corrugated Board Association, Kanniston Leipomo, Kuulas Research Agency, HK Ruokatalo, Metsä Board, Myllyn Paras, Saarioinen, Stora Enso, Verman, and Westpak. The study of 2020 was supported by the following companies: Elopak, Finnish Packaging Association, HKScan, Metsä Board, Orkla, Paulig, Spices Chef and UPM Raflatac.

References

[1] Ray, P.H. and Anderson, S.R. "The Cultural Creatives: How 50 Million People Are Changing the World". New York: Harmony Books. 2000.

[2] Korhonen V. Package Value for LOHAS Consumers—Results of a Finnish Study. In: 18th IAPRI World Packaging Conference, Proceedings. 2012. p. 156.

Appendix 1: Pro-environmental behaviors in LOHAS groups and Finnish population 2020 (2014), Independent Samples T-Test. (1 = does not describe me or my actions at all; 7 = describes me or my actions very well)

			LOHAS groups				T-Test	
	LOHAS heavy n=171 (99)	LOHAS medium n=279 (248)	LOHAS light n=161 (159)	Not interested n=329 (386)	Anti-LOHAS n=60 (107)	**Finnish population N=1000 (1000)**	**t**	**Sig.**
I sort household waste carefully.	6.4 (6.5)	6.0 (6.0)	5.4 (5.3)	4.8 (4.8)	3.7 (3.1)	**5.4 (5.2)**	**2.5**	**0.01**
I try to avoid products that are packed in too many packages.	6.2 (6.2)	5.5 (5.6)	4.8 (4.6)	4.3 (3.9)	3.0 (2.8)	**5.0 (4.6)**	**4.9**	**0.00**
When choosing detergents, I consider their impact on the environment.	5.9 (5.9)	4.9 (5.3)	4.2 (4.1)	3.6 (3.3)	2.5 (2.6)	**4.4 (4.2)**	**2.7**	**0.01**
I prefer eco-friendly products.	6.4 (6.4)	5.6 (5.8)	4.8 (4.8)	4.1 (3.9)	2.7 (2.8)	**4.9 (4.7)**	**2.9**	**0.00**
I prefer organic products.	5.7 (5.8)	4.6 (4.8)	3.7 (3.8)	3.2 (3.1)	2.3 (2.6)	**4.0 (3.9)**	**1.9**	**0.06**
I prefer local products.	6.0 (6.4)	5.4 (5.6)	4.5 (4.8)	4.2 (4.2)	3.0 (3.0)	**4.8 (4.8)**	**0.6**	**0.55**
I try to avoid unnecessary driving.	5.7 (5.8)	5.2 (5.1)	4.3 (4.5)	4.0 (3.9)	2.7 (2.8)	**4.6 (4.4)**	**2.2**	**0.03**
I recycle empty cans and bottles.	6.9 (6.9)	6.8 (6.8)	6.6 (6.6)	6.4 (6.4)	6.0 (5.1)	**6.6 (6.5)**	**2.1**	**0.04**
I avoid using chemical fertilizers in yard/garden/balcony plants.	6.1 (6.3)	5.4 (5.5)	4.9 (4.5)	4.3 (4.0)	2.6 (2.8)	**4.9 (4.6)**	**3.9**	**0.00**
I avoid flying if possible.	5.5 (4.9)	4.7 (4.6)	4.0 (3.9)	3.8 (3.4)	2.7 (2.5)	**4.3 (3.9)**	**4.4**	**0.00**
I prefer non-toxic products.	6.5 (6.4)	5.8 (6.0)	5.4 (5.3)	4.8 (4.6)	3.5 (3.1)	**5.4 (5.1)**	**4.0**	**0.00**
I only buy products that are not tested on animals.	5.6 (5.4)	4.7 (4.6)	4.0 (3.8)	3.7 (3.2)	2.7 (2.7)	**4.3 (3.9)**	**5.5**	**0.00**
I want the products I buy to be made of recyclable or reusable materials.	6.2 (5.9)	5.3 (5.0)	4.7 (4.2)	4.1 (3.5)	2.9 (2.8)	**4.8 (4.2)**	**7.8**	**0.00**
I prefer energy-efficient appliances.	6.3 (6.2)	5.9 (6.0)	5.3 (5.4)	4.8 (4.8)	3.9 (3.5)	**5.4 (5.3)**	**2.0**	**0.05**
I prefer products whose production and/or use consumes less water.	5.7 (5.5)	5.1 (4.8)	4.4 (4.0)	4.0 (3.6)	3.1 (2.8)	**4.6 (4.1)**	**6.5**	**0.00**
I prefer products made of natural/ organic materials.	6.1 (6.0)	5.3 (5.1)	4.4 (4.3)	3.8 (3.6)	2.8 (2.8)	**4.7 (4.3)**	**5.1**	**0.00**

Appendix 2. Packaging value dimensions 1/4		2020								2014							
		Total N=1000	LOHAS heavy N=171	LOHAS medium N=279	LOHAS light N=161	Not interested N=329	Anti-LOHAS N=60	**F**	**Sig**	**Total N=1000**	LOHAS heavy N=99	LOHAS medium N=248	LOHAS light N=159	Not interested N=386	Anti-LOHAS N=107	**F**	**Sig**
Item	**Functional value**																
1	I prefer packages that provide long shelf life.	**5.5**	5.9	5.7	5.6	5.3	4.9	**11.7**	**0.00**	**5.0**	5.5	5.1	5.3	5.0	4.2	**13.9**	**0.00**
2	I always choose a package from which I can clearly see that no-one has opened it before me.	**5.5**	5.8	5.7	5.7	5.2	5.1	**8.7**	**0.00**	**5.1**	5.4	5.4	5.4	5.1	4.4	**9.7**	**0.00**
3	I prefer light packaging materials in order to avoid heavy shopping bags.	**4.6**	5.2	4.8	4.7	4.4	3.9	**11.6**	**0.00**	**4.5**	5.0	4.8	4.5	4.2	3.8	**13.6**	**0.00**
4	I often choose packages based on their functionality.	**4.8**	5.3	5.1	4.8	4.6	4.2	**12.5**	**0.00**	**4.6**	5.1	4.8	4.8	4.3	3.9	**18.9**	**0.00**
5	I like buying pre-packaged food products because they are clean and have a long shelf life.	**4.8**	4.8	4.8	5.1	4.8	4.7	**1.8**	**0.12**	**4.2**	4.0	4.2	4.4	4.3	4.0	**1.9**	**0.11**
6	I can think of several packages that I avoid buying because they are too difficult to open.	**4.1**	4.6	4.4	4.0	3.7	3.6	**12.7**	**0.00**	**4.1**	4.6	4.3	4.2	3.7	3.5	**11.0**	**0.00**
7	It's hard for me to find small enough package sizes in the stores.	**3.9**	4.4	3.9	3.6	3.8	3.6	**5.5**	**0.00**	**3.9**	4.1	4.0	4.0	3.7	3.6	**2.5**	**0.04**
	Mean	**4.8**	**5.2**	**4.9**	**4.8**	**4.5**	**4.3**	**18.8**	**0.00**	**4.5**	**4.8**	**4.7**	**4.7**	**4.3**	**3.9**	**22.9**	**0.00**
	Cronbach alpha	**0.73**								**0.66**							
	Informational value																
8	I prefer packages that clearly show the producer and origin of the product.	**5.1**	6.3	5.7	5.1	4.6	3.7	**75.3**	**0.00**	**5.0**	5.9	5.5	5.1	4.5	3.9	**45.9**	**0.00**
9	I always check the producer and country of origin when I buy private label products.	**4.4**	5.9	5.0	4.1	3.8	3.1	**65.7**	**0.00**	**4.5**	5.5	5.1	4.5	4.0	3.6	**29.9**	**0.00**
10	Before buying, I carefully read product descriptions on packages.	**4.4**	5.7	4.9	4.2	3.8	3.2	**61.4**	**0.00**	**4.3**	5.1	4.8	4.2	3.8	3.5	**25.6**	**0.00**
	Mean	**4.7**	**6.0**	**5.2**	**4.5**	**4.1**	**3.3**	**98.5**	**0.00**	**4.5**	**5.5**	**5.1**	**4.6**	**4.1**	**3.7**	**50.7**	**0.00**
	Cronbach's alpha	**0.82**								**0.77**							

Appendix 2. Packaging value dimensions 2/4		2020								2014							
		Total N=1000	LOHAS heavy N=171	LOHAS medium N=279	LOHAS light N=161	Not interested N=329	Anti-LOHAS N=60	**F**	**Sig**	**Total N=1000**	LOHAS heavy N=99	LOHAS medium N=248	LOHAS light N=159	Not interested N=386	Anti-LOHAS N=107	**F**	**Sig**
	Environmental value																
11	To avoid wasting food, I prefer appropriate package sizes.	**5.5**	6.2	5.8	5.6	5.1	4.6	**35.7**	**0.00**	**5.4**	6.0	5.9	5.7	5.2	4.3	**36.0**	**0.00**
12	I value reusable packaging.	**5.2**	6.2	5.6	5.1	4.7	4.2	**50.5**	**0.00**	**5.2**	5.9	5.8	5.4	4.8	4.0	**43.8**	**0.00**
13	I like buying products with recyclable packaging.	**5.1**	6.3	5.8	5.1	4.5	3.8	**94.9**	**0.00**	**5.0**	5.9	5.7	5.1	4.5	3.6	**61.1**	**0.00**
14	I feel guilty buying environmentally harmful packages.	**3.9**	5.4	4.7	3.9	3.3	2.4	**76.0**	**0.00**	**4.2**	5.3	4.9	4.0	3.4	3.2	**51.8**	**0.00**
15	Environmentally harmful packaging stops me from buying a product.	**3.7**	5.3	4.2	3.6	3.1	2.5	**79.3**	**0.00**	**3.9**	5.0	4.2	3.6	3.2	3.3	**33.3**	**0.00**
16	I'm willing to pay a higher price per kilo for products with environmentally friendly packaging.	**3.5**	4.7	4.1	3.1	2.9	2.5	**64.5**	**0.00**	**3.7**	4.9	4.1	3.3	2.9	3.3	**43.8**	**0.00**
	Mean	**4.6**	**5.7**	**5.0**	**4.4**	**3.9**	**3.3**	**167.8**	**0.00**	**4.5**	**5.5**	**5.1**	**4.5**	**4.0**	**3.6**	**94.8**	**0.00**
	Cronbach's alpha	**0.81**								**0.80**							
	Aesthetic/design value																
17	When I'm shopping for presents, I want top-quality product packaging.	**4.9**	5.5	5.3	5.0	4.8	4.1	**14.8**	**0.00**	**5.0**	5.3	5.3	5.3	4.9	4.1	**13.0**	**0.00**
18	I appreciate hand-packed products.	**4.3**	5.3	4.7	4.1	4.0	3.6	**36.9**	**0.00**	**4.2**	4.9	4.4	4.2	3.8	3.6	**16.9**	**0.00**
19	I think that packaging quality also says something about the quality of the actual product.	**4.7**	5.3	5.0	4.8	4.4	4.1	**15.8**	**0.00**	**4.2**	4.3	4.3	4.4	4.1	3.8	**2.8**	**0.03**
20	Good packaging strengthens my brand loyalty.	**4.5**	5.1	4.9	4.6	4.2	3.5	**21.7**	**0.00**	**4.0**	4.1	4.3	4.0	3.8	3.8	**4.1**	**0.00**
21	I value good design in packaging.	**4.5**	5.1	4.7	4.5	4.4	3.6	**12.9**	**0.00**	**4.1**	4.5	4.3	4.0	4.0	3.6	**4.7**	**0.00**
22	I like to shop in stores where product packages are displayed with thought and attention.	**4.2**	4.8	4.4	4.2	3.8	3.6	**17.4**	**0.00**	**4.1**	4.6	4.4	4.1	3.9	3.7	**8.1**	**0.00**
23	I pay attention to packaging when I'm shopping for myself.	**3.9**	4.6	4.3	3.8	3.7	3.2	**15.4**	**0.00**	**4.0**	4.6	4.2	4.1	3.7	3.6	**9.3**	**0.00**
	Mean	**4.5**	**5.1**	**4.8**	**4.4**	**4.2**	**3.7**	**40.1**	**0.00**	**4.2**	**4.6**	**4.5**	**4.3**	**4.1**	**3.8**	**15.4**	**0.00**
	Cronbach's alpha	**0.82**								**0.79**							

Appendix 2. Packaging value dimensions 3/4		2020								2014							
		Total N=1000	LO HAS heavy N=171	LO HAS medium N=279	LO HAS light N=161	Not interested N=329	Anti-LO HAS N=60	**F**	**Sig**	**Total N=1000**	LO HAS heavy N=99	LO HAS medium N=248	LO HAS light N=159	Not interested N=386	Anti-LO HAS N=107	**F**	**Sig**
Item	**Social/Expressive value**																
24	I often buy products with packaging that stands out from the others in a positive way.	**3.8**	4.3	4.0	3.7	3.5	3.3	**12.0**	**0.00**	**3.5**	3.8	3.7	3.4	3.2	3.5	**4.5**	**0.00**
25	On the street, I easily notice people carrying packages or bags of brands.	**3.0**	3.3	3.1	3.0	3.1	2.7	**1.3**	**0.27**	**3.2**	3.3	3.1	3.2	2.9	3.4	**2.3**	**0.05**
26	I avoid buying cheap-looking packages.	**3.3**	3.5	3.5	3.2	3.3	2.8	**3.4**	**0.01**	**3.3**	3.4	3.4	3.1	3.1	3.5	**2.5**	**0.04**
27	I could pay more for individually packaged products.	**2.9**	3.3	3.1	3.0	2.7	2.4	**7.3**	**0.00**	**3.0**	3.1	3.2	2.8	2.7	3.3	**6.0**	**0.00**
28	I'm willing to pay more for packaging designed by famous designers.	**2.5**	3.0	2.7	2.4	2.4	2.1	**5.5**	**0.00**	**2.6**	2.8	2.6	2.4	2.4	3.0	**4.7**	**0.00**
29	I seldom look at the price tag, if a product has an especially appealing package.	**2.5**	2.7	2.6	2.3	2.4	2.4	**2.3**	**0.06**	**2.6**	2.4	2.6	2.3	2.3	3.2	**7.1**	**0.00**
	Mean	**3.0**	**3.3**	**3.2**	**2.9**	**2.9**	**2.6**	7.0	**0.00**	3.0	**3.1**	**3.1**	**2.9**	**2.8**	**3.3**	**6.1**	**0.00**
	Cronbach's alpha	**0.85**								**0.84**							
	Emotional value																
30	Packages that I keep are often connected with a particular experience or story.	**3.3**	4.1	3.7	3.4	2.9	2.6	**17.5**	**0.00**	**3.6**	3.9	3.7	3.5	3.4	3.6	**1.8**	**0.14**
31	I keep some packages because they're pretty.	**3.3**	4.0	3.5	3.4	3.0	2.6	**9.3**	**0.00**	**3.6**	3.8	3.6	3.5	3.4	3.7	**1.0**	**0.41**
32	I collect unusual packages.	**2.3**	2.8	2.4	2.2	2.2	2.0	**4.9**	**0.00**	**2.6**	2.3	2.5	2.5	2.4	3.1	**4.1**	**0.00**
	Mean	**3.1**	**3.7**	**3.2**	**3.0**	**2.7**	**2.4**	**13.7**	**0.00**	**3.2**	**3.3**	**3.3**	**3.2**	**3.1**	**3.5**	**2.1**	**0.08**
	Cronbach's alpha	**0.81**								**0.72**							

Appendix 2. Packaging value dimensions 4/4		2020								2014							
		Total N=1000	LOHAS heavy N=171	LOHAS medium N=279	LOHAS light N=161	Not interested N=329	Anti-LOHAS N=60	**F**	**Sig**	**Total N=1000**	LOHAS heavy N=99	LOHAS medium N=248	LOHAS light N=159	Not interested N=386	Anti-LOHAS N=107	**F**	**Sig**
	Price value																
33	The appearance of packaging is not important to me, it's the price that counts.	**5.2**	4.9	5.1	5.2	5.2	5.4	**1.6**	**0.18**	**4.9**	4.6	5.0	5.2	5.2	4.6	**5.5**	**0.00**
34	With food products, I often prefer the cheapest package sizes, and I preserve/freeze a portion of the food.	**5.1**	5.6	5.4	5.2	4.8	4.5	**14.6**	**0.00**	**4.8**	5.1	5.1	4.9	4.8	4.3	**6.5**	**0.00**
34	I buy all products based on the cheapest package size available per kilo.	**4.8**	5.1	5.0	5.1	4.8	4.2	**5.4**	**0.00**	**4.7**	5.0	4.9	4.7	4.8	4.2	**4.6**	**0.00**
	Mean	**5.1**	**5.2**	**5.2**	**5.2**	**4.9**	**4.7**	**5.1**	**0.00**	**4.9**	**4.9**	**5.0**	**4.9**	**4.9**	**4.4**	**6.0**	**0.00**
	Cronbach's alpha	**0.58**								**0.63**							
	Instrumental value																
35	I only consider packaging as protection for products.	**4.8**	4.6	4.7	5.0	4.9	5.0	**2.6**	**0.03**	**4.8**	4.9	4.8	4.9	4.9	4.7	**0.5**	**0.77**
36	I often throw away packages without paying them any special attention.	**4.5**	3.8	4.2	4.5	5.0	5.2	**19.9**	**0.00**	**4.3**	3.8	4.2	4.2	4.6	4.6	**7.4**	**0.00**
37	I don't care what material packages are made of.	**3.8**	2.7	3.1	3.9	4.3	5.1	**58.1**	**0.00**	**3.7**	2.9	3.3	3.8	4.1	4.3	**21.9**	**0.00**
	Mean	**4.3**	**3.7**	**4.0**	**4.5**	**4.7**	**5.1**	**37.5**	**0.00**	**4.3**	**3.8**	**4.1**	**4.3**	**4.6**	**4.5**	**11.2**	**0.00**
	Cronbach's alpha	**0.60**								**0.57**							

CHAPTER V
Testing analysis & quality control

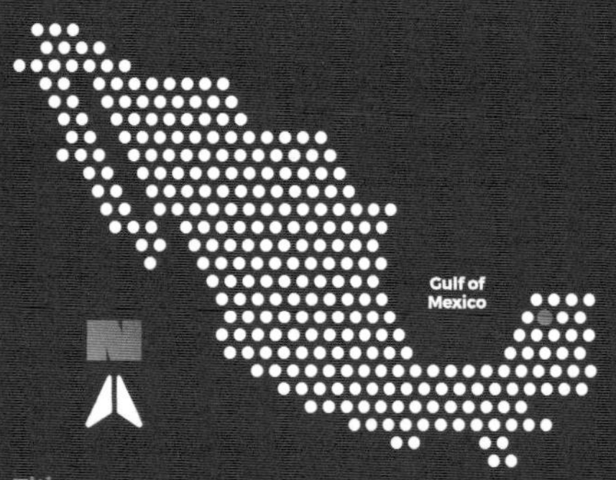

Title:
Red Pool for Salt Production

Author:
Jess Kraft (jkraft5)

Location:
Las Coloradas, YUCATÁN

Description:
Las Coloradas is a small, whimsical fishing port that seems to be a portal towards somewhere magical. Famous for its virgin beaches and abundant mangroves, its flora and fauna makes you think of a modern-day Eden, where man and nature are one in complete balance.

A novel mechanical-shock fragility test of a product for simple stochastic cushioning design [11]

Shogo Horiguchi *1,2, Katsuhiko Saito 3
1 Ph.D. Student, Graduate School of Maritime Sciences, Kobe University, Kobe, Japan
2 Osaka Research Institute of Industrial Science and Technology, Izumi, Japan
3 Transport Packaging Laboratory, Kobe University, Kobe, Japan

Abstract: Proper cushioning is required to prevent product damage during transport and to prevent over-packaging. Effective cushioning design must take into account the mechanical-shock fragility of the product. Furthermore, improved cushioning design can be achieved by performing stochastic cushioning design investigations using mechanical-shock fragility statistics. However, to obtain statistics with mechanical-shock fragility testing of a product, testing that is composed of critical velocity change tests and critical-acceleration tests (the "conventional method"), many samples are required and, in many cases, the required number of samples cannot be prepared. Thus, the research reported here is designed to develop testing methods requiring half the number of samples of the conventional method. We propose a statistical method (the "proposed method") by improving a test procedure, namely "mechanical-shock fragility test of a product with one sample." The proposed method is one in which the shock of a single velocity change (the "test velocity change") is given by increasing the acceleration in a step-wise fashion, and the results indicate the failure rate resulting from the velocity change and provide the critical-acceleration statistics. In these experiments, the critical-acceleration statistics for test velocity changes larger than the critical velocity change were equivalent to those from the conventional method. The relationship between the test velocity change and the failure rate was clarified so it can be used as a criterion for determining the requirements of cushioning design. Moreover, examples are given in which the results of the proposed method are applied to simple stochastic cushioning design.

Keywords: mechanical-shock fragility test; cushioning design; shock test; statistical analysis; damage boundary curve.

***Correspondence to:** Shogo Horiguchi, Osaka Research Institute of Industrial Science and Technology, Izumi 5941157, Japan. E-mail: HoriguchiS@tri-osaka.jp

Oral / Testing analysis and quality control

Industrial leak testing of dangerous goods packagings [46]

Eva Schlick-Hasper *, Marcel Neitsch, Thomas Goedecke
Federal Institute for Materials Research and Testing (BAM), Berlin, Germany

Abstract: The Dangerous Goods Regulations currently do not include limit leakage rates or sensitivity requirements for industrial leak testing procedures that are equivalent to the bubble test, which is the prescribed test method for design type testing of dangerous goods packagings. During series production of such packagings, various methods are used, which often do not meet the requirements of the bubble test with regard to important criteria.

Sensitivity, flow direction, pressure level and automatability are particularly important factors when selecting a suitable industrial leak testing method. The following methods are in principle both suitable and equally effective as the bubble test: pressure rise test (vacuum chamber), ultrasonic bubble leak detection and gas detection methods (pressure technique by accumulation and vacuum chamber technique).

To ensure a uniform test level during design type testing and production line leak testing and therefore a comparable safety level as required by the Dangerous Goods Regulations, it is necessary to include a more precise specification in these regulations. This requires, on the one hand, information about the sensitivity of the bubble test and, on the other hand, the inclusion of a list of suitable, equally effective industrial test methods with their specific boundary conditions.

Keywords: bubble test, dangerous goods packagings, industrial leak testing, leakproofness test, series production

PTS Special Edition: https://onlinelibrary.wiley.com/doi/10.1002/PTS.2502

***Correspondence to:** Eva Schlick-Hasper, Federal Institute for Materials Research and Testing (BAM), Berlin, Germany. E-Mail: eva.schlick-hasper@bam.de

CHAPTER XI
Packaging education

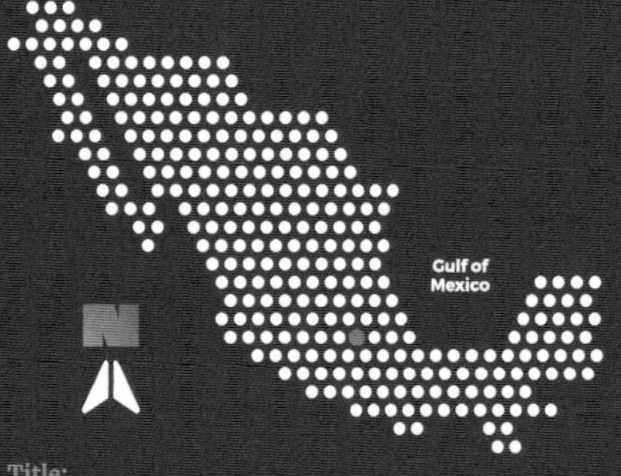

Title:
México Análogo (Analogue Mexico)

Author:
Sarai Cuello Gutiérrez

Technique:
Analogue photography, fujifilm iso 200,
Kyoskko processing, scanned.

Location:
Downtown, MEXICO CITY

Description:
Mexico is a country of many layers, some metaphorical, some literal. If you visit Mexico City's downtown, you can actually see the ruins of the preColombian buildings covered up with Colonial structures, speckled here and there with contemporary details. History is ever-present and very much alive in Mexico City's downtown.

Mapping Class Learning Outcomes to University Learning Goals at Michigan State University's School of Packaging [48]

Rafael AURAS*, Eva ALMENAR, Laura BIX, Alyssa HARBEN, Ronald IWASKIEWICZ, Paul KONING, Donatien Pascal KAMDEM, Monireh MAHMOUDI, Laurent MATUANA, Patrick McDAVID, Muhammad RABNAWAZ, Ricky SPECK, Susan SELKE, Uruchaya SONCHAENG, Cimberly WEIR, Dennis YOUNG

School of Packaging, Michigan State University, East Lansing, MI, USA

Abstract: The class learning outcomes (CLO) of the packaging bachelor's degree at the School of Packaging (SoP) at Michigan State University (MSU) were mapped to competency-based, programmatic learning outcomes (CPLO), which are aligned with the broad learning goals of the University (MSU-LG). Six CPLOs were developed using group consensus building for the core curriculum: CPLO-1: Evaluate packaging systems; CPLO-2: Analyze tradeoffs in packaging systems; CPLO-3: Design innovative and sustainable packaging systems; CPLO-4: Manage projects in diverse teams; CPLO-5: Communicate effectively considering diverse audiences; CPLO-6: Conduct oneself in a professional and ethical manner. Relationships, from specific to broad, (CLOs to CPLOs to MSU-LGs) were mapped during several group sessions with SoP packaging educators utilizing the same consensus-building process. This mapping scheme (class-specific CLOs supporting broader program CPLOs and, ultimately, MSU-LGs) was developed to guarantee alignment of expectations for learning from the course to the packaging program to the University level.

During fall 2018, and spring and fall 2019, assessment tools, including rubrics, questionnaires, and activity/assignments intended to evaluate learning were developed to evaluate core and elective courses offered by the SoP. Data collection of each student's performance in the core and selective elective courses was conducted and assessed utilizing Watermark's VIA software.

Assessment of student performance related to each of the CLOs and related CPLO and MSU- LG provided objective evidence of learning across the SoP curriculum as well as how CLOs, delivered and assessed at the individual student level, translate into competence achieved at the programmatic and university levels. As more instruments were implemented to assess students' performance, areas of improvement became increasingly evident and a path forward for curriculum adjustment and development manifested.

Keywords: programmatic; correlation; assessment; evaluation; students; STEM education

***Correspondence to:** Rafael Auras, 448 Wilson Road, School of Packaging, Michigan State University, East Lansing, MI, USA, 48824. E-mail: aurasraf@msu.edu

1. Introduction

Packaging is an interdisciplinary field integrating science, engineering, technology and management to protect and identify products for distribution, storage, sale and use. It is a critical component of all value chains and affects product quality, safety, price and cost. Hence, packaging is rich area for research and collaboration [1]. The School of Packaging (SoP) at Michigan State University (MSU) currently offers Bachelor of Science (BS), Master of Science (MS), and Doctor of Philosophy (PhD) degrees in packaging and has conferred over 10,000 degrees to date as can be seen from the cumulative number of SoP graduates in Figure 1.

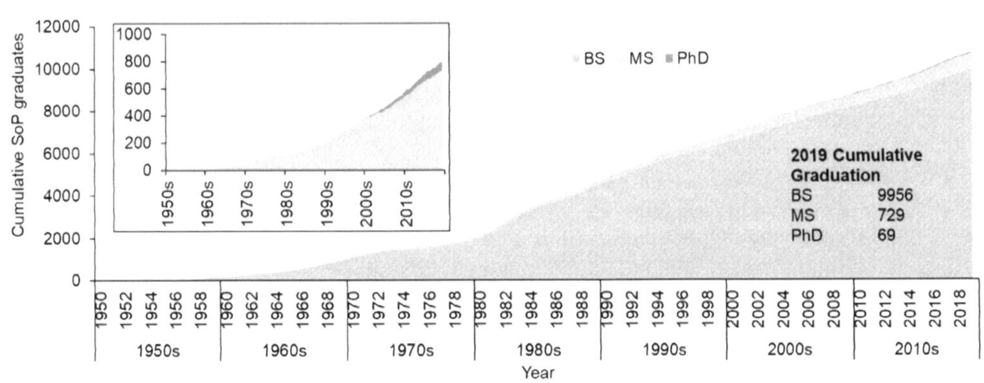

***Figure 1** Cumulative graduates by year graduating with Bachelor of Science (BS), Master of Science (MS), and Doctor of Philosophy (PhD) degrees from the School of Packaging (SoP) at Michigan State University. The inset shows cumulative graduates of the MS and PhD degrees, excluding the BS degree.*

Michigan State University's BS program in packaging has historically been an enrollment- limited program to keep the number of students at a manageable level. The readily understandable context of the major, together with an ability to combine a passion for innovation, design, and sustainability into practical applications have made it a long-popular choice. Furthermore, interest has been fueled by excellent job opportunities and relatively high salaries offered to BS graduates [1]. To strive for the best quality of the courses taught in its BS program, the SoP recently conducted a major planning to rebalance, realign, and develop a strategic plan for the deployment of efforts and resources and to improve interpersonal competencies. The current packaging curriculum (i.e., the academic content taught in SoP program) consists of ten core and twelve elective packaging courses as shown in **Figure 2**. All the core courses are required for the degree; however, the students can choose to focus on the Packaging Science or Packaging Value Chain Management for their elective courses. The Packaging Science electives emphasize the technical competencies required of those in packaging while the Packaging Value Chain Management electives emphasize the role of packaging in the value chain and the need to understand economics and business functions [2]. Each of these two concentrations (Packaging Science and Packaging Value Chain Management) have mandatory courses designated appropriately within **Figure 2**.

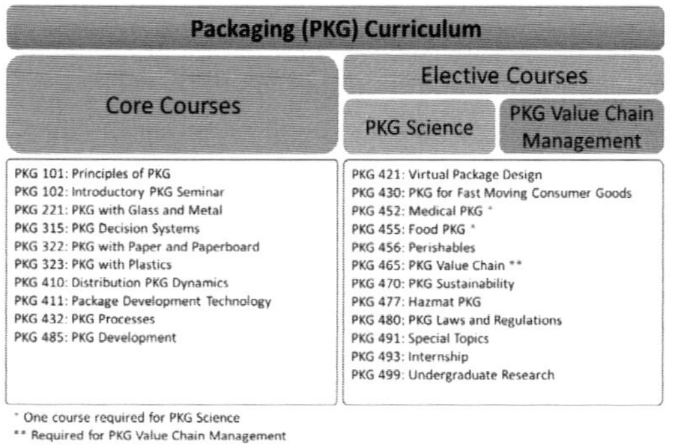

***Figure 2** The current School of Packaging curriculum including core and elective courses.*

Curriculum and learning assessment methods have been extensively used to evaluate students' learning [3,4]. Outcomes-based approaches to curricular framing and learning assessment have been utilized in education for decades [5,6] and employed by various disciplines [7-9]. The approach, kindred to that used in a backward design process, emphasizes the exit outcomes needed by students rather than the objectives when designing a curriculum [5,6,10,11]. Under this paradigm, learning outcomes are defined as the knowledge or skills the students should acquire by the end of a particular assignment, class, course, or program [12]. Work presented herein includes a full evaluation of the packaging curriculum, exit surveys of students, and feedback from the external packaging industry advisory board and the alumni association to a) develop the class learning outcomes (CLO); b) develop the competency-based programmatic learning outcomes (CPLO), which are the outcomes that students should master; and c) map them to the Michigan State University learning goals (MSU-LG) [13], to ultimately use them to assess learning. We framed our work as an outcomes-based approach. In our curricular mapping, the CLOs were mapped to the CPLOs at the SoP and also to the broad MSU-LGs. The various levels of the learning outcomes that were assessed for the packaging curriculum are shown in **Figure 3**. Traditional curriculum maps are presented in a tabular format or a list [14,15], but recently they are also shown in graphical formats [3,16]. The tabular and graphical formats were implemented to the SoP curriculum map.

***Figure 2** Different levels of learning outcomes for the packaging curriculum mapping at the School of Packaging, Michigan State University.*

This paper presents the methodology that we used to conduct the mapping and reports the results from the curriculum assessment.

2. Methodology

2.1. Learning outcome mappings

As part of the curriculum assessment plan, eight CPLOs that had consensus agreement regarding their importance as competencies for exiting students were utilized as shown in Table 1. CPLO- 1 to CPLO-6 were determined to be requisite for all packaging students, and, as such, assigned to the packaging core courses (listed in Figure 2). CPLO-7 and CPLO-8 were assigned to the Packaging Science and Packaging Value Chain Management electives (also listed in Figure 2), respectively. CPLO-1 to CPLO-6 were initially approved by the SoP voting instructors. CPLO- 7 and CPLO-8 were approved in a second iteration. The following results and discussion section concentrates on the core curriculum and CPLO-1 to CPLO-6 excluding CPLO-7 and CPLO-8 and the elective courses. Nonetheless, the mapping and evaluation process for them are the same as those of CPLO-1 to CPLO-6 for the core courses.

Table 1. School of Packaging Bachelor of Science degree competency-based programmatic learning outcomes (CPLO).

CPLO-1: Evaluate packaging systems
Evaluate and choose materials, packaging systems, and components by applying and interpreting scientific tests, writing and interpreting specifications, and using and recommending appropriate test protocols.
CPLO-2: Analyze tradeoffs in packaging systems
Analyze and prioritize product, packaging line, distribution system, environmental footprint, marketing, financial implications, user needs and additional tradeoffs to create and/or to provide innovative, efficient, sustainable, legally compliant and cost-effective packaging systems.
CPLO-3: Design innovative and sustainable packaging systems
Design innovative and sustainable solutions to package and packaging systems related problems and future needs.
CPLO-4: Manage projects in diverse teams
Formulate and manage projects with the ability to work in diverse teams to achieve common and successful outcomes.
CPLO-5: Communicate effectively considering diverse audiences
Communicate effectively considering diverse audiences in a variety of situations with a variety of media.
CPLO-6: Conduct oneself in a professional and ethical manner
Conduct oneself in a professional and ethical manner, exhibiting values such as civility and respect for others, honesty, integrity, accountability, maintenance of confidentiality, etc.
CPLO-7: Design legal and efficacious packaging systems
Design, analyze and prioritize the legality and efficacy of packaging systems while considering the nuances imposed by stakeholders such as industry, government, NGOs and end-users.
CPLO-8: Make decision in packaging
Design supply chains using different packaging systems considering various constraints that may be encountered by suppliers, manufacturers, distributors and consumers.

Each SoP instructor initially developed CLOs for packaging courses for which they had primary responsibility; drafted CLOs were discussed, revised and approved by all the instructors. Relationships among the CLOs were established by the instructors based on the prerequisite linkages between and within courses, similar to the data visualization models previously described [16,17]. An excerpt of a packaging course (PKG 101)'s CLOs is shown in Table 2. Graphical data visualization in a form of hierarchical circular layout [18] (hereafter referred to as a chord diagram) of the CLO relationships was created based on a modified schemaball code [19] using MATLAB program R2018b (MathWorks, Natick, MA, USA). Relationships between the CPLOs and the MSU-LGs (listed in Table 3), and the CLOs and CPLOs were initially established in table formats and later transformed into a graphical format.

Table 2. An excerpt of the School of Packaging Bachelor of Science degree class learning outcomes (CLO) for PKG 101.

PKG 101 (Principles of Packaging) CLO
PKG101-1: Understand the history and evolution of packaging, and its ever-changing role in society.
PKG101-2: Understand the School of Packaging history and opportunities of packaging as a professional career.
PKG101-3: Understand the functions and classifications of packaging.
PKG101-4: Understand the role of packaging in marketing.
PKG101-5: Understand the basic properties of packaging materials and systems, types, structures, pros/cons, performance, attributes, design, decoration, manufacturing, machinery, distribution, cost, testing, environmental, regulatory, and anti-counterfeiting fundamentals.
PKG101-6: Understand various industry packaging segments, their needs and requirements, and their current packaging technologies and challenges.

Table 3. Michigan State University learning goals (MSU-LG) [13].

Analytical Thinking
AT1: Acquires, analyzes, and evaluates information from multiple sources.
AT2: Synthesizes and applies information within and across disciplines.
AT3: Identifies and applies, as appropriate, quantitative methods for defining and responding to problems.
AT4: Identifies the credibility, use and misuse of scientific, humanistic and artistic methods.
Cultural Understanding
CU1: Reflects on experiences with diversity to demonstrate knowledge and sensitivity.
CU2: Demonstrates an awareness of how diversity emerges within and across cultures.
Effective Citizenship
EC1: Understands the structures of local, national, and global governance systems and acts effectively within those structures in both individual and collaborative ways.

EC2: Applies knowledge and abilities to solve societal problems in ethical ways.
Effective Communication
ECO1: Identifies how contexts affect communication strategies and practices.
ECO2: Engages in effective communication practices in a variety of situations with a variety of media.
Integrated Reasoning
IR1: Critically applies liberal arts knowledge in disciplinary contexts and disciplinary knowledge in liberal arts contexts.
IR2: Uses a variety of inquiry strategies incorporating multiple views to make value judgments, solve problems, answer questions, and generate new understanding.

2.2 Learning outcome assessments

Rubrics and questionnaires to evaluate packaging core and elective courses were created and implemented using a learning outcomes measurement tool (VIA by Watermark , Watermark, NY, USA). Data were gathered during fall 2018, spring 2019, and fall 2019 academic semesters.

3. Results and Discussion

3.1. Learning outcome mappings

Figure 4 shows relationships within and between packaging courses as established by the instructors based on the prerequisite linkages [16,17] of the curriculum. Chord diagrams were created based on these relationships as shown in Figure 5 where the lines inside the diagram show the relationships while the numbers after each course in the label represents the CLOs of that course.

The intensity of the color of each node (i.e., where the lines are connected to the CLO) represents how many lines are linked to that node. At these nodes, the brighter the red color indicates the higher the number of links. The graphical mapping aids in visualizing which CLOs have greater coverage in the curriculum, and whether there are gaps that need to be filled.

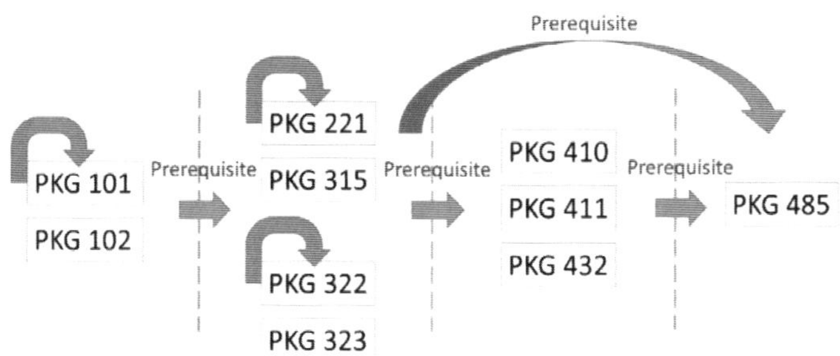

Figure 4 Prerequisite and correlation between CLOs in the core packaging curriculum.

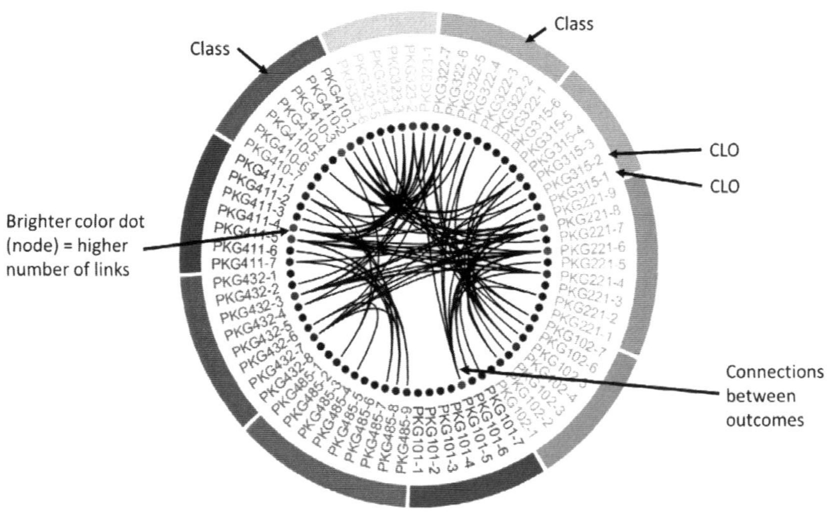

Figure 5 An example of a chord diagram showing relationships among the class learning outcomes (CLO) of packaging (PKG) core courses.

Relationships between the MSU-LGs and the SoP CPLOs were also established by the instructors, as shown in **Figure 6a.** Then, a matrix indicating the mapping of CLOs to CPLOs to MSU-LGs was created. An excerpt of the matrix is shown in **Figure 6b**. The full graphical relationship is shown in **Figure 7** where the thicker lines between CPLOs and packaging classes indicate a higher number of linkages. This data visualization helps to determine if CPLOs or MSU-LGs are linked to some courses (through the CLOs) more than other courses, and the curriculum can be adjusted for a better balance following CLOs all the way to MSU-LGs.

a

Competency-based programmatic learning outcomes (CPLO)	Michigan State University Learning Goals (MSU-LG) →	AT1 Acquires, analyzes, and evaluates information from multiple sources	AT2 Synthesizes and applies information within and across disciplines	AT3 Identifies and applies, as appropriate, quantitative methods for defining and responding to problems	AT4 Identifies the credibility, use and misuse of scientific, humanistic and artistic methods	CU1 Reflects on experiences with diversity to demonstrate knowledge and sensitivity	CU2 Demonstrates an awareness of how diversity emerges within and across cultures	EC1 Understands the structures of local, national, and global governance systems and acts effectively within those structures in both individual and collaborative ways	EC2 Applies knowledge and abilities to solve societal problems in ethical ways	ECO1 Identifies how contexts affect communication strategies and practices	ECO2 Engages in effective communication practices in a variety of situations with a variety of media	IR1 Critically applies liberal arts knowledge in disciplinary contexts and disciplinary knowledge in liberal arts contexts	IR2 Uses a variety of inquiry strategies incorporating multiple views to make value judgments, solve problems, answer questions, and generate new understanding
CPLO-1	Evaluate packaging systems	✓	✓	✓									✓
CPLO-2	Analyze tradeoffs in packaging systems	✓	✓	✓					✓				✓
CPLO-3	Design innovative and sustainable packaging systems	✓	✓	✓								✓	✓
CPLO-4	Manage projects in diverse teams	✓	✓	✓	✓	✓	✓			✓			
CPLO-5	Communicate effectively considering diverse audiences					✓	✓			✓	✓	✓	✓
CPLO-6	Conduct oneself in a professional and ethical manner				✓	✓	✓	✓	✓				

b

		Michigan State University Learning Goals (MSU-LG)					
		AT1, 2, 3; IR2	AT1, 2, 3; IR2; EC2	AT1, 2, 3; IR1, 2	AT1, 2, 3, 4; CU1, 2; ECO1	ECO1, 2; IR1, 2; CU1, 2	AT4; EC1 ,2; CU1, 2
		Competency-based programmatic learning outcomes (CPLO)					
Class-CLO	Description	CPLO-1	CPLO-2	CPLO-3	CPLO-4	CPLO-5	CPLO-6
PKG 101-1	Understand the history and evolution of packaging, and its ever-changing role in society						
PKG 101-2	Understand the School of Packaging history and opportunities of packaging as a professional career						
PKG 101-3	Understand the functions and classifications of packaging	✓	✓				
PKG 101-4	Understand the role of packaging in marketing	✓	✓				
PKG 101-5	Understand the basic properties of packaging materials and systems, types, structures, pros/cons, performance, attributes, design, decoration, manufacturing, machinery, distribution, cost, testing, environmental, regulatory, and anti-counterfeiting fundamentals	✓		✓			
PKG 101-6	Understand various industry packaging segments, their needs and requirements, and their current packaging technologies and challenges		✓				

***Figure 6** a) A matrix mapping the School of Packaging competency-based programmatic learning outcomes (CPLO) to Michigan State University learning goals (MSU-LG) and b) An excerpt of a matrix mapping packaging course learning outcomes (CLO) to CPLO to MSU-LG.*

3.2 Learning outcome assessments

Figure 8 and **Figure 9** show the assessment for fall 2018, spring 2019, and fall 2019 semesters of CPLO-1 to CPLO-6 for the packaging core courses and the MSU-LGs, respectively. The courses utilizing the VIA software and collecting assessment outcomes related to the CLOs, CPLOs and MSU-LGs were ramped between fall 2018 and fall 2019; hence, the total number of reported assessments by semester is not the same. The results were normalized as percentage as shown in the x-axis of the figures. The CPLO assessment in Figure 8 shows that more than 95% of the students met all the CPLOs in fall 2019. The "met" criteria were allocated to 70% passing of the outcomes. The MSU-LG assessment in Figure 9 shows that all MSU-LGs except the EC2 achieved a 90% met status in fall 2019. The results imply the importance of mapping across the curriculum and not only in selected courses since a robust measurement system allows for determining learning gaps in early courses.

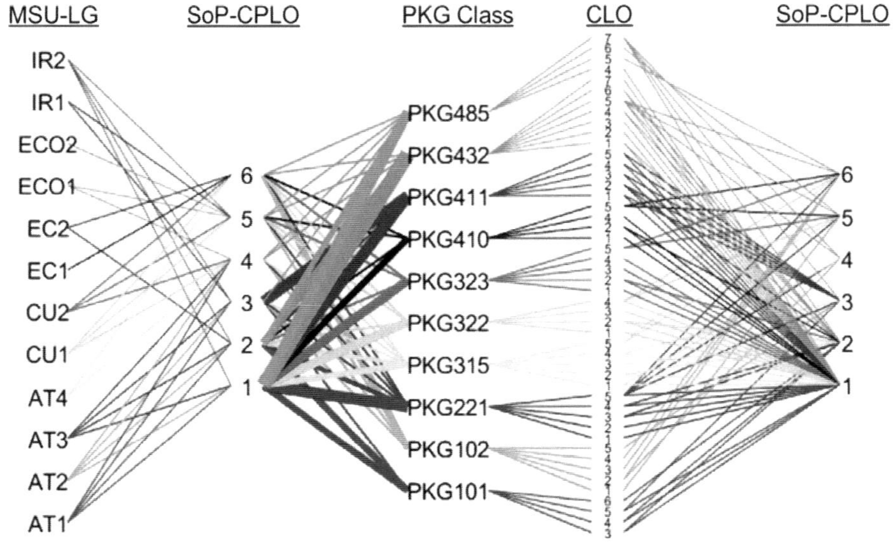

Figure 7 *A graphical representation of relationships between packaging (PKG) course learning outcomes (CLO), the School of Packaging (SoP) competency-based programmatic learning outcomes (CPLO), and Michigan State University learning goals (MSU-LG).*

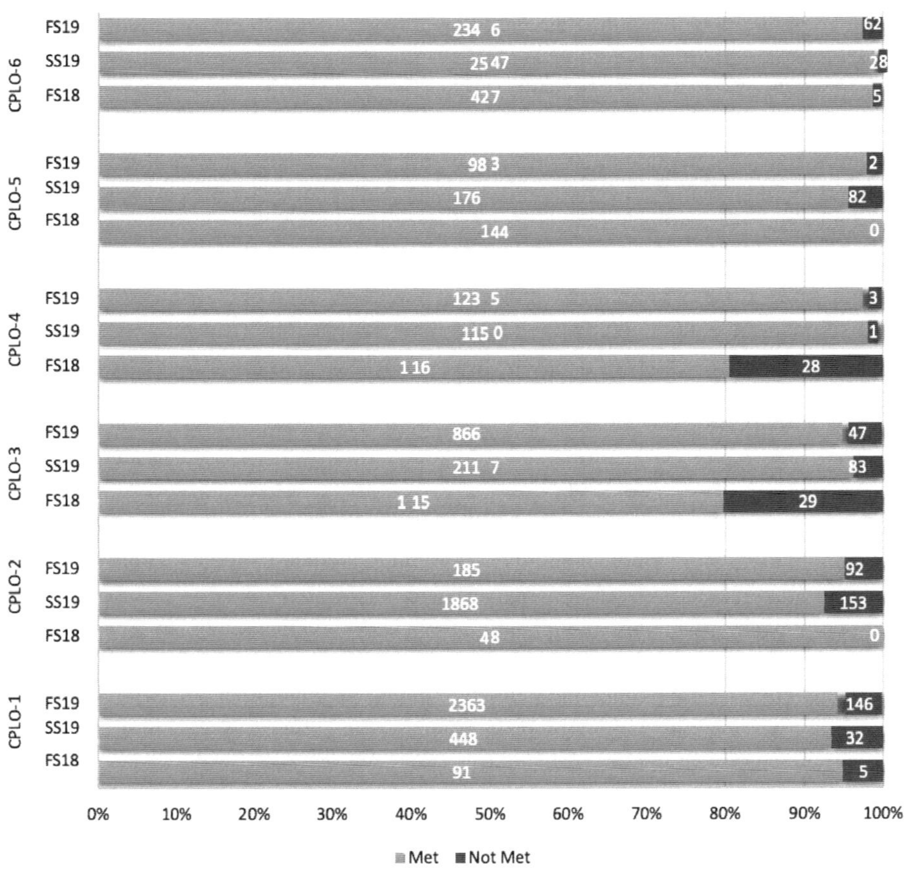

Figure 8 *Competency-based programmatic learning outcomes (CPLO) assessment for fall 2018 (FS18), spring 2019 (SS19), and fall 2019 (FS19). The number inside the bars indicate the number of times that the developed tools were assessed through the curriculum.*

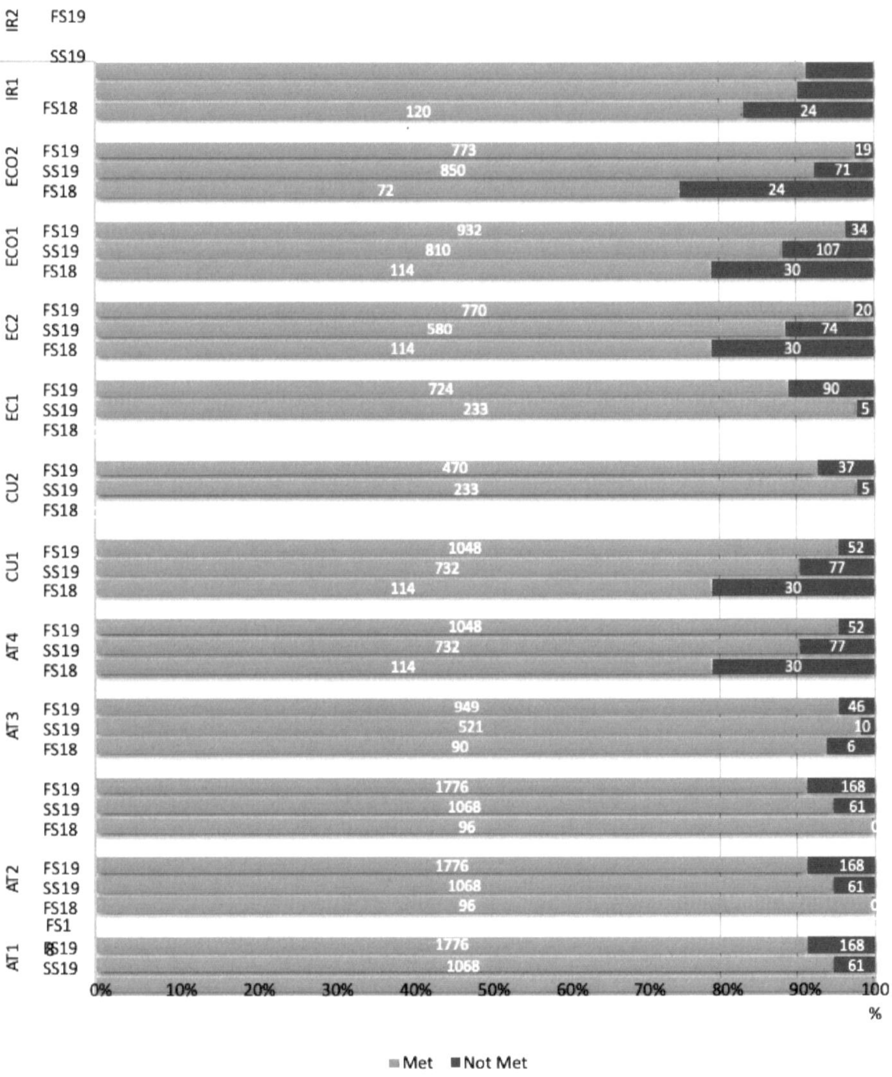

Figure 9 *Michigan State University learning goals (MSU-LG) assessment for fall 2018 (FS18), spring 2019 (SS19), and fall 2019 (FS19). The number inside the bars indicate the number of times that the developed tools were assessed through the curriculum.*

4. Conclusion

The curriculum assessment for any academic program is a journey and requires continuous evaluation and adjustment so that it keeps relevant and up to date. We have shown the SoP initial steps on this journey and a methodology for assessing and mapping CLOs to CPLOs to MSU- LGs. Collection of data in this fashion offers the promise of evaluating learning at several levels. It can potentially be used: a) at the student level to assess learning and growth over time; b) at the classroom level to assess how pedagogical changes (over time) impact student learning; and c) at the program level to assess how well the curriculum is meeting stakeholder demands and disciplinary requirements for student learning. Ultimately, this type of data can be used to assess and improve the curriculum. Although we have not yet measured the effectiveness of changes on the student experience, the process of identifying outcomes and mapping the curriculum has been fruitful in revealing gaps that we can effectively bridge.

5. References

[1] School of Packaging. Academic Program Review School of Packaging - Michigan State University Spring 2020.

[2] Michigan State University. Michigan State University Office of the Registrar Undergraduate Degree - Packaging. https://reg.msu.edu/academicprograms/ProgramDetail.aspx?Program=0405 (Accessed May 12, 2020).

[3] Spencer D, Riddle M, Knewstubb B. Curriculum mapping to embed graduate capabilities. High Educ Res Dev. 2012;31(2):217-231. doi:10.1080/07294360.2011.554387

[4] Herrmann T, Leggett T. Curriculum mapping: Aligning content and design. Radiol Technol. 2019;90(5):530-533.

[5] Spady WG. Organizing for Results: The Basis of Authentic Restructuring and Reform. Educ Leadersh. 1988;46(2):4-8.

[6] Harden RM. AMEE Guide No. 14: Outcome-based education: Part 1-An introduction to outcome-based education. Med Teach. 1999;21(1):7-14. doi:10.1080/01421599979969

[7] Uchiyama KP, Radin JL. Curriculum mapping in higher education: A vehicle for collaboration. Innov High Educ. 2009;33(4):271-280. doi:10.1007/s10755-008-9078-8

[8] Harden RM. AMEE Guide No. 21: Curriculum mapping: a tool for transparent and authentic teaching and learning. Med Teach. 2001;23(2):123-137. doi:10.1080/01421590120036547

[9] Wang C-L. Mapping or tracing? Rethinking curriculum mapping in higher education. Stud High Educ. 2015;40(9):1550-1559. doi:10.1080/03075079.2014.899343

[10] Harden RM. Learning outcomes and instructional objectives: Is there a difference? Med Teach. 2002;24(2):151-155. doi:10.1080/0142159022020687

[11] McNeir G. Outcomes-based education. Res Roundup. 1993;10(1):2-5.

[12] Centre for Teaching Support & Innovation University of Toronto. Developing Learning Outcomes. https://teaching.utoronto.ca/teaching-support/course-design/developing-learning-outcomes/ (Accessed March 20, 2020).

[13] Michigan State University. Undergraduate Learning Goals - Undergraduate Education. https://undergrad.msu.edu/programs/learninggoals (Accessed February 24, 2020).

[14] Perlin M. Curriculum Mapping for Program Evaluation and CAHME Accreditation. J Health Adm Educ. 2011;28(1):33-53.

[15] Kelley KA, McAuley JW, Wallace LJ, Frank SG. Curricular Mapping: Process and Product. Am J Pharm Educ. 2008;72(5):100. doi:10.5688/aj7205100

[16] Seering J, Willcox K, Huang L. Mapping outcomes in an undergraduate aerospace engineering program. ASEE Annu Conf Expo Conf Proc. 2015;122nd ASEE(122nd ASEE Annual Conference and Exposition: Making Value for Society):1-7. doi:10.18260/p.24467

[17] Willcox KE, Huang L. Network models for mapping educational data. Des Sci. 2017;3(e18):1-23. doi:10.1017/dsj.2017.18

[18] Holten D. Hierarchical Edge Bundles: Visualization of Adjacency Relations in Hierarchical Data. IEEE Trans Vis Comput Graph. 2006;12(5):741-748. doi:10.1109/TVCG.2006.147

[19] Komarov O. File Exchange Okomarov/schemaball. https://www.mathworks.com/matlabcentral/fileexchange/42279-okomarov-schemaball (Accessed September 14, 2018).

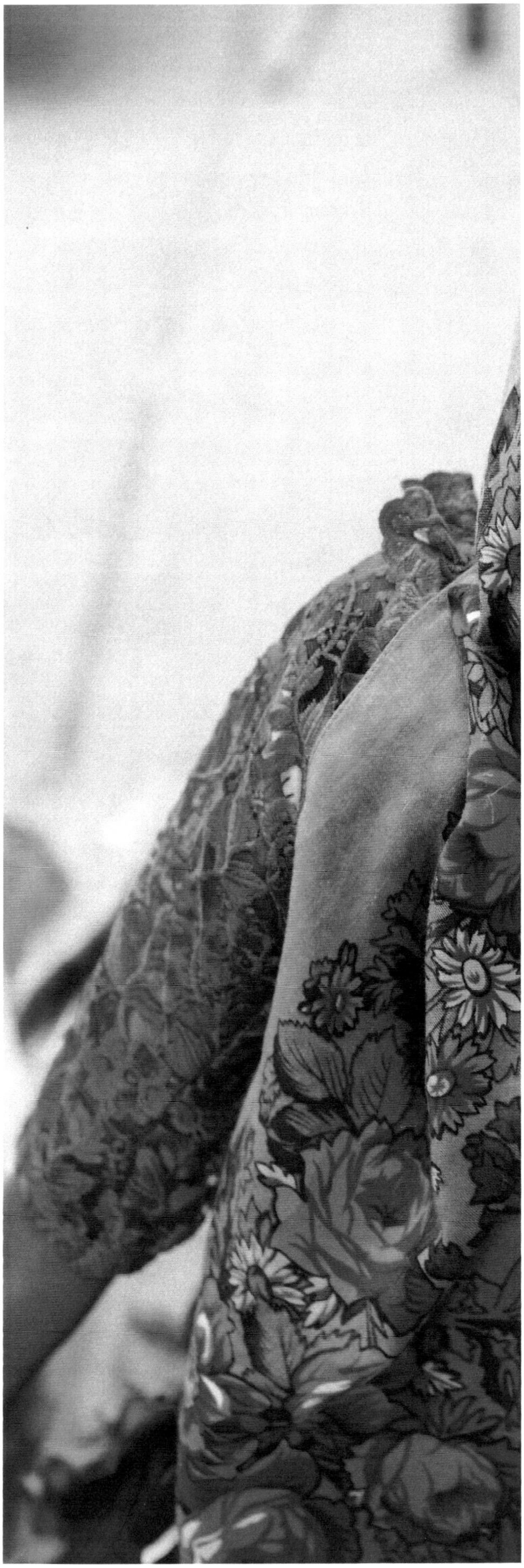

CHAPTER XII
Posters

Title:
Mujer en mercado de Tlacolula
(Woman at Tlacolula's market)

Author:
Rolando Angulo

Location:
Oaxaca, OAXACA

Description:
Color is an intrinsic aspect of Mexican culture. We find it manifesting itself in our gastronomy, our biodiversity and even on our outfits. This woman's shawl can't help but make anyone that watches it feel happy and joyous, thanks to the rich and vibrant colors and organic patterns.

IAPRI MEXICO 2020
WORLD PACKAGING CONFERENCE

Study and characterization of palletizing films used in the field of freight transport

Elora Leguebe[1,2,3], Marie Le Baillif[2,3], Victor Huart[1], Jean-Baptiste Nolot[3], Nicolas Krajka[1], Jérôme Pellot[1], Damien Erre[2,3]

1 METROPACK , 2 ITheMM/Université de Reims Champagne-Ardenne, 3 ESIREIMS-ESIEC, France

1. Introduction

The present study focused on the understanding of wrapping material properties during transportation constraints.

The most commonly used wrapping material is the linear low density polyethylene (LLDPE), either manually or through mechanical equipment. Both types of films were investigated.

Mechanical properties of the materials were measured in order to understand their behaviors during wrapping applications, and to check their possible anisotropy.

2. Preparation of specimens

Specimens of LLDPE films were prepared according IS 14995 standard.

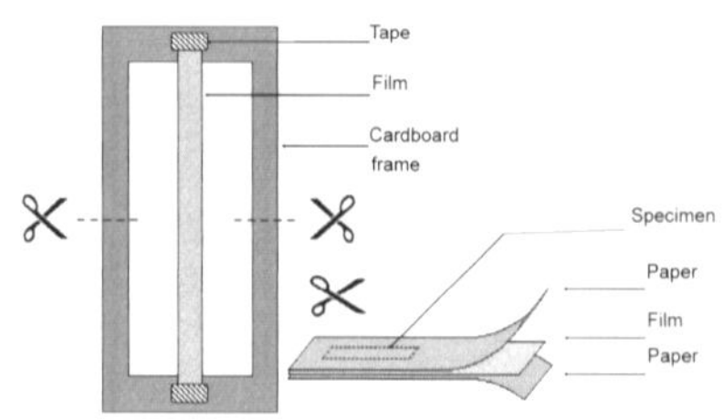

Figure 1: Assembly and cutting of test specimens

- No catching during cutting
- Easy manipulation of specimen
- No stress prior testing

2. Tensile Properties

MTS tensile machine according ASTM D882 standard.

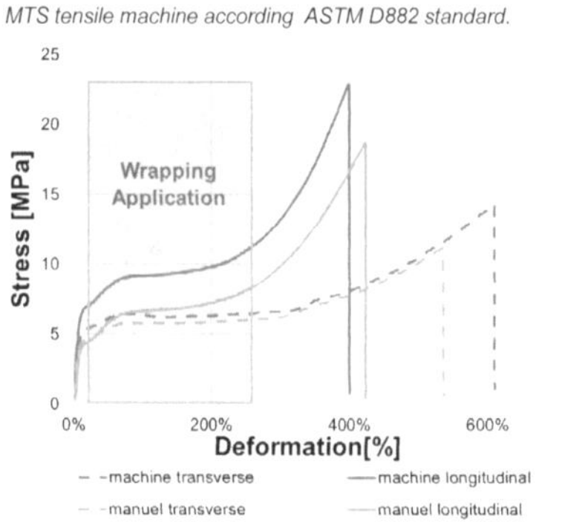

Figure 2: Traction curve of two types of stretch film in both directions

- Both materials showed anisotropic properties.
- No significant difference between machine and manual films.
- Longitudinal tensile strength and modulus were higher than the transverse ones, but the elongation at break was lower for the longitudinal direction.

3. Stress Relaxation

MTS tensile equipment according to ASTM D882.

Effect of strain level

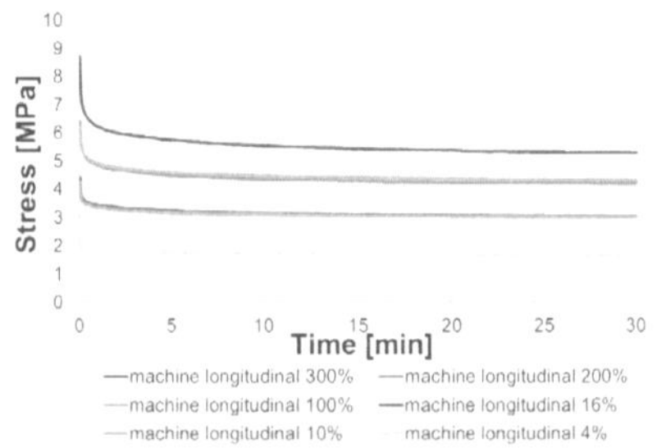

Figure 3: Relaxation test of one film for different deformations

- Measurements showed expected tendencies.
- After 15 minutes, residual stresses were achieved, even for high strain levels.
- Residual stresses increased with increased strain levels as expected.

Effect of film application system

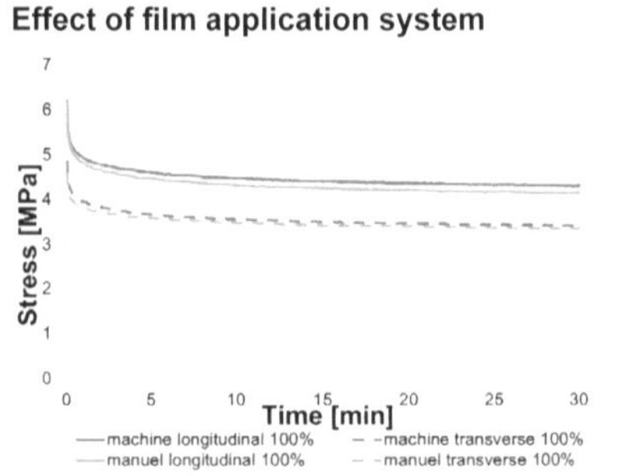

Figure 4: Relaxation test of different films for one deformation

- No significant difference between machine and manual films.

Residual stresses compared with tensile properties

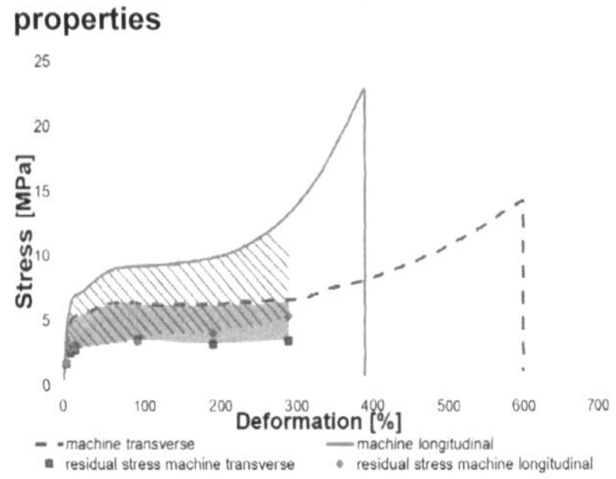

Figure 5: Points of residual strain with traction curve

- Only about half of the initial stress remain after relaxation.
- Load stability during transportation was affected by relaxation

4. Future Research

Initial straining + Dynamic stress

Material behaviors
Tearing
Load stability

? ?

- Combine pre-straining and dynamic testing.
- Use transport frequencies
- Make library of film defects

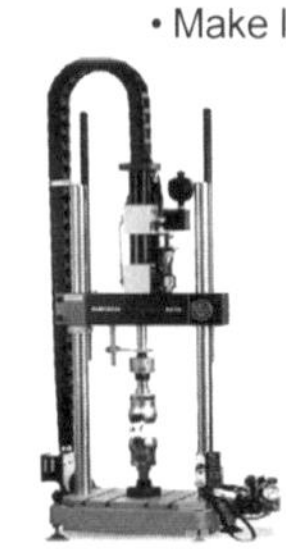

Figure 6: INSTRON 8872 servo-hydraulic machine

Figure 7: Pictures of defects on wrapping pallets

5. Conclusion

- Mechanical properties of machine and manual wrapping films were measured.
- Both films showed similar and anisotropic properties.
- Residual stress during relaxation was achieved after 15 minutes only.
- Residual stress was depending on film direction and pre-straining level.
- Relaxation will strongly affect the load stability.
- Dynamic testing must be performed to understand real transportation stresses.

6. References

- G. M. Mcnally and al - The Effect of Polymer Properties on the Mechanical Behavior and Morphological Characteristics of Cast Polyethylene Film for Stretch and Cling Film Applications - Journal of Plastic Film and Sheeting, 2005, 21.
- J. V. Bisha, "Correlation of the Elastic Properties of Stretch Film on Unit Load Containment", Ph.D. thesis, Virginia Polytechnic Institute and State University, 2012.
- Klein, Daniel & Stommel, Markus & Zimmer, Johannes, "Influence of the stretch wrapping process on the mechanical behavior of a stretch film", AIP Conference Proceedings, 2018.
- Park, Jonghun & Horvath, Laszlo & White, Marshall & Araman, Philip & Bush, Robert, "The influence of stretch wrap containment force on load bridging in unit loads", Packaging Technology and Science, 2018.

iapri

IAPRI MEXICO 2020
WORLD PACKAGING CONFERENCE

UDEM

Kurtosis response spectrum analysis of Gaussian random vibration derived from vehicle vibration

Akira Hosoyama, Kazuki Tsuda, Shogo Horiguchi

Osaka Research Institute of Industrial Science and Technology, Japan

1. Introduction

Packaging vibration tests are conducted to evaluate the durability of packaged products against vibrations by simulating the vibration environment during actual transportation. To this end, currently, the test standards recommend the use of a random vibration test which is performed considering a single power spectral density. Recently, the ISO 4180 and ASTM D 4169 standards were revised to specify a method involving the conduction of sequential tests under multiple power spectral densities. Although the revised test standard specifies a method involving sequential tests, it is assumed that the vibrations having the same power spectral density (PSD) and probability density function (PDF) are equivalent. In other words, it is assumed that the actual-transport-derived vibrations are equivalent to those generated using the vibration controller. Nevertheless, the equivalence of the vibrations with the same PSD and PDF has not been conclusively established yet.

2. Research Goal

The purpose of this study was to verify the equivalence of vibrations with the same PSD and PDF, derived during actual transport and by using a vibration controller. In particular, a kurtosis response spectrum analysis was performed to determine the response kurtosis for a single degree of freedom (SDOF) system in the natural frequency range of interest. Moreover, the difference between the two types of derived vibrations was clarified.

3. Research Method

The vertical acceleration occurring on the vehicle bed of a small van (Daihatsu HIJET) traveling on a local road in Japan was measured. The acceleration RMS was calculated in intervals of one second and decomposed into several Gaussian random vibrations. A specific decomposed Gaussian random vibration was used as the actual-transport-derived Gaussian random vibration. The vibrations corresponding to the vibration controller were generated to have the same PSD as that of the transport-derived Gaussian random vibration, similar to the process followed in current testing approaches. The kurtosis response spectrum analysis was performed for both the types of vibrations, and the difference between the two vibrations was examined.

4. Results and Conclusions

Input

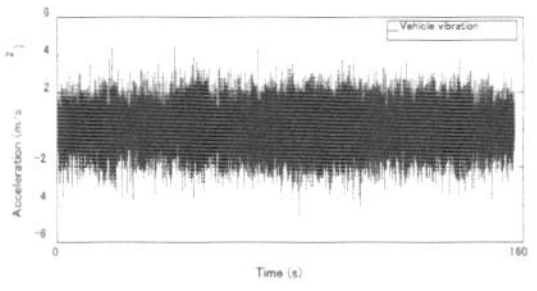

Gaussian vibrations derived using an actual vehicle

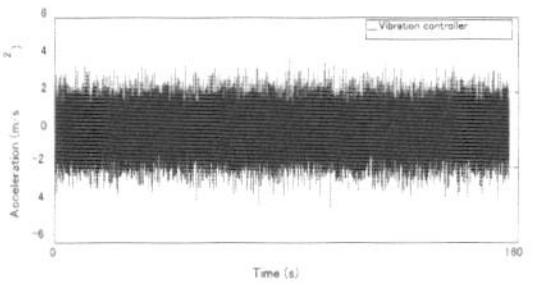

Gaussian vibrations derived using vibration controller

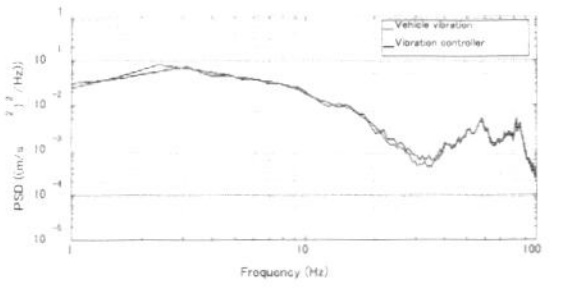

PSDs of Gaussian vibrations derived using an actual vehicle and vibration controller

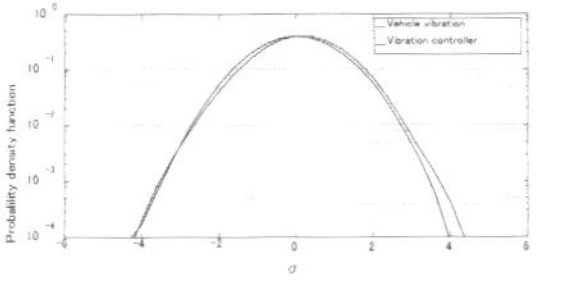

PDFs of Gaussian vibrations derived using an actual vehicle and vibration controller

Kurtosis response spectrum analysis

14 Hz

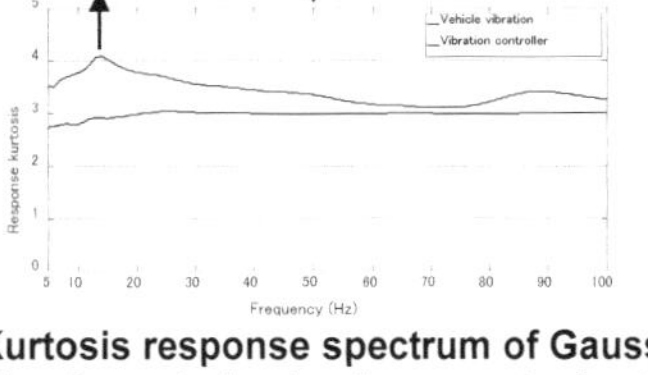

Kurtosis response spectrum of Gaussian vibrations derived using an actual vehicle and vibration controller

f = 14Hz
ζ = 0.15

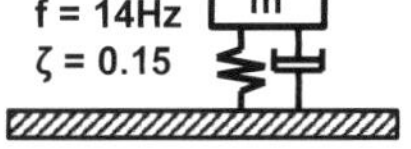

The PDF of the SDOF response to the vibration-controller-derived vibration remains Gaussian, whereas that of the SDOF response to the actual-transport-derived vibration changes from Gaussian to non-Gaussian.

Even for the vibrations with the same PSD and PDF, the PDF of the SDOF response may be different.

Therefore, to accurately reflect the vibrations, it is necessary to consider not only the PSD and PDF, but also the PDF of the SDOF response.

SDOF Response

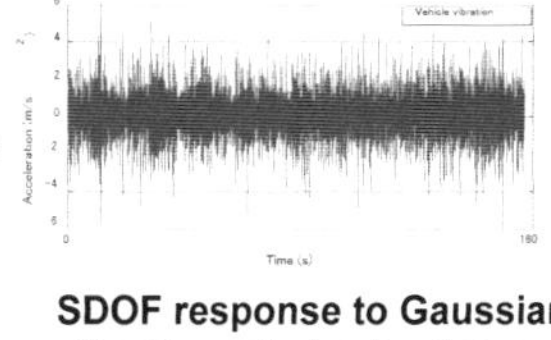

SDOF response to Gaussian vibrations derived using an actual vehicle

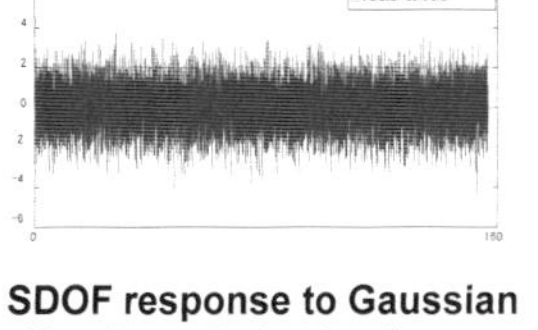

SDOF response to Gaussian vibrations derived using vibration controller

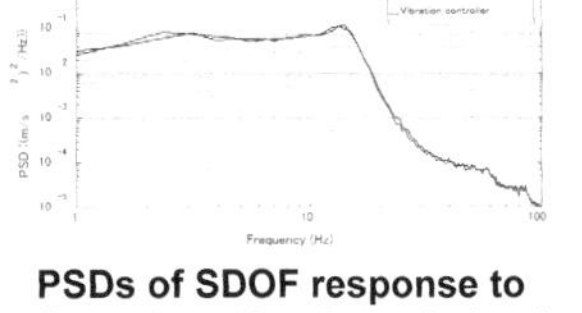

PSDs of SDOF response to Gaussian vibrations derived using an actual vehicle and vibration controller

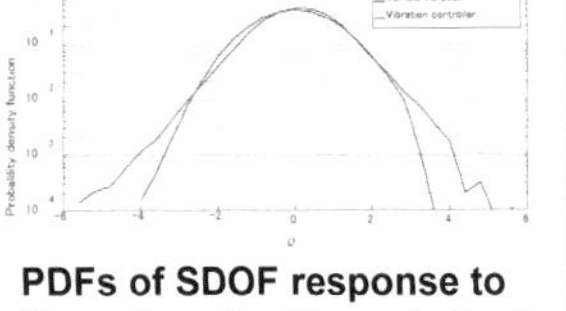

PDFs of SDOF response to Gaussian vibrations derived using an actual vehicle and vibration controller

5. Future Research

The current vibration controller cannot generate random vibrations, considering the non-Gaussian nature of the response. In future work, it is desirable to develop a method to generate random vibrations considering the non-Gaussian nature of the response.

iapri

Inverse Method for Estimating Diffusion Coefficient of Oxygen in Different Polymeric Packaging Materials

IAPRI MEXICO 2020
WORLD PACKAGING CONFERENCE

UDEM

Anbuhkani (Connie) Muniandy[1], Ferhan Ozadali[1,2], Patnarin Benyathiar[3], Dharmendra Mishra[1]

[1]Department of Food Science, Purdue University, West Lafayette, IN | [2]Mead Johnson Nutrition, Reckitt Benckiser Health, Evansville, IN | [3]Islander Consulting and Engineering, West Lafayette IN

PURDUE UNIVERSITY

1. Abstract

Oxygen diffusion across polymeric packages is an important parameter needed for different research and commercial applications. This is particularly important for the food industry because excessive diffusion of oxygen can be detrimental to the quality of food. The reaction of oxygen with food can change the sensory quality and degrade the nutrients present in the food. Hence, understanding diffusion of oxygen under various circumstance is crucial. **The aim of this study was to study the diffusion coefficient of oxygen in High Impact Polystyrene (HIPS) and High-Density Polyethylene (HDPE) packaging materials under heat and pressure.** Both HIPS and HDPE containers were filled with water and flushed with nitrogen to keep oxygen level below 2%. Samples were kept at three different conditions, 1) room temperature, 2) 40°C, and 3) at 40°C under oxygen pressure. The changes in the headspace oxygen over time was monitored using OxySense 520i. The diffusion coefficient was estimated based on Fick's 2nd Law using inverse problems approach. After 20 day, the headspace oxygen level in samples kept at room condition did not change. For HIPS, the headspace oxygen level reached 2.77% at 40°C and 14.47 % at 40°C at 5 psig pressure in 20 days. Similarly, in HPDE the headspace level was at 3.2 % and 12.57 % at 40°C in 20 days and 40 °C with 20 psig pressure in 15 days, respectively. The diffusion coefficient for HIPS with and without pressure at 40°C is 1.01 x10-14 m^2/s and 6.56 x10-15 m^2/s, respectively. For HDPE the diffusion coefficient was slightly higher, 1.26 x10-13 m^2/s and 8.46 x10-14 m^2/s for with and without pressure, respectively. The use of higher temperature coupled with pressure increased the diffusivity of oxygen through polymeric packaging materials. The results are helpful for food industry in determining product shelf life at different distribution and storage conditions.

2 . Introduction

Migration of oxygen in food packaging

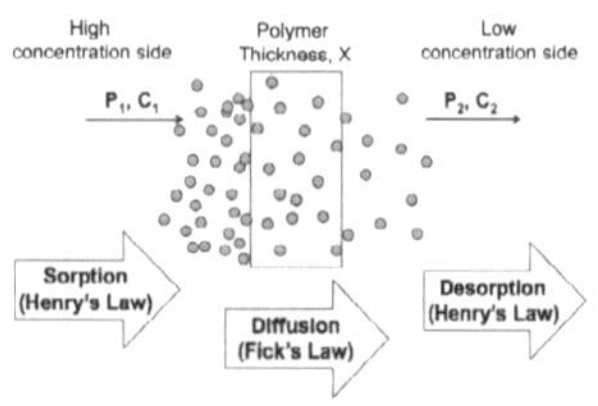

- Governed by Fick's 2nd Law of Diffusion

$$\frac{\partial C_p}{\partial t} = D\frac{\partial^2 C_p}{\partial x^2}$$

C_p Concentration at t in the direction x
t time
D diffusion coefficient

3. Methods

Samples

- High-density polyethylene (HDPE)
- High impact polystyrene (HIPS)

Sample preparation

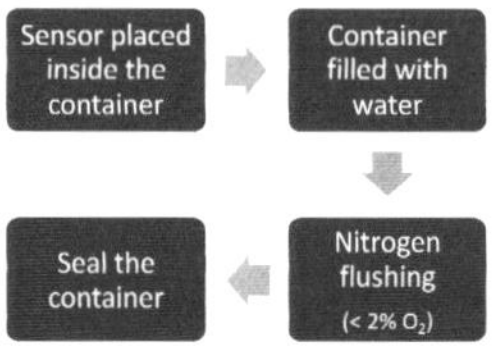

3. Methods

Treatment conditions

- 40 °C
- 40 °C + oxygen pressure

Headspace oxygen measurment

- OxySense 520i was used to monitor oxygen level for 20 days

Simulation of oxygen transfer

- COMSOL, finite element software, was used to predict the oxygen transfer by solving Fick's 2nd law of diffusion numerically based on a 2D model
- Boundary conditions: The concentration at the surface of the membrane (x =0) remains constant at 51.92 (mol/m^3)
- Initial conditions: Concentration of oxygen inside the packaging is uniformly distributed < 2% oxygen

Estimation of D using Inverse Problems

- Scaled Sensitivity Coefficient (SSC)
  - Magnitude change of the response variable due to changes in the parameter
  - Must be large, uncorrelated with other parameters and sum of SSC is not zero

$$X_i' = \beta_i \frac{\partial \eta}{\partial \beta_i}$$

- Sequential estimation
  - Matrix inversion lemma based on Gauss minimization method with prior information

$$S = [Y - \hat{Y}(\beta)]' W [Y - \hat{Y}(\beta)] + [\mu - \beta]' U [\mu - \beta]$$

Y Experimental response variable
$\hat{Y}$ Predicted response variable
μ Prior information
β Parameter vector
W Inverse covariance matrix of errors
U Inverse covariance matrix of parameters

4. Results & Discussion

Estimation of diffusion coefficient, D

Example of inverse problems plot

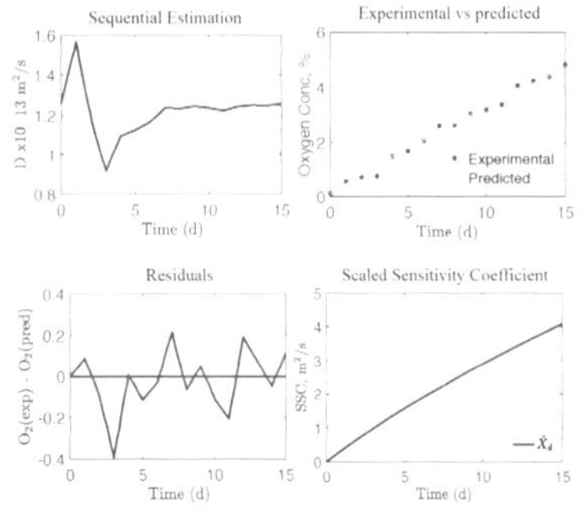

Figure 1: Inverse problems plot; Sequential estimation of D, experimental vs predicted oxygen concentration, residual analysis and scaled sensitiviy coefficient

4. Results & Discussion

Accumulation of headspace oxygen

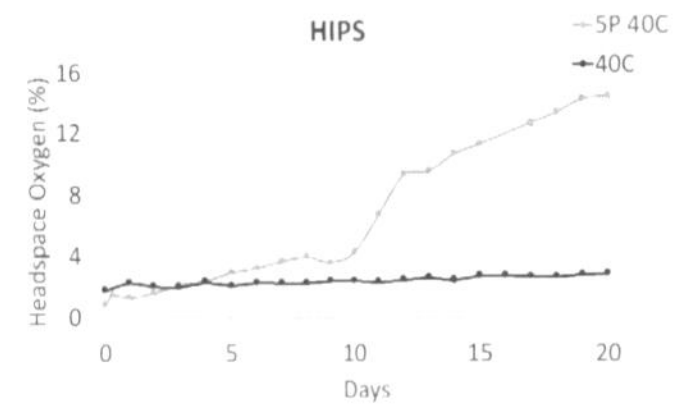

Figure 2: Increase in headsapce oxygen in HIPS container

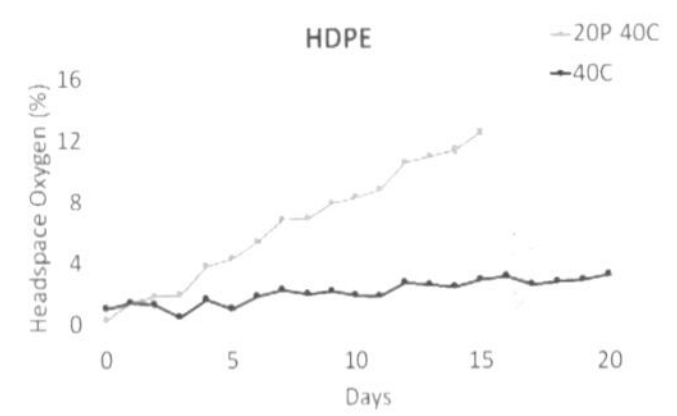

Figure 3: Increase in headsapce oxygen in HDPE container

- For both HDPE and HIPS, oxygen transfer to the packaging was rapid when the samples were placed under oxygen pressure
- Samples kept at ambient pressure did not show much increase in oxygen over time
- Addition of oxygen pressure increased the rate of oxygen transfer through polymeric packaging

Estimation of diffusion coefficent, D

Sample	O_2 Pressure (psig)	D (m^2/s)	95% CI	RSME
HDPE	20	1.26×10^{-13}	$(1.21,1.29) \times 10^{-13}$	0.158
	-	8.46×10^{-14}	$(7.34,9.59) \times 10^{-14}$	0.156
HIPS	5	1.01×10^{-14}	$(0.98, 1.05) \times 10^{-14}$	0.38
	-	6.56×10^{-15}	$(5.88,7.24) \times 10^{-15}$	0.094

- When oxygen pressure is applied, the value of D increased for both HDPE and HIPS containers
- Estimation of D using inverse problem was successful given the tight 95% confidence interval and low RSME values

5. Conclusion

- The use of high temperature coupled with oxygen pressure increased the diffusivity of oxygen through polymeric packaging
- Inverse probles approach was used to determine the diffusion coefficient
- The study is beneficial for the food industry to select packaging materials with optimal barrier properties

6. Reference

1. Beck, J. V., & Arnold, K. J. (1977). Parameter Estimation in Engineering and Science. New York: John Wiley & Sons.

2. Samsudin, H., Auras, R., Mishra, D., Dolan, K., Burgess, G., Rubino, M., ... Soto-Valdez, H. (2018). Migration of antioxidants from polylactic acid films: A parameter estimation approach and an overview of the current mass transfer models. Food Research International, 103, 515-528. doi:https://doi.org/10.1016/j.foodres.2017.09.021

iapri

Development of peach waste-filled polyolefin bio-composite with maleic anhydride coupling agent.

IAPRI MEXICO 2020 WORLD PACKAGING CONFERENCE

UDEM

Caralyn Wong1, Stephanie Jung1, Ajay Kathuria2, Joongmin Shin2

1. Food Science and Nutrition, California Polytechnic State University, USA
2. Industrial Technology and Packaging, USA

1,2 CAL POLY
College of Agriculture, Food & Environmental Sciences

1. Introduction

- US produces roughly 103, 515 tons of peach waste annually.
- Peach waste is primarily landfilled, which generally leads to landfill gas and leachate production with the risk of contaminating ground water [1].
- Agro-waste contains cellulose and lignin, which can be utilized as a filler in plastic packaging to reduce carbon footprints and material cost.
- Drupe seeds contain nearly twice as much lignin as wood and possess high mechanical properties, which opens opportunities for drupes in materials research [2].

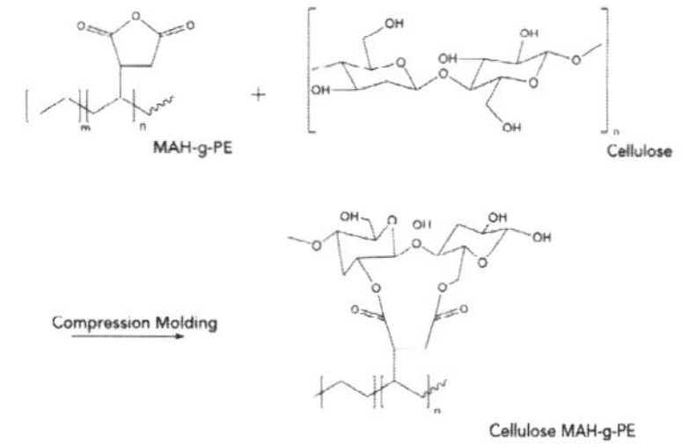

Figure 1: Hypothesized mechanism for MAH-g-PE and cellulose bond

2 . Objectives

- To develop peach flour (PF) -filled biocomposites with an HDPE matrix using MAH as a coupling agent resulting in a biocomposite with maximum tensile strength.
- To investigate the biocomposites' physico-mechanical, thermal, and water resistance properties.

3. Methods

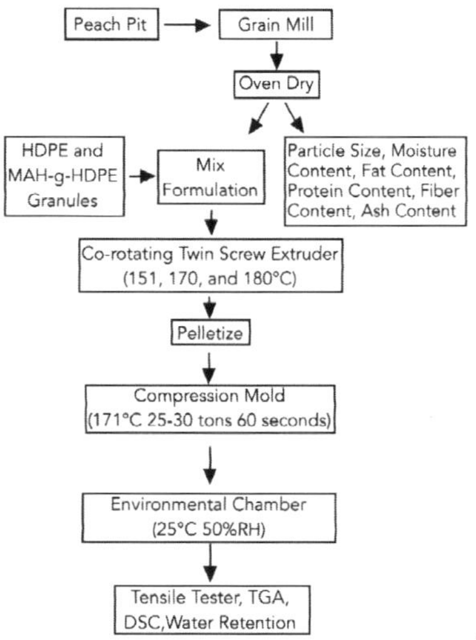

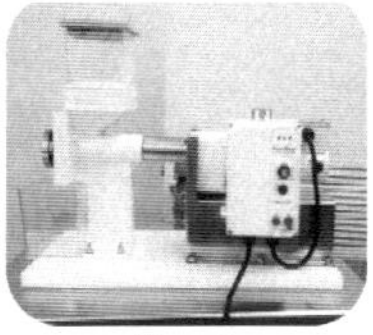

Figure 2: Grain mill

Figure 3: Molten biocomposite

Figure 4: Tensile testing sample

Figure 5: DSC Instrument

Figure 6: TGA Instrument

Mechanical Properties

Formulation	Tensile Stress (MPa)	Extension at Break (mm)	Young's Modulus (MPa)
PE 0	14.9^{A}	15.5^{A}	1403.1^{A}
PE 2.5	16.2^{A}	8.6^{AB}	1180.3^{A}
PE 5	12.0^{A}	8.7^{AB}	836.0^{A}
PE 10	14.7^{A}	4.1^{AB}	1092.8^{A}

Table 1: Mechanical properties of PF-HDPE biocomposites

DSC

Formulation	T_c	Enthalpy of cold crystallization (j/g)	T_m	%Crystallinity
PE 0	118.7	210.7	133.9	77.0%
PE 2.5	118.6	196.5	134.4	73.4%
PE 5	119.8	186.0	133.4	67.4%
PE 10	118.3	148.4	134.6	53.2%

Table 2: Thermal properties of PF-HDPE biocomposites

TGA

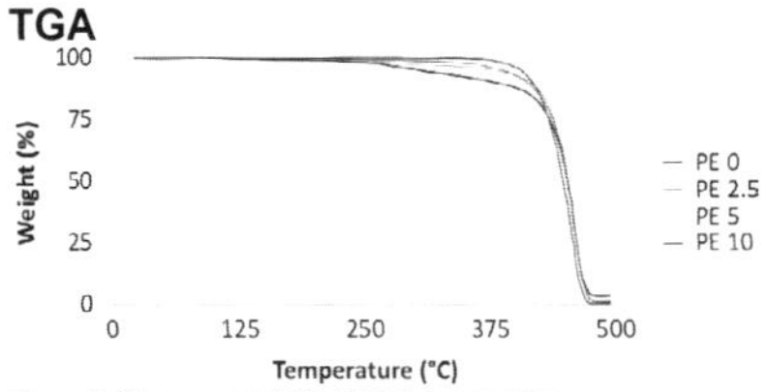

Figure 7: Thermogram of PF-HDPE biocomposites

Water absorption

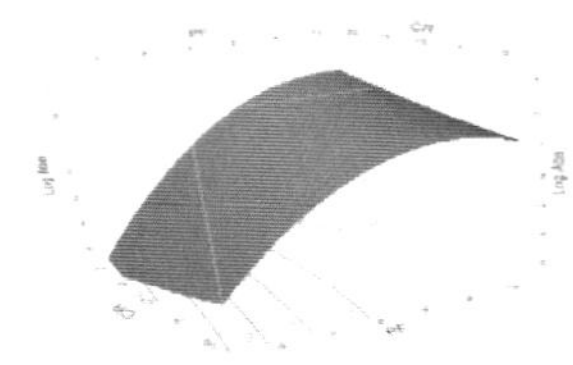

Figure 8: Response surface profile of water absorption for PF-HDPE biocomposites

5. Results and Discussion

Thermal Stability

- PF-HDPE biocomposites displayed no change compared to their control, except for PE5, which may be attributed to sample variability.
- PF addition immediately decreased biocomposite crystallinity as fibers may act as an obstacle for crystal formation as it limits polymer chain movement [3]
- PF had no influence on Tc , Tm, and Td suggesting there was negligibly weak interaction between filler and matrix.

Mechanical Properties

- PF addition decreased tensile strength, extension at break, and young's modulus.
- Poor adhesion between filler and polymer will concentrate stress and accelerate sample break [4]
- Rigid particles and coupling agents ultimately decrease polymer plasticity to decrease the extension at break.
- Decrease in Young's modulus may be due to the weak interactions between polymer and fiber.

Water Absorption

- Absorption increased with fiber loading.
- An increased amount of hydrophilic cellulose increases the interfacial area for absorption.

6. Conclusion

The addition of PF into an HDPE matrix is best with a 2.5% fiber loading. A 2.5% PF composite could divert approximately 2,500 tons of organic waste from landfill and used for non-structural commodities such as packaging, construction, and automotive parts.

7. References

[1] Kaur G et al. (2019) Bioresour Technol 289:121698.
[2] Mendu V et al. (2011) Biotechnol Biofuels 4:43.
[3] Perinović S et al. (2010) Thermochim Acta 510:97–102.
[4] Essabir H et al. (2014) J Biobased Mater Bioenergy 8:344–351.

iapri

IAPRI MEXICO 2020
WORLD PACKAGING CONFERENCE

UDEM

Packaging and its impacts on the value chain towards circular models

Irma Elizabeth Peñúñuri García

Universidad de Monterrey, Universitat Politècnica de València.

1. Research Goals

This article presents a study of topics and concepts related to the Product Value Chain (PVC) with a focus on packaging and its relevance in circular economy models. This exploratory research generates a preamble of existing concepts and methodologies for the development of products with a life cycle approach, comparing systemic methodologies in relation to packaging-product development and circular strategies of packaging.

2 . Objectives

- Analyze the concepts related to packaging from an integral approach to circular economy considering stakeholders.
- Compare packaging development methodologies and sustainability assessment in the PVC and life cycle.

3. Materials and Methods

The purpose of this exploratory and descriptive research is to generate the preamble for the comparison of concepts, tools and methodologies related to the circular economy (CE), as well as the impact of packaging on the PVC. This comparative diagnosis of tools for the development of product-packaging, will allow to move towards the development of a proposal for future application and validation.

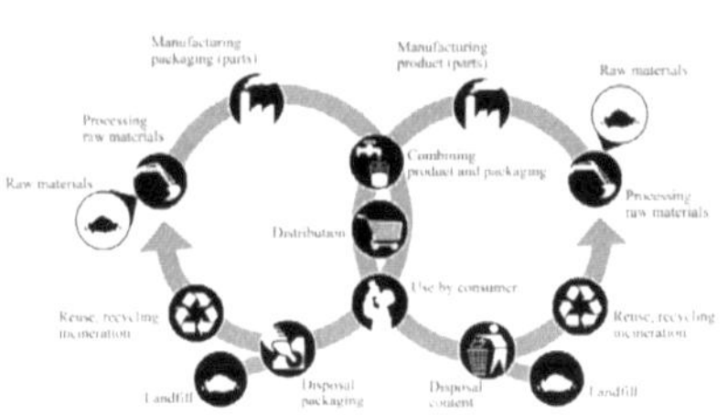

Figure 1: Global product/packaging life cycle. Luttinkhuis, E., et al. 2013

4. Results and Discussion

Packaging is a critial element when conducting Life Cycle Assessment (LCA) studies. Packaging impacts in several phases of the life cycle. In some cases the efficient use of the product depends directly on its packaging and this correlation and interdependence generates the product-packaging combinations (PPC).

Numerous sustainability assessment tools exist for product-packaging development. These tools, as shown in Figure 2. are divided into four large groups, differentiated by the type of results and the stage of maturity of the project for accessing information required during the application of each of these.

Tools like the family of "Design for X" where "X" is a characteristic to improve or a key development feature used in circular strategies, favor the use of qualitative data to enhance 4 R's: Recycling, Reuse, Renewal and Redesign, and need clear and cumulative actions throughout the packaging design process.

Another group describes guidelines or principles applied in packaing design with a life cycle approach regarding the product packaging system.

When considering intermediate qualitative-quantitative results we find tools like the MET Matrix (Materials, Energy and Toxicity), which is an analysis tool used to classify information on qualitative terms, this allows you to structure information for the inventory required for the LCA. An alternative matrix is the Quality Function Deployment (QFD), that provides a structured approach to define requirements with a focus on sustainable considerations.

Another side of the tool spectrum, we have ecoindicators and LCA that use inventories and calculations to provide quantitative information of potential environmental impacts, which allows an objective scenario comparisons. However, they require precise data of the scenario with certain confidence as a result these tools are usually used on the final stages of the product development cycle.

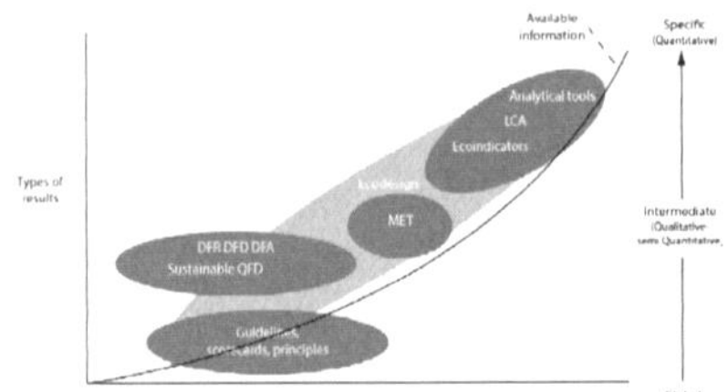

Figure 2: General vision of tools and applicability. Modified from Luttinkhuis, E., et al. 2013

All these considerations, add to the complexity of the product-packaging system, which highlights the importance of selecting and correctly applying these tools, especially in the early stages. A better understanding of the environmental aspects to improve on a specific product-packaging development will allow for a appropriate tool selection at the time of the development of the product-packaging.

The packaging ecodesign challenge is to articulate and integrate systemically to improve circular model proposals. Adapting circular model requirements and reaching the environmental performance of product-packaging and PVC to the early design and development processes.

5. Conclusions and Future Research

Packaging decision making requires reaching the environmental performance and the translation of CE objectives and standards to early design and development processes and these definitions need to be aligned to the sustainability goals without leaving aside technical feasibility, functional optimization, competitiveness and market needs. However, in practice these applications are not obvious, because of the particularities of the packaging LC or PPC. As shown in Figure 3. the incorporation of design methodologies and guidelines for the application of actions and environmental quantitative-qualitative input that improve desirable characteristics for circular strategies like: recyclability, separability, compatibility, disassembly, as well as the use of materials with post-consumer or renewable content should be considered in the development of packaging. These methodologies should also consider an integration of value chain and stakeholders parallel to the maturity of the design project itself.

Future research could use a technical and qualitative perspective to develop a methological proposal incorporating circular design strategies during earlier design phases. When discussing CE, we need to look further than just the product-packaging, to the critical role of the consumer behavior, which is ofter underconsidered in LCA. The successful implementation of a CE model relies on the consumer during the end of life, since he is either wholly or partially responsible for classifying and managing waste.

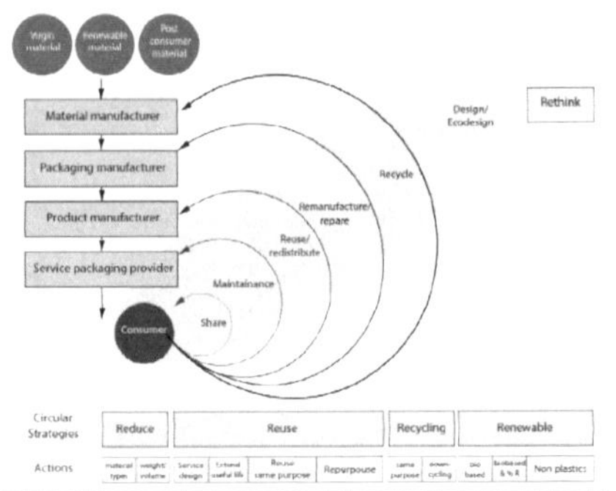

Figure 3: Circular economy diagram with packaging strategy and action adaptation. Adapted from Ellen Mcarthur Foundation (2014).

iapri

Study on adhesion properties of superhydrophobic coatings on aluminum substrates

UDEM

IAPRI MEXICO 2020 WORLD PACKAGING CONFERENCE

Ruomei Wu, Shuai Wu ,Zigong Chang, Haiyun Jiang, Zhiqing Yuan, Qinghua Chen

College of Packaging and Materials Engineering, Hunan University of Technology

Introduction

The adhesion of the layer includes the adhesion of the organic coating and the metal surface of the substrate and the cohesion of the organic coating itself. Low adhesion will cause the coating to fall off the surface of the matrix;The coating with poor cohesion tends to crack and lose its effect. Only by increasing the adhesion of the organic coating to the metal surface and the cohesion of the coating itself can the metal be provided with good protection.

Characterization

Scanning electron microscopy (SEM, HITACHIS-3000N) was used to characterize the surface structure and morphology. Film adhesion tester (QFZ-2)and grid method was used to analyze the adhension between film and aluminum matrix.

Results & Discussion

the contact angle between the surface of aluminum alloy and the water drop after the film coating is greater than 150°. All the samples have superhydrophobic property. the superhydrophobic surface with needle-like microscopic appearance prepared by anodic oxidation method has the best adhesion, the lowest film shedding area (only 35%), and the shedding area of other samples exceeds 50%. Therefore, the aluminum matrix with needle-like surface micro morphology has better bonding performance to the superhydrophobic film layer.

Conclusions

1) At room temperature, the surface microscopic shape of superhydrophobic aluminum alloy has little effect on wettability.
2) The surface of aluminum alloy with needle-like microstructure prepared by anodic oxidation method has the best bonding property with the film layer. The rate of coating spallation area of this sample is 35%, and the film adhesion level is 2B. This shows that the microstructure of the surface of aluminum alloy has a great influence on the bonding force between the superhydrophobic film layer and the aluminum alloy matrix.

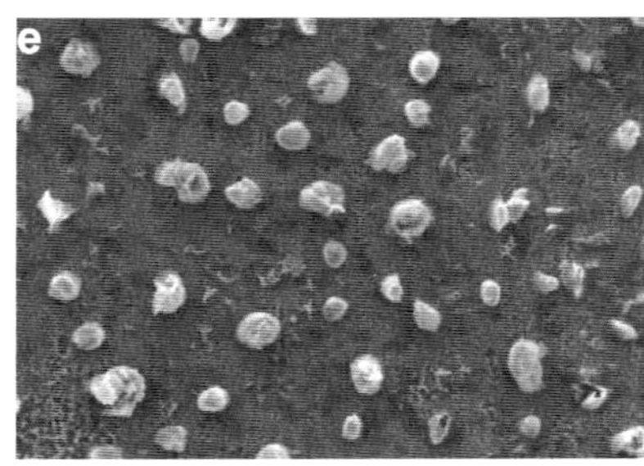

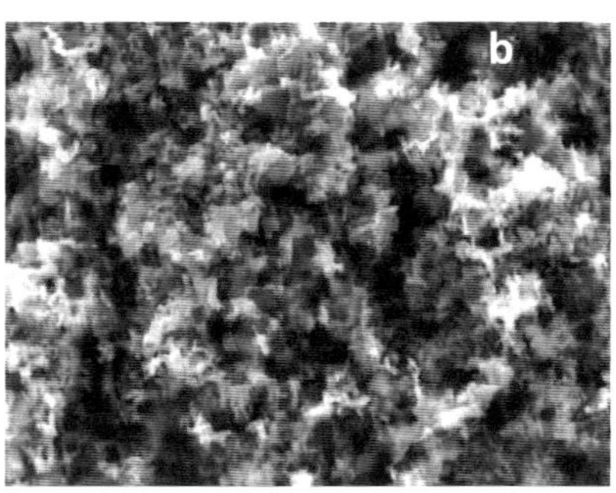

micro morphologies of superhydrophobic aluminum alloy
(a)step-shaped(b) needle-shaped(c) ellipsoid(d) columnar (e) triangle

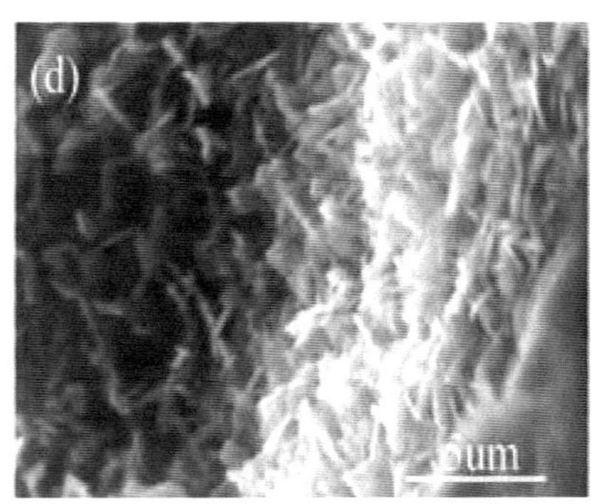

iapri

Circular "on-the-go" packaging

Kristina Wickholm, Annika Lindström

RISE, Research Institutes of Sweden

1. Introduction

In May 2018, EU countries approved several measures on waste legislation as part of the overall strategy for a circular economy. The purpose is to prevent waste and, when it is not possible, to significantly increase the material recycling of municipal solid waste and packaging. In a circular economy the collection of material is crucial. Single-use packaging and goods create major problems in society and in nature, partly because they are collected only to a limited extent and therefore contribute to littering. Furthermore, as these disposables are not collected, they are not recycled either which makes the resource efficiency low. These disposables end up high on the top 10 list of the most common litter on land and in the ocean. Much of the litter found in measurements performed annually by The Keep Sweden Tidy Foundation, in urban environments, parks and beaches in Sweden, is from packaging from "on-the-go" products. Most of the packaging from on-the-go consumption from public places ends up in waste incineration and have the potential to be handled more resource effective through increased material recycling and reuse.

2. Research Goals/Objectives

The project goals were to develop new solutions to decrease littering and increase reuse and recycling of packaging from on-the-go consumption. The aim is to create behavioral changes both by consumers and stakeholders in the value chain, so that disposable packaging from on-the-go consumption are handled more circularly, ie source sorted, reused and recycled to a higher degree than today and also so that the recycled material is demanded and used to a greater extent.

3. Research Method

The project gathered actors along the packaging value chain in Sweden to collaborate with the aim to develop new solutions, based on user needs, for collecting and sorting packaging from on-the-go

Figure 1: Used on the go packaging that has ended up as litter instead of being recycled.

Activities performed during the project were:

1. Analysis of the current situation. An analysis of the current situation in Sweden and in other countries were performed in the beginning of the project. The purpose was to get insight in other activities in the field.
2. Waste analysis in parks in the city of Örnsköldsvik, Sweden. This was done to see what kind of packages that end up in the parks.
3. Consumer surveys
   a. To get an understanding about consumer behavior and needs an online survey was conducted with respondents all over Sweden. 892 answered the survey and of them 811 respondents completed the survey. The result from the survey served as input to the idea generation workshops.
   b. A survey was conducted in parks and online in Örnsköldsvik. The purpose of the survey was to get insights in how to improve the collection of packaging from on-the-go consumption in the parks.

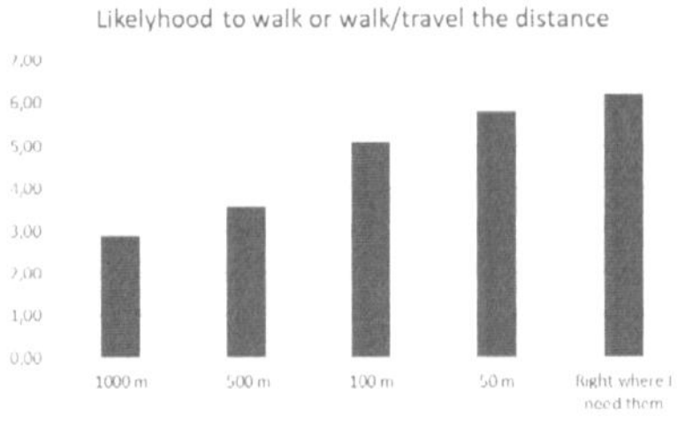

Figure 2: Mean for how far respondents in the consumer survey were willing to walk to sort packaging from on-the-go consumption. The scale ranged from 1 (not likely at all to 7 (very likely).

4. Idea generation workshops: In the workshops the actors along the packaging value chain were gathered to develop new solutions for more circular use of packaging from on-the-go consumption. Results from the consumer surveys and learnings from the analysis of the current situation served as input and the idea generation workshops.
5. As a last step, in- depth interviews with consumers were conducted to verify the new solutions.

4. Results and conclusions

The results show that consumers want to sort packaging on-the-go if sorting is offered in public places. Many of the respondents stated that they experienced a lack of possibility to sort the packaging from on-the-go consumption, so the waste ended up in waste bins.

Results also showed that it is important that the sorting is close by and that it is easy to understand how to sort the packaging. Even though the consumers are willing to sort their packaging, results show that it is important that the collection bins are not too far away.

Deposit gives an added value to the used packaging and results from the consumer survey showed that packaging with a deposit were recycled to a higher extent. In the parks included in the waste analysis, a complete absence of deposit bottles and -cans was noted. A small test was conducted; bottles and cans with deposit were placed in ten of the parks' bins. Detailed analysis of the collected waste showed that all were removed within 24 hours.

In idea generation workshops new solutions were created, that was built upon the results from the activities in the project. The new solution that we chose to continue with is based on providing the possibility to sort on-the-go packaging, within a reasonable distance and with clear information on how to sort them. In addition, offer deposit as incentives to recycle and reuse these packaging. This should be accomplished through an app that also facilitates the sorting for the consumers by providing information on how to sort the packaging. Furthermore, the app will make it easy for the user to find the closest recycling station and it also offers the possibility to register new recycling stations.

The solution could also be feasible in other countries because the app solution uses the collection system available in the specific country. However, since the collection system differs between countries the solution would need to be tested in the specific country and with their current collection system. The solution also needs to be adjusted to the collection system in that country to reach its full potential.

5. Future Research

Future research should test the effects of the solutions in a real environment. The focus should be to evaluate levels of collected packaging, the quality of the material and how the solution could be adjusted to reach its full potential from both a consumer- and system perspective.

6. Funding

This research was funded by Vinnova, Sweden's innovation agency, and the Swedish Environmental Protection Agency.

Figure 3: Project partners

IAPRI MEXICO 2020
WORLD PACKAGING CONFERENCE

Encapsulation Efficiency in Cyclodextrin Metal Organic Frameworks for Active Packaging

Ajay Kathuria[1], Travis Lang[2], Trevor Harding[2]

1. Industrial Technology and Packaging, California Polytechnic State University, San Luis Obispo, CA, USA
2. Materials Engineering, California Polytechnic State University, San Luis Obispo, CA, USA

UDEM

CAL POLY

1. Background

Aliphatic acids, aldehydes, alcohols and ethers have been widely studied for antifungal and antimicrobial activity. Acids and aldehydes have been observed as most active groups. Various researchers studied the structure-antimicrobial activity relationship of such active species. It was observed that the order of antimicrobial activity follows the order of aldehydes>ketones>alcohols. Hexanal; an antimicrobial C6 aldehyde; is generally regarded as safe (GRAS) low molecular weight fruity flavor, however it has cytotoxic potential at elevated concentrations

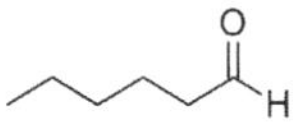

Figure 1: Chemical structure of Hexanal

Porous materials have been widely studied for encapulation and release of active species for packaging application. This study is examining the encapsulation efficiency of hexanal in γ-cyclodextrin metal organic frameworks (γ-CDMOFs) as a mechanism for potential active packaging applications. γ-CDMOFs were synthesized by vapor diffusion process. Hexanal was encapsulated within the γ-CDMOFs using vapor diffusion process. The synthesized γ-CDMOFs were characterized both before and after the encapsulation of hexanal using x-ray diffraction (XRD), scanning electron microscopy (SEM), and thermogravimetric analysis (TGA). XRD characterization results matched literature values which confirmed uniform γ-CDMOF crystallinity and a successful synthesis. SEM images were used as an additional confirmation of the γ-CDMOF crystallinity which matched those of previous γ-CDMOF structures. TGA characterization results revealed an encapsulation efficiency of about 5%.

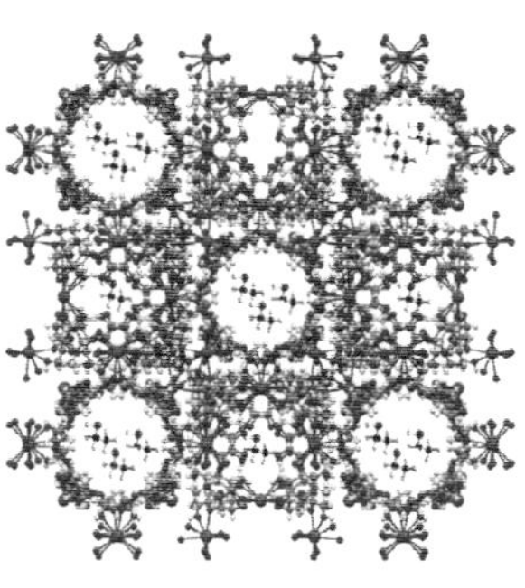

Figure 2: Porous γ-CDMOF host with small organic guest molecule

2. Objectives

1. To synthesize structurally stable γ-CDMOF
2. Encapsulate hexanal in γ-CDMOF
3. Quantify the hexanal encapsulation efficiency of γ-CDMOF

3. Materials and Methods

The γ-CDMOF crystals were synthesized using vapor diffusion of methanol into a solution γ-CD and potassium hydroxide (KOH).

Synthesis of γ-CDMOF

1.30 g of γ-CD and 0.45 g of KOH (1 mol γ-CD : 8 mol KOH) and 20 mL of deionized water were added into a 50 mL beaker to create a γ-CD + KOH solution. The solution was stirred at room temperature for 6 hours at 600 rpm. The 50 mL beaker containing this solution was then placed inside a 250 mL beaker containg 50 mL of methanol. Vapor diffusion was allowed to occur for 7 days to nucleate and grow the γ-CDMOF crystals. After vapor diffusion synthesis, the γ-CDMOF crystals were filtered and soaked in methanol for 3 days to remove any unlinked potassium ions from the γ-CDMOF crystals.

Encapsulation of Hexanal

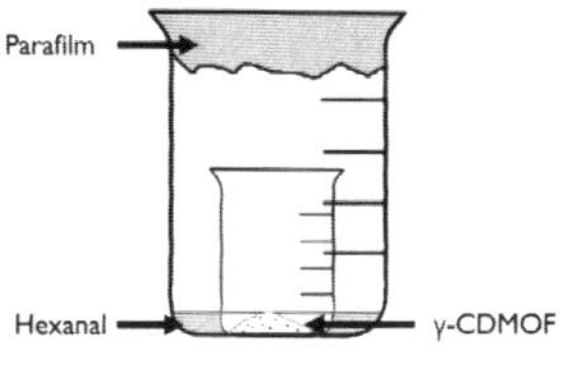

Figure 3: Schematic representation of encapsulation of hexanal in γ-CDMOF

4. Results and Discussion

Highly crytalline porous γ-CDMOF crystals were obtained as observed in XRD and SEM, represented in Figure 3 and Figure 4 respectively.

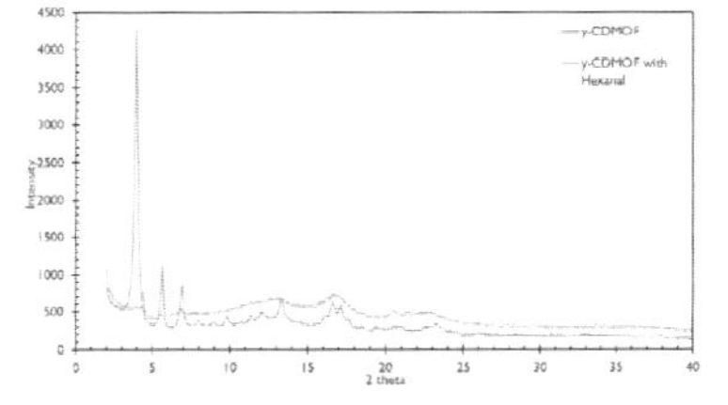

Figure 3: TGA of γ-CDMOF and hexanal encapsulated γ-CDMOF

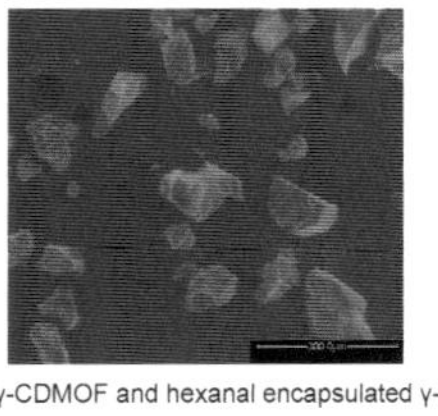

Figure 4: TGA of γ-CDMOF and hexanal encapsulated γ-CDMOF

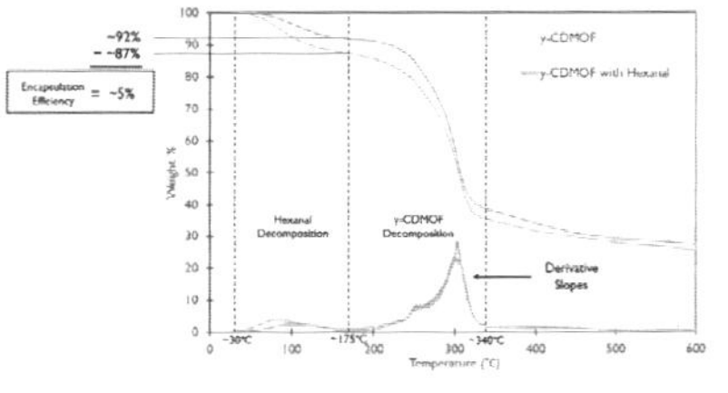

Figure 5: TGA of γ-CDMOF and hexanal encapsulated γ-CDMOF

As observed in the TGA thermograms in Figure 5, weight loss ~ 175°C in encapsulted γ-CDMOF is 5% higher.

This increase weight loss of volatile compounds can primarliy be ascribed to volatile hexanal

5. Conclusions

Hexanal molcules were successfully encapsulated in γ-CDMOF crystals

Encapsulation efficieny of hexanal was observed to be ~ about 5% as observed using TGA

iapri

Filamentous Fungi

UDEM

IAPRI MEXICO 2020
WORLD PACKAGING CONFERENCE

Author: Daniela Guadalupe Fernández Leal
Advisers: UDEM's Microbiology Laboratory

Universidad de Monterrey

1. Plastic Pollution

Given its mechanical and chemical properties, plastic substituted other materials.In 2015 the production of plastic is over 310 million tons. (PlasticsEurope, EPRO, 2015) Since it´s used mainly as packaging and single-use products, it represents 10% of the municipal waste globally. (K. A. Barnes, Galgani, C. Thompson, y Barlaz, 2009) About 275 million tons of waste were registered worldwide in 2010 (Ritchie, Roser, 2018). Creating a way for this plastic to enter ecosystems that didn´t live with this pollutant. By introducing itself to marine habitats, it costs between $3,300 to $33,000 dollars per ton globally (J. Beaumont et al, 2019). The fact that we use plastic to dispose of it after a single-use, mainly in landfills or open dumps, creates greenhouse gases (Royer S-J et al, 2018) and microplastics. These micro and nano-plastics are ingested first by the organisms living in our environment, especially the ocean, and later (through our food) by us. (Rochman et al, 2016). This intrinsic but sometimes invisible relationship we have created with plastic has changed our ecosystem, creating the plastisphere.

2 . Plastisphere

The plastisphere is the ecosystem created by living organisms to adapt and live in the presence of man-made plastics. Many species have developed methods to cope and thrive in the presence of plastic.Some studies analyze organisms present in the soil which degrade plastic, ranging from bacteria to fungi. (Zettler, Mincer y Amaral-Zettler, 2013) Fungi present the most degradation potential due to the enzymes they produce (Barratt et al, 2003). Representing an opportunity to harness the power of nature to reduce our plastic footprint.

Figure 1: Fllamentous fungi growing in plastic substrate (Author,2019)

3. Proof of concept

Mycelium is the vegetative body of the fungi. It is made from singular multicellular strands called hyphae. Through the tips of the hyphae, the fungus delivers enzymes to digest its surroundings and absorb the nutrients. These strands branch out, creating a vast network called mycelium (Crosby, 2018). Mycelium is being used as a solution to decrease the use of EPS as packaging.

The objective of this research is to validate if filamentous fungi can degrade PS and create a sustainable material.

To evaluate if the fungus could grow with plastic in its substrate, a natural medium was made, composed of agave fibers, coffee, wood, and flour. Different proportions shredded polystyrene, not exceeding 5mm in length, were added. The proportions made by weight began at 0%, 5%, 10%, 20%,30%,40%,50%,60%,70%, and 80% of plastic present in 100 grams of substrate.

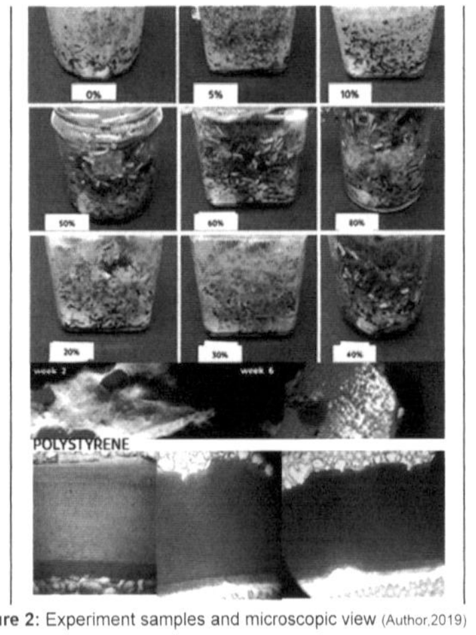

Figure 2: Experiment samples and microscopic view (Author,2019)

After the samples are sorted, they are sterilized in an autoclave and inoculated with 10 grams of germinated seeds and left to grow in a space where the temperature was 25°C.These samples were in a space with air conditioning for 6 weeks.

After 2 weeks, the fungus grew in all the samples of the substrate. After 4 weeks fruiting bodies were visible. Figure 2 demonstrates the branching of the mycelium was reduced as the percentage of PS present grew. All samples had mycelium, but the presence of the plastic changed how it behaved. Microscopic samples were made, viewing fragmentation and hyphae on the outer layers of the plastic were the fungus had grown.

4. Results

It can be concluded that the fungus it's affecting the plastic at a microscopic level, since some porosity and melting on the outer layers of the plastic samples are visible. But the percentage of plastic in the substrate can affect the behavior of fungus growth, and it is taking longer than estimated to have an effect on the plastic. Further research is required to promote mycelium growth and degradation.

5. Future possibilities

This research presents some feasibility to use filamentous fungi as a bioremediation, but several next steps should be made first. Knowing the chemical composition of the plastic samples and mycelium will be key to be able to determine which are the byproducts resulting, and if there is any degration at a molecular level. And the evaluation of the byproducts will show if its better or worse to do the degradation process, given that some chemical components of plastic may be worse alone than in the stabilized molecule of the polymer.

There should also be an analysis to show if the cutinase is the one changing the plastic or if it is a combination of enzymes. This would help to know how to further improve the process.

The main reason this research is relevant in packaging is because it offers an alternative end of life to most of the packaging used. Considering even unrecyclable paper and plastic products as substrate, to eradicate the concept of waste in the end of life of a packaging. Including that the byproduct could present itself as an alternative to plastic foamed materials.

Figure 3: Compilation of possible product samples already available comercially. (Ecovative)

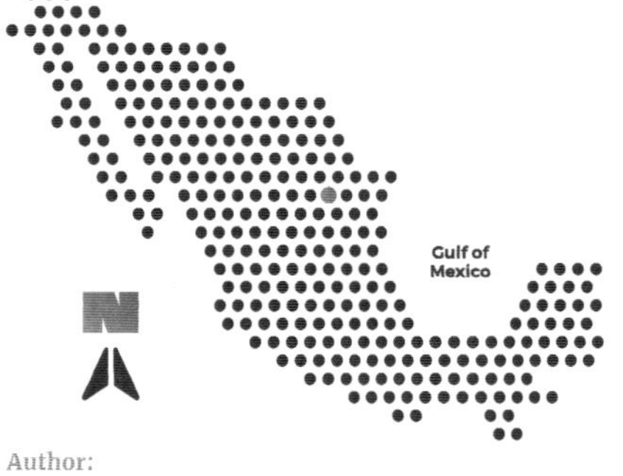

Author:
Turismo NL/OCV MONTERREY

Location:
García, NUEVO LEÓN

Description:
El Fraile y *San Miguel*, a group of mountains in the town of García, house the mystical and famous Grutas de García (Garcia's Grotto), part of a natural state park, where one can watch in awe the passage of time and nature's wonderful work.

MONTERREY

MÉXICO

CONVENTION AND VISITORS BUREAU

UNIVERSIDAD DE MONTERREY

HOMO HOMINIS IN MINISTERIO PERFICITUR

IAPRI MEXICO 2020

22ND WORLD PACKAGING ONLINE CONFERENCE

Industry 4.0 - UDEM

IAPRI Team

Cristina F. Guzmán Siller
Laura Lozano Montemayor
Diana Sofía Chapa Chapa
Paola Ivonne Cáceres Alvarado
María Fernanda Márquez Culebra
Verónica Lucía Fuentes Peña
Melissa de la Luz Díaz Quiroz

Special Collaboration

Concept & Graphic Design
JEROME AND ZIMMERMAN

Social Media & Marketing
Marketing Code 98

Website Design & Programming
Coddica

Video Edition & Production
SismoMedia

Universidad de Monterrey
Av. Ignacio Mornoes Prieto 4500 Pte.,
San Pedro Garza García,
N.L. México. C.P. 66238

ISBN 978-1-7138-5251-3

9 781713 852513

CURRAN ASSOCIATES INC.
proceedings.com

International Conference on Computer Graphics, Visualization, Computer Vision and Image Processing 2020; Big Data Analytics, Data Mining and Computational Intelligence 2020; and Theory and Practice in Modern Computing 2020

Held at MCCSIS 2020 (Held online due to COVID-19)

Lisbon, Portugal
21 - 25 July 2020

iadis